IDEAS AND INSTITUTIONS
OF
VICTORIAN BRITAIN

GEORGE KITSON CLARK

Ramsey & Muspratt

IDEAS AND INSTITUTIONS
OF
VICTORIAN BRITAIN

☆

Essays in honour of George Kitson Clark
edited by
ROBERT ROBSON

LONDON
G. BELL & SONS, LTD
1967

Printed in Great Britain by
The Camelot Press Ltd, London and Southampton

Contents

Preface

This volume is published in honour of Dr George Kitson Clark on the occasion of his retirement as Reader in Constitutional History at Cambridge. Its contributors are only a few from the long list of those who have reason to be grateful for his guidance while they were serving their apprenticeship as historians, and who remember with affection the fruitful talks they had with him across the friendly hearth of his room above the Great Gate of Trinity or on afternoon walks through the colleges and countryside of Cambridge.

During the last twenty years Dr Kitson Clark has been one of the most notable and successful supervisors of research students in the History Faculty at Cambridge, and his pupils are now scattered in universities all over the world, from Canberra to California, from Edinburgh to East Anglia, from Oxford to Cambridge. His genial personality and enthusiasm, his wide reading and capacious memory, his imaginative sympathy and sensitive appreciation of new problems and new approaches, his suspicion of glib generalizations, and a Yorkshireman's endowment of the uncommon gift of common sense all fitted him to be an ideal research supervisor. And his gifts have been fully exploited. His influence on his pupils has been considerable, but he has never sought to mould them; no dogma is imposed on those who belong to what has been called 'the Kitson Clark school'.

It would have taken a massive volume indeed to do full justice to the catholicity of Dr Kitson Clark's interests, and to have accommodated all those who would have wished to express at greater length the gratitude they have already briefly recorded in the prefaces and footnotes of the many books and articles he has stimulated and inspired. Only a few of the many themes of nineteenth-century British history that interest him are touched upon in this book. Its authors know better than anyone how much these essays would have been improved if they had been submitted before publication to the author of *The Making of Victorian England*.

14 June 1966   R. R.
Trinity College,
   Cambridge

Parliamentary Parties and the 'Independent' Member, 1810–1860

I

IN Sir Lewis Namier's Romanes lecture, 'Monarchy and the Party System', is to be found a brilliant and famous brief analysis of the growth of constitutional monarchy in Britain since the eighteenth century. This is its central paragraph:

> What are the basic elements of constitutional monarchy? A Sovereign placed above parties and policies; a Prime Minister and Government taking rise from Parliament, and received rather than designated by the Sovereign, yet as 'H.M. confidential servants' deriving from the Royal Prerogative that essential executive character which an elected legislature could not impart to them; and an unpolitical Civil Service whose primary connexion is with the Crown, and which, while subordinated to party-governments, is unaffected by their changes: the two permanent elements, the Crown and the Civil Service, which not by chance together left the political arena, supply the framework for the free play of parliamentary politics and governments. Under royal government the sovereign was the undisputed, immediate head of the executive; under parliamentary government, it is the prime minister; but no clear-cut formula is possible for the intervening period of 'mixed government', during which the direction of government gradually passed from the sovereign to the prime minister by a process that can be logically defined but eludes precise dating. The

prime minister replaced the sovereign as actual head of the
executive when the choice of the prime minister no longer
lay with the sovereign; the sovereign lost the choice when
strongly organized, disciplined parliamentary parties came
into existence; and party discipline depends primarily on
the degree to which the member depends on the party for
his seat.   The sovereign can keep clear of party-politics
only so long as it is not incumbent on him or her to choose
the prime minister.   Thus constitutional monarchy as
now understood hinges to a high degree on the working
of the modern party system.

The next sentence seems to define the chronological limits of
the process: 'In 1761 not one parliamentary election was
determined by party, and in 1951 not one constituency
returned a non-party member'.[1]

The object of the present essay is to consider one factor in
this development, the Parliamentary party, in the crucial
period, from roughly 1810 to roughly 1860.   An attempt will
be made to show, through a review of the recent secondary
literature on the subject, especially the fundamental work of
Professor Gash, what progress has been made towards establishing the main lines of the story; and some suggestions will be
put forward on certain points still unsettled.

Namier was never able to write the book on 'The Rise of
Party' which he planned,[2] and his Romanes lecture and the
whole tenor of his published work emphasized the persistence
into the late eighteenth and early nineteenth centuries of
elements of 'royal government' rather than the emergence over
that period of features of 'parliamentary government'.[3]
Richard Pares, however, filled out Namier's analysis of the
growth of constitutional monarchy in the last chapter of his
marvellous Ford lectures, 'The Decline of Personal Monarchy'.
He argued that, soon after 1812,

---

[1] L. B. Namier, *Monarchy and the Party System* (Oxford, 1952), pp. 3-4 (reprinted
in Namier, *Personalities and Powers* (London, 1955), pp. 13-14 and Namier, *Crossroads of Power* (London, 1962), pp. 213-14).

[2] See Namier, *England in the Age of the American Revolution* (new ed. London, 1961),
p. 418.

[3] Perhaps I may refer to my article 'Sir Lewis Namier and the Party System'
in *Cambridge Review*, vol. LXXIX (1957-8), pp. 599-603.   Apart from 'Monarchy
and the Party System', Namier's most important contribution to the theme of this
essay is 'Country Gentlemen in Parliament, 1750-84' (Enid Muir lecture, 1954)
in *Personalities and Powers*, pp. 59-77 and *Crossroads of Power*, pp. 30-45.

the consolidation of the country's patriotic and Conservative forces in the revived tory party created a bloc so powerful, and (in spite of the friction over Catholic Emancipation and Canning's personal ambition) so well united that the king's power to divide or desert it began to be questioned;

that the 'King's Friends' declined greatly between 1807 and 1827; that 'promotion in the public services was becoming more strictly professional'; and that there was evident 'a *tendency* to a two-party system'. 'Between 1807 and 1841, the man without a party label almost disappeared from the House of Commons.' True,

> it was not for nothing that the generation between the first and second Reform Acts was known as the golden age of the private M.P. Yet, though the parties of Grey's and Peel's time were loose and weak compared with those of Gladstone and Disraeli, they were, at least, pretty nearly inclusive; and this fact, too, was beginning to reduce the sovereign to registering the results of general elections.[1]

Professor Aspinall identified more precisely a point of culmination: 'Melbourne . . . was leader of the Whig party in April 1835. He, not Pitt, was the first Prime Minister to be chosen by the people, since, with Radical and Irish support, he was backed by a majority of the House of Commons.'[2] In Dr Kitson Clark's own words,

> This was in its way the end of the old personal monarchy; the end of the principle that the King, however straitened in choice by Parliamentary necessities and in action by legal restrictions, ought to appoint the executive government of the country. . . . After 1830 the realities of the constitution had decisively changed; never again would a ministry retain power simply because the monarch wished it to do so.

Dr Kitson Clark stresses also the significance of the united Conservative opposition of more than 300 M.P.s which 'at the election of 1841 achieved a majority with the result that Peel its leader came into office *against* the wishes of the

[1] R. Pares, *King George III and the Politicians* (Oxford, 1953), ch. VI, pp. 182–207; quotations from pp. 185, 189, 191, 192.
[2] A. Aspinall, 'The Cabinet Council, 1783–1835', *Proceedings of the British Academy*, vol. XXXVIII (1952), p. 249.

Queen. This was indeed the shape of things to come.'[1]

In Professor Gash's article of 1951, 'Peel and the Party System', the emphasis is on the weakness of parties and the party system between 1830 and 1850. He quotes with approval an article in the *Edinburgh Review* of 1840 which maintained that 'the whole current of development in fact was setting away from and not towards a stronger party system'. Peel's ministry of 1841–5 provided an exception to the trend.

> The surprising feature is not that his party broke up when it did, but that it lasted so long and that it ended on a note of achievement rather than failure. With its disruption the basic elements in the political situation were once more laid bare. Indeed, the disintegration of the Conservative party in 1846, so far from creating an abnormal situation, may with some justice be regarded as a return to normality.

'The Aberdeen coalition . . . was the natural outcome of a quarter of a century of politics in which the party system had shown itself almost uniformly incapable of supporting strong government.'[2] In this article Professor Gash accepts as a statement of historical fact Peel's claim in his first speech in the reformed House of Commons that the two-party system had existed in the 1820s and had since disappeared, and accepts also at its face value Peel's declaration that in the altered circumstances he is going to abandon traditional party warfare and instead seek to strengthen the Whig Government.[3] It is further suggested that there was a drift of M.P.s from the Whig to the Tory side between 1833 and 1841.[4]

In *Politics in the Age of Peel*, published in 1953, Professor Gash was concerned chiefly with developments outside Parliament, but in his masterly introduction he ranged more widely.

> In this unprecedented situation three features of the political system were outstanding: the oligarchic tradition of government, fundamentally administrative in outlook; the party system, moving slowly towards a programme as well as a philosophy of action; and the external forces of

---

[1] G. Kitson Clark, *Peel and the Conservative Party* (new ed. London, 1964), pp. xvi, xix.

[2] N. Gash, 'Peel and the Party System, 1830–50', *Transactions of the Royal Historical Society*, 5th series, vol. I (1951), pp. 64, 65, 69.

[3] *Ibid.*, pp. 52–9.

[4] *Ibid.*, pp. 51–2, 67–8.

public opinion. . . . By the end of the century the party
system was to emerge as the strongest of the three, having
destroyed the aristocratic concept of 'the King's Government' on the one hand, and having made itself (at the cost
of some concessions) the main channel of public opinion
on the other. But in the age of Peel party was far from
being in that dominant position, and between the three
forces there existed a rough balance of power.

It was true of course that party took on a firmer outline
after 1830. A remarkably continuous tradition of party
in British parliamentary politics had existed since the
seventeenth century and even before the Reform Act the
party system had by no means been devoid of either
principle or organization. The technical post-1830 developments, however, together with the issues thrown up
by the reform crisis, immeasurably strengthened its control over politics.[1]

These technical developments, in fact—registration societies,
constituency associations, the great political Pall Mall clubs,
the central party agent—mark 'the real emergence of the party
system in its modern form'.[2]

The first volume of Professor Gash's biography of Peel, *Mr
Secretary Peel*, which appeared in 1961, deals only with the
period before 1830 and is not particularly full on the general
political situation. There is, though, one especially interesting
passage on the subject:

Parliament itself had not yet evolved a party system
capable of producing alternative sets of ministers. The
existence of a formed whig opposition was an exception,
not a contradiction, to the characteristic shapelessness of
politics. They had excluded themselves, and by some
were regarded as rightly excluded, from participation in
government; but this was historical accident rather than
constitutional principle. The Whigs in fact were in the
anomalous position of forming a party in a non-party
political system. In the first twenty years of Peel's
political career, they were never able to offer an alternative to the existing government and on occasion came near
to absorption in it.[3]

[1] N. Gash, *Politics in the Age of Peel* (London, 1953), p. xviii.
[2] *Ibid.*, p. xiii.
[3] N. Gash, *Mr Secretary Peel* (London, 1961), p. 9.

Professor Gash's Ford lectures, published in 1965 under the title *Reaction and Reconstruction in English Politics, 1832–52*, contain his most complete statement on the parties and the party system of the period, and on the development of the constitution. In a fine first chapter, 'The End of the Hanoverian Monarchy', he shows that 'the crisis of 1834–5 became in retrospect a constitutional landmark only because about seven years later the Crown began effectively to detach itself from party politics'. The Bedchamber crisis must be given due place. 'There can be little doubt that Victoria prolonged and William, had he lived, would have curtailed the duration of Whig power'. 'It was Albert,' and not until after the change of government in 1841, 'who weaned the Queen from her early partisan ties towards his conception of a supra-party constitutional monarchy.'

> The contrast between the behaviour of the Crown in 1832, 1834, and 1839 and its behaviour in December 1845, in 1846 and in 1852 is one between isolation and co-operation, between legal power and political influence, and between obstruction and mediation. . . . It was the difference between working with, and against the grain of politics.[1]

'The grain of politics' is discussed in chapters V and VI. Here the interpretation of party history put forward in the article of 1951 is in some points reversed. In the 1820s 'party was the basis neither of Government nor of any Opposition likely by itself to become a Government'.

> On Catholic Emancipation, foreign policy, fiscal policy, administrative reform, it was increasingly difficult to distinguish liberal elements in the Cabinet from those in opposition; and the lines of division in the House of Commons had to be redrawn on almost every issue.

The immediate result of the Reform Bill crisis 'was if anything an even greater weakening of party and executive influence'. Peel's remarks of 1833 contrasting the strength of parties in the 1820s with their weakness in the Reformed Parliament are quoted in support of this statement, but with the *caveat* that 'the significance of this comment . . . relates more to the state

[1] N. Gash, *Reaction and Reconstruction in English Politics, 1832–52* (Oxford, 1965), pp. 15, 21, 28–9, 29 and the whole first chapter.

of the legislature in 1833 than in the previous decade'. 'The year 1832 was the point of origin for a new party system in the sense of a redefinition of party.' 'Nevertheless, the reconstruction of parties . . . dates less from 1831–2 than from 1834–5, following two confused sessions in which party was at a discount in parliamentary politics.' After 1835, however, 'it would be a mistake to lay the emphasis on the laxity and indiscipline of party life'. There were few Parliamentary floating voters. 'The Government was brought down at last in 1841 not so much in the House of Commons as at the polling booths; the party was solid to the last.'[1]

II

As far as the strength of Parliamentary parties from 1835 to 1845 is concerned, it is Professor Gash's more recent view that must be endorsed. What has evidently much influenced Professor Gash in his change of attitude is statistical study of Commons voting. Professor Aydelotte, whose work dominates this field, has lately modified his own approach. In his earlier writing his chief object was to relate the votes of M.P.s to their economic interests.[2] It is only in his latest and most original article that he has stressed the importance of party ties.[3] 'The results suggest,' writes Professor Gash, 'that party attitudes on issues in the 1840s showed a considerable degree of consistency and that ideological differences were much more closely related to party in this period than has always been acknowledged.'[4] Issues can be divided into two groups. On issues of the first group, by far the larger, which includes questions as various as Free Trade and most financial matters, religious matters, flogging in the army, educational and sanitary reform, 'party affiliation was closely related to votes'. The parties were not usually solid on these issues, and the divisions on them were not often party divisions in the sense that the line of disagreement coincided with the line between the parties. But, for example, on many occasions the more extreme Liberals voted on one side,

---

[1] *Ibid.*, pp. 119, 120, 121, 121n., 122, 123, 126, 185.
[2] W. O. Aydelotte, 'The House of Commons in the 1840's', *History*, vol. XXXIX (1954), pp. 249–62.
[3] Aydelotte, 'Voting Patterns in the British House of Commons in the 1840s', *Comparative Studies in Society and History*, vol. V (1962–3), pp. 134–63.
[4] Gash, *Reaction and Reconstruction*, p. 217.

and the rest of the House on the other. 'The common frame of reference, the set of shared assumptions about the ordering of issues, which in modern America or modern France appears to extend only to individual parties, extended in mid-nineteenth-century Britain to the entire legislative body.' On issues of the second group, which 'consists principally of divisions on the regulation of working hours in factories and on the Poor Law', 'party affiliation was almost entirely unrelated to the voting'.[1]

Comparison of the division lists for three of the main divisions of 1840-1, with other evidence, led Professor Gash to his revised view that there was very little drifting from one Parliamentary party to the other during the period.[2] Further, the number of M.P.s considered 'doubtful' by the Conservative Whip at the beginning of 1840 was very small: eight, plus eight 'Radicals'.[3]

There is another piece of published work offering additional proofs of the strength of party during these years. President Lowell, as long ago as 1901, brought out a remarkable comparative study of 'The Influence of Party upon Legislation in England and America'. In an elaborate analysis of division lists, he found a surprisingly high degree of party solidarity in the House of Commons of 1836, lower than in 1871 and later, but higher than in 1850 and 1860, and higher than was usual in American legislatures.[4]

Other evidence is easily adduced to strengthen the case. The three divisions compared by Professor Gash were that on the no-confidence motion of January 1840, that on the sugar duties in May 1841 and that on the no-confidence motion of the following month—all before the General Election. It is worth while to extend the comparison. If, first, the division of June 1841, in which the Conservatives had a majority of one in a House of 627, is compared with the division on the Address

---

[1] Aydelotte, *Comparative Studies in Society and History*, vol. V, pp. 151, 155, 157 and *passim*.
[2] Gash, *Reaction and Reconstruction*, pp. 127, 214-16.
[3] *Ibid.*, p. 202.
[4] A. L. Lowell in *Annual Report of the American Historical Association for the Year 1901*, vol. I, pp. 321-542. The results are summarized in his *The Government of England* (London, 1912), ch. XXXV (vol. II, pp. 71-100). There is a contemporary *Atlas of the Divisions of the House of Commons . . . 1836* (London, 1836), with tables showing the votes cast in every division by every M.P.

in August 1841—after the Election—in which they had a
majority of 91 in a House of 633, it will be found that no M.P.
changed sides. The whole difference in the position of the
parties between the two divisions is due to the intervening
Election. If earlier divisions are brought into the comparison,
for instance those on the Speakership and on the Address
immediately after the General Election of 1835 (while Peel was
still Prime Minister) and that on the Speakership in 1839—
all great party divisions in which the Whigs had small majorities
in Houses of over 600—it will be found that party alignment
over the whole period is remarkably stable. Not one Member
who voted Whig in the Speakership division of 1835 voted
Tory either in the no-confidence division or in the division on
the Address in 1841. There was, though, some transfer of
votes in the other direction as between these divisions. Thirteen M.P.s who voted Tory in the Speakership division of 1835
voted Whig in the no-confidence division of 1841, and seven
survived the subsequent Election to vote Whig on the Address.
But most of these Members had become Whig supporters very
soon after the formation of Melbourne's second Government,
and only one was still voting Tory as late as 1839. As between
the Speakership division of 1839 and the divisions of 1841
there is a small transfer of votes from Whig to Tory: four M.P.s
who voted Tory in 1841 had voted Whig in 1839, one of them
the Tory candidate for the Speakership who had sportingly
voted for the other man. Those eight M.P.s whom the
Conservative Whip in 1840 considered 'doubtful' have voting
records which justify the adjective. But seven of the eight
Radicals whom he seemed to couple with the 'doubtfuls' were
consistent Whig supporters.[1]

[1] The complement of the House of Commons over this period was 658. My figures
of the number taking part in a division include the tellers, but not the Speaker.
This is the list of the divisions considered:

1. 19 February 1835, Choice of Speaker: Whigs 316, Tories 306.
2. 26 February 1835, Amendment to the Address: Whigs 309, Tories 302.
3. 27 May 1839, Choice of Speaker: Whigs 317, Tories 299.
4. 31 January 1840, No-confidence motion: Whigs 308, Tories 287.
5. 4 June 1841, No-confidence motion: Whigs 311, Tories 312.
6. 27 August 1841, Amendment to the Address: Whigs 269, Tories 360.

Some comments on individual M.P.s seem in place. Goulburn was the Tory candidate for Speaker in 1839. Wall was the Whig of 1840–1 who was still voting Tory
in 1839. In his analysis of the division of 31 January 1840, Professor Gash states
(*Reaction and Reconstruction*, p. 205) that, of the eight Radicals listed by the Whip,

What has happened to the 'independent' M.P.? 'Independence' is an imprecise concept. For the purpose of analytical discussion of the rise of party its meaning ought to be limited to 'non-partisanship'. But the word was often used in the eighteenth and nineteenth centuries to connote or denote other things: economic independence; representation of a more or less 'open' constituency, especially a county constituency; unwillingness to receive favours from ministers; unwillingness to accept office. It was possible to give consistent support to a party, even to accept office, and yet claim to be considered 'independent'.[1] Moreover, when a man asserts 'independence' in the sense of 'non-partisanship', his claim must be tested against the evidence of his political behaviour. It is notorious that most of those who have called themselves Independents in twentieth-century British politics have been hard to distinguish from Conservatives, and this phenomenon has a long history.

The eighteenth-century House of Commons has been represented as an assembly in which a body of 'independent' M.P.s or 'country gentlemen' held the balance between rival groups of politicians, and the role of the 'independents' has been compared with that of the modern electorate choosing

only Fielden voted on the Tory side, and that Grote and Jervis were absent. With regard to Fielden, it should be appreciated that this is the only one of the divisions considered in which he voted at all. With regard to Jervis, it was not the Radical Jervis who was absent, but his namesake; the Radical Jervis voted on the Whig side. In his analysis of the 'sugar division' of 18 May 1841 and the division of 4 June 1841 Professor Gash mentions (*ibid.*, p. 215) that Long and Bennett changed sides between the 1830s and the 1840s, and that their Tory vote on 4 June 'marked their secession from the Liberal party'. This seems doubtful, at least for Long, who voted on the Whig side only on the Address in 1835, otherwise on the Tory side.

Division lists were printed by authority of the House only for the session of 1836 and subsequent sessions. The official lists are surprisingly difficult to come by. The British Museum has only one or two years; the Cambridge University Library seems to have none. However, once official lists were published, the accuracy of the lists in *Hansard* greatly improved. In fact, in at least one case *Hansard* has the better list; the official list for the division on Canada on 7 March 1838 is one short on the Tory side, while *Hansard* gives the missing name, Lord Norreys. Before 1836 the position is difficult. Often only one side, usually the minority in opposition, is listed. It was claimed in the House of Commons (3 *Hansard*, XXI, 562–5, 18 February, 1836) that unofficial lists were sometimes wildly inaccurate. It can only be hoped that, once lists were being published for a reasonable number of divisions each session, the errors were not generally great. I have relied on the lists in *Hansard*.

I have been much helped in this and the next section by the work of some of my pupils at Harvard University, especially J. S. Donnelly, jun., for the election and the divisions of 1835, and J. Humphreys, for the election of 1841.

[1] Cf. J. Brooke and L. B. Namier, *History of Parliament, 1754–90* (London, 1964), vol. I, pp. 195–6.

between alternative governments.[1]   There is little sign of any such 'independence' in the years 1835–45.   There were very few 'non-party' men, either those who at any particular moment were doubtful or those who changed from one side to the other during the period.   Further, the politicians who made the strongest assertions of 'independence' at this time were not country gentlemen, but Radicals,[2] and this, rather than their observed behaviour, presumably accounts for the Whip's associating them with the 'doubtfuls'.   The true 'doubtfuls', on the other hand, were not usually, like the Radicals, politically active M.P.s critical of both parties.   Often the doubt about their allegiance arose from their casual attitude to their Parliamentary duties.   Greville wrote of the no-confidence motion of June 1841:

> For the last day or two it was a complete toss-up which side won, and it evidently depended on the few uncertain men who might or might not choose to vote.   As it was, it all turned on an accident.   John Russell wrote to Sir Gilbert Heathcote (who never votes), and begged him to come up on Thursday, and to vote.   Sir Gilbert did come, but, as there was no division that night, he went home again, and his vote was lost.[3]

Professor Aydelotte distinguished two types of division. Other distinctions ought to be made.   Among the divisions in his first group, in which alignment was related to party differences, were some in which the Government took no stand; some in which, though it took a stand, defeat would not bring it down; and some in which defeat would result in the Government's resignation.   The last group included some issues of policy.   On the question of the disposal of the surplus revenues of the Irish Church, voting was on strict party lines.   It was the issue on which the alliance between Whigs, Radicals and Irish had been made in 1835 and on which the Whig Cabinet had split

---

[1] *Ibid.*, vol. I, p. 191.

[2] This emerges from newspaper reports of the General Election campaigns of 1835 and 1841 (Harvard seminar papers).

[3] C. C. F. Greville, *Journal of the Reign of Queen Victoria from 1837 to 1852* (London, 1885), vol. II, p. 11, 9 June 1841.   Sir G. Heathcote, with Sir R. Howard, seem to be the best examples here.   Two of the so-called 'doubtfuls' were regular voters (Chetwynd and Wall), one of them (Chetwynd) consistently for the Whigs.

in 1834. It made a good cry, and it had the further advantage for a party issue that it was of no practical significance: there was no surplus. On many other issues of policy the Administrations of these years were surprisingly successful in imposing their will on the House. The Government Whips, for instance, were defeated only once in the session of 1836.[1] There are well-known cases when Ministers forced the House to reverse itself.[2] But they did not expect support from the rank and file of their party on every issue of policy, only 'general' or 'regular' support. The touchstone of party allegiance was not voting on issues of policy, but voting on motions devoid of policy content: in Speakership elections, on amendments to the Address, on explicit votes of no-confidence. It was well understood that parties existed not just to marshal opinion, but to marshal it behind alternative governments.[3]

III

Before 1835 and after 1845 the position is less clear. It is convenient to take the later period first. The rigidity of parties between 1835 and 1845 did not endure. From 1846 to 1859 there were always more than two parties in the House of Commons. Within parties discipline was weakened; parties were inclined to split; government defeats were more frequent.[4] Great party trials of strength were rare. There was some rejoicing at the decline of party.[5] However, parties and party loyalty did not disappear. There were those who regretted the disorganization of parties, most notably and articulately Gladstone.[6] The Peelites were conscious of themselves as a party, and the leaders at least were most reluctant to join either

[1] Lowell, *Annual Report of the American Historical Association for the Year 1901*, vol. I, pp. 328, 356. Lowell believed that the Government Whips were tellers in 91 of the 186 divisions of the session of 1836, and that the appearance of the Whips as tellers indicated that the Government took a stand on the matter concerned.

[2] Gash, *Reaction and Reconstruction*, p. 125.

[3] E.g., *ibid.*, pp. 126–7.

[4] See J. B. Conacher, 'Party Politics in the Age of Palmerston' in P. Appleman, W. A. Madden and M. Wolff (ed.), '*1859*': *Entering an Age of Crisis* (Bloomington, Indiana, U.S.A., 1959), pp. 163–80. Lowell, *Annual Report of the American Historical Association for the Year 1901*, vol. I, pp. 326–9. J. H. Whyte, *The Independent Irish Party, 1850–9* (Oxford, 1958).

[5] E.g. Sidney Herbert in 3 *Hansard* CLIV, 334 (10 June 1859).

[6] The main references are in Conacher, in '*1859*': *Entering an Age of Crisis*, p. 164 and n.

the Protectionists or the Liberals.[1]   But by 1859 they had done so, the other party splits of the 1850s had been repaired, and it was possible to rally 637 M.P.s into a party division in which there was little cross-voting.[2]   The behaviour of the politicians was less wayward than has sometimes been suggested.   Protectionists and Liberals declined to collaborate with one another.   The category of 'Liberal-Conservatives' was less independent' than the name implied, and perhaps the use of the name in preference to 'independent' reflects the acceptance of party labelling.   As Lowell found:

> Of these men, some had really become Liberals and some Conservatives; but the task of classifying them is rendered less difficult by the curious psychological fact that most of them, though disliking to call themselves by a party name, were unusually constant in going into the lobby with the party whip.[3]

The true 'non-party' man is hard to find.

It is the period before 1835 which poses the most difficult and interesting problems.   Here also Professor Gash has modified his earlier views, though in the opposite sense.   He now sees the generation before 1835 as a period of weak party ties, a period indeed when 'the whigs . . . were in the anomalous position of forming a party in a non-party political system'.[4]   Much work will have to be done before a definitive study of party in this period can be written.   But some general considerations can be put forward, and supported by evidence which is fairly readily available, to suggest that Professor Gash's opinion is open to question.

First, it is unreasonable to expect to discover steady general trends in party history.   Periods of strong parties may alternate with periods of weak parties.   Even in an age of mass parties there may occur party splits, three or more parties may co-exist, solidarity may be much reduced.   There may also be coalitions.   The politics of the years 1929–32 afford sufficient

---

[1] Conacher, 'Peel and the Peelites, 1846–1850', *English Historical Review*, vol. LXXIV (1958), pp. 431–52. J. Morley, *Life of Gladstone* (London, 1903), vol. I, pp. 417–23, 540–1. Cf. other Peelite biographies.

[2] See D. Beales, *England and Italy, 1859–60* (London, 1961), pp. 82–3. The House now numbered 654 at maximum.

[3] Lowell, *Annual Report of the American Historical Association for the Year 1901*, vol. I, p. 326.

[4] Gash, *Mr Secretary Peel*, p. 9.

proof of all these statements. In the nineteenth century, it cannot be doubted that the period 1835–45 was one of more rigid party alignment than the periods immediately preceding and following. But there is no reason to suppose that the position remained constant from 1810, say, to 1835. It has usually been held that the last years of Liverpool's Administration were a period of exceptionally clear party division. Professor Gash cannot prove his contention that parties were of trifling importance in the reign of George IV with evidence taken only from before 1822 and after 1827, as in his Ford lectures.[1]

Again, he is inclined to identify what actually happened too closely with what had to happen. 'In the first twenty years of Peel's political career,' he claims, the Whigs 'were never able to offer an alternative to the existing government.'[2] It is of course true that they never formed a government during the years concerned, 1809–29. But they certainly might have done. In 1811 and 1812 not only did they think so, but the Regent and their opponents thought so too.[3] There were widespread expectations of a Whig Government at later dates also.[4]

Professor Gash points out, in support of the view that party hardly mattered in the 1820s, that then 'the lines of division in the House of Commons had to be redrawn on almost every issue'.[5] The same could be said of voting in the 1840s, but Professor Aydelotte, by showing that there was none the less a general relationship between party differences and the various lines of division on most issues, has reconciled the fact with the idea that parties were relatively strong. There is reason to think that this could be done for the 1820s also. Division lists are comparatively rare and unreliable for the earlier period, but there are some valuable contemporary analyses of voting based on them. Though their material was inadequate and though they were written to expose the effect of 'influence', they can provide evidence about party solidarity. A summary table from one of these analyses has found its way, *via Hansard*,

---

[1] Gash, *Reaction and Reconstruction*, pp. 119–21.
[2] Gash, *Mr Secretary Peel*, p. 9.
[3] M. Roberts, *The Whig Party, 1807–1812* (London, 1939), ch. V.
[4] For example, in 1820–1. See W. R. Brock, *Lord Liverpool and Liberal Toryism, 1820–7* (Cambridge, 1941), pp. 121–3.
[5] Gash, *Reaction and Reconstruction*, p. 120.

into *English Historical Documents*, vol. XI.[1] According to this table, during the sessions of 1821 and 1822 320 M.P.s voted with Ministers, 226 against them, 23 both ways and 89 not at all. Examination of the pamphlet in which the analysis originally appeared shows that it is based on full lists for not more than nine divisions.[2] Still, it remains striking that the number of M.P.s voting both ways should be so small, especially by comparison with the number not voting at all. A more thorough analysis was published later, using more complete lists for the session of 1823.[3] In this case no summary table was appended, but it can be calculated from the data that in fifty divisions about 98 voted both ways and about 51 not at all. Just over 500 M.P.s, then, voted consistently one way or the other. It must be said, though, that the number of Members who voted less than five times altogether is so great —250, including the fifty-odd who did not vote at all—that the force of this conclusion is somewhat weakened. However, the figures do not suggest that the House of Commons was anarchic in these years.[4] To take a particular issue, while the dividing-line between supporters and opponents of Catholic Emancipation was not the same as that between the parties, the two lines were closely related: nearly all the Whigs and the generally more progressive Tories were for it, and the rest of the Tories against.[5] Laments were common in the 1820s that parties were not fighting about what mattered.[6] But they were common also in the 1830s and the 1950s.

There are many other signs of the importance of party in the 1820s. The Government side of the House was becoming more conscious of being a party, and more ready to acknowledge the name 'Tory'.[7] Party organization was well

[1] Ed. A. Aspinall and E. A. Smith, *English Historical Documents, 1783–1832* (vol. XI) (London, 1959), p. 254. See 2 *Hansard*, XV, 697–8 (speech of J. C. Hobhouse, 27 April 1826).

[2] *Alphabetical List of the Members of the Commons House of Parliament* . . . (London, 1823), reprinted in *The Pamphleteer*, vol. XXI, pp. 293–316.

[3] *Analysis of the British House of Commons* . . . (London, 1823), reprinted in *The Pamphleteer*, vol. XXII, pp. 451–74.

[4] I say 'about 98', and so on, because it is difficult to be exact in these computations.

[5] G. I. T. Machin, *The Catholic Question in English Politics, 1820 to 1830* (Oxford, 1964).

[6] E.g., *The Elector's Remembrancer* (London, 1822), reprinted in *The Pamphleteer*, vol. XX, p. 236n.

[7] Pares, *King George III and the Politicians*, p. 185. A. S. Foord, *His Majesty's Opposition, 1714–1830* (Oxford, 1964), pp. 443–51.

developed in the House of Commons, and growing in the House of Lords.[1] Closely related to these developments was the increasing role of the Government in legislation, and the sheer growth of Parliamentary law-making.[2]

An earlier pamphlet, John Ranby's *Inquiry into the supposed increase of the influence of the Crown*, of 1811, though its statistics are crude, offers interesting indications of the strength of party even at that date. Here is a ministerialist asserting the importance of party ties and questioning the right both of '*no-party* men' and of 'conscientiously wavering neutrals' to these designations. Like the Liberal-Conservatives of the 1850s, they in fact voted consistently.[3] Ranby had a very clear grasp of the concept of 'regular support': on the one hand, Ministers depended on the general backing of a Commons majority; on the other, M.P.s might vote as they pleased on questions which were not considered party matters.[4]

If much can be urged against Professor Gash's view of party for the last third of Liverpool's Administration and even for earlier years, the problem of the period between 1827 and 1835 remains peculiarly difficult. Peel's remarks about 'strong government' in 1833 must be carefully construed. In the first reformed Parliament Tories were 'few and scattered', many of them discontented with Peel's leadership. By the test of its normal majority, no Government has ever been stronger than Grey's. It was strong when it was a matter of putting certain reforms through the House of Commons. The kind of strength which Peel could assert it lacked was strength to uphold law and order, that is, resist radicalism.[5] Manifestly, the political situation was most confused. Grey's Government was a coalition; before it was formed, between 1827 and 1830, there were the Canningites, the ultra-Tories and two Whig groups

---

[1] A. Aspinall, 'English Party Organization in the Early Nineteenth Century', *English Historical Review*, vol. XLI (1926), pp. 389–411. D. Large, 'The Decline of "the Party of the Crown" and the Rise of Parties in the House of Lords, 1783–1837', *ibid.*, vol. LXXVIII (1963), pp. 669–95.

[2] Pares, *King George III and the Politicians*, pp. 195–6. P. Fraser, 'The Growth of Ministerial Control in the Nineteenth-century House of Commons', *English Historical Review*, vol. LXXV (1960), esp. pp. 454–5.

[3] J. Ranby, *Inquiry into the supposed increase of the influence of the Crown* (London, 1811), esp. pp. 41–5.

[4] *Ibid.*, p. 12.

[5] C. C. F. Greville, *Journal of the Reigns of George IV and William IV* (London, 1875), vol. II, pp. 353–4. R. Gooch, *The Book of the Reformed Parliament* (London, 1834). This last deserves further study.

operating with more or less independence and cohesion in the House of Commons, as well as the supporters of Wellington's Government; after Grey's Government left office, in 1834–5, 'the Derby Dilly' acted to some extent as a separate party.[1] But the most recent treatment of the change of the government in 1830 gives prominence to 'the activity of the established parties'.[2] It may be significant that the rebellious county members at that time were known as 'Ultra-Tories' rather than 'independents'. Perhaps it is this which is the chief importance of Althorp's elevation to the leadership first of the Opposition, then the House: that a natural 'independent' should be propelled by other natural 'independents' into office.[3] The incident resembles those of 1784 and 1788, when country gentlemen tried to bring about a coalition;[4] but it differs from them in this vital respect, that in 1830 the country gentlemen were prepared to take part in the coalition. Finally, it would seem to be during the Reform Bill debates— at one bound rather than by a slow process—that the majority of hitherto 'non-political' Members, those who had been accustomed not to vote at all, became involved in politics. The largest division before 1831, it appears, was on Tierney's motion for a committee on the state of the nation in 1819, in which 539 M.P.s took part.[5] The first reading of the Reform Bill was carried by one vote in a House of 607. Thereafter, divisions in which over 600 M.P.s voted were not uncommon. Political involvement is more than half-way to party affiliation.

A related development was the disappearance of the sort of 'non-political' Member who has been likened to a civil servant, the Under-Secretary or Civil Lord whose tenure of office was unaffected by changes of government and who always

[1] A. Aspinall, 'The Canningite Party', *Transactions of the Royal Historical Society*, 4th series, vol. XVII (1934), pp. 177–226. Aspinall, 'The Last of the Canningites' *English Historical Review*, vol. L (1935), pp. 639–67. D. C. Moore, 'The Other Face of Reform', *Victorian Studies*, vol. V (1961), pp. 7–34. D. W. J. Johnson, 'Sir James Graham and the "Derby Dilly"', *University of Birmingham Historical Journal*, vol. IV (1953–4), pp. 66–80.
[2] C. Flick, 'The Fall of Wellington's Government', *Journal of Modern History*, vol. XXXVII (1965), pp. 62–71.
[3] Cf. Gash, *Reaction and Reconstruction*, p. 165n. and Aspinall, *English Historical Review*, vol. XLI (1926), p. 393. Although the letter quoted by Gash from Le Marchant's *Althorp* describes a very limited 'election' as leader, it is evident from that book that the incident had a wider significance.
[4] See Namier, *Personalities and Powers*, pp. 30–2, and *Crossroads of Power*, pp. 227–9.
[5] Foord, *His Majesty's Opposition*, pp. 457–8.

supported the government of the day.   Some of these, together
with some Household officers, made up the core of the 'King's
friends'.   The change of government in 1830 revealed that this
type of 'non-political' Member no longer existed, though it is
difficult to determine precisely when he had left the scene.
The last Parliamentary stronghold of this type was among the
Household officers in the Lords, where their position was
regularized in the 1830s.[1]   In the Commons, 'the aristocratic
concept of "the King's Government" ' would seem to have
been overborne by the party system even before 1830.

IV

The 'independent' Member, then, in the sense of the 'non-
party' Member, scarcely existed between 1835 and 1845, and
two 'strongly organized, disciplined parliamentary parties' all
but divided the House of Commons between them.   Though in
the generation after 1845 parties were weaker, and for much of
the time more numerous, there was little sign of 'non-party'
Members.   In the generation before 1835 also, parties were
weaker, and for much of the time more numerous; and until
around 1830 there was a considerable body of 'non-political'
M.P.s.   But almost all those who were politically active were
party men.

These conclusions make it possible to comment on Namier's
summary of the whole development of constitutional monarchy.
It is plain that the party discipline of these years did not arise
from Members depending on party for their seats.   In many
constituencies the improved central party organs had no
influence, and many Members were elected on account of their
personal or hereditary position.   Yet such Members, like
many peers, obeyed a party whip.

It is plain too that, at least in 1835 and 1841, parties were
strong and disciplined enough to impose Prime Ministers on
the monarch.   But that is not to say that he thereby at once
totally lost the choice of the Prime Minister.   'Queen Victoria
never took a more active part in choosing a Prime Minister
than when she laid her commands upon the Peelite Lord

[1] Namier, *Crossroads of Power*, pp. 220–3, and *Personalities and Powers*, pp. 22–5.
G. Kitson Clark, '"Statesmen in Disguise": Reflexions on the History of the
Neutrality of the Civil Service', *Historical Journal*, vol. II (1959), pp. 27–8, 34.
Large, *English Historical Review*, vol. LXXVIII (1963), pp. 685–90.

Aberdeen.'[1]   George V in a sense chose MacDonald to lead the National Government in 1931; Elizabeth II in a sense chose Macmillan in 1957 and Home in 1963.   Instances similar to the last two are unlikely to recur, now that the Conservative Party as well as the Labour Party has a procedure for the election of a leader in such circumstances.   But there may still be occasions when no party has a majority in the House of Commons or a coalition is demanded and the monarch has to select the Prime Minister.   On the other hand, even before 1830 there were occasions when the monarch had no real choice.   Professor Gash has given the best formulation of what happened in the 1830s and 1840s.   In 1834 William IV, and in 1839 Victoria, were still making choices 'against the grain of politics'.   After the experience of 1841 Victoria and Albert took a conscious decision to place themselves above parties— though not above policies.   The symbol of this determination was their surrender of their electoral patronage in 1845.   The Queen was certainly very active in promoting the formation of the Aberdeen Government in 1852, but she was now working *with* the grain of politics.[2]   It may be suggested that, but for their conviction that they ought to be neutral as between the parties, Victoria and Albert might have succeeded in the political confusion of the 1850s in making good a choice of Prime Minister dictated by personal predilection rather than by constitutional propriety.   However, by the time, after Albert's death, that the Queen had half-forgotten their good resolution, the parties were again few and disciplined enough to give her little opportunity to assert her personal views.

Consideration of this subject provokes this final thought. Thanks to the work of Dr Kitson Clark among others, the 1830s and 1840s are comparatively well understood.   But the previous period, though so evidently vital in constitutional as in other branches of history, is still to a surprising degree unknown.

[1] Pares, *King George III and the Politicians*, p. 191.

[2] Gash, *Politics in the Age of Peel*, esp. ch. XIV, and *Reaction and Reconstruction*, ch. I.

☆ 2 ☆

Social Structure, Political Structure, and Public Opinion in Mid-Victorian England

I

AS Dr Kitson Clark noted in his Ford lectures, historians have occasionally used 'generalizations . . . inherited from contemporaries of the events themselves, who might have been strong partisans of one side or other in the conflicts of the period. . . .'[1] In consequence of this procedure events have sometimes been described less in terms of how they in fact occurred than in terms of how certain protagonists wished it to be believed they occurred, or—what often comes to the same thing—how these men themselves believed they occurred. In English history this is particularly true for the nineteenth century and, among nineteenth-century phenomena, for those having to do with the development and functioning of parliamentary government. In effect, historians have only rarely considered the public relations aspects of their problems. In particular, they have tended to ignore the functional imperatives which politicians faced who were trying to deal with a widening electorate in such a manner as to guarantee their own survival. Instead, historians have tended to accept contemporary interpretations of events at face value especially when these interpretations are consistent with certain models of electoral behaviour which were widely accepted during the nineteenth century—indeed, which can almost be said to have been produced during the century, and which are among the more important conceptual legacies of the century.

[1] *The Making of Victorian England* (London, 1962), p. 3.

Two such conceptual models may be specified, the individual model and the class model. According to the one, voters behave as individuals, their behaviour conditioned by their objective understanding of the ways in which their individual interests might be furthered within the context of the problems which issues represent. According to the other, voters behave as members of classes, their behaviour conditioned by their objective understanding of the needs of the classes to which they belong. Each of these models raises serious difficulties. Yet whatever the number of persons who actually behave as the individual model requires, on one level this model raises fewer difficulties than the class model. Individuals enjoy an *a priori* existence which classes do not enjoy. Of course, class lines can always be drawn with varying degrees of precision depending upon the social, economic or other circumstances existing at the time, and upon the criteria used for the purpose. But such classes do not always possess internal cohesion. Marxist theory notwithstanding, aggregates of persons possessing similar economic or other attributes do not automatically constitute political groups. Unfortunately, however, many historians tend to assume that they do. In consequence, historians have often treated the groups with which they deal as if these groups were both logically and chronologically antecedent to the issues in terms of which they behaved. In short, historians have tended to ignore the possible rôles which issues played in conditioning the existence of these groups themselves. They have also tended to assume that the men who defined these issues were simply the spokesmen of these groups, that the issues themselves had little to do with the rôles of these men *vis-à-vis* their respective groups.

In dealing with the world today most sociologists and political scientists have found that the individual model is totally inadequate: voters seldom formulate their own opinions. Superficially, the inadequacies of the class model have been somewhat less apparent. Yet because many voters do not behave according to what might be called their objective economic or other interests, many social scientists have come to regard classes and other groups as the products of diverse social, economic and ideological phenomena. But historians have been almost totally untouched by the various empirical findings which have prompted many of their colleagues in other disciplines to discard the individual model *in toto*, and to amend the class model so as to allow for the rôles of issues, ideologies and leaders in conditioning the membership and cohesion of the effective behavioural groups which exist at any given time.

If the reason for this has to do with the fact that historians cannot use the same social survey techniques which others have used to test their own models, the reason is not always as compelling as it might seem.   Indeed, for English historians of the period before 1872 a body of evidence exists for which many social scientists would give their eyeteeth.   Until the adoption of the secret ballot, voting in England was open. When they went to the polls English voters declared their choices publicly, before all to see and hear.   And—lest anyone forget what he had seen or heard—after almost every contested election in almost every constituency a list was published indicating the voters' names and the votes they cast.   Most of these poll books identify each voter by his place of residence, some by the location of his electoral qualification. Some poll books also specify each voter's principal occupation. But all of them contain the basic electoral information by which the behavioural groups in each constituency might be defined and, in some cases, by which the factors might be specified which conditioned their cohesion.   By generally ignoring this body of evidence historians have not only deprived themselves of valuable information; they have also deprived themselves of the opportunity of assimilating the implications of its existence.   These implications have an important bearing upon the relationships among social structure, political structure and, for lack of a better term, 'public opinion' during the period for which poll books are available.   In addition, they have an important bearing upon the reasons why, shortly after the second Reform Act was passed, poll books ceased to be published.

II

In many cases poll books—especially county poll books— reveal patterns of electoral behaviour which are scarcely compatible with either the individual model or the class model.

County poll books show that many men, when they went to the polls, behaved not as individuals but as members of clearly definable groups. But the groups these men composed cannot be defined in class terms. Criteria of wealth, status, or relationship to the means of production are effectively useless as means of distinguishing the men who voted together. But in many cases these men can be distinguished in geographic terms. Hence the importance of the fact that county poll books listed those men together who either resided in the same parish or whose electoral qualifications were located in the same parish. In effect, because of their own geographic organization, county poll books provide a means of distinguishing the different groups of voters from one another. But they do more than this. Poll books also suggest that the principal factors which conditioned the behaviour of each electoral group— which defined it as a group—were endogenous to the localities in which the group existed. At any given election many examples of local electoral unanimity, and many more examples of near unanimity, can be found in every county poll book. Furthermore, if and when the voters in a given parish changed their political orientation they tended to do so as a bloc. Before considering the internal dynamics of these blocs—what it was which held them together and defined their orientation —it will be useful to look at certain examples of these blocs themselves.

At the five contested elections in Cambridgeshire between 1826 and 1835 the great majority of the voters in the parishes of Stetchworth, Thorney and Royston polled as separate blocs clearly distinguishable from one another in consequence of their differing political orientations (Table A, p. 24).

The same is true of the voters resident in the Northamptonshire parishes of Aldwinkle and Lowick. The two parishes are directly adjacent to one another. Yet each contained a distinct behavioural group (Table B, p. 26).

Whether the orientations of the local electoral groups were politically simple, as in Stetchworth, Royston, Aldwinkle and Lowick, or complex, as in Thorney, where all but one of the local voters split his votes between the Whig and Tory candidates in 1830, such patterns of local unanimity and near unanimity can be seen fairly often. Indeed, they are so

TABLE A

Polls for the parishes of Stetchworth, Thorney and Royston at the elections of 1826, 1830, 1831, 1832 and 1835.[1]

	1826				1830				1831 (by-election)			1832					1835				
	voters in the parish	votes for Manners (Tory)	votes for Osborne (Whig)	votes for Adeane (Independent)	voters in the parish	votes for Manners (Tory)	votes for Osborne (Whig)	votes for Adeane (Independent)	voters in the parish	votes for Yorke (Tory)	votes for Townley (Whig)	voters in the parish	votes for Yorke (Tory)	votes for Townley (Whig)	votes for Childers (Whig)	votes for Adeane (Independent)	voters in the parish	votes for Yorke (Tory)	votes for Eaton (Tory)	votes for Townley (Whig)	votes for Childers (Whig)
Stetchworth	3	3	0	0	2	2	0	0	7	7	0	13	13	0	0	0	20	20	20	0	0
Thorney	5	3	5	0	12	11	12	0	19	0	19	57	3	57	57	8	53	0	0	53	53
Royston	21	6	16	12	19	3	16	15	34	3	31	25	7	20	20	16	22	6	4	18	19

¹ These polls, and those for other Cambridgeshire parishes and towns mentioned below, are taken from *The Poll for Election of Two Representatives in Parliament for the County of Cambridge* (Cambridge, 1826), *The Poll for two Knights of the Shire for the County of Cambridgeshire* (Cambridge, 1830), *The Poll of an Election of a Representative in Parliament for the County of Cambridgeshire* (Cambridge, 1831), *The Poll of the Election of Three Knights of the Shire for the County of Cambridgeshire* (London, 1833), and *The Poll of the Election of Three Knights of the Shire for the County of Cambridgeshire* (Cambridge, 1835). At the general election of 1826 Manners and Osborne were returned; at that of 1830, Osborne and Adeane. No contest occurred in the county at the general election of 1831. But a contest did occur at a by-election in October when Townley was returned. At the general election of 1832 Yorke, Townley and Childers were returned, at that of 1835, Yorke, Eaton and Townley. Thereafter, no contest occurred in the county until 1857 when, if the tables were enlarged, similar patterns would be apparent as they would be again for the contest of 1868. During the period to which this paper refers, each voter could vote for as many candidates as there were seats to be filled at the election. Each of the constituencies whose poll books are cited below was a two-member constituency except for Cambridgeshire, which, after 1832, had three members. Thus, at the Cambridgeshire elections before 1832, and at the elections in Northamptonshire and Huntingdonshire, twice as many votes could be cast as there were voters to cast them. In Cambridgeshire between 1832 and 1868 three times as many votes could be cast as there were voters to cast them. Since it was not possible to cast more than one vote for any one candidate, the number of votes received by a candidate could not exceed the total number of voters. However, since an elector was not required to use all his votes, the number of votes cast at a general election, when there was more than one seat to be filled, was not necessarily equal to the number of votes which might have been cast.

c

TABLE B

Polls for the parishes of Aldwinkle and Lowick at the elections of 1831, 1832 and 1835.[1]

	1831					1832					1835 (by-election)		
	voters in the parish	votes for Cartwright (Tory)	votes for Knightley (Tory)	votes for Althorp (Whig)	votes for Milton (Whig)	voters in the parish	votes for Brudenell (Tory)	votes for Tryon (Tory)	votes for Milton (Whig)	votes for Hanbury (Whig)	voters in the parish	votes for Maunsell (Tory)	votes for Hanbury (Whig)
Aldwinkle	15	0	0	14	15	29	4	5	25	24	30	8	22
Lowick	4	4	4	0	0	12	12	12	0	0	11	11	0

[1] The polls for these parishes are taken from *A Copy of the Poll of the Freeholders as taken at the Election of Knights of the Shire for the County of Northamptonshire, 1831 ...* (Northampton, 1831); *Copy of the Poll, for Two Knights, for the Northern Division of the County of Northamptonshire ...* (Kettering, 1833), and *Copy of the Poll taken at the General Election for the Northern Division of Northampton* (Northampton, 1835). The poll book of 1835 was mistitled. There was no contest in North Northamptonshire at the general elections in January 1835. But there was a contest at the by-election in December 1835. It was this contest to which the poll book referred.

pervasive as to raise the question whether the modern concept of 'public opinion' is a useful means of dealing with early and mid-nineteenth-century elections.   For practical purposes, the impact of 'opinion' cannot be distinguished from the impact of those other factors which conditioned the existence of these various groups.   As a rule, the changes in the total constituency polls which account for the return of one candidate at one election and for another candidate at another election were the products of local changes of orientation of the various electoral groups, most of which retained their own cohesion. The Huntingdonshire polls books of 1826, 1831, and 1837 provide a case in point.

According to the electoral behaviour of the majority of their residents at these elections the various parishes in Huntingdonshire can be distinguished fairly readily into ten different groups.   According to what might be called 'party' consistency, or ideological consistency, three of these groups of parishes can be distinguished from the remainder.   In one of these three groups the majority of the voters polled for the two Tory candidates at each of these elections.   In another, the majority of the voters cast single votes for the Whig candidates in 1826 and 1837 but split their votes in 1831 between the two reform candidates, one of whom was a Whig, the other a Tory.   And in another, the majority of the voters polled for the two Tory candidates in 1826 and 1837 but cast single votes in 1831 for the Tory candidate who opposed the Bill.   But in the remainder of the parishes in the county—48 of the 104 from which voters polled at these elections—majorities of voters either split their votes across the lines of both 'party' and ideology, in some cases voting for both the pro-reform and anti-reform candidates in 1831, changed their orientations between elections from Tory to Whig, or Whig to Tory, or split their votes and changed their orientations.   To a large extent the returns of different candidates at these elections should be attributed to these changing orientations.   But the point to note is this: in most of the parish groups the voters tended to poll as blocs whatever their orientation in any given election.   In 1837 the different electoral groups in the county tended to sort themselves out more in terms of parliamentary alliances: split votes across 'party' or issue lines were less

TABLE C

Total polls of the Huntingdonshire voters at the elections of 1826, 1831 and 1837, who can be readily identified with the various parishes in the county.[1]

1826		1831		1837	
voters	1,281	voters	1,214	voters	2,266
votes for Mandeville	759	votes for Mandeville	717	votes for Fellowes	1,381
	(Tory)		(Tory)		(Tory)
votes for Fellowes	689	votes for Rooper	619	votes for Thornhill	1,322
	(Tory)		(Whig)		(Tory)
votes for Russell	608	votes for Strathavon	496	votes for Rooper	985
	(Whig)		(Tory)		(Whig)

[1] These totals and those cited in Table D are taken from *A Copy of the Poll for Two Knights of the Shire for the County of Huntingdon* (Huntingdon [1826]), *The Poll for Two Knights of the Shire for the County of Huntingdon* (Cambridge [1831]), and *Copy of the Poll taken at the General Election for the County of Huntingdon* (Huntingdon [1837]). Unfortunately, for 1826 and 1831 there are sizeable numbers of voters who cannot readily be identified with any parish in the county. These were the 'outvoters', those men who, while owning property in the county, resided outside the county. The problem of their geographic assignment arises in 1826 and 1831 from the fact that the Huntingdonshire poll books for these years were organized on the basis of the parish of residence. In 1837, when the poll book was organized on the basis of the parish of qualification, this problem does not arise. Thus, for 1826 and 1831 the totals of votes revealed in the Tables fall somewhat short of the totals of votes which the sheriff reported. These were as follows: in 1826, Mandeville 968, Fellowes 911, and Russell 858; in 1831, Rooper 841, Mandeville 813, and Strathavon 575. For 1837 there are smaller—indeed negligible—discrepancies between the two sets of figures, which probably derive either from errors of the men who kept the records on which the poll book was based, from errors in the sheriff's office, or from both. As announced in 1837, the final poll was as follows: Fellowes 1,392, Thornhill 1,332, and Rooper 990.

Except in 1831, the totals of votes announced by the sheriff and the totals of votes cast by voters who can be identified with the various parishes in the county assign the same relative standings to the various candidates. In 1831, counting only the votes cast by voters resident in the county, Mandeville received more votes than Rooper. But if the outvoters be included, Rooper received a few more votes than Mandeville. Unfortunately, again, there was another contest in the county during this period—in 1830—for which the poll book was not available when the research was being pursued upon which this paper is based. At this contest the same candidates stood as in 1831. But in 1830 Mandeville and Strathavon were returned. On this occasion, including the votes cast by the outvoters, Mandeville received 1,012, Strathavon 943, and Rooper 759. The unavailability of this poll book is particularly unfortunate since it obviates what might have been an extremely revealing comparison between the geographical bases of support of Strathavon and Rooper in 1830 and 1831. But neither the unavailability of the poll book of 1830 nor the omissions of the outvoters in 1826 and 1831 affects the behavioural patterns which Table D reveals.

frequent than they had been before. But the returns of different candidates at different elections cannot be attributed to the decisions of individual voters affected by shifting tides of cosmopolitan 'opinion'. In certain groups of parishes local electoral agreement was less pronounced in 1831 or 1837 than it had been in 1826. But the general pattern of local electoral agreement remained. In some cases it was even stronger in 1837 than in 1826 or 1831.

The cumulative effects of these changing orientations are apparent from the total polls of the voters who can be readily identified with the various parishes in the county. But these total polls obscure their own essential components. In consequence, they also obscure the nature of the factors which produced them (Table C).

Among the politically consistent parishes was a group of thirty-three in which large majorities of voters polled for the Tory candidates, Viscount Mandeville and William Henry Fellowes, in 1826, for Mandeville and Lord Strathavon in 1831, and for the Tory candidates, Edward Fellowes, the son of the former member, and George Thornhill in 1837. From these parishes the Whig candidates, Lord John Russell and John Bonfoy Rooper received relatively few votes (see Group 1 of Table D, p. 30). Also among the politically consistent parishes was a group of twenty in which majorities of the voters polled strongly for Russell or Rooper. In 1831, however, a large proportion of the voters in these parishes split their votes between Rooper and Strathavon, thus, presumably, rewarding Strathavon for his vote in Parliament in support of the first Reform Bill, and trying to defend him against the opposition of many of his erstwhile friends (see Group 2 of Table D). Clearly, certain of Strathavon's erstwhile friends can be seen in three parishes where overwhelming majorities of votes were cast for the *two* Tory candidates in 1826 and 1837, but where most of the voters cast single votes for Mandeville in 1831 (see Group 3 of Table D).

In the remainder of the parishes in the county the majorities of the local voters either changed their political orientations between elections, or, at one election or another, voted irrespective of both normal 'party' lines and the ideological lines reflected in the behaviour of the voters in the parishes in

TABLE D

An analysis of the Huntingdonshire poll books of 1826, 1831 and 1837, showing the patterns of behaviour of the resident voters.[1]

	1826				1831				1837			
	number of voters in the group	votes for Mandeville (Tory)	votes for Fellowes (Tory)	votes for Russell (Whig)	number of voters in the group	votes for Mandeville (Tory)	votes for Strathavon (Tory)	votes for Rooper (Whig)	number of voters in the group	votes for Fellowes (Tory)	votes for Thornhill (Tory)	votes for Rooper (Whig)
Politically or ideologically consistent parishes												
Group 1	477	368	381	99	463	351	297	130	768	596	579	191
Group 2	158	22	18	141	133	11	61	102	354	103	95	267
Group 3	52	52	39	7	59	57	3	9	93	82	83	11
Politically or ideologically inconsistent parishes, and those in which majorities of voters changed their political orientations between elections												
Group 4	175	110	107	73	167	104	32	113	220	140	137	91
Group 5	117	87	29	83	100	65	17	66	220	144	138	90
Group 6	168	43	47	129	183	71	36	144	296	115	110	197
Group 7	54	29	36	22	40	12	10	33	116	75	67	48
Group 8	48	27	11	38	41	32	28	6	108	84	76	33
Group 9	23	17	14	8	18	8	7	11	69	30	25	45
Group 10	9	4	1	8	8	3	5	3	22	12	12	12
Poll book totals	1,281	759	683	608	1,212	714	496	617	2,266	1,381	1,322	985
Totals announced by the sheriff		968	911	858		813	575	814		1,392	1,332	990
Totals of votes cast by the voters in Groups 3–7.	566	321	258	314	549	309	98	365	945	556	535	437

The groupings of the parishes covered by Table D are:

Group 1: The parishes of Brampton, Bury, Little Catworth, Chesterton, Conington, Covington, Diddington, Everton with Tetworth, Eynesbury, Little Gidding, Steeple Gidding, Graffham, Haddon, Hamerton, Hemingford Abbots, Hemingford Grey, Huntingdon, Keyston, Leighton, Luddington, Offord Darcy, Oldhurst, Orton Longville, St Neots, Little Paxton, Ramsey, Stow with Catworth, Little Stukeley, Upton, Upwood, Waresley, Wooley, and Wyton.

Group 2: The parishes of Colne, Denton, Earith, Farcet, Fletton, Great Gidding, Glatton, Lutton with Washingley, Morbourne, Water Newton, Orton Waterville, Great Paxton, King Ripton, Sawtry All Saints, Sawtry St Andrew, Sawtry St Judith, Sibson with Stibbington, Stilton, Toseland, and Yaxley.

Group 3: The parishes of Barham, Kimbolton, and Swineshead.

Group 4: The parishes of Abbotsley, Godmanchester, Great Gransden, Hail Weston, Hilton, Offord Cluny, Southoe, Warboys, and Yelling.

Group 5: The parishes of Alconbury, Brington, Buckden, Great Catworth, Copingford, Easton, Spaldwick, Great Staughton, Old Weston, and Winwick.

Group 6: The parishes of Bluntisham, Buckworth, Elton, Holme, St Ives, Pidley with Fenton, Somersham, and Woodhurst.

Group 7: The parishes of Broughton, Fenstanton, Great Faveley, Abbot Ripton, Great Stokeley and Wistow.

Group 8: The parishes of Bythorn, Ellington, Molesworth, Papworth Agnes, Stanground, Thurning, Woodstone, and Woodwalton.

Group 9: The parishes of Hartford, Holywell with Needingworth, Houghton, and Midloe.

Group 10: The parishes of Alwalton, Caldecot, and Folkesworth.

Groups 2 and 3 of Table D. In nine parishes which were otherwise Tory—although not heavily so—the obvious vendetta against Strathavon in 1831 produced somewhat anomalous majorities for Rooper, the pro-Bill candidate, and Mandeville, the anti-Bill candidate (see Group 4 of Table D). In ten other parishes this pattern of vote-splitting across 'party' lines was already apparent in 1826. It remained strong in 1831. But it vanished in 1837. The parishes became Tory—although not heavily so (see Group 5 of Table D). In eight parishes where Russell received heavy majorities in 1826 and where Rooper received smaller proportionate majorities in 1837, a significant number of voters also split their votes between Rooper and Mandeville in 1831 (see Group 6 of Table D). In six parishes which were Tory both in 1826 and 1837—although not heavily so—there was a strong swing to Rooper individually in 1831 (see Group 7 of Table D). In eight parishes the pattern of split votes between Russell and Mandeville, apparent in 1826, was replaced by strong Tory majorities in both 1831 and 1837 (see Group 8 of Table D). In four parishes where sizeable Tory majorities are apparent in 1826 the majority of the voters polled for Rooper in both 1831 and 1837 (see Group 9 of Table D). And, finally, in three parishes the clarity of political orientation evident in the strong majorities for Russell in 1826 became dissipated by 1837 (see Group 10 of Table D). Especially in view of the rôle of the outvoters, it somewhat exceeds the implications of the evidence to say that Strathavon was defeated in 1831, and Rooper defeated in 1837 solely because of the endogenous factors which conditioned the existence and orientation of the behavioural groups in the various parishes in Groups 3, 4, 5, 6 and 7 of Table D. On the other hand, the importance of these factors as well as of those which conditioned the existence and orientation of the other behavioural groups in the other parishes in the county can scarcely be ignored.

Of course, Huntingdonshire may be something of a special case. In both Cambridgeshire and Northamptonshire there were many parishes in which behavioural patterns analogous to those in Huntingdonshire cannot be seen in the poll books. Possibly, in such parishes cohesive behavioural groups did not exist. On the other hand, what may be lacking is the appropriate evidence which would reveal their existence.   As a rule, the towns and villages in which analogous patterns cannot be seen in the poll books contained large numbers of voters. Thus, the problem becomes extremely complicated of trying to distinguish the voters within them into the various groups which they may have composed.   Such a problem does not arise in the Cambridgeshire parish of Soham.   In spite of the number of voters in the parish the existence of a behavioural group is obvious.   But it does arise in the town of Cambridge (Table E, p. 34).   Possibly, the voters in Cambridge comprised behavioural groups equally as cohesive as those in Stetchworth or Thorney, but groups whose existence is obscured by the total polls for the town much as the existence of the Stetchworth, Thorney and Royston groups would be obscured if the poll books themselves did not reveal them.   Indeed, many voters in the town *seem* to have behaved as members of groups.   At successive elections the same men can usually be found voting together for the same candidates.   But in the town of Cambridge—at least with the evidence currently available—such behavioural patterns cannot be attributed to anything more than the coincidental agreement of individuals.

In many rural parishes this is not the case.   There, the patterns of local electoral agreement can often be seen for what they are, measures of the social significance of the communities which the parishes themselves represented.   The parish of Thorney, for example, was effectively congruent with the boundaries of an estate belonging to the Whig Dukes of Bedford.[1]   Undoubtedly, the cohesion of the Thorney voters was a measure of Bedford's influence among them, an influence transmitted through the agency of the estate and fairly well circumscribed by its limits.   Confirmation of this hypothesis lies in the relative uniqueness of the political progression of the Thorney voters, and the close relation between their political progression and the political vagaries of the sixth Duke.   In the summer of 1830 Bedford abandoned his normal Whig affiliations to vote with Wellington on the regency

[1] Information on Cambridgeshire landownership has been taken primarily from Robert Gardner, *History, Gazetteer and Directory of Cambridgeshire* (Peterborough, 1851), supplemented by E. P. Kelly, *The Post Office Directory of Cambridgeshire* (London, 1846).

TABLE E

Polls for the parish of Soham and the town of Cambridge at the elections of 1826, 1830, 1831, 1832 and 1835.

	1826				*1830*				*1831* (by-election)			*1832*				*1835*					
	voters in the parish or town	votes for Manners (Tory)	votes for Osborne (Whig)	votes for Adeane (Independent)	voters in the parish or town	votes for Manners (Tory)	votes for Osborne (Whig)	votes for Adeane (Independent)	voters in the parish or town	votes for Yorke (Tory)	votes for Townley (Whig)	voters in the parish or town	votes for Yorke (Tory)	votes for Townley (Whig)	votes for Childers (Whig)	votes for Adeane (Independent)	voters in the parish or town	votes for Yorke (Tory)	votes for Eaton (Tory)	votes for Townley (Whig)	votes for Childers (Whig)
Soham	109	109	2	0	155	129	25	34	130	123	7	222	199	30	32	27	202	176	181	34	34
Cambridge	378	171	260	195	456	217	325	245	471	168	303	376	225	231	184	185	394	216	196	238	199

question.   But he returned to the Whig fold the following year.[1]
In only three other Cambridgeshire parishes did a significant
number of voters poll *à la* Thorney in 1830.   In only one of
these, Doddington, did a majority of the voters follow an
identical progression in all five elections.   There, the cohesion
and orientation of the local behavioural group were undoubtedly a measure of the social significance of the Peyton
estate.   The Peyton family, the predominant landowners in
the parish, had close connexions with the Russell family.[2]
In Wimblington, where the majority of the twenty-four voters
who polled in 1830 split their votes between Osborne and
Manners, analogous factors were probably responsible.   Both
the cohesion and orientation of the relevant group were
probably measures of the local property interests of the Duberly
family of Huntingdonshire.   However, in the town of March,
where forty-two of the hundred voters who polled in 1830
split their votes between Manners and Osborne, a number of
questions arise which, with the available evidence, cannot be
answered.   For March, no clear nexus is apparent which
might account for the cohesion of these men or for their
peculiar orientation.

While the rarity of split votes between Osborne and Manners
in 1830 serves to isolate the groups in which they occurred and
—except in March—to suggest the factors to which they
should be attributed, the fact that other electoral progressions
were more usual does not in itself imply that different types
of factor were responsible for them when they occurred.   In
many other parishes majorities of voters were obviously just

[1] From Huntingdonshire, where Bedford had considerable property as well,
and thus where his own political alliances had considerable impact, Capt. James
Duberly wrote to Lord Milton, '. . . no one can comprehend the Duke of Bedford's
vote'.   (5 July 1830, Fitzwilliam Papers, Northamptonshire Record Office.)   Three
days later the Marquis of Tavistock provided a possible explanation of his father's
behaviour when he observed—also to Milton—that enough mischief had been
done by strong Governments, and that Wellington's Government was 'too weak
for evil, & yet strong enough to carry through any good measure that may be
forced upon them'.   (8 July 1830, Fitzwilliam Papers, Northamptonshire Record
Office.)

[2] The Reverend Algernon Peyton, later described as 'the great dry nurse of
Whig candidates' in the county, (Cambridge *Chronicle*, 21 March 1857) was a
frequent chairman of local Whig meetings at which Bedford could not preside
because of his status as a peer, e.g., in 1831, to choose a 'reform candidate' upon
Osborne's resignation.   (Cambridge *Independent Press*, 8 October 1831.)   In 1844
Peyton's daughter, Elizabeth, was married to Lord Francis-John Russell, son of
the sixth Duke of Bedford.

as isolated from the tides of 'opinion' as they were in Thorney. In Stetchworth, where not a single Whig or Liberal vote was cast between 1826 and 1868, the cohesion and orientation of the local behavioural group were obviously a measure of the ramifications of the Eaton estate. The Eaton family, whose Toryism was unimpeachable, were the predominant land-owners in the parish. In the latter 'thirties the behaviour of the majority of the Soham voters was attributed to the influence of the Tory Dobede family, the predominant landowners in the adjacent parish of Exning.[1] In Aldwinkle, the predomin-ant landowner was the Whig, Lord Lilford; in Lowick, the predominant landowner was the Tory, W. B. Stopford.[2] Among the parishes in Group 3 of Table D was Kimbolton, the seat of the Earls of Sandwich, whose interest in 1831 was exerted against Strathavon, the apostate Tory, as well as against Rooper.[3] Nor did the tides of 'opinion' flow with any greater force in Royston than in Stetchworth. What dis-tinguished the two parishes was the orientation and, probably, the essential basis of cohesion of the local behavioural group. Tory votes in Royston were almost as rare as Whig votes in Stetchworth. But while the cohesion and orientation of the Stetchworth voters were undoubtedly due to the Eaton estate and the politics of the Eaton family, the cohesion and orienta-tion of the great majority of the Royston voters were probably a measure of the electoral implications of their religious non-conformity. Royston was a well-established Congregational centre.

In all probability poll books provide for these places a measure of the electoral importance of what might be called the 'deference community', the community of men who lived in close contact with one another, who had the same occupation or were connected by the same 'interest', and—most important of all—who recognized the same individual, or individuals, as their social, economic and ideological leader or leaders. But if these poll books reveal the electoral importance of these

[1] Such was the opinion of 'Screwdriver'. See his letter to the editor, Cambridge *Advertiser*, 14 August 1839.

[2] Information on Northamptonshire landownership has been taken from William Whelan and Co., *History, Gazetteer and Directory of Northamptonshire* (London, 1849).

[3] William Page and Granville Proby, 'Parliamentary History', *Victoria History of the County of Huntingdon* (London, 1932), vol. II, p. 54.

communities it is only because these communities were definable in geographic terms, and because these poll books distinguished the various parishes from one another in which they were located. Had they not done so—had the Stetchworth and Royston voters been lumped together with no means provided to disentangle them—each community would have eclipsed the other. This possibility suggests the inherent difficulties of using poll books to discover whether cohesive groups analogous to those in Stetchworth and Royston existed, and had the same electoral importance, in those places where a single behavioural group was not predominant, and where the factors responsible for its predominance are not fairly clear.

With the evidence currently available, borough poll books tell very little—merely that the men who voted in the borough disagreed with one another politically. The assumption is probably valid that the economic, religious and other groupings of urban society overlapped one another less frequently than was the case in the countryside. In all probability, when E. P. Frost observed in 1852 that not a single dissenter resided in the Cambridgeshire parish of West Wratting,[1] he was citing the effects of one of the principal criteria by which many landlords chose their tenants.[2] The sociological consequences —and hence the political consequences—of only allowing those men to become tenants on an estate who had the same religion and politics as their prospective landlord are obvious. Such a practice would tend to reinforce the cohesion of the estate at a time when, for purposes of administration, many estates

[1] His statement was reported in Cambridge *Chronicle*, 22 May 1852.

[2] Unfortunately, when statistics on the geographical distribution of the various religious groups were assembled in 1851 they were assembled on the basis of the registration district, not the village or parish. Because the registration districts were relatively large, the differences are thus obscured which, probably in many cases, existed among the several villages contained in the same district. For Cambridgeshire, no districts are shown in which absolutely no one attended a nonconformist service on 31 March 1851. Yet in all probability many individual villages were not so heterogeneous. As it is, the range of variation shown by the census in the proportions of dissenters among the different registration districts is great enough to suggest that the range of variation among individual villages, or parishes, was far greater. The proportion of dissenters varied from 40·0 per cent to 78·7 per cent. It is significant that the former proportion obtained in the south of the county, in the district of Linton, where most of the parishes were enclosed and where landownership was largely concentrated in the hands of Anglican squires. The latter proportion obtained in the fenland district of North Witchford where a number of parishes were unenclosed. Religious Worship, Sessional Papers, 1852–3, vol. LXXXIX, pp. 341–2.

were becoming far more organized than they had ever been before.[1] Whatever the accuracy of the Duke of Rutland's later argument, that most agricultural labourers preferred to live in their own communities—'near the church, and near his club'—and walk to work rather than live in 'close' parishes, those in which landownership was concentrated, and where they might not feel at home,[2] his argument itself reflects the strength of his belief that the geographic units in the country-side had broad sociological significance.　But even for the towns, it was widely assumed that men would sort themselves out according to analogous criteria.　Indeed, in 1843, the Radical William Ewart was able to prove—at least to his own satisfaction—how many Anglicans and how many dissenters were employed in certain cotton mills simply by specifying the numbers of men employed by Anglican and dissenting mill owners.[3]　He left it to his audience to complete his syllogism by supplying his major premise, that no Anglican would employ a dissenter and no dissenter an Anglican.

In all probability, townsmen were more anonymous than their rural cousins, less involved in such stable and multiple nexus as existed on many rural estates.　But until adequate studies are made of urban electoral behaviour the various and possibly changing factors which conditioned this behaviour must remain unknown.　Obviously, for the towns, the principal means by which the poll books identified the various men whose names they contained do not in themselves provide a key to these factors.　Urban street addresses did not define effective social, religious or economic communities in the same ways in which rural addresses defined them.　But while the nature of the poll book evidence prevents—at least for the present—any firm generalizations bearing upon the nature of electoral behaviour in the towns, the same evidence suggests that for many rural voters the local or neighbouring estate, or the local church or chapel, provided the essential channel through which politics impinged upon them.　Primarily, the votes they cast were social gestures.

---

[1] On this point see especially David Spring, *The English Landed Estate in the Nineteenth Century: Its Administration* (Baltimore, 1963).

[2] 3 *Hansard*, CLXXX (12 June 1865), 25.

[3] 3 *Hansard*, LXVII (24 March 1843), 1423.

III

In most cases in the counties such deference communities were fairly small. Their electoral impact was not individual but cumulative, the result of the coalitions in which their leaders engaged, coalitions whose dynamics were sometimes those of economic interest, religion, or personal relationship. Hence, the electoral importance of the new varieties of local political grouping which emerged both during and after the reform crisis, which were generally organized by the élites in the various constituencies, and which were generally focused upon the ideological issues in terms of which the various local élites tended to coalesce among themselves.[1] On occasion, however, a single deference community had important ramifications, particularly when its political orientation was changed. Largely because such occurred in East Norfolk, the two Conservative members for the division refused to fight for their seats in 1857, thereby allowing two Liberals to replace them quietly. The circumstances were somewhat unusual: the first Lord Wodehouse was an ardent Tory; his grandson and heir was an ardent Liberal. Thus, when the first Baron died his 'property and character' were debited from the Conservatives and credited to the Liberals.[2] Somewhat later, when Palmerston began to attract the support of certain important East Norfolk Conservatives, the local politicians became convinced that the division was no longer a Tory stronghold. Thus, when two appropriate Liberal candidates were found, the two Conservatives simply retired. In West Cornwall, in 1881, the Falmouth interest did not in fact change sides. But the assumptions of the deference community made some people

[1] E.g., the organization of the Northamptonshire Association for the Protection of Agriculture, in 1835, by the same men who, in 1832, had formed a Conservative Club in the county and who, in 1831, had agreed to advance the money necessary to start a local newspaper in the interests of the 'high Tory Party'. Concerning the newspaper, see the agreement of 27 October 1831 between William Cartwright, Sir Charles Knightley, Sir Henry Gunning, and William Wiles, Knightley Papers, K. CLVIII, 1391–1404, Northamptonshire Record Office. Concerning Cartwright's activities in the Club see J. S. Bentor to Cartwright, 16 June 1833, Cartwright Papers, Box 12, Northamptonshire Record Office. Concerning Gunning's activities on the protectionist association—he was the first chairman—see *The Times* (London), 26 January 1835.

[2] The phrase and description come from the discussion of the background of the uncontested election of 1857, which itself provided the background of the contested by-election of 1858. *The Poll for a Knight of the Shire for the Eastern Division of the County of Norfolk* (Norwich, 1858), pp. vi–xv.

believe it had: one of Lord Falmouth's tenants resigned his
office in his local Liberal association. Coming on top of the
rumours that Falmouth was deeply disturbed by the presence
of Bright and Chamberlain in Gladstone's second Cabinet, the
tenant's resignation produced consternation among the local
Liberal wirepullers. They thought the Falmouth interest had
switched. They were only satisfied that the tenant spoke for
himself alone, and that his behaviour might be a measure of
his health, not his politics, when one of the two Liberal members
for the division had an interview with Falmouth. But lest the
same evidence prompt their Conservative opponents to contest
the division at the next election—no contest had occurred in the
division since the first Reform Act had created it—they were
careful to advertise that Falmouth was still on their side.[1]

In all probability it was a matter of public knowledge who
was connected with the various major estates. Clearly—at
least in the case of one man—certain Liberals in Cornwall
knew. Clearly—at least in the case of several men—certain
Conservatives in Cambridgeshire knew also. And, by applying their knowledge within the context of their community
assumptions, they concluded—whether accurately or not is
another question—that the Duke of Rutland was opposed to
the prospective candidacy of the protectionist dissenter,
Edward Ball, in 1852. To them the evidence was clear: not
a single one of Rutland's tenants had attended a meeting in
support of Ball.[2] But for other types of community nexus
and, perhaps, for the lesser estates, such knowledge could only
be had by sending men out to get it.

Taking the counties as a whole, poll books probably obscure
as many of the effective behavioural groups as they reveal. An
accurate calendar of such groups would not be based on the
institutional form in which they often appeared, but on the
personal, or quasi-personal, relations from which they derived.
The astute local politician assembled his knowledge of such
relations wherever he could. Indeed, until fairly late in the
century the major function of local political organizations was

---

[1] See Henry Grylls, jun., to Arthur Pendarves Vivian, 25 and 26 May 1881,
and Vivian to Grylls, 26 May 1881 (copy), Vivian Papers, DDPV.I.8., Cornwall
Record Office.
[2] See the comments of Mr Cotton reported in the Cambridge *Chronicle*, 8 May
1852.

to provide the channels by which this knowledge could be gathered. Such was the rôle of the canvass. As the author of an electoral handbook explained, in 1826, the object of the canvass was not only to learn the exact number and names of the electors, and whether or not they were assessed to the land tax,[1] but also how each elector was disposed, whether he was favourable to the particular candidate for whom the canvasser was working, against him, uncertain, or neutral. And, if the elector fell into one of the latter three categories, it was the canvasser's job to learn what influences might be brought to bear upon him to promote him to the first.[2] In effect, it was the canvasser's job to discover the patterns of hierarchical relationship within the constituency. The only difference between this canvass and those which took place later in the century lay in the fact that after 1832 the canvassers had electoral registers at their disposal. They already knew the number and names of the electors. But it remained their job not only to learn that Richard Burrow, of Cullompton, in North Devonshire, would probably not vote in 1868, and that Thomas Grant, also of Cullompton, would probably vote for the Conservative candidates, Sir Stafford Northcote and Thomas Walrond, but also why. Concerning Burrow, the canvasser's comments are somewhat cryptic. He merely noted that Burrow was 'afraid' to vote because he was employed by a certain Mr Mortimore. Concerning Grant, his report is more revealing. Possibly, however, what he reported was already public knowledge: Grant was one of Walrond's tenants.[3] Frequently, of course, analogous information was available from the intimate local knowledge which some men already possessed. In 1868, for example, Edwin S. Coleridge informed the Liberal agent in North Devonshire that the Hon. Colin Lindsay of Brighton—he included his full address— might help overcome the adverse influences in the village of Honiton if he could be induced to bring influence to bear upon his own tenants within the village.[4] Presumably, a letter to

---

[1] G. Butt, *Suggestions as to the Conduct and Management of a County Contested Election* (London, 1826), p. 64.
[2] *Ibid.*, lvii–lviii.
[3] Liberal Canvassing Book for Cullompton [1868], Burrow Papers, 74B/MV3, Devonshire Record Office.
[4] See his letter of 26 August 1868, Burrow Papers, 74B/MV54.

D

Lindsay from the proper person went off by the next post. In forwarding his report to the local Liberal registration agent, in 1882, the Reverend Henry Fox Strangeways explained that his conclusions about the political opinions of the new electors who had recently been added to the register derived from his knowledge of 'their associations, and the influence that is likely to be brought to bear upon them'.[1]

While poll books were published and hence exist today in fairly large numbers, only a few such canvassing books and such private communications have survived the immediate period of their usefulness. Where they have survived, they reinforce the picture which the poll books themselves frequently reveal. They illustrate the degree to which electoral politics were attuned to the hierarchical structure of society. Political agents used their knowledge of this structure in a variety of ways, in choosing which men to propose for inclusion in the electoral register and which men to oppose, in recommending whether or not a contest would be advisable on a given occasion, and, of course, in bringing pressure to bear where it might be effective.

The importance of this knowledge is reflected in the extent of the organized efforts which were sometimes made to obtain it. In south west Yorkshire, for example, the Liberals had a network of committees, one in each polling district, by which —at least in theory—each voter in the district was canvassed before each contested election, by which the results of the canvass were sent to the central committee sitting in Wakefield, and—when possible—by which steps were taken to secure the promise of the votes of those men who, initially, were either neutral or doubtful. Before the election of 1865 the central committee sent to each polling district committee a marked copy of the electoral register for the district,[2] as well as other, unmarked copies. According to the instructions of the central committee, the unmarked copies were to be used to index the canvassing books which each district committee was to prepare. Against each name in the register the district committee was to enter the number of the canvassing book in which the name was inscribed and the number of the name within the book.

---

[1] Covering letter, 6 July 1882, accompanying the report for Silverston parish, Burrow Papers, 74B/MV48.

[2] Unfortunately, no copies of these have been found. Thus, what information the marks conveyed is not known.

Then, having compiled their canvassing books, and having done so in duplicate, each committee was to give one copy of each book to 'some intelligent and influential individual, or if possible, two in each [sub] District, to canvass every Voter'. Each evening the canvassers were to report in to the committee. At that time the information they had gathered, and which they had entered in their own books in pencil, was to be entered in ink in the copies of the canvassing books which the committee had retained. Possibly—although this was not indicated—these 'permanent' copies were ultimately forwarded to Wakefield where they provided the basis upon which the marked registers were drawn up before the subsequent election. But in the meantime, and also on a daily basis, the numerical results of the canvass were to be forwarded to the central committee. However, the canvassers' job did not end with a simple report of who had promised to vote for the Liberal candidates, who was neutral, who was doubtful, and who was against them. As the central committee explained, it was the canvassers' 'indispensable duty . . . [to] make further efforts to secure the support of neutral and doubtful voters'.[1]

Besides the mention of the marked registers—which, of course, may have been marked from previous poll books—no specific evidence is available either to show what the Liberals did with all this information once they had it, or even what their assumptions were in gathering it. For the Conservatives in the division, however, considerable evidence exists. In 1868 they had a similar network of committees. Every few days during the canvass the principal Conservative agent in the division met with his local agents—usually the secretaries of the polling district committees—both to spur them on and to learn, for example, that of the twenty-two doubtful voters in the parish of Thornhill 'about 5 will be Cons. but if *Searle* does not interfere more than 5, perhaps 1/2'.[2] On four occasions

[1] Circular letter from J. W. Childers, chairman, and R. J. Gainsford, secretary, Ramsden and Fitzwilliam Committee Room, Wakefield, 19 June 1865, Hinkleton Papers, A4/42. I wish to express my gratitude to Lord Halifax for permission to quote from these Papers, and to Mr Thomas Ingram for having arranged that I might use them.

[2] Report of the meeting of 22 October 1868, Nostell Papers, D3.8.1. I wish to express my gratitude to Lord St Oswald for permission to quote from these Papers, and to Mr Thomas Ingram for having arranged that I might use them. The potent Searle has not been identified.

during the course of the canvass the results of the canvass were arranged in tabular form showing, for each polling district, the total number of registered voters, the total number of votes promised to each of the candidates, Liberal as well as Conservative, the number of double entries in the register, the number of doubtful or neutral voters, the number of men on the register who had died since the register was compiled, and the number of men remaining to be canvassed. Of the 19,908 men on the register in 1868, the Conservatives claimed that only 1,890 were unaccounted for at the end of their canvass.

But the statements accompanying the final tabulation, and the social assumptions and realities which they reflect, are even more striking than the claim to have canvassed over 90 per cent of the voters in the division. 'Our usual experience,' the Conservatives declared, 'has been that we poll within 5% of our promises.'[1] On this basis they predicted the return of both Conservative candidates. Obviously, within the immediate context of the electoral situation, the rationale of the canvass lay in its usefulness as a means of appealing to the voters through the nexus of the groups they composed, and of obtaining firm promises of their support at the polls. But if the voters failed to make good on their promises—in effect, if the disciplinary agencies in the society broke down upon which the whole conduct of the canvass was based, the canvass would lose its essential value. And, as the Conservatives noted in 1868, 'at the last election exceptionally we lost 11–1/4 [per cent]'. But what they described as 'exceptional' was becoming the rule. At least in large part their predictions were wrong in 1868—their candidates were both defeated— because over 9 per cent of the voters who had promised to vote for them failed to do so.

Who these voters were they never specified—at least in the evidence which has been found. But in 1870, following the revision of the electoral register, the Conservatives adopted a new method of tabulation of gains and losses which is highly suggestive of who they *thought* these voters were. As before, they distinguished the new voters in political terms, 'Conservative', 'Radical', and 'Doubtful'—in effect, they tried to keep an annual running count of the balance of political power

[1] 'Mr Baxter's calculations,', 21 November [1868], Nostell Papers, D3.8.1.

in the constituency. But beginning in 1870 they also distinguished—as they had not done before—between the £12 occupiers, the men enfranchized by the second Reform Act, and the 'old qualifications'. In the tabulation of these latter, the number whose politics were described as 'doubtful' in 1870 was relatively small. Of those whose claims to be registered were sustained before the revising barrister, they described 700 as 'Conservative', 568 as 'Radical', and only 62 as 'Doubtful'. But among the 5,886 £12 occupiers whose claims were sustained, they described 1,126 as 'Doubtful'.[1] Similar proportions are apparent in subsequent years. Clearly, the Conservatives in south west Yorkshire had recognized the need to adopt a new method of tabulation which reflected a new set of social conditions. Yet, whether or not the criterion itself was valid by which the Conservatives tried to separate those men whose politics could generally be specified from those whose politics could not be specified so generally, it would be wrong to attribute the new political conditions occasioned by the advent of these latter solely to the second Reform Act. Even before 1865 something had happened which rendered the Conservatives' 'usual experience' obsolete as a model for the future. Whatever the reason—either because many voters were no longer members of cohesive behavioural groups, or because the Conservatives' canvassing techniques were no longer appropriate to the behavioural groups to which many voters belonged, or both—the expectations which they had based upon their 'usual experience' had already been disappointed in 1865.

IV

That electoral influence survived the first Reform Act is scarcely a novelty to historians familiar with the work of Professor Norman Gash and Professor H. J. Hanham. But the implications of its survival have not been adequately considered. As a rule, before Professor Gash and Professor Hanham did their work, influence was treated either as something of a joke or, at most, as a bit of residual corruption which could not totally be rooted out all at once. As Professor Gash and Professor Hanham have both shown, such treatments

[1] 'Revision—1870', Nostell Papers, D3.8.1.

confuse the distinction between the 'temporary and specific devices [of corruption, and the] permanent disposition of circumstances [implicit in influence]'.[1] Yet while illustrating the differences between corruption and influence, and while showing how long they both survived the traditional dates of their expiry, neither man has considered the crucial nature of the relationship between influence and ideology. Possibly, the reason for this lies in the strength of two assumptions which have informed a great deal of work in nineteenth-century history and which both men appear to share, first, that parliamentary reform was a single process which, although requiring close on a century to achieve the goal of individualistic democracy, was somehow focused upon this goal from the start, and secondly, that the rôle of electoral influence was clearly distinguishable from the rôle of public opinion.

In large part, the first of these assumptions was undoubtedly responsible for obscuring certain important provisions of the first Reform Act with which it is scarcely compatible, in particular those concerning constituency boundaries, the rights of borough freeholders to vote in the counties, and the new residential requirements for the borough franchise. When these provisions are noted, and when their functions are noted within the context of accelerating industrialization, accelerating population movement, and growing intellectual ferment, it becomes apparent that these phenomena did not provide the dynamics of the Act except as symptoms with which the Ministers sought to deal. The Ministers were not trying to create a political structure in which urban interests would enjoy predominant weight. Nor were they trying to encourage the growth of political individualism.[2] When their handiwork is seen both in its entirety and against the background of the social, political and intellectual movements of the early nineteenth century, it becomes clear that their primary concern was to perpetuate the political pre-eminence of the landed interest and the hierarchical structure of English society in town as well as countryside. In particular, their efforts in this

---

[1] Norman Gash, *Politics in the Age of Peel* (London, 1953), p. 173. See also H. J. Hanham, *Elections and Party Management* (London, 1959).

[2] These questions are dealt with at greater length in the author's 'Concession or Cure: the sociological premises of the first Reform Act', *The Historical Journal*, vol. 9, no. 1 (1966), pp. 39–59.

latter direction are apparent from their attempts to define each constituency socially and geographically—by franchise and boundaries—so that it would provide representation for the interest it principally symbolized.

In 1832 a new constituency structure was created, one in which the various local élites might legitimize their own local status by identifying themselves with the interests their constituencies symbolized, and by clarifying these interests in ideological terms appropriate to their own rôles within them. However, the relationship between this structure and the various opinion groups throughout the Kingdom has been almost totally obscured both by the neglect of those provisions of the Act which were primarily responsible for the structure itself, and by the weight of the Benthamite assumption that influence and ideology—or influence and public opinion—were distinct and even opposing phenomena. For conceptual purposes, of course, deferential behaviour should be distinguished from behaviour motivated by economic, social or religious interest. In practice, however, in most constituencies for most of the century this distinction cannot be made. While Bedford remained a Whig, most of the other major landowners in Cambridgeshire coalesced to form a 'landed party' which not only monopolized the representation of the county during the middle years of the century, but which also provided an ideological justification of the rôles and status of these men themselves. Analogous phenomena can be seen in many other counties and in many urban boroughs. In effect, in most cases, opinion and ideology cannot be distinguished from the rationalizations of influence appropriate to the communities in which it obtained. The social results of this are clear: until fairly late in the century the spokesmen of the various interest groups were the same men who, in another capacity, were the leaders of the various deference communities of which these interest groups were composed.

The reformers of 1832 had intended this result. But certain of its consequences were not intended. In all probability, the constituency structure of 1832 helped to solve the related problems of social discipline and social cohesion. But it only did so by intensifying the rivalries in Parliament between, or among, the various interests, or interest coalitions, whose definition it directly or indirectly affected. As Russell explained, in 1854, the first Reform Act had 'tended to divide the country in a way it was not divided before; in short, into opposite camps according as the districts might be connected with land or trade'.[1] And, he went on—with the events of the previous decade obviously in mind, '. . . Since the passing of the Act we have seen—what had not occurred before—we have seen county Members too generally exclusive in respect of the interest they cared for, and Members for the great cities too exclusive also for theirs.'[2]   In large measure the Bill he was then introducing was designed to correct what he had come to believe was a 'defect' of the first Reform Act.   To prevent future crises of confrontation in Parliament he proposed to make the various constituencies—in particular the county constituencies— more heterogeneous.   He proposed to introduce elements into their respective electorates which, as he explained, would significantly affect the 'special character' of their representation.[3]

In reality, of course, the problems with which Russell sought to deal in 1854 were far more complicated than his proposed solution.   The interests which the various constituencies symbolized were not fixed entities.   To a large extent they were social and ideological constructs.   Within limits, the definition of the interest each constituency symbolized might be affected both by the registration of specific electors and by the organized dissemination of specific ideologies among them. As a rule, however, in the post-reform period, politicians sorted themselves out in terms of the constituency framework which the reformers had created.   Sir William Molesworth, for example, the Radical member for East Cornwall, refused to contest his seat in 1837 after he had fallen out with various of his former supporters among the local gentry.   True, he still enjoyed the confidence of the voters in the Hundred of Trigg.[4] It was there his own estates were located.   But for electoral purposes he withdrew to the more congenial borough of Leeds. In effect, since the structure itself was conceived as a means of

[1] 3 *Hansard*, CXXX (13 February 1854), 498.
[2] *Loc. cit.*
[3] *Ibid.*, 504.
[4] W. Brian Elvins, The Reform Movement and County Politics in Cornwall, 1809–52 (Unpublished M.A. thesis, University of Birmingham, 1959), chapter VII, p. 9.

defining constituencies in terms of interests, it also served to intensify the very interests on which it was based.   Furthermore —and it was here that the real problem lay—by providing clear channels of representation for the spokesmen of rival interest groups, it encouraged the formulation of issues in terms of which the status of these men within their respective deference communities might be legitimized or threatened.

As Russell recognized, the intensity of the corn law crisis in Parliament was largely the consequence of the constituency structure of 1832.   What he failed to recognize—or at least to mention—was the reciprocal nature of this relationship, how the corn law question enhanced the solidarity of the various interest groups which the reformers of 1832 had sought to strengthen.   He also ignored the functional relationship between the solidarity of these various interest groups and the solidarity of the principal types of deference community they contained.   Yet in all probability it was what he failed to mention which explains the intransigence he deplored.   Within each of the two major interest groups, the urban and the rural, the corn law question carried the burden of the argument according to which the prosperity of the constituent classes was primarily affected—or primarily threatened—not by the relations of these classes with one another but rather by their corporate relations with a rival interest group.   In effect, while new productive techniques were focusing attention upon class unity, and the lines of division between classes, the corn law question provided a means of assimilating the consequent class tensions within the fabric of traditional society.

In all probability, it was this rôle which the corn laws played which explains why the changing nature of the corn law question, and the actual means by which the corn laws were repealed, have both been so effectively obscured.[1]   As a rule, the context in which the corn laws were discussed was defined by two related notions, first, that rural prosperity could only be had on the basis of high arable prices, and second, that the main threat which the domestic producer faced was not his neighbour's increasing efficiency but the foreigner's lower costs of production.   This context was reinforced by the social

[1] The following questions are dealt with at greater length in the author's 'The Corn Laws and High Farming', *The Economic History Review*, 2nd Ser., vol. XVIII, no. 3 (1965), pp. 544–61.

problems inherent in trying to adapt rural society to the exigencies of high farming, especially when prices had fallen from the levels which the corn laws projected. But it was also reinforced by certain assumptions of the classical economists according to which the essential purpose of the corn laws could not have been other than what most urban spokesmen declared it to be, that of perpetuating high agricultural prices, and hence high rents, at the cost of low real wages in the towns and, possibly, of general urban depression. On one point in particular, Adam Smith, Sir Edward West, David Ricardo, and even Thomas Malthus were substantially agreed, that while investments in industry were inherently capable of reducing the unit costs of production, investments in agriculture would inevitably increase these unit costs.[1] In all probability, it was the prestige which these men enjoyed which obscured the essential rationale of protection as Sir Henry Parnell conceived it. According to Parnell—he was the principal sponsor of the corn law of 1815—if domestic producers were given a monopoly of the domestic market, they would so increase their investments as to increase their production and *lower* their unit costs.[2] While the corn laws scarcely served the purpose he had in mind—as efforts to support prices and thereby encourage investments they were effectively cancelled out by deflation and rising productivity itself—his argument was essentially

---

[1] See Adam Smith, *The Wealth of Nations* (London: Everyman's Library; 1910, reprinted 1950), vol. I, p. 6; Sir Edward West, *Essay on the Application of Capital to Land*, Jacob H. Hollander, ed. (2nd impression, John Hopkins Press, 1934), pp. 10–11; David Ricardo, *Influence of a low price of corn on the profits of stock, Economic Essays*, E. C. K. Gonner, ed. (London, 1923), pp. 247–51; T. R. Malthus, *An Enquiry into the Nature and Progress of Rent* (London 1815), pp. 54–5.

[2] His clearest statement on this question was made in 1813 while introducing the report of the Corn Law Committee of 1812–13. As he then explained, '. . . If the agricultural capital is considerably increased, its effects on the quantity produced, and the expence [sic!] of production, and also in lowering prices, will be the same as when employed in manufactures. Every one knows how it operates in increasing the quantity of manufactures; and that those who employ it in manufactures can afford to sell them at very reduced prices, in consequence of the reduced expenses at which with its help they can make them. In the same way the farmer by being able to render his land more productive in proportion as he improves it, and at a small expense according as he makes use of good implements, will be able to afford to sell his corn at reduced prices; . . .' *Hansard*, XXVI (15 June 1813), 645. The following year he reiterated this argument while replying to the arguments of those who contended that heightened protection was solely designed to perpetuate high prices. '. . . As the effect of the measure,' he explained, 'would be to encourage tillage, and to promote the growth of corn, by which means a greater supply would be obtained, it must finally occasion a reduction of the price.' *Ibid.*, XXVII (5 May 1814), 708.

accurate, that the law of diminishing returns did not apply to agriculture any more than it did to industry. Of course, at the time he voiced this belief most agriculturalists were unconvinced. And, believing that any reductions in price would not only drive the marginal producer to the wall but would also invalidate any prior investments others had made, they elaborated arguments in defence of the corn laws which served both to enhance the cohesion of their own interest group and to reinforce the logic of the urban case against them.

By the 'forties, when high farming had become an organized movement, the situation had changed radically. By then, certain agriculturists were proclaiming to the world that they no longer needed protection.[1] But their very success aggravated the problems of the others. These latter tended to deny the economic value of high farming.[2] Yet in view of the obvious success which many high farmers enjoyed, the arguments of these latter must be recognized for what they were, rationalizations which served to cloak their own reluctance to disturb the traditional relationships of rural society in ways which high farming often required.[3]

By 1846 the polemical importance of the corn laws required that something be done about them. At the same time it served to obscure exactly what was done. Large segments of the population—especially those which made the most noise—focused their attention upon that one element in Peel's legislative package which they had projected into prominence. Their behaviour suggested that corn law repeal should be conceived within the context of those polemical arguments to which its prominence was due. In consequence, those other elements of the package—in particular the drainage loan—were effectively ignored, which might have suggested another context, one having to do with the relations between those agriculturists on the one hand who no longer had any fears of foreign competition and those on the other whose fears of foreign competition were really a measure of their inability to compete

[1] E.g., Sir Thomas Lethbridge before the Bath and West of England Society, *Farmers' Magazine*, New Series, II, 1 (January 1839), pp. 77–8.

[2] E.g., Robert Baker before an anti-malt tax meeting, *ibid.*, 2nd series, XI, 1 (January 1845), pp. 23–5.

[3] On this question see the author's 'The Corn Laws and High Farming', especially pp. 549–53.

with their neighbours.   In effect, while the Anti-Corn Law
League helped to make repeal essential by enhancing the
solidarity of the urban and landed interests, and by raising
the tensions between them to a point of imminent explosion,
it was the progress of high farming which made repeal possible.
But to a large extent this progress itself contributed to the need
for repeal.   With their hopes still focused upon the prices
which the corn laws still symbolized, many agriculturists had
done little or nothing to adapt themselves to the low prices of
which they complained and which in large measure were
attributable to their neighbours' increasing efficiencies.

V

In 1846 Peel sought to extricate the kingdom from the
polemical consequences of Ricardian economics by implement-
ing a policy based on the concept of economic growth which
the high farmers had shown to be valid.   Russell's concerns
in 1854 were similar.   He sought to deal with those elements
of the constituency structure in 1832 by which these polemical
consequences had been channelled into Parliament.

Russell's over-all scheme was fairly simple.   But certain of
its crucial aspects have scarcely been noted, perhaps because
the problems themselves have not been noted to which these
aspects are related, perhaps because Russell proposed to deal
with these problems in a negative way.   He proposed to
ignore them.   Yet by ignoring them he made them a part of his
Bill itself.   Primarily, these problems were the consequence
of the population overspill by which the essential rural nature
of many county constituencies was being diluted.   In 1831,
commissioners had been appointed who had been charged
with the task of drawing the boundaries of the various constituencies, boundaries whose essential significance is revealed
by the new residence requirements for the borough franchise,
and by the so-called borough freeholder clause, that by which
many freeholders whose properties lay within the confines of
a borough lost their rights to vote in the county in which the
borough was located.[1]   In 1831, in dealing with the major
boroughs—the major urban constituencies both old and new

---

[1] On this question see the author's 'Concession or Cure: the sociological premises
of the first Reform Act'.

—these commissioners had been instructed to pay close attention 'to the direction in which . . . [the] Town . . . [was] increasing . . .; and [to make] a liberal allowance . . . for the extension of the Town in such direction; so that the boundaries determined today may not require alteration tomorrow'.[1] But Russell's Bill of 1854 contained no similar provisions. He proposed to redistribute sixty-two seats which he hoped to obtain by disfranchising the smallest boroughs entirely and by reducing the representation of the slightly larger boroughs. Of these sixty-two seats he proposed to assign forty-six to the counties. But no dams were to be built to protect the counties from the electoral consequences of urban overspill. Indeed, the electoral urbanization of the counties was to be further enhanced by reducing the occupation franchise in the counties from £50 to £10. As others had noted, and would note again, such occupiers were primarily concentrated in the suburbs and the unenfranchised towns.[2] As Russell explained in 1854, with such an electorate it was 'obvious that the county representation will have less of a special character than heretofore'.[3]

Conceptually, the Bills introduced by subsequent Liberal Governments in 1860 and 1866 were similar to Russell's Bill of 1854. Each of them was designed both to accede to the renewed urban penetration of the counties, and to facilitate this penetration. Each of them provided for the enfranchisement of new categories of county elector whose essential orientations would have been urban. None provided for the redrawing of constituency boundaries in such a fashion as to re-isolate the rural from the urban constituencies. In this respect, they differ radically from both the Conservative Bill of 1859 and the second Reform Act. Not only would the Conservative Bill of 1859 have provided for boundary commissioners who, as Disraeli explained, would 'rearrange [the boundaries] according to the altered circumstances of the time',[4] it would also have provided a defence against another

[1] 'Instructions, etc. . . . addressed to the Gentlemen engaged in collecting Information respecting the Boundaries of the Cities and Boroughs of England and Wales', 23 August 1831, Sessional Papers, 1831–2, vol. XXXVI, p. 13.
[2] See Locke King's arguments for assimilating the county to the borough franchise, 3 *Hansard*, CXII (9 July 1850), 1146ff.; *ibid.*, CXIV (20 February 1851), 850ff.; and *ibid.*, CXLIV (19 February 1857), 841ff.
[3] *Ibid.*, CXXX (13 February 1854), 504.
[4] *Ibid.*, CLII (28 February 1859), 992.

form of urban penetration of the counties, that which derived
from the exploitation of the amended borough freeholder
clause of 1832.   Had the first Bill been passed which Russell
introduced in March 1831, no borough freeholder would have
been able to vote in a county election if, in respect of his
property, either he or anyone else had been able to qualify to
vote in the borough.   Later, in consequence of the Ministers'
failure to defeat the so-called Chandos clause, that by which
£50 tenants-at-will were enfranchised in the counties, this
clause was amended.   According to the amended clause, each
borough freeholder might qualify in the surrounding county
if the specific property for which he might claim a county vote
did not qualify him to vote in the borough.[1]   By 1859, as
Disraeli noted, in some instances these borough freeholders
far outnumbered the £50 tenants-at-will.[2]   Oddly enough,
even though the Conservative Bill of 1859 was defeated on this
issue,[3] the relevance of the issue itself has scarcely been noted.
Nor has the basic point of similarity been noted between the
Bill of 1859 and the Act of 1867.   In 1867 the Conservatives
did not repeat their efforts to restore the initial borough freeholder clause of 1831.   But they did repeat their efforts to
re-isolate the rural counties from the urban boroughs.

The real paradox of 1867—if such, indeed, it should be
called—was not the franchise but the boundaries.   As had
been noted in 1860, the £6 borough franchise which the
Palmerston Government was then proposing was effectively
the same as household suffrage because, at least in the larger
towns, few premises were available at a rent of less than 2s. 6d.
a week, which the £6 franchise represented.[4]   Thus, on the

---

[1] On this question see the author's 'Concession or Cure: the sociological premises
of the first Reform Act'.

[2] 3 *Hansard*, CLII (28 February 1859), 990.   The process to which he referred
can be seen, for example, in South Leicestershire.   While the total number of
registered electors in the division increased between 1852 and 1865 from 5,118
to 6,238 the number of these who qualified in respect of property in the borough of
Leicester increased between 1852 and 1866 from 1,318 to 2,316.   Accounts and
Papers, 1852, vol. XLII, pp. 303–4; 1865, vol. XLIV, pp. 427–8; and 1866, vol.
XLII, pp. 15–16.

[3] See 3 *Hansard*, CLIII (21 March 1859), 389ff.

[4] On this question see the testimony of Sidney Smith, the secretary of the City
of London Liberal Registration Association, before the Select Committee of the
House of Lords appointed to inquire what would be the probable increase of the
number of electors in the counties and boroughs of England and Wales from a
reduction of the franchise. . . . Transmitted to the Commons, Sessional Papers
1860, vol. XII, especially q. 658.

borough franchise, there was little to choose between the Palmerston Bill of 1860 and the Derby–Disraeli Bill of 1867, as the latter was finally amended.   Nor was there really much to choose between the £10 occupation franchise in the counties which Russell proposed in 1860, and the £12 occupation franchise in the counties which the Act of 1867 finally provided. But there was much to choose between the two measures on the question of constituency boundaries.   The paradox of 1867 lies in the fact that the Liberal majority in the Commons not only agreed to the appointment of boundary commissioners. They also agreed to instruct these commissioners to enlarge the boroughs 'so as to include within the limits of the borough all premises the occupiers of which ought, due regard being had to situation or other local circumstances, to be included therein for Parliamentary purposes . . .'.[1] Apparently, they only realized what they had done when the commissioners took their instructions to heart, and when a Boundary Bill was introduced based on their report by which every important borough was so enlarged as to absorb its suburban overspill.   To the Con-servatives, whose symbolic basis of power lay in the counties, and who, perhaps, were more at home than many Liberals in a hierarchical society, such a measure was essential as a means of restoring the world they knew.   To many Liberals, on the other hand, who appreciated its electoral consequences, it was a simple gerrymander.   But having agreed to the Reform Bill itself—the measure containing the boundary commissioners' instructions, and which would not be complete without the Boundary Bill based on their report—the Liberals found themselves in something of a dilemma when they refused to approve the Boundary Bill.

Apart from their political embarrassment their problem was largely one of timing.   When they became fully aware of the provisions of the Boundary Bill, it was too late to reopen the whole boundary question if elections under the Act were to be held in the autumn of 1868.[2]   There was no real escape from the dilemma.   But the Liberals did force the appointment of a select committee to reconsider the more important boundary cases.[3]   In all, the committee only considered thirty-three

---

[1] 3 *Hansard*, CLXXXVIII (25 June 1867), 528.

[2] See Gladstone's analysis of this problem, 3 *Hansard*, CXCII (14 May 1868), 253.

[3] *Ibid.*, (14 May 1868), 248ff., and (18 May 1868), 427.

cases, and only recommended serious changes in the boundary commissioners' scheme in fifteen.[1] But they did something that was possibly more important. Symbolically, they drew the curtain upon the political world which the first Reform Act had created.

VI

In truth, however, this world had already passed. The class lines which earlier issues had tended to dull had become too sharp; interest groups had become too jumbled; in many significant respects social and economic categories had ceased to overlap. In these circumstances, borough and county were no longer adequate symbols of homogeneous urban and rural communities. Nor did the various deference communities still provide adequate agencies of social discipline, or adequate points of ideological reference. Thus, the refusal of the Liberal M.P.s to approve the Boundary Bill was not the cause of the end of the mid-century politics. But it was the symbol. Shortly thereafter, poll books ceased to be published in which the basic social factors of mid-century politics had been reflected. With the passing of the deference community their continued publication had become impossible.

The Parliament which passed the Ballot Act was not very different in membership from those which repeatedly had refused to do so before. What had changed was not the men but the structure of society in which these men operated, and, consequently, the conduct of electoral politics. As different groups of men became more interspersed, and as the groups to which they belonged ceased to re-inforce one another, local political leaders no longer recognized the same inhibitions as they had before. The elections of 1868 were contested in far more constituencies than any previous elections. In many cases contests occurred simply because local politicians realized the inadequacy of their knowledge of how voters would behave if a contest did occur. In effect, an actual contest was their only means of discovering the relative strengths of the different political groups in the constituency. And, in conducting these contests, many local leaders tried—as never before—to exert influence where it was not recognized as the legitimate

[1] See the discussion of their recommendations, *ibid.* (11 June 1868), 1405–44.

attribute of an *a priori* community. Of course, the ballot cannot be removed from the context of individualistic political theory. But the point should not be forgotten that one of James Mill's major arguments for the ballot had to do with his belief that it would prevent illegitimate influence from weakening the strength of legitimate influence.[1]

Because the passage of the Ballot Act obscured the evidence of its effects it is impossible to determine whether it served in England more to protect the individual from the electoral pressures of landlord or employer, or to protect the residual deference communities from the men who, increasingly, were trying to undermine them. Whichever its greater effect, social, economic and ideological influences did not disappear immediately. Indeed, they are still a part of the British political world. But the nature of influence changed as the groups changed through which it was channelled. In the middle years of the century the major function of local political organization had been to discover the hierarchical patterns of society through which influence might be transmitted. The new organizations and the new organizers were different. Unable to depend upon the cohesion of *a priori* communities of a hierarchical nature these latter had no alternative but to try to recruit the voters directly. And, in many cases, they tried to do so in terms which encouraged the voters to group themselves on either side of the class lines which were becoming increasingly important and upon which the redistribution and boundary schemes of 1885 were largely based.

---

[1] 'Thoughts on moderate reform in the House of Commons', *Westminster Review*, vol. XIII (1830), pp. 5–7.

☆ 3 ☆

Coal Mines Regulation: the First Decade
1842–1852

SAFETY in coal-mines had been the subject of quasi-official inquiry and intermittent public discussion for a generation before a Commons select committee was set up to explore the possibilities of statutory regulation in 1835.[1] The need for regulation was clearly established by the evidence before this committee; but so too were the great difficulties of prohibitions, and the utter confusion (not to say contradictions) of scientific opinion on safety methods and devices.[2] The committee shrank from proposing legislation. Soon afterwards, a voluntary committee was set up in South Shields to review the whole matter more thoroughly and professionally,[3] and this had still not reported when the first Mines Act was being hammered out. The 1842 Act sprang, instead, from the report of the Commission on Child Employment inquiring into the mining districts which was issued earlier in the same year.[4] It was concerned essentially with the well-being of children;

[1] For a general description of the earlier nineteenth-century activities, see R. N. Boyd, *Coal Mines Inspection: its History and Results* (London, 1879), especially chap. II, and D. Morrah, 'A Historical Outline of Coal Mining Legislation', in *Historical Review of Coal Mining* (London, 1924), pp. 301–8.

[2] *Rep. sel. comm. accidents in mines*, 1835 (603), v.

[3] This was the South Shields Committee formed in 1839 after an explosion at the Hilda pit, South Shields, in which 52 lives were lost. Some of its members (especially the very able secretary, James Mather) were highly experienced in mining questions, and its main subjects of investigation were safety lamps, ventilation, scientific instruments, infant labour, plans and sections, scientific education for miners and government inspection. It reported early in 1843, *Report of the South Shields Committee* (London, 1843). See also *Mining Journal* 25 February, 4, 18 and 23 March 1843; *Rep. Lords sel. comm. accidents in coal mines*, 4, 1849 (613), vii.

[4] *1st rep. commissioners mines*, 13–17, 267–71, 1842 (380), xv.

safety entered the picture incidentally, and almost accidentally, only because the employment of children in certain tasks endangered their own as well as miners' lives. An additional proposal to exclude women from underground work was a sort of lateral extension of 'moral principle'. From first to last, the safety of the miners, as such, was scarcely mentioned.[1]

The first shot in the 1842 campaign, the Bishop of Norwich's speech in presenting petitions for action upon the Commissioners' report, indicated what was to follow. It was on the Commissioners' description of women and children, 'chained . . . to their labour of dragging small vehicles loaded with coal through narrow apertures or passages, in which they were obliged to crawl upon their hands and knees, their garments drenched with water', that the Bishop lingered.[2] Ashley, originally responsible for the Commissions on Child Employment, and the natural executor of their recommendations, followed the same path in composing and introducing his bill to terminate the iniquities. He assumed that no one could possibly dispute that such practices were intolerable in a civilized state.

> Now, Sir, to remove or even to mitigate, these sad evils requires the vigorous and immediate interposition of the Legislature. That interposition is demanded by public reason, by public virtue, by the public honour, by the public character, and I rejoice to add by the public sympathy; for never, I believe, since the first disclosure of the horrors of the African slave-trade, has there existed so universal a feeling on any one subject in this country, as that which now pervades the length and breadth of the land in abhorrence and disgust of this monstrous oppression.
>
> In [my] bill I propose, in the first place, and at once, to cut off the principal evils. Much, no doubt, may be left for future legislation; but there are some of the evils of so hideous a nature, that they will not admit of delay— they must be instantly removed—evils that are both

---

[1] All that was said was that fearful accidents were common, due to negligence and parsimony in raising and lowering the cages, in providing ventilation, in using safety lights and in propping; and that 'another frequent cause of fatal accidents in coal mines is the almost universal practice of intrusting the closing of air-doors to very young Children', *ibid.*, 269.

[2] 3 *Hansard* LXIII, 196, 198, 6 May 1842.

disgusting and intolerable—disgusting they would be in a heathen country, and perfectly intolerable they are in one that professes to call itself Christian.

Ashley's speech concluded on the same note, with a scriptural appeal, 'to break off our sins by righteousness, and our iniquities by showing mercy to the poor . . .'[1] Unlike the Lords (some of whose mine-owning members were of sterner stuff), the Commons quailed before such a declaration. None in the mining lobby ventured to question Ashley's pre-suppositions. Some argued that it was the miners rather than the owners who maintained the evil system; others, that the evils were localized, not general. But this was the extent of their initial reservations.[2] Meanwhile the non-committed members tumbled over one another in expressing their abhorrence of female and child labour, and their veneration of the author of the proposed reform. Graham, the Home Secretary, apart from postponing the details of two of the proposals for further consideration, appeared to accept the bill officially. In the name of the cabinet, he assured 'his noble Friend that Her Majesty's government would render him every assistance in carrying on the measure'.[3]

Red sky at dawning, shepherd's warning: Ashley's early triumph was his last. Centred upon the Coal Trade Office at Newcastle-upon-Tyne, opposition to his bill grew rapidly.[4] This was based partly upon a denial of the facts alleged in the Commissioners' report, and partly upon an assertion that wholesale changes in the supply of labour would ruin the industry. Ashley attempted to settle, once for all, with these opponents, at a meeting on 20 June at the House of Commons, when he hammered out a compromise which, he understood, would bring the resistance to an end. He made one very large concession. In place of his original proposal to prohibit

---

[1] *Ibid.*, 1320–52, 7 June 1842. Ashley specifically grounded his case on the Commissioners' report, beginning his indictment with, 'Sir, it is not possible for any man whatever be his station, if he have but a heart within his bosom, to read the details of this awful document without a combined feeling of shame, terror and indignation', *ibid.*, 1321.
[2] See the speeches of Lambton, Egerton, Turner and Ward, *ibid.*, 1352–61.
[3] *Ibid.*, 1357–9.
[4] The first rebuttal of the charges made by the Child Employment Commission was issued by the Coal Trade Office on 25 May. For the text, and comments, see *Mining Journal*, 10 June 1842.

the employment of boys under 13 years, he agreed to lower
the age limit to 10 years (provided that those between 10 and
13 worked only three, and alternate, days a week), and to
permit boys over 9 years who were currently working to
continue.[1] The group whom he met included Lord Wharncliffe,[2] who was a member of the cabinet with mining interests,
Hedley Lambton, M.P. for Durham, and John Buddle,
the principal agent of the colliery owners of the North East;
so that Ashley had very good reason for his conclusion that he
had reached a final agreement with both the government and
the trade. The amended bill passed the Commons unscathed.
In the debate on the third reading, however, one mining
member raised cheers with the ominous remark, 'He fervently
rejoiced that there was another House,'[3] and Palmerston tried
to stiffen the ministry in advance by observing that it 'would
be nothing more than mockery if the promised support [of the
Government] were not to be given elsewhere'.[4]

These implicit hopes and tacit fears were well justified. The
Lords at once referred the bill to a select committee, from which
it emerged badly mutilated. The restriction of the hours of
work of children between 10 and 13 years was altogether
abandoned. The apprenticing of pauper children, which
Ashley's bill had prohibited—'here', he had exclaimed, 'you
have a number of poor children, whose only crime is that they
are poor, and who are sent down to these horrid dens, subjected
to every privation, and every variety of brutal treatment'—
was practically reallowed.[5] The minimum age for tending

[1] 3 *Hansard* LXIV, 426, 22 June 1846 (Ashley).
[2] Wharncliffe was lord president of the council.
[3] This was Ainsworth, whose speech also included the observation, 'Mr Buddel
[sic] had explained how it was that the noble Lord [Ashley] had obtained the
support of some of the proprietors of mines; his supporters were those who worked
thick mines; but those who have to work thin mines could not but object to the
practice of the boys labouring only three days a week', *ibid.*, 999–1002, 5 July 1842.
[4] *Ibid.*, 1008. There had been two divisions on whether the debate should be
adjourned before the house was asked to pass the third reading, but both motions
for adjournment were defeated. Later there was some dispute on whether support
for adjournment constituted opposition to the bill in its current form. Gladstone
was one of the supporters of adjournment.
[5] Under the apprenticeship system, most common in Yorkshire, Lancashire,
Staffordshire and the west of Scotland, pauper boys of eight or nine years were
assigned by the workhouse masters as apprentices to butty colliers (in effect,
sub-contractors) to serve until they were twenty-one years old. The butties kept
what the apprentice earned, and virtually controlled his life: hence the references
to 'white slavery' by the reformers. The Lords' amendment allowed the apprenticing of paupers, up to the age of eighteen years, to continue.

winding machinery was lowered from 21 to 15 years. Other clauses were emasculated after the second reading.[1] Even this failed to satisfy diehards like Lords Londonderry and Radnor; but it was quite enough to make Ashley declare that the amendments of the House of Lords had both invalidated the general purposes of the bill and rendered what was left unenforceable. Naturally, he felt—and said publicly—that he had been sold. But Wharncliffe had told the Lords, as soon as the bill came up for their consideration, that 'the Government had taken no part whatever with respect to this bill. The Government intended to remain perfectly passive . . .'; while Londonderry denied, and induced Buddle to support him in denying, that the meeting on 20 June had reached a binding agreement. What weight precisely to attach to misunderstanding, and what to treachery, it is difficult to say. Certainly, Graham's and Wharncliffe's respective declarations on behalf of the ministry could not be reconciled; and Lambton confirmed Ashley's understanding of the compact with the trade—'It must be self-evident that you would only consent to make these concessions on condition of receiving our support'.[2] But however the blame is distributed, the 1842 Act was a sad ghost of the original proposal.

Essentially, the lopped measure prohibited the employment of females of all ages, boys under 10 years and apprentices over 18 years, in coal-mines; and the employment in machine-tending of all persons under 15 years.[3] Apart from a novel wages clause,[4] this was all. Of course, three great principles,

[1] The most important change was permitting women and young children to *enter* coal mines, while still prohibiting their employment there. Ashley had originally proposed their total exclusion from the mines, and the amendment, of course, increased the difficulty of preventing their being employed underground.

[2] 3 *Hansard* LXV, 3-7 (Londonderry and Wharncliffe), 12 July 1842; 84-6 (Palmerston and Graham), 13 July 1842; 102-4 (Londonderry and Clanricarde), 120-2 (Wharncliffe) 14 July 1842; 1096-9 (Ashley, Palmerston, Graham and Peel) 6 August 1842; *The Times*, 6 August 1842. Lambton's letter ended, 'I recollect you distinctly said, at the close of your discussions: "Well, If I make all these concessions, will you all support the bill?" Lord Wharncliffe should have protested then.' Apart from the dispute as to the measure of agreement reached at the private meeting, the whole affair reveals the confusion of current conceptions of the collective responsibility of a ministry, and the bonds of party in the respective houses.

[3] 5 and 6 *Vic.* c. 99, secs. 1, 2 and 4. The commencement date of the new provisions was 1 March 1843.

[4] *Ibid.*, sec. 10. The payment of wages in public houses, beer shops and places of entertainment was forbidden; any such payment made was to be void; and the penalty for such payment was £5 10s. for each offence.

two of them new to English law, had been carried.[1]   But just
as much had had to be abandoned; and the executive clauses
were defective.[2]   Much, however, still depended on how the
clause empowering the Home Secretary to appoint inspectors
to examine and report upon collieries, the 'condition' of the
miners and the operation of the Act, was interpreted and
carried into effect.   Here the important fact was that the bill
originated outside government.   Whatever Ashley had had in
mind in inserting this provision—probably no more than a
vague desire to imitate the factory legislation—Graham was
nonplussed.   In fact he made but a single appointment, that of
H. S. Tremenheere,[3] an assistant poor law commissioner.
Tremenheere, who was to serve for sixteen years without
either colleague or successor, was called indifferently in the
official papers 'Commissioner' and 'Inspector'; and this
epitomizes the ambiguity of his position.   He did undertake
some prosecutions under the 1842 Act, noted its weaknesses,
pressed intermittently for their amendment and reported
annually.   But he regarded the examination of the social
problems of the mining districts as his main function.   In
fact, he often wrote as if it were his business to discover and
neutralize the causes of dangerous discontent.   Not that he
saw himself as the tool of the employers.   Within his limitations, he was disinterested and humane.   But limitations there
certainly were: occasionally at least, he spoke as if he abhorred
unionism, despised miners and regarded the costs of coal, the
staple of national energy, as inflated through excessive wages.

[1] These were the exclusion of adult women from certain employments; the
exclusion of certain persons from the management of machinery; and the prohibi-
tion of child labour in a new field.
[2] *Ibid.*, secs. 5–7, 11–12. Amongst the weaknesses were these: the employment
of women and children 'above ground' was completely exempted from the Act;
J.P.s might find that owners or their agents *bona fide* acted on wrong information
provided by parents about children's ages, in which case they were not to be fined;
the owner's agents might be rendered personally liable for paying wages in
forbidden places and the owner exempted from penalty, if the J.P. were satisfied
that the offence took place without the owner's consent or personal knowledge;
and the Act contained no provision for the summoning of witnesses.
[3] H. S. Tremenheere (1804–93), Winchester and New College, Oxford, Fellow
of New College, 1824–56. Called to the bar, 1834. Revising barrister, Newport,
investigating the Frost affair, 1839. Inspector of Schools, 1840–2. Assistant Poor
Law Commissioner, 1842. Coal Mines 'Inspector' or 'Commissioner', 1843–59.
Commissioner of Inquiry into various forms of female and child labour, 1855–70.
For an account of Tremenheere's character and some of his work, see R. K. Webb,
'A Whig Inspector', *Journal of Modern History*, XXVII, pp. 352–64.

Set loose with only general instructions, he was thenceforth practically independent of the Home Office. His salary, no less than his social standing and his conduct as an administrator, indicated the status of commissioner. So too perhaps did the immediate reason for his appointment—in effect he was kicked upstairs to release the Home Office from an entanglement with angry dissenters.[1] Yet he contributed as much perhaps as any other single person to the first form of the second mining inspectorate, that which supplied much of what his régime omitted, and superseded even his own work in the end.

Tremenheere pressed for a new inspectorate as early as 1845,[2] and crystallized his project in a letter to Sir George Grey, the new Home Secretary, at the end of 1846.[3] Tremenheere was moved to act by the colliery explosions at Aberdare and Risca, South Wales, in 1845–6,[4] in which many lives were lost. Having canvassed the subject with mining engineers and managers, he was convinced 'that *Inspection* of the mode of Ventilation in each Colliery, by a properly qualified Government Officer, *without powers of interference* would tend greatly to diminish the risk'. Tremenheere's conception of the inspector's utility (it matched his view of his own function) was that of teaching by superior knowledge and soft words, rather than coercion. He quoted with warm approval one

---

[1] Tremenheere's own account of the affair in his journal was as follows: 'Kay Shuttleworth and I had devised nearly the whole of my employment as Inspector from the beginning, with a view to the manner in which our ideas on Educational improvement could best be brought before the public. The topics were nearly exhausted. The B and F Society were not likely to work harmoniously with the Govt while I continued Inspector. Yet the Govt could not with any justice set me aside; they had indeed supported me thro'out with the utmost steadiness. It was necessary for them to provide for me some other employment, which should be a Promotion, before they proposed any new arrangements for Inspection to the B & F Society. This they have honourably done by offering me the Inspectorship of Mines and Collieries, with an additional salary of £100 a year, & the promise of Sir J. Graham that I shall have the duty of attending to the District Schools, as Asst P. L. Comr pro tem.', Webb, *op. cit.*, p. 356.

[2] The first coherent proposal of an inspectorate came from the South Shields Committee in 1843, who appear to have been most impressed by the numerous and long-standing continental precedents for such a step. The Committee advocated 'two or three practical qualified inspectors' to examine mines and recommend improvements to be arbitrated upon by the courts or some other authority if the owners refused to adopt them. A bill presented in 1844 also proposed a mines inspectorate, but this was merely for the examination of mining plans and maps. Earlier, some of the witnesses before the 1835 select committee had suggested the appointment of inspectors.

[3] H.O./O.S. 1490, Tremenheere: Grey, 31 December, 1846.

[4] 28 lives were lost in the first, and 35 in the second of these explosions, Boyd, *op. cit.*, p. 247.

engineer who said that periodic inspection by men with experience of 'fiery' colleries 'would have a wonderful effect in saving life. Such a man would say, "Here you have a bad plan, if you don't alter it you will have an accident". They would say, "Why, what are we to do?" "Why, do what they are doing at such and such a Colliery, and you will get on very well." A master would feel awkward after that if any accident happened.' A similar idea expressed by the manager of the Rhymney Iron Works was used by Tremenheere as an example of how the employers' *amour propre* and fear of adverse publicity might be worked upon.

> When the Proprietors knew they would be subject to remarks from a Government Officer they would take care to have it all right. For when a thing of that kind is likely to be known, such as endangering the men from penuriousness or neglect of the Employer, he would not like to be found out, and to be seen to be behind his neighbours, and if any accident should happen, and the fact came out, it would tell greatly against him.

Tremenheere's answer to the problem of explosions was then a technically qualified inspectorate, visiting and reporting on the safety precautions in various mines, advising colliery managers and inducing them to emulate each other. But he also asked, as a result of his experiences as inspector, for an amendment of the 1842 Act in three particulars: first, that boys under ten years be required to attend school for some specified time;[1] secondly, that magistrates be given power to summon witnesses in prosecutions under the 1842 Act;[2] and, thirdly, that all explosions involving loss of life should be reported to the Home Secretary. The absence of the second from the Act had been responsible for the failure of many prosecutions in the North of England and South Wales, with the consequence that women, and little boys, still continued to work in mines in these districts; and Tremenheere argued that 'not even Lord Londonderry' would dare to oppose a clause necessary to the execution of these statutory prohibitions.[3]

---

[1] Tremenheere intended that the certificates for the required school attendance should be examined and checked by the inspectors.

[2] The latest factory act contained such a provision, 7 & 8 *Vic.* c. 15, sec. 49.

[3] Tremenheere had apparently recognized the need for these amendments as early as 1843, but felt that to reopen the question 'in the first two or three years' might have 'revived the opposition dangerously'. His fear may not have been

Grey's endorsement on the letter, 'Is any power required to be given by Act of Parliament for such inspection?', points to one of the mysteries of the business. On the face of it, there was no reason why the Home Secretary should not have appointed the new inspectors straightaway. The Act gave him discretion to appoint as many inspectors as he pleased, and gave inspectors powers to examine any machinery or workings;[1] and the only executive functions envisaged by Tremenheere concerned existing legislation: in safety matters the inspector would merely advise and 'diffuse knowledge about ventilation matters'. Yet Tremenheere's recommendation, originally put forward in 1846, and published in his annual report in 1847,[2] was not carried out until 1850, and then only through the medium of a new statute. Meanwhile the subject of mines inspection was brought forward repeatedly after 1846. The Home Office papers contain several protests of this kind for the years 1847–9: 'All parties as well as the public were disappointed no one attended the inquest on the part of the government.' 'Had there been Inspection this accident could not have occurred—The Inspector would not have suffered the colliery to be worked under the circumstances—It is hoped that the accident will urge on the appointment of Inspectors.' 'The Jury . . . are further of the opinion, that the recurrence of accidents involving so large a loss of human life . . . would justify Parliament in framing such a Code of Regulations as would give greater security to persons employed in Mining operations.'[3] Agitation in the House of Commons was continuous. No less than four private members' bills, proposing more or less stern intervention by an inquisitorial and repressive inspectorate, were introduced in 1847 and 1849. The bills mainly derived from, and were mainly supported

---

groundless. An attempt was made in 1843 to permit women over 21 years to work underground in coalmines, although the motion for leave to bring in such a bill was defeated by 137 votes to 23, 3 *Hansard*, LXVIII, 429–81, 16 May 1843.

[1] 5 & 6 *Vic.* c. 99, sec. 3. The clause empowered inspectors to examine the works, machinery, buildings, etc., of any colliery, and required proprietors to furnish all means necessary for such examination. The debate on the introduction to this clause makes it quite clear that underground inspection was intended, although Tremenheere appears to have assumed that his powers did *not* so extend. See 3 *Hansard*, LXV, 891–3, 1 August 1842.

[2] *4th rep. commissioner appointed under 5 & 6 Vic. c. 99*, 1847 (844), xvi.

[3] H.O. 45/O.S. 1830, 1831, 1873, correspondence addressed to Sir G. Grey, 8 March, 18 July and 4 December 1847, respectively.

by radicals, Duncombe, Wakley, Hume, Bright and others (it was Hume who drew the distinction between legislative interference with wage contracts, which was objectionable, and 'ventilating mines', which was 'another matter'); but they were also supported by some members of a very different type, such as Colonel Sibthorp. The cry of class discrimination was raised. Wakley observed that whenever a measure to help the working classes was introduced, it was staved off as long as possible. 'Why,' he concluded (perhaps truly) 'if a noble Lord were blown out of a coal mine, there would be legislation on the subject the very next day the Parliament assembled.' Similarly, Duncombe complained that however obdurate the cotton lords had proved, the coal lords promised to be worse. The Parliamentary coal interest was blamed for the failure of reform; and it was hinted that Grey himself was influenced by his family connection with mine-owners. Grey never opposed the principle of mine inspection outright. Each time he pleaded for postponement—because of the gravity and complexity of the issue; because the mine-owning members had left town; because the recommendations of eminent scientists were awaited; because the session was too late— because of any and every cause he could lay hands on. Occasionally he threw out generalities about vexatious minute interference and the prodigious size of the service which would be required. But since the demand for reform had been first raised in the Commons as early as 1844 (before Grey had even taken office), and since several dramatic explosions took place and hundreds of lives were lost in each succeeding year, his excuses gradually wore thin. In 1847, Duncombe replied to an objection that safety legislation was the business of the government, that he quite agreed, but that if the government refused to act, some-one else must do so. In the same debate, Ferrand asked whether the House could be surprised if Grey, during the recess, had 'to send down the military to keep the peace [in mining districts], and all because the House refused to legislate'?[1]

What is the explanation of the protracted failure to act? Six main reasons can be ascribed. First, the coal interest was

[1] All the references to parliamentary discussion of the 1847 and 1849 bills are covered by 3 *Hansard*, XCIII, 1071–8; XCIV, 307–14; and CVI, 1250, 1335–42. The details of the bills are to be found in *Parl. pap.*, 1847, i(626); ii(509) and iii(626); 1849 iv(369) and (459).

wealthy, powerful and strategically situated in Parliament. In the north-east it was thoroughly organized, with a permanent secretariat; in the Commons, in the Cabinet and, most of all, in the Lords it could work for procrastination and the emasculation of bills with devastating effect; and a mere reference to the industry as *the* commanding height of British manufacture invariably gave pause. Second, the agitation for an inspectorate was originally sustained, at least in part, by the new trade unions, and was sometimes pressed in the idiom of class conflict. This cut both ways. The sense of hardly-suppressed violence in the background was certainly a goad to action. But the opposite feeling, against any concession to organized labour lest its appetite should grow with feeding, was generally more powerful in the 1840s. On balance, union support was probably still a liability on this issue.

The other four retarding factors were more enduring, being problems of peculiar difficulty, special to the regulation of coal mining. The first was that of scale. There were nearly two thousand collieries scattered throughout Great Britain, many with several pits. All were more or less difficult of access. Some were three thousand feet underground; in others, miles of passageway had to be traversed to reach the working faces. To have each pit inspected thoroughly, say, quarterly, reported on and re-examined where changes in working methods were proposed, would have needed an executive corps running perhaps into hundreds. Where were such immense numbers of qualified men, where was the money to pay their salaries, to come from? Next was the variety of the measures needed. To take the single question of ventilation as an example, the airflow which contemporaries deemed necessary for safety in 'fiery' mines might vary by a factor of ten or even more from case to case; moreover, even these figures depended on the degree to which the current was unobstructed, and no one could tell what further allowance should be made for the possible range of changes in barometric pressure. In short, it was impracticable to set down any particular anemometric reading as prerequisite. Thus the framing of specific regulations, either comprehensive or special, seemed extraordinarily difficult—at first sight, virtually impossible. Another factor, scientific ignorance, reinforced the last. Exact knowledge of the causes of explosions was, as one inspector later observed, still in its infancy. Educated opinion realized how little had been established so far, and at the same time assumed that scientific certainty would eventually be attained. On both counts, this operated against immediate statutory intervention. Finally, there was the matter of 'responsibility'. This was a double-edged weapon against the establishment of an inspectorate. On the one hand it was argued that any diminution of the managers' responsibility would weaken the miners' best protection against death and injury; on the other, that inspectors would not assume the burden (which would inevitably attach to them if they could lay down what was to be done) so long as they lacked the power either to make a full assessment of the deficiencies, or to ensure that their own recommendations were carried out. These last four difficulties, those of scale, heterogeneity, scientific uncertainty and responsibility without power, would not disappear overnight, or even for decades after the establishment of state controls. They were lasting governors of, or at least continuing influences upon, the entire question.

But however strong the array of opponents, some ostensible reform was unavoidable. Disasters multiplied in 1847–9, attracting more and more newspaper publicity in snowball fashion; memorials and petitions for government action rained in; the ministerial defences for delaying legislation became less plausible with each sterile session. The government's main shield against the assaults was the practice, begun without forethought, of appointing one or two 'eminent scientific men' to investigate and report upon various of the mine disasters. The first pairs, Lyell and Faraday, and Sir Henry de la Beche (Director of the Geology Museum) and Lyon Playfair (a first step towards becoming a sort of National Adviser upon Science), were appointed to report on Welsh colliery disasters in 1844 and 1845. With the addition of Professor Phillips of Newcastle-upon-Tyne and two established mining consultants, Warrington Smith and Kenyon Blackwell, they constituted, in effect, a panel from which the government drew commissioners of inquiry. The inquiries[1] not only established the causes of particular disasters (though this never led to further action)

---

[1] See *Rep. Lyell and Faraday*, 1845 (232), xvi; *Rep. gases and explosions collieries*, 1846 (529) xliii; *Reps gases and explosions collieries, de la Beche, Playfair, Warrington Smith*, 1847 (815), xvi; *Rep. explosion Darley Main*, 1849 (1051), xxii.

and provided general observations upon safety. They also helped to ward off criticism of the government for doing nothing, by suggesting that the whole matter was *sub judice*, and even comment consequently improper. In the long run, however, the effect of the special commissions was to increase the pressure for state action. Though quite closely confined to the matter in hand, the commissioners could not but indicate the appalling, general state of ignorance amongst both managers and working miners, and the necessity for some form of supervision. By 1849 the need for a fresh statute and a new inspectorate was practically established. Thus, the force of scientific authority was now added to the pressures which had first been exerted within the administration (by Tremenheere), by reformers (primarily, the South Shields Committee) and through the mining unions, several years before. The upshot was a Lords Committee in the spring of 1849 'to inquire into The Best Means of preventing the Occurrence of Dangerous Accidents in Coal Mines . . .'[1]

We might term the most important witnesses, from the standpoint of our present interest, official, reformist and trade unionist respectively. The 'officials', headed by the mandarin de la Beche, favoured the Tremenheere form of inspectorate: qualified, discreet men visiting particular collieries and recommending safety precautions appropriate to each case, on an altogether advisory basis. De la Beche carefully observed the current orthodoxies: he did 'not know that the name "Inspector" is a good one'; ' "Interference" I should certainly not like'. But he also justified his caution by the conservative 'state of opinion at present', and revealed that he had consulted Grey beforehand.[2] Playfair agreed with de la Beche that it

---

[1] Amongst the petitions which constituted the immediate occasion of this select committee was one from James Mather, the secretary of the South Shields Committee, and one from the Northumberland and Durham Miners Union. The Lord Wharncliffe who was chairman of the Lords' Committee, and said that he had recently abandoned his opposition to an inspectorate after reading of Belgian practice (3 *Hansard* CV, 1335, 15 June 1849), was a son of the peer who had played an equivocal part in the emasculation of the 1842 measure, *D.N.B.*

[2] *Rep. Lords sel. comm. accidents in coal mines*, 4–19, 1849 (613), vii. Referring to his recommendations as commissioner inquiring into various of the recent mines accidents, de la Beche observed, 'we suggested that properly qualified persons should be appointed to the various districts, who should use considerable discretion in the mode of recommending what should be done in different Collieries, not employing compulsory powers, none being given them by which they could act hostilely, but simply by advice', *ibid.*, 5.

would be unwise to give inspectors enforcing powers (with the corresponding responsibilities), and that their work should be essentially that of report and advice. Otherwise, however, he was more radical: he recommended the policing of underground work to ensure that safety precautions were observed; the transference of the burden of proof to the owners in 'bad' districts;[1] and empowering the inspectors to enter mines at will, see (and correct where necessary) the working drawings, and publish their views upon the safety of a mine's operations.[2] Playfair concluded by proposing a farthing per ton tax on all coal mined to pay for the executive corps: the reporter noted the Committee's evident consternation at this point.[3]

The most interesting 'reformist' was Matthias Dunn, a Durham mining engineer, who had agitated for several years for colliery reform, by pamphlets, books and public speeches. Dunn was no firebrand; he had examined the French system of controls, studied the French mining reports and been introduced in 1847 by Robert Stephenson to the Society of Engineers where he had spoken on mine accidents. His proposals were correspondingly moderate. He asked for regulations, but 'as few and as simple as possible'. He hedged on whether the inspectors should have the power to stop workings where the safety precautions which they thought necessary were not being observed. But he inclined more than any of the 'official' witnesses towards executive powers for the inspectors, and he made it clear that further advances in legislation should be made as 'the state of opinion' ripened.[4] Dunn also argued (Playfair and Tremenheere made virtually the same plea) for high technical and scientific qualifications for the inspectors, and for attempting to improve the managers' and viewers' standard of scientific education through Schools of Mines.[5] John Atkinson of Jarrow spoke for the working

---

[1] Playfair's proposal was that in districts with bad accident records, certain practices and devices should be prohibited, unless and until the owners could demonstrate their safety. He did not indicate how such a demonstration might be made!

[2] *Ibid.*, 66–71.

[3] *Ibid.*, 70. This proposal had been a feature of one of Duncombe's bills, which doubtless did nothing to endear it to the peers.

[4] *Ibid.*, 494–7, 501–3, 513–15.

[5] At this stage, the Museum of Practical Geology in London was the nearest British equivalent to the French School of Mines. Cf. H. T. de la Beche, 'Inaugural Discourse . . .', *Royal School of Mines Records* (London, 1852), I, pt i, pp. 2–11.

miners, who favoured the strongest and most instant powers
for inspectors. Atkinson testified that both inspectors and
sub-inspectors were badly needed; that it should be 'their duty
to go and inspect the colliery . . . as the supervisor visits the
excisemen, not to give any notice whatever when he is coming';
and that both inspectors and sub-inspectors should themselves
have the power of imposing fines on the spot—'it could not be
done otherwise with any satisfaction'.[1]

The whole spectrum of the testimony, from de la Beche to
Atkinson, was not after all very wide. The Committee noted
that there had been a remarkable consensus in favour of
inspectors with rights not merely to enter and inspect mines
but also to call for and examine working plans. The only
essential difference of view—although it was an important
one—was whether the inspectors should have powers 'to order
and to enforce penalties'. The Committee endorsed what was
undoubtedly the majority opinion, that the inspectors should
merely advise, lest managers and owners shuffle off that
'responsibility which naturally belongs to them, and which it
is not only desirable not to withdraw, but rather, if possible,
to increase'. Sympathy with the working miners' objectives
was expressed; but the Committee contended that vexation
and disappointment could be the only fruits of a coercive
executive.

> If there were no other reasons against such powers, the
> cases to be dealt with are too various in their conditions,
> opinions as to the fittest remedies in each particular
> instance are occasionally too doubtful, and the difficulty
> and cost of applying them often too great, to justify the
> positive enforcement of the views of a Government
> Officer, however competent, against, perhaps, no less
> experience and knowledge in the properly responsible
> parties. In addition to this, it would appear to be next
> to an impossibility that an Inspector should make himself
> thoroughly acquainted with the working of a large Mine,
> without the willing assistance of those who manage it;
> and, finally, that many remedies and safeguards would
> require a continued superintendence to render them
> effectual, which it is clear that no attainable staff of

[1] *Rep. Lords sel. comm. accidents in coal mines*, 520–4, 1849, (613), vii.

Inspectors employed over the whole mining operations of England, Wales and Scotland, could possibly supply.[1]

But, with these qualifications, the Committee came out strongly in favour of an inspectorate, however much owners and managers might object to an inquisitor roaming about their workings, questioning their men, scrutinizing their drawings, criticizing their procedures and telling them (and the Home Secretary) what changes they should make. There might, the Committee allowed, be reasonable and substantial objections to inspection; but these could not outweigh 'the imperative duty of Parliament and the Executive' to protect the miners' lives, limbs and health, both by inspection and direct enactment, so far as practicable.[2]

Though its positive recommendations were few, and its analysis of the inspectorial system was superficial, the report at least aired and balanced the best contemporary opinions; and it wisely recognized both the extent of its own ignorance and the uncertainty which still surrounded the entire question. The argument on the inspectorate was confused. But this was mainly because the contestants had confined their choice to the somewhat unreal alternatives of advising or coercive officers. The advisory service was in fact a *pis aller*. It tried to reconcile two contrary impulses, hesitation to legislate at all in such a matter at such a stage, and the need at least to appear to take remedial action. The compromise was essentially of the same type as the common practice in the 1830s and 1840s of rendering an initial reforming measure permissive, but not compulsory. If Tremenheere's peculiar view of his functions originated, the scientific commissions spread, the idea of regulation by advice; and it happened to fill the immediate need conveniently. The establishment of a *coercive* service in England in 1849 was inconceivable, nor could it have worked in a legal and political system alien to it at every point. On the other hand, advising officers were anomalous. What no one discussed was the type of inspectorate natural to and already established in the British environment: an executive corps which saw to it that a law was executed, and whose experience

---

1 *Ibid.*, vii.
2 *Ibid.*, viii.

and recommendations helped to shape that law. The reason for this omission was, really, the unwillingness of most parties to commit themselves yet to constraining and prohibitory legislation: in this respect, the proposed advisory inspectorate was simply the latest in the series of devices to put off the awkward choice.

Even the Lords' Committee report was not immediately sufficient to produce legislation. While the Committee still sat, Grey appointed Blackwell and Phillips to inquire generally into safety measures;[1] and subsequently argued that legislation should await their recommendations.[2] Two months later— after further mine disasters in the meanwhile—a gigantic miners' meeting was held at Black Fell, co. Durham, to petition for legislation in the next session. The chief speaker was Wyld, the member for Bodmin, a mining constituency. Wyld had, fruitlessly, introduced a bill to set up a safety inspectorate in July 1849.[3] He now presented himself as the miners' friend, battling against the 'large number of [mine-owners'] nominees in the House'. 'England,' he continued, 'spends half a million annually to prevent the slave trade. Has she a drop of sympathy for white slaves at home?' It was ten to one that the soldier would survive: the miner's chance was merely even. Wyld, and also Jude, the secretary of the Northumberland and Durham Miners Union, were openly sceptical of the Blackwell–Phillips inquiries—in fact, of the whole process of inquiry by commission.[4] At a second mass-meeting at Black Fell in February 1850, this scepticism was elaborated by another trade unionist, George Reynolds: Home Office officials were despatched to write bluebooks simply to enable the Home Secretary to fend off awkward questions with, 'the hon. gentleman is all wrong—the Government Commissioner has been down the mine and here is the result of his investigation'. The second meeting was reassured, however, by Jude's reading aloud a letter from Wyld announcing that

---

[1] *Instructions Professor Phillips and J. K. Blackwell*, 1849 (427), xiv.

[2] *Newcastle Chronicle*, 15 June, 6 and 13 July 1849; 22 March 1850.

[3] In introducing his bill (which was negatived without a division, although Wyld had declared his determination to put the matter to a vote), Wyld objected to the appointment of 'theoretical geologists' to conduct the latest inquiry.

[4] *Newcastle Chronicle*, 21 September 1849. A later meeting appointed a deputation to confront Phillips with the miners' objections to his procedure. Apparently, Phillips was able to satisfy the deputation, *Mining Journal*, 17 November 1849.

Grey had promised him that he would introduce a mines inspection bill.[1]

Blackwell and Phillips reported at last in May 1850.[2] In effect, they repeated the findings of the previous inquiries, and concerned themselves largely with what facilities commissioners such as themselves required to perform their investigations. The government had now nothing to fall back on, and a bill was finally introduced in July—in the Lords, not the Commons, and by the under-secretary, Carlisle, instead of Grey. The bill proposed a mild version of the 'advisory' inspectorate. The Home Secretary might appoint inspectors, who would be empowered to enter any coal-mine, examine its operations and recommend changes where he adjudged existing practices or machinery to be unsafe. If the owner or manager refused to adopt the changes within a reasonable time, the inspector was to report the case to the Home Secretary. The only other significant provision was that owners or managers were required to report fatal accidents to the Home Secretary within 24 hours, and that coroners were to give the Home Secretary 48 hours' notice before holding an inquest in such a case. The only penalties prescribed were for obstructing inspections and failing to report accidents;[3] and the operation of the Act was to be limited to five years. Although there was little debate, there was some opposition and a division in both houses. Carlisle, introducing the second reading, repeatedly stressed the absence of 'interfering powers', the owners' continued liberty to work their mines as they wished and the fact that the inspection would cost them nothing. But the 'Ditchers' were not appeased. Lonsdale scorned the 'eminent men of science' whom Carlisle had paraded to justify the measure, and added (prophetically) that 'if they adopted this Bill, they would hereafter be told they had admitted the principle of interference

---

[1] *Newcastle Chronicle*, 22 February 1850. If Grey made such a promise, he evidently did not consider it binding. A month later he told Wyld that the question of legislation must await the Blackwell–Phillips reports; and in May 1850, the Northern miners sent a deputation to Grey to discover whether the government intended to legislate, *Mining Journal*, 4 May 1850. See also *Newcastle Chronicle*, 7 June 1850.

[2] *Rep. ventilation mines J. Kenyon Blackwell*, 1850 (1214), xxiii; *Rep. ventilation mines John Phillips*, 1850 (1222), xxiii.

[3] The proposed penalties were small: £5–10 for obstructing an inspector in any of his duties; and £10–20 for failing to notify the Home Secretary of a fatal accident and its probable cause.

and that further powers would be asked for'. Londonderry opposed every dot and comma of 'the most mischievous and unjust measure that could possibly be imagined', but dwelt longest on the iniquity of exhibiting to the world at large 'the interior concerns of his [the owners'] work, all his wealth, all his property'. Brougham objected, catholically, in the names of both labour and property, and pressed his resistance to the point of a division.[1] Grey's introductory speech in the Commons was still more lukewarm than Carlisle's but the Commons' opposition, rather less absurd than that in the House of Lords, was mainly directed at procuring yet another postponement of legislation.[2] But talk of unseemly haste was unconvincing after five or six sessions of inaction. At any rate, the bill passed intact, except for a handful of concessions made by Grey in favour of the coal interest, and it received the royal assent on 14 August.[3] Three months later, Grey appointed four inspectors[4] and divided Great Britain into four areas of inspection.[5]

Two of the new inspectors, Blackwell and Dunn, are familiar, and had long been prominent in the discussion upon an inspectorate; the others were established mining engineers.[6] Blackwell's appointment reinforced the idea (which had also coloured the Blackwell–Phillips inquiries) that the inspectors were more permanent commissioners of inquiry than executive officers. But if so, the salary was not commensurate with the status. £400 p.a., even with travelling expenses, was less

---

[1] 3 *Hansard*, CXII, 1239–45, 11 July 1850; CXIII, 3–4, 19 July 1850.

[2] *Ibid.*, CXIII, 603–4, 31 July 1850; 759–60, 2 August 1850; 1009, 10 August 1850. Disraeli, reiterating his protest against 'this interposition between labour and capital', pressed for a postponement until 1851: the current bill, he declared, was 'a piece of hasty and ill-considered legislation'.

[3] As 13 & 14 *Vic.*, c. 100.

[4] *Gazette*, 22 November 1850.

[5] *Copy instructions inspectors coal mines*, 401–2, 1851, xliii. The initial instructions emphasized the diplomatic and advisory character of the inspectors' task, 'While therefore, you will afford to any parties who may solicit it, such advice or suggestions as your knowledge and experience may enable you to offer them, you will abstain from dictation or any unauthorized interference . . . You will not fail to act with courtesy and forbearance in your official intercourse with all parties, and you will encourage a good feeling and understanding between the miners and their employers', *ibid.*, 401.

[6] They were Charles Morton and Joseph Dickinson. Morton had been an underviewer in Durham, R. Fynes, *Miners of Northumberland* . . . (reprinted, London, 1923) p. 142; and Dickinson, a viewer in both South Wales and Scotland, *Rep. sel. comm. coal mines*, 50, 1852 (509), v; *Rep. sel. comm. mines*, 238, 1866 (431), xiv.

than half the salary of a good mine manager or engineer. This
was a source of trouble from the start. Men resigned from the
service to take up better posts—Blackwell himself resigned
within a year[1]—and for a time some supplemented their
incomes by acting as consultants or arbitrators. Even when
the salary was raised in 1853 to £600 p.a., the complaints of the
inspectors did not cease—presumably adding to the difficulty
of recruiting able and energetic men. If the rewards were
much too small, the inspection areas were much too large.
Initially each inspector had over 400 collieries in his district;
a single thorough inspection of, and report upon, each pit
might have taken a man three or four years to accomplish.
Even when the corps was increased, in 1855, to twelve,[2] the
inspection regions were still too extensive for regular, even
annual, visits to every mine. Despite all these inadequacies,
legislative and administrative alike, the first inspectors
(especially the most active, Herbert Mackworth and Joseph
Dickinson) laid the foundations of a real system of control.
It was established almost at once that the inspectors should
prosecute for breaches of those clauses of the Act to which
penalties attached. This was a critical precedent. Neither
the Act itself nor the preceding arguments[3] had made it clear
that the inspectors should act as the executors of the legislation
in this sense. The new decision was not immediately important. The subjects on which prosecutions could be under-
taken were very few before 1860. But amending legislation
increased the number of offences—and all this apart, the
recognition of his rôle as enforcement officer specified the
inspector's function and secured his standing. Nor was
the 'advisory' work necessarily negligible, at any rate where
owners had been already cowed by fatal accidents upon their
properties. One of the first such cases, at Heys Colliery early
in 1851, illustrates what might be achieved in very favourable

[1] In September 1851. He was succeeded by Herbert Mackworth, who had
worked as both a civil and a mining engineer, and who had received his 'scientific
education' at King's College, London, *Rep. sel. comm. coal mines*, 36, 1852 (5–9), v.

[2] Meanwhile, in 1852, the number of inspectors had been increased to six,
H.O. 45/O.S.3790, Grey: Treasury, 15 December 1851. When the corps was
doubled again, to 24, in 1873, the number of districts remained the same, and each
inspector was given an assistant.

[3] 'All that was asked by the Bill', Carlisle declared when introducing it, 'was a
power of inspection, and a right of demanding plans', 3 *Hansard*, CXII, 1241,
11 July 1850.

conditions. Six men having died there in an explosion on 17
March, Dickinson inspected the pits within a fortnight and
reported to both the owners and the Home Secretary that they
were in a 'very unsatisfactory state and still attended with
considerable danger'. All the airways were ineffective;
pockets of stagnation produced 'magazines of gas' at various
places; and leakages in the ventilating system, the wrong
positioning of the boiler, insufficient air courses, insecure
stoppings and the foreman's negligence all contributed further
to the danger. Dickinson furnished a lengthy list of detailed
recommendations, adding ('although it scarcely falls of my duty
to allude to it') a criticism of the firm's practice of contracting-
out the maintenance of their ventilation system. So far from
being stung into an angry rejoinder, the Company expressed
its gratitude to Dickinson and promised to adopt his suggestions.
On Grey's instruction, he re-visited Heys to make sure that his
recommendations had been carried out, and on 17 May
reported that the gas had been removed and the colliery
rendered safe.[1] Of course, all this was after the damage had
been done; it was also in the salad days when owners did not
realize quite how circumscribed the powers of an inspector really
were; and other collieries were by no means so submissive. But
it indicates, none the less, what remarkable things the state
might achieve, although powerless to inflict a legal penalty.

Next, the inspectors provided, almost *de novo*, the statistics
of their subject. Hitherto, even the mortality from accidents
was only vaguely guessed at, and its causes still less explored.
The systematic collection of information gradually made it
clear, for example, that fatal accidents were much more
numerous than had been supposed, that explosions were not
in fact the major source of fatalities, and that occupational
diseases killed many more miners than the disasters. The
foundation of accurate knowledge, even if still of a most
elementary kind, was now being laid. The fourth—and if the
things were comparable at all, most important—achievement
of the early inspectors was to provide a professional and continuous evaluation of the problems of regulation: the various

[1] H.O.45/O.S. 3501. Report by J. Dickinson, 3 April 1851, and Grey's endorsement; Manager, Heys Colliery: Dickinson, 5 April 1851; and Dickinson: Grey,
17 May 1851. See also O.S. 3976, Dunn: Grey, 2 April 1851.

inquiries preceding their appointment had been (as was usual in such cases) irregular and superficial. The first opportunity to turn the new advantage to account came in August, 1852, when all the inspectors were asked to comment upon a recent report of a Commons select committee inquiring into safety in collieries.[1] By then, there were six inspectors, three of whom had served already for twenty months, and two of whom had visited France, Germany and Belgium on a study-tour of the continental systems of control. Before forwarding their individual replies to the Home Office,[2] the inspectors met and discussed the report, a general meeting foreshadowing the later annual and even more frequent gatherings. Generally, the inspectors agreed in both their criticisms of the Committee's report and their own recommendations for new legislation. As to the latter, they were practically unanimous. They agreed that inspectors should be empowered to stop the working of any colliery which they considered unsafe, and which the owners refused to reform;[3] that the Act should cover iron-stone mines as well as collieries (the evils being substantially the same in each); and that owners be required, under heavy penalties, to fence off all abandoned workings. Further, they discovered, and proposed the amendment of, the same body of defects in the existing legislation. They asked for a time limit (with penalties for failure to perform) to be prescribed for the production of maps and plans by mine-owners; for sufficient intervals and notice to ensure that inspectors had an opportunity to attend all colliery inquests and adjourned inquests; and for the rectification of other clauses where it had proved impossible to recover the damages which they specified.[4]

[1] *Rep. sel. comm. coal mines*, iii–x, 1852 (509), v.

[2] H.O. 45/O.S. 4105, reports by J. Dickinson, 24 August; H. Mackworth, 24 August; W. Lancaster, 26 August; M. Dunn, 27 August; and T. Wynne, 28 August.

[3] This was coupled with a scheme of subsequent arbitration: after the workings had been stopped, the owner was to appoint some one to adjudicate the matter with the inspector; if they disagreed, they should appoint a third party as umpire; and if they could not agree even on an umpire, the Home Secretary should appoint one over their heads. A similar arbitration arrangement was in fact enacted in 1855 to cover disputes over the Special Rules which were to govern each particular colliery, 18 & 19 *Vic.*, c. 108, sec. 5.

[4] The penalty proposed for failure to perform in such matters as fencing and the production of plans was £1 per diem during the delay. The inspectors also proposed that coroners should give at least six days, instead of 48 hours, notice of their intention to hold an inquest on a fatal colliery accident, and that notice should be sent to the district inspector as well as to the Secretary of State. There were several other minor recommendations.

So far there was consensus. It was in a modest but significant area, covering established flaws in the existing Act, two patently desirable extensions and the crucial question of sanctions for the inspectors. The other issue, compensation for the relatives of those killed in colliery accidents, produced three different types of solution. William Lancaster, observing that in England most widows got only a coffin and a sovereign from the mine-owners, and many not even that, looked to an amendment of Lord Campbell's Act,[1] which would increase the damages recoverable and permit proceedings to be instituted in the county courts, as the remedy. Dunn recommended empowering coroner's juries to levy a deodand for a victim's survivors, both parties having a right to appeal to quarter sessions. If this was ingenious, it was certainly outstripped by the third proposal, Mackworth's. He argued for a tax of £10 per death on the owners of mines in which fatal accidents occurred. Survivors should receive £5—£100 according to the degree of culpability on the part of the management, and the remainder of the £15,000 which such a tax would raise annually should go towards supporting the costs of the inspectorate. Mackworth also pointed out that, if such things could be quantified, miners' diseases and non-fatal accidents represented a still greater evil. To cover these very numerous cases, he suggested an ingenious scheme of regular medical inspection and reports, with up to three-quarters wages for the victim, as the levy upon negligent owners. Actually, compensation was only one of Mackworth's purposes in making this recommendation. He also hoped that a body of precise information on miners' health and working conditions might be built up from the medical reports. 'I feel the want of accumulated and acknowledged facts given under authority, which might bear down all question of opposition.' But his most important object was to bring into being self-acting checks, in the shape of penalties and damages, which would induce owners and managers to safeguard the lives and well-being of the workers. At first blush, Mackworth's proposals might seem to smack of the doctrinaire. But in fact he was

---

[1] 9 & 10 *Vic.* c. 93. This gave a right of action to the near relatives of a deceased person, if they suffered pecuniary loss by his death and if he would have had a right to action had he been merely injured instead of killed. In practice, this right was difficult to exercise successfully in such cases as mines accidents.

led to them partly by Belgian precedents (especially in the plan
of medical inspection); partly by analogy with the fines which
were imposed as a matter of course on miners for breaches of
colliery regulations (Mackworth saw his scheme as but a
natural corollary); and partly by his belief that inspection
per se could only touch the surface of these interior problems.

A second facet of the inspectors' achievement under this
head was the sweeping away of many of the misconceptions
which had characterized the discussion on mining regulations
down to that time. The lengthy and detailed reviews by
Dickinson and Mackworth of the report of the 1852 Committee
furnish an example. First, they showed that the committee
(like every previous inquiry) had exaggerated greatly the
importance of explosions as a cause of mortality amongst miners.
In their experience, explosions accounted for some 20 per cent
of the deaths, instead of the 66 per cent asserted by the
Committee. The Committee was equally astray in believing
that afterdamp caused 75 per cent of the deaths arising from
explosions: Dickinson's figures suggested 7 per cent. Mackworth
pointed out, moreover, that in concentrating upon 'fiery' mines,
the Committee had ignored over two-thirds of the collieries in
Great Britain. This type of basic information, never formu-
lated systematically, if indeed known, before, made it possible to
define the problems with some precision, and established valid
general perspectives for the first time. Next, the inspectors
dissipated myths about the use of science. The Committee
had misunderstood and wildly exaggerated what science could
do at that time to improve mine regulation—here again
reflecting a prevalent general error. For instance, the Committee had assumed (as almost everyone who had spoken or
written on the matter hitherto had assumed) that ventilation
was the key to safe working; that one or other of the methods
of artificial ventilation must be superior to all the rest; and that
the minimum velocity of air-current necessary for safety could
be determined. The inspectors had no difficulty in demolish-
ing these *jejune* assumptions. Dickinson observed that the
belief that ventilation was the sole significant factor was, in
fact, the distinguishing error of all 'theorists': in reality,
ventilation was 'but one item of a catalogue'; the 'best airflow'
would be worthless without adequate airways, or if some of the

underground regions were cut off from the main stream. Similarly, it was folly to search for a minimum 'safe' rate of current, or a minimum 'safe' sectional area. 100,000 cubic feet per minute were needed in some mines, 5,000 would suffice in others. A sectional area of 50 square feet for air-flow would be too small in many places, 25 too large elsewhere. Again, the select committee, after a lengthy and (one might almost say) eager discussion of the merits of the various systems of artificial ventilation had plumped for the steam jet as superior to all the rest, and in particular to that most commonly employed, the coal furnace. The inspectors pointed out that the entire question of ventilation mechanisms was still, scientifically speaking, *sub judice*; and that in any case it could not be sensibly discussed without considering the comparative costs of operating the various systems. As Mackworth wrote, 'In the ever varying circumstances of depths of shafts, and resistance of airways, each system has cases to which it is most applicable, and in which it is the most economical. It is to this end that all inquiries of the kind should be directed.' The real question was not how a few very large collieries might best increase their ventilation, but how the large number (nearly 40 per cent of the whole) which still trusted to the 'caprice of the wind', might be induced to adopt any form of artificial ventilation.

Both the inspectors, but Mackworth especially, stressed the very backward state of British science in their field, which, they agreed, rendered it imperative to set and maintain the inspectorate at a high level of technical proficiency. It was for this reason that they disapproved of any other of the select committee's recommendations, that a Board with wide dis-cretions and large powers be established. They believed that sufficiently expert members could not—or at any rate would not—be found. Instead, Mackworth argued for the initiation, so far as practicable, of the 'superlative' French system, which embraced over two hundred experimental scientists, engineers and trained mine-guards. The French Department of Mines, he wrote, was staffed by men of the first quality, 'constantly occupied in promoting all real improvements', preventing the duplication of research and the repetition of experiments which had failed, and adding systematically to the knowledge and economy of the mining industry. The lack of defined goals, co-ordination and competent inquirers, and the all-pervasive, ramshackle amateurism of law-making opinion in Great Britain, formed a dispiriting contrast. Nor was it technical ineptitude alone that fired the inspectors' indignation. On choke-damp mines, for example, which the Committee had ignored, Dickinson wrote, 'There is an almost total want of air, and life is quietly sapped away—nipping from men's lives probably a greater annual total than is lost by explosions of firedamp'; yet there was nothing to hinder the installation of effective ventilation, except a trifling expense and trouble for the management. On the same theme, Mackworth declared that the carbonic acid and other gases, 'silently numbering their victims', killed and incapacitated many more men than the explosions. 'In some [choke-damp] mines medicine is constantly taken by the men. The greatest injury is no doubt produced on the boys who after the age of 10 years are worked from 8 to 10 hours per day. In Pembrokeshire where the ventilation is very deficient, the colliers in some mines earn about 15*d*. per day and the younger boys 4*d*. or 4½*d*.'[1]

All this is not meant to suggest a species of 'God said, *Let Newton be!* and All was *Light*.' Some of the inspectors' proposals had been put forward already by laymen; others, like Dunn's deodand or Mackworth's death-tax, were obviously unlikely to succeed. The next essential reform, the subjection of all collieries to both General and Special Rules, which was to be enacted in 1855, was not so much as mentioned in 1852; and this applies to many other subsequent innovations. Improvement, moreover, was to be slow and painful. Although each of the intermediate measures, the acts of 1855, 1860 and 1862,[2] added materially to the inspectors' powers and range of work, twenty years were to pass before new legislation established a fully effective system of control.[3] Almost twenty years were to pass before sufficient data was accumulated to draw firm statistical conclusions. 'Expertise'

---

[1] Further light is thrown on Mackworth's and Dickinson's views about this time by their evidence before the 1852 and 1853 select committees on coal mines accidents, especially *Rep. sel. comm. coal mines*, 42–3, 48, 59, 64, 1852 (509) v; *1st rep. sel. comm. mines accidents*, 6–48, 55, 1852–3 (691), xx.

[2] 18 & 19 *Vic.*, c. 108; 23 & 24 *Vic.*, c. 151; 25 & 26 *Vic.*, c. 79.

[3] By a consolidation and amendment act, 35 & 36 *Vic.*, c. 76.

was a gradual acquisition, the fruit of protracted field work, observation and comparison. If this was what lay ahead, the statutory powers of the inspectors were negligible in 1852. The 1850 Act, wrote the best contemporary critic of mines legislation, 'did little more than provide for the appointment of inspectors, who were few in number, and not invested with much authority. They could do little more than record the number of accidents, and act as assessors to the coroners holding inquests on the victims of accidents.'[1]

None the less, by 1852 the inspectorate had become in effect a corps, already transforming itself into an executive arm of the ordinary kind. It had begun to concert its activities, and to perform creative, no less than regulatory, work. The publication of regular annual reports, which clarified and determined the inspectors' philosophy of reform and prepared educated opinion for further changes, commenced. Moreover, the want of formal powers did not necessarily mean the absence of effective powers. In the Heys Colliery type of case, for instance, the inspectors anticipated powers which they were later to enjoy—or more precisely achieved as much by informal means as they could have done under statutory authority. Dickinson, the main mover in 1852 of the proposal to require all disused workings to be fenced to the inspector's satisfaction, had reported a little earlier that in 22 of the 23 such cases which he had recently encountered, the owners had complied without demur to his requests.[2] 'Public opinion', suspicious unionists, the parliamentary question and a reckless press were useful assistants. Moreover, if progress was slow, it was also continuous and apparent from the start of the inspectorate. In 1851, 19·35 deaths occurred in collieries per million tons of coal mined; in 1861, the figure was 10·95 and in 1871, 9·15. During the decade 1851–60, the accident mortality amongst miners was 1 per 245 employed; in 1861–70, it was 1 per 300; and in 1871–5, 1 per 430. Moreover, the fall in mortality was steepest in those classes of accident which the inspectors could do most to influence. Explosions, for example, accounted for 24 per cent of the accident deaths in 1851–60, but only 17·8 per cent in 1871–5. Conversely, deaths from

---

[1] Boyd, *op. cit.*, p. 156.
[2] *Reps. Dunn, Dickinson and Morton, Inspectors*, 541, 1851 (1422), xxiii.

roof and wall falls, which the inspectors could do least to
check, rose from 37·6 to 41 per cent of the totals over the same
periods.[1]

1852 did not represent even the beginning of the end so far
as safety in collieries was concerned.   But (as the phrase goes)
it was the end of the beginning.   After nearly two decades of
serious concern, and one of formal statutory intervention, the
stage had been reached at which, at last, the interior momentum
of government could come significantly into play.   Perhaps
the most interesting general lesson of the pre-history of this
development is its demonstration that inspectorates do not
necessarily spring fully grown upon the scene, but may evolve.[2]
In this case, there were two quite separate offices, one formed
in 1842, the other in 1850; and they coincided for nine years,
until the second took over all the duties of the first.   One was
conceived of initially as an executive rather than an investigative or advisory service.   In fact, social inquiry of the most
general character became almost its sole function.   The other
was conceived of as investigative and advisory rather than
executive.   Yet it turned at once in the opposite direction.
Indeed, the second inspectorate set about transforming itself

[1] *Reps. Inspectors Mines*, 433, 1875 (c. 1216), xvi; 81, 135, 1876 (c. 1499), xvii;
Boyd, *op. cit.*, pp. 237–40.   It is not, of course suggested that a simple causal relationship between the work of the inspectors and the fall in mortality can be established.
Other factors operated on either side.   Safety mechanisms improved, and scientific
knowledge grew, throughout these years.   But coal mining also became more
and more dangerous, as work was carried on at ever-deeper levels, and in less
accessible places.   There can be little doubt that the inspectorate contributed
substantially to the reduction in the accident rate, but no certainty as to the precise extent of their contribution.

[2] There were, of course, some other striking features.   For example, in one
branch of the subject, that involving sexual degradation and cruelty to very little
children, mere 'revelation' was enough; even Lord Londonderry and the Newcastle Coal Office made no attempt in 1842 to resist the clauses which prohibited
female and (in the popular sense of the word) infant labour.   In the other branch,
however, the pressure had to be cumulative.   Doubtless, as Morrah suggests (*op.
cit.*, p. 310), it was the great Darley Main disaster of 1849 which set off the final
chain of events which issued in the Act of 1850.   But obviously the disaster would
not have had so powerful an effect, had it not been preceded by several similar
catastrophes, and the consequential inquiries.   Again, superficially, the sequence
seems topsy-turvy in one important area.   One might almost say—it is certainly not
a grievous exaggeration—that, in this field executive officers operated before there
was a law for them to execute; that they were, on occasions, carrying into force
legislation before it had been passed!   Certainly, the substance of the General and
Special Rules provision of the 1855 Act (18 & 19 *Vic.*, c. 108, sec. 4) was enforced
in places in 1853–4; and even before that, as we have seen, the distinction between
an officer's 'advice' and an instruction was often formal.   Cf. for a similar and
contemporaneous case, see O. MacDonagh, *A Pattern of Government Growth 1800–60*
(London, 1961), p. 250.

almost from the beginning. By 1852, the officers were con-
certing their demands, and in particular demanding that they
be given power to stop workings which were, in their opinion,
dangerous. Of course they did not want absolute powers,
and with them absolute responsibilities. As one of them
observed in 1869, 'Much as the question of more inspection . . .
may be desirable, I have often thought that many of the
casualties herein reported might have happened while I was
in the mine. Often I have found men working in great danger
for want of their places being propped and spragged when
props and sprags in abundance were lying out of use within a
few yards.'[1] Equally, of course, there was nothing sinister
or conspiratorial in their proposals for a change in the formal
character of the inspectorate. The advisory service was
inherently unstable. There could be no lasting half-way
ground between no coercion and a statute prohibiting bad
practices, and providing for its own enforcement.[2]

[1] Boyd, *op. cit.*, p. 184. The inspector in question was Peter Higson, who was
appointed in 1855, and whose district was West Lancashire and North Wales.
[2] The first factory 'inspectors' are another interesting case of administrative
evolution. They were not, initially, inspectors at all, as the term is ordinarily
understood by historians. More precisely, they were as much special magistrates
as executive officers, and as much commissioners of inquiry as special magistrates.
This three-headed animal was ill-fitted to the British constitutional and govern-
mental environment, and naturally failed to survive. But it was ten years before
the office was statutorily reformed, MacDonagh, *op. cit.*, pp. 332–3.

☆ **4** ☆

Cobden and Bright in Politics
1846–1857

THE object of this essay[1] is to discuss the political fortunes of Cobden and Bright in the years between the repeal of the Corn Laws and the General Election of 1857. These years saw a transformation in their standing; in 1846 Cobden at least was widely regarded as a political figure of very great importance, while in 1857 the two men were reduced to the rôle of leaders of a forlorn hope, voices crying vainly in what was for them the moral wilderness of Palmerstonian England.

In the spring and early summer of 1846, with the Corn Laws doomed, the leaders of the Anti-Corn Law League seemed to occupy a position of immense significance in British politics. Among these leaders Cobden was clearly recognized as the leading spokesman and mainspring of the organization, while the previous few years had seen Bright achieve in and out of Parliament recognition as the most eminent of Cobden's coadjutors. At first sight the hopes of these men that they might continue to play an important rôle in national politics seemed well founded. The past few years had seen the League which they led rise from an ineffective minor agitation into the most fully organized political machine which Britain had yet seen, with a degree of sophistication in its arrangements for administration and propaganda that was not to be equalled for many years. The impression which this Leviathan of

[1] I am grateful to the late Professor W. L. Burn and to Professor G. F. A. Best for discussing this paper with me, and for the helpful suggestions they made about it.

agitation had made was reflected in the importance accredited to its leaders.   Peel himself heightened this impression when, in his resignation speech in the House of Commons on 29 June, he unequivocally credited Cobden with responsibility for the repeal of the Corn Laws.   This view of the situation was widely shared at the time.   A few days later *The Times* asked

> What is to be done with the said Richard Cobden?   Is he to be treated as the dangerous agitator, or the successful deliverer?   Is he to have the benefit of the régime which he has himself established?   There must be something hypocritical in these praises if the object of them, after all, is unworthy of rank, office or trust.   Is he too great, too glorious, too plebian, too successful for a Whig ministry? . . .[1]

When the repeal legislation was safe in Parliament Cobden set off for an extensive tour on the Continent; during his absence his activities were watched with eager and flattering interest by observers both at home and in the countries he visited.   Everywhere he went abroad he was received as a visitor of importance, while British newspapers devoted a good deal of space to his travels.   For example, *The Times* in the summer of 1847 paid tribute to his missionary activities in the following terms:

> . . . In England, honour to him is superfluous.   But out of England in foreign states and courts, each impression of English opinion has a weight and effect beyond what we dream of here.   Mr Cobden has been the undiplomatized but not unacknowledged internuncio of a new economic creed, which his country was the first to profess.   He has been received with the respect due to an ambassador, and the reverence which belongs to a discoverer. . . .   The cause which first found disciples at Manchester has sent its chief apostle on a high mission to Naples, to Piedmont, and to France.   It does become us then as a nation to do honour to this man; for in honouring him we show our zeal and devotion for principles which are as yet only beginning to gleam over the rugged Alps and the Pyrenees of Continental Protection . . .[2]

[1] 1 July 1846.
[2] 7 August 1847.

It may seem hard to maintain that both Sir Robert Peel and *The Times* were wrong in their assessment of the position, but it is hoped that this essay will adduce sufficient evidence to cast doubt upon their appreciation.

In 1846, however, both Cobden and Bright had high hopes for the future. For both of them repeal of the Corn Laws had always been seen as merely the first step in a much more far-reaching programme. It seemed possible that the forces which had rallied to the League might be kept together behind a wider programme and that a 'Manchester party' might continue to play a prominent part. For this purpose it was necessary to put forward an attractive programme for both domestic and foreign policy, proposals which could rally and maintain support now that the slogan of the Corn Laws was no longer available. Here the two leaders hit the first serious snag. They themselves were agreed on the desirable development of British foreign and colonial policy, but they found it much more difficult to reconcile their views on the next target in domestic affairs. The divergence in view here was in some degree a reflection of differences in temperament. Cobden was the more practical and shrewd of the two men, and he favoured practical reforms in the field of national finances as the first objective to be aimed at in a new agitation. He had grave doubts as to the likelihood of further Parliamentary Reform proving conducive to the forwarding of the aims of the Manchester School. He was, as a deft politician, perfectly capable of writing plausible letters when necessary explaining how much he relied on the good judgement of the British people, but much more typical of his correspondence is a strong vein of doubt, increasingly justified in these years, as to the bellicose and extravagant tendencies of most of his fellow countrymen. Rather than aim at Parliamentary Reform, Cobden went to a good deal of trouble to work out a 'National Budget', whereby the burdens laid on the British producers were to be lightened by cutting down taxation, primarily at the expense of the armed forces, bodies which to Cobden and Bright were on the one hand mere extensions of the aristocracy's pension list, and on the other standing temptations to war.

Bright took a different line. At this time a facile optimism and an ebullient self-confidence are prominent in his activities;

G

from the beginning he did not share Cobden's doubts about the efficacy of Parliamentary Reform, and argued that the first place in any new agitation should be given to a further extension of the suffrage.   After Cobden's return from his travels, many months were consumed in a lengthy correspondence between the two men as to their future line in domestic policy, the eventual result being an unhappy compromise to run Parliamentary and Financial Reform in harness, an expedient which did not succeed, for little enthusiasm was roused for these objectives in the late 1840s, and the organizations formed to forward them proved weak and ephemeral.   These divergences were one factor—among many—which made it so difficult to provide the League with a strong posterity in radical agitation.

Foreign and colonial policies proved awkward too, but not in this case because of any lack of agreement; in this field Cobden and Bright saw eye to eye, and indeed for both of them this was in many ways the most important field for the application of their ideas.   Here, however, it was the inherent nature of their views which militated against the creation of a powerful political force.   For both men the objectives of peace and international co-operation were right in the forefront of their policy.   For them the acceptance of a Free Trade policy by Britain was only the first step.   Everything possible should be done to facilitate the acceptance of this system by other states, not simply for the sake of economic advantage, but mainly so that the whole world might be bound together by links of mutual inter-dependence, chains of commerce so vital that war would become impossible and armaments wither away.   Cobden felt

> . . . how impossible it is to ensure the peace of the world, and guarantee us against all the burdens which our present warlike attitude entails upon us by any means excepting a free commercial intercourse between all nations. . . .[1]

To forward this policy Cobden and Bright advocated the adoption by this country of foreign and imperial policies aimed

---

[1] Cobden/Bright, 24 October 1846. Copy in Cobden Papers at Dunford. Note the clearly private nature of this and the following letter cited, which argues sincerity.

at the attainment of peaceful co-existence between nations, and the scrupulous avoidance of unnecessary friction. In a letter of 1847 Cobden expounded for the benefit of George Wilson, once the very efficient Chairman of the League, how he had framed his views on foreign policy:

> From the moment that I could form my notions into a theory of statesmanship—and it is nearly 20 years ago— I came to the following conclusions on our public policy —1st that Ireland was the great domestic difficulty— 2nd. That our intervention in the state-politics of the Continent was the chief source of our heavy taxation and financial difficulties—and 3rdly that the United States, and not any Continental power, was the quarter from whence rivalry for England was to be apprehended. Every year's experience has since confirmed me in those views, which I published, crudely enough, twelve years ago. I thought free trade would have been the prelude to a wiser foreign policy—that common sense would have been admitted to a seat at Downing Street—But we seem to be playing the fool in our foreign policy worse than ever. We are now actually employing a fleet larger than the whole American navy in the mere personal service of that little petticoat puppet who can't rule over two millions of beggarly Portuguese without our taxpayers' money to coerce them. It is enough to make an Englishman of sense turn hermit, let his beard grow, and live in a cave. Oh, I wish the English people knew how little good their 800 millions of debt had done for foreign nations, and how little the people of the Continent feel indebted to us for our sacrifices . . .[1]

A corollary of these views on foreign policy was that it was clearly wrong to spend energies in the conquest of colonies abroad; commerce rather than empire was at once Britain's interest and moral duty. Cobden and Bright found much to criticize in these years; in 1852 the former complained of the Whigs that

> . . . they are committed to our present expenditure, and a prospective increase in the item (military) on which alone there could be a sensible diminution. Whilst professing free-trade principles to serve the end of party, they seem

---

[1] 21 June 1847. In Wilson Papers, Manchester Central Library.

to be quite unable or unwilling to accept its logical consequences, for they are extending our territorial dominions
in all directions—buying Danish possessions in Africa;
talking of assuming authority in South Africa from the
Cape to the Line; endorsing the piratical adventures in
Sarawak, Lagos, etc., and all this when the most elementary powers of common sense would have dictated a
gradual disentanglement from our existing colonial responsibilities.[1]

On the whole the ideals which moved Cobden and Bright in
colonial affairs were creditable. Cobden complained about
British India that

> . . . I find the common epithet applied to our fellow
> subjects in Hindostan is *nigger*. One of those ladies took
> some credit for her condescension in allowing a native
> officer, answering to the rank of subaltern, to sit down in
> her presence when he came for orders to her husband.
> All this might have been borne, though with difficulty,
> if the English with whom the natives came into contact
> displayed exalted virtues and high intellectual powers.
> But I fear that the traits most conspicuous in our country-
> men have been of a very different character . . .[2]

This does not seem absurd or exaggerated, but it is not the
whole story. The strength of the feelings which Cobden and
Bright had on these matters all too frequently led them to go
further than their brief justified, and in consequence the effect
of their generous enthusiasm was often impaired by uncritical
and exaggerated zeal. For example, the previous letter on
India might be compared with Cobden's declaration that

> . . . the world never yet beheld such a compound of jobbing,
> swindling, hypocrisy, and slaughter, as goes to make up the
> gigantic scheme of villainy called the 'British rule in
> India' . . .[3]

All too often Cobden and Bright seemed to start from the
prejudice that anything done by their fellowcountrymen
abroad was likely to be evil, while conversely they were ever-
ready to accord to headhunters in Borneo or to a Burmese

[1] Cobden/Bright, 30 August 1852. Copy in Cobden Papers.
[2] J. Morley, *Life of Cobden* (1906 ed.), p. 673.
[3] Cobden/Bright, 18 October 1850. Copy in Cobden Papers.

king all the attributes of the noble savage. During the fighting in Burma in 1853 both men assumed at once that Britain was in the wrong, and Bright asked

> . . . What a dreadful business is the Burmese war! Who is responsible for the murder and famine and misery which now ravage Pegu? . . .[1]

It did not occur to either of them apparently that the Burmese might conceivably bear some of this responsibility. Another good example of the same sort of thing is the vendetta carried out against Rajah Brooke, a campaign in which Cobden was joined by Joseph Hume.[2] Despite warnings from such informed friends as Joseph Parkes[3] that there were some 'queer customers' among the 'colonial reformers' with whom Cobden and Hume were concerned in the Sarawak affair, the radical politicians involved continued to launch attacks on Brooke based on evidence accepted credulously from personal enemies of the Rajah, in a way which recoiled upon them later when the truth came to light. Cobden and Hume believed that Brooke, with the connivance of the Royal Navy, was launching bloody attacks on peaceful natives, whereas the natives against whom Brooke fought seem to have been in fact headhunters of a markedly uncongenial nature. Cobden and his allies in this business refused to be convinced even when one of their informants literally lost his head in the area concerned. Cobden still saw the problem in clearly defined, if erroneous, moral terms. He wrote about the Sarawak business that

> . . . It shocks me to think what fiendish atrocities may be committed by English arms without any conscientious resistance at home, provided they are only far enough off, and the victims too feeble to trouble us with their groans. . . . There must be a public and solemn protest against this wholesale massacre. . . .[4]

This kind of obstinacy in error diminished the chances of an

---

[1] 17 November 1853, in Cobden Papers.
[2] For the Sarawak affair, see the accounts given in *The White Rajahs*, by Sir Steven Runciman (Cambridge, 1960), and *James Brooke of Sarawak*, by Emily Hahn (London, 1953).
[3] Parkes/Cobden, 5 January 1850. In Cobden Papers.
[4] Cobden/Bright, 6 December 1849. Copy in Cobden Papers.

effective propagation of the programme put forward by Cobden and Bright.

A greater weakness, however, was that the whole tenor of the foreign and colonial policies espoused by these radicals at this time was alien to the dominant ethos of Palmerstonian England. Some of the reasons for this will be explored later, and it may suffice here to say that both in domestic and in overseas policies Cobden and Bright never again commanded such an impressive and attractive 'cry' as the Corn Laws had been. This was one reason why in the years after 1846 the old leaders of the League found it impossible to rally sufficient strength to make their activities effective. Instead of a great new political alignment, the years after 1846 saw Cobden and Bright at the head of a diminishing band of devoted followers, while other issues and other cries proved more attractive to their fellow countrymen. The 'Manchester Party'—increasingly, as we shall see, a misnomer—was in practice Cobden and Bright and the few for whom they acted as spokesmen; the 'party' was never more than a handful in the House of Commons backed by diminishing support in the country at large. In these years Cobden and Bright were never within measurable distance of effective political power.

A consideration of the political situation in the years after 1846 points to another factor in the impotence of Cobden and Bright. It has already been suggested that the importance accorded to the League leaders in 1846 was exaggerated. After all it was not Cobden and the League who were primarily responsible for the repeal of the Corn Laws; had it not been for Peel's decision they would have continued to exist, for the plain fact was that in the existing political system, dominated by the older sources of property and influence, the agitation for Free Trade was unable from its own resources to amass sufficient political power to ensure victory. Exaggeration of the League's strength was a weapon deliberately used by its own supporters, but the number of constituencies which it could effectively influence was a tiny minority, and it was only by Whig and Peelite votes that repeal was effected. The key decision was that of Peel, and thus the importance so often assigned to the League leaders in this respect was something of an illusion from the beginning. The Leaguers were never

able to command anything like the serried ranks in Parliament
of the old parties.   Corn had been a key problem of the 'forties,
disturbing established groupings and producing an extraordinary political alignment in 1846.   Perhaps the extent to
which Corn dominated the politics of the early 'forties is sometimes exaggerated—there were many other problems about
at home and abroad for British politicians—but what is not
in doubt is that the disappearance of Corn as an immediate
political issue put the initiative in British politics back firmly
in the hands of the established parties, and marked something
of a return to a more normal pattern of politics.   It is true that
the party system had been disturbed, but the dominance of
the landed interest remained; once again a weak position had
been abandoned in time, and opposition had been disarmed by
concession.   A main advantage of the Corn Laws as a cry was
that here was an appeal capable of attracting wide and varied
support.   It was this advantage which enabled the League to
grow as it did.   The fight for the repeal of the Corn Laws
rallied to its standard manufacturers directly concerned with
economic policy, others moved by arguments of the political
economists, humanitarians concerned with the Staff of Life,
and many interests which joined battle because it seemed such
an effective weapon with which to attack the social and political
pre-eminence of the territorial aristocracy.   Even if the League
did exaggerate its strength it was not a negligible force in
politics in 1845 and 1846 while it commanded support from
diverse elements, some of which at least possessed property
and influence.   This strength could not be held together after
the Corn Laws disappeared.   Whigs and Tories continued to
dominate British politics because they possessed more of the
reality of political power, that is more property and influence,
while radicals could not rally enough strength to mount an
effective challenge to the 'Establishment'.   These points may
emerge more clearly from a consideration of the electoral
fortunes of Cobden and Bright.

The electoral fortunes of the two radical leaders in 1846–7
were one aspect of the myth of real strength which surrounded
them at that time.   If the newly installed Whig government
showed little respect for the radicals, doling out only very
meagre scraps in the shape of minor office for Villiers and

Milner Gibson, two of the most aristocratic of the League's members, the General Election of 1847 provided one of the most remarkable compliments of the day. The West Riding of Yorkshire, one of the most highly esteemed constituencies in the country because of its great concentration of wealth in various forms, elected Cobden as one of its Members in his absence and without any personal connection or canvass. This return was the most striking result of all in that election, but here, as with the ex-Leaguers' position in general, the reality was very different from the apparent strength. The background of this singular result has been lucidly analysed by F. M. L. Thompson,[1] who has shown that the nomination of Cobden was in great part the reflection of dissension among the different 'liberal' groups in the Riding, and in particular friction between the Whig country interest led by Lord Fitzwilliam and the urban liberals led by men like Edward Baines of Leeds. The latter group was responsible for nominating Cobden, partly as a deliberate demonstration of their own power and ability to act independently of the country interest, which reluctantly accepted a *fait accompli* in this instance. It was clear, however, that the liberal bloc could only maintain its hold on the West Riding if a cordial co-operation between the various groups could be established, and this was to prove very difficult in these years. Although outwardly his election for the West Riding was a remarkable testimony to the strength of Cobden's position, the recipient himself from the beginning had no illusions about the hollowness of the honour done to him. At the time he declared to his old Stockport constituents that

> . . . there is no advantage whatever to me in representing the West Riding of Yorkshire after representing Stockport. Whatever I can do in Parliament as the representative of the West Riding I believe I could do equally well as the representative of Stockport. . . . I consented to sit for the West Riding, because when I returned home I found that I had no alternative but to do so . . . had I been in England at the time they proposed to put me in nomination I should not have consented to their doing so. . . . [2]

[1] 'Whigs & Liberals in the West Riding', *English Historical Review*, vol. LXXIV, 1959.
[2] *The Times*, 13th December, 1847.

He could not reject the proffered honour, but his position in the West Riding was a vulnerable one if his prestige should sag, or disunity imperil the liberal control of the constituency. From the beginning Cobden knew that he had no secure hold on the seat he held in the Commons. After the disaster of 1857 he wrote that

> . . . the real cause of my finding myself at this moment out of the House is to be traced as far back as 1847, when, owing to the over-zealous kindness of my friends, I was, whilst a thousand miles distant from England, returned for both the West Riding and Stockport. On my return home, at the urgent request of these friends, I reluctantly dissolved my connection with the Borough, and elected to sit for the West Riding—I should have been but a coldblooded politician had I acted otherwise—But I had a full foresight of the consequences, for I was the first to declare that it would be impossible after the free trade question was settled, that the largest County Constituency in the Kingdom, should continue to be represented by one unconnected with it by birth, property, or residence. . . .[1]

The last few words of this passage show an appreciation of the hard realities of the politics of the day. Unfortunately for Cobden's Parliamentary tenure, not only did his own prestige decline markedly during the next ten years, but in addition liberal disunity in the Riding worsened. The principal villain in the piece was Edward Baines. Not only did differences persist between Whig country interest and urban liberals, but in the years after 1846 the urban liberals in the West Riding were themselves bitterly divided as a result of the narrow and fanatical line followed by Baines on the education question; this question, with its overtones of religious duty and sectarian rivalry, played a major part in Yorkshire politics in these years, and indeed aroused more energies than Cobden was able to enlist for his policies. On the question of state interference in education, Cobden was completely at odds with Baines, who, in the face of all evidence and argument, continued to assert that the need for increased facilities in education could be adequately met by voluntary bodies. It is probable that the Baines line commanded only minority support among the

---

[1] Cobden/Alexander Laing (Hawick), 30 April 1857, in Cobden Papers.

liberals in the Yorkshire towns, but he was certainly able to
disrupt the unity of the liberal front on which Cobden's seat
depended.   Already in the 1847 General Election, for example,
the education question divided the liberals at Leeds, Bradford
and Halifax.   The same cause was responsible for a Conservative victory in a by-election for the other West Riding seat in
1848, which completely exposed the weakness of Cobden's
position in the county.   Cobden declined to take a prominent
part in this election, although he was willing as a pacific gesture
to vote for Eardley, the eccentric candidate put forward by the
Baines party.[1]   After the election Cobden wrote to Baines,
with whom he tried hard to keep on friendly terms, that

> . . . the result of the W. R. election did not I presume
> surprise our friends.   With three or four great rents in the
> liberal party, it was wonderful that the defeat was not
> more signal. . . .[2]

In another letter of the same day—this time to Bright—he
was not so polite.

> . . . Now doing as much justice as any man to Baines'
> usefulness in the Corn Law struggle I look upon his present
> position in the West Riding as a misfortune to the liberal
> cause.   If he were not there, I could undertake to rally
> the party tomorrow and in two years beat both the Tory
> and Whig aristocracy.   Literally speaking, he and he
> alone is the obstacle.   By hereditary prestige, rather than
> by any native qualities for leading such a constituency,
> he occupies a position from which he cannot be
> deposed . . .[3]

Cobden went on to declare, wrongly as it happened, that he
would never stand for the Riding again, and even to say that
he preferred Garnett of the *Manchester Guardian* to Baines and
the *Leeds Mercury*, a statement the significance of which will
emerge a little later.   The division between Cobden and
Baines was not healed within the period considered here, and
as the years went by Baines rather widened the breach.   In
the late 'forties the *Leeds Mercury* was on the whole courteous

[1] Cobden/Baines, 13 December 1848.   Copy in Cobden Papers.
[2] *Ibid.*, 21 December 1848.
[3] In Cobden Papers.

even when disagreeing with Cobden and Bright, but in their years of difficulty after 1852 the *Mercury* adopted a more disagreeable tone, sometimes patronizing and sometimes downright offensive towards these old allies. The whole affair made Cobden's position in the West Riding hopeless; by the end of 1849 he wrote to George Wilson that

> . . . the West Riding is a source of embarrassment to me in every possible way, and I do not see my way out of the trouble—excepting on the corn question, I do not see that I could with propriety contest it—Yet my friends there will not hear of anything else, and at the same time they are not preparing the register for a successful fight— This is a sad mess for me. . . .[1]

If one were to name one constituency in which the ex-Leaguers might be expected to be firmly in the saddle Manchester would at once come to mind. Yet surprisingly enough at that other pole of industrial England, Bright was in just about as sad a mess in these years.[2] Manchester had always contained a good deal of Conservative and Whig elements among its influential inhabitants and although it had never yet returned a Tory, the liberal members for Manchester had usually been very respectable, solidly based men of substance. The rôle of Manchester as cradle of the League had given an exaggerated impression of its devotion to the radical group which came to bear the town's name. Well before the General Election of 1847 Bright had set his heart on occupying one of the town's two seats, in spite of the fact that he was not liked by many of Manchester's most influential citizens. He was too radical and too brashly self-confident and too self-righteous for many moderate liberals in the town. In 1847 the opposition to Bright's candidacy was unavailing, but it is instructive to note where the dissidents looked for a rival candidate. They sought to bring forward instead the Earl of Lincoln, Peelite heir to the Tory Duke of Newcastle. If these plans had succeeded Manchester, that supposed centre of radicalism, would have been represented in the House of Commons by two recent converts from Conservatism, the Suffolk squire Milner Gibson,

---

[1] 24 December 1849. In Wilson Papers.
[2] I have profited from discussions with Mr John Skinner on the representation of Manchester in these years.

and the Earl of Lincoln. Lincoln's candidacy was pushed
vigorously, and by February 1847 his supporters claimed 4,725
pledged votes for him.[1]   Cobden loyally used all his influence
in the town in Bright's favour, despite his knowledge of the
fact that Bright was certainly not the best candidate the
liberals could find there.   It is fairly clear that if Cobden had
consented to stand for Manchester he would have been elected
without much fuss, for he was much more popular in the town
than Bright, and he was always a man of more charm and tact
that Bright was ever to possess.   Bright's candidacy was pushed
principally by the old League organization in Newall's Buildings under George Wilson's indefatigable leadership.   These
agents succeeded in amassing behind Bright many more
pledges than the Lincoln party claimed, and when faced with
the clear threat of an open breach in the liberal ranks if he
came, Lincoln dropped the idea of standing for Manchester,
and Bright and Gibson were elected.   Yet dissatisfaction
rankled in the town, and from the beginning there was a large
bloc of old Leaguers who would not support Bright, as well
as elements further to the right which had held aloof from the
League.   Opposition to Bright was kept up to the mark in
these years by Garnett's *Manchester Guardian* which normally
took a moderate or Whiggish line, and wielded a vitriolic pen
against Bright whenever opportunity offered; the *Guardian*
provided the opposition to Bright among Manchester liberals
with a more effective Press mouthpiece than the sitting members
were ever able to acquire.   Bright had owed his election in
1847 in great measure to the twin factors of Cobden's whole-
hearted support and the work of Wilson's organization, but
the value of these supports declined in the next few years.
Cobden never became quite as unpopular in Manchester as
Bright did in the mid-'fifties; but as he settled in the South, and
became to some extent disillusioned with northern politics, he
ceased to be in as close touch with Manchester groups, and less
influential in the town.   His increasing remoteness from local
politics was a serious loss to Bright's position in Manchester.

The organization in Newall's Buildings continued, for
although the League ostentatiously dissolved itself after the
victory of 1846, Wilson kept a nucleus of the organization in

[1] *The Times*, 27 February 1847.

being with the object of providing Bright and Gibson with a political machine which could continue to work in the politics of Manchester and other neighbouring constituencies. In the years after 1846, however, these activities came to be a mixed blessing. The failure to dissolve the League machinery completely, despite the numerous promises that this would be done after repeal, aroused suspicions among moderate liberals who had been dubious about the League's political activities already. Moreover, the way in which the Newall's Buildings group claimed to speak and work on behalf of all the liberals in Manchester was irritating to Manchester Whigs. For example, Wilson continued to receive and distribute the official patronage in the area which was channelled to him by the sitting members,[1] so that the government patronage for Manchester came to be confined to keen supporters of Bright and Gibson, a monopoly irksome to those denied a share. While it was perfectly true that Wilson and his helpers were skilled political manipulators, their activities tended to arouse irritation in some influential quarters, and in any event they could not control the constituency without the cordial support of the men of substance in the town. Apart from these factors, the fundamental reason for Bright's increasing weakness in Manchester was, of course, that the policies which he and Cobden advocated were increasingly out of tune with dominant opinion here as elsewhere, and Bright had no local strength or influence capable of counteracting this situation.

The position of strength which Cobden and Bright seemed to occupy in 1846 dissolves when tested in their constituencies. Yet these two areas, with their concentration of the new manufacturing wealth and influence, were surely the very places where we might expect the free trade radicals at their strongest. If their position was in jeopardy in Manchester and the West Riding, how much more tenuous was their influence in the great majority of other constituencies, most of which were still dominated in these years by the landed interest. The propertied classes in these years retained with ease the reality of power and were not prepared to accept the doctrines

---

[1] Two examples of this: Milner Gibson/Wilson, 14 February 1853, asking for names for Manchester Post Office appointments, and Alexander Henry (M.P. South Lancs)/Wilson 5 January 1848, asking for names for Tax Commissioner appointments in the county. Both in Wilson Papers, with others to similar effect.

advocated by Cobden and Bright. Instead, political power
was for the most part firmly in the hands of established parties,
and these parties contained men perfectly capable of assessing
the real weakness of the 'Manchester' party. It was not
possible in the years after 1846 to build up a structure as strong
as the League, let alone anything more enduring and powerful.
There was not the strength available to build an independent
party of any size, and so in practice, however unwillingly,
Cobden and Bright were forced to act for the most part as one
element in the loose bloc of Whigs and various radical groups.
They were not usually among the more powerful elements in
this coalition, and did not find their position at all to their
liking. There is no single year in this period when the correspondence of Cobden and Bright does not contain bitter
denunciations of the Whigs, yet the hard truth was that the
Whigs were stronger, and that without Whig votes the radicals,
even in the unlikely event of their agreeing among themselves,
were helpless. The Whigs for their part had no intention of
falling into the hands of the radicals, so that in these years
Cobden and Bright were remote from the real business of
policy making. In these circumstances the feelings of the
two leaders were vented in vitriolic though impotent correspondence. As early as May 1848, Bright was writing that:

> . . . It would be a capital thing if the government men
> could be thrown out . . .[1]

and in the next year he informed Wilson of

> . . . great dissatisfaction with the govt. among our friends,
> on a/c of their almost insolent treatment of any question
> touching upon *reform*. . . .[2]

In 1851 Bright's tale is the same.

> . . . Lord John is sinking into a state of hopeless imbeci-
> lity. . . . I believe him to be incurable, and the sooner he
> is banished from politics, the better for the Country. . . .[3]

Cobden was in full accord with these strictures; later in 1851
he told Bright that:

> . . . The Whigs are an impossible party to govern upon our

---

[1] Bright/Wilson, 5 May 1848. In Wilson Papers.
[2] *Ibid.*, 12 July 1849.
[3] *Ibid.*, 12 March 1851.

principles.   In fact they only keep office by the prostitution of the radicals, and if they remain a few years more
in office, there will not be above a dozen Liberals who
will not have yielded to their impure embraces. . . .[1]

From time to time the frustration engendered by the reluctance
of the Whigs to pay any attention to their remonstrances led
Cobden to look longingly to the other side.   He told Bright
in 1852 that:

> . . . It is my opinion that, taking Free Trade as an estab-
> lished fact, *accepted by all parties*, you would be much more
> likely to get a reduction of taxation and expenditure, a
> revision of our colonial system, a thorough reform of the
> laws affecting real property, and a diminution of our
> standing armaments, from the Tories than the Whigs . . .[2]

These doubts were to persist.   During the minority Conservative government of 1858 a sympathizer mentioned to
Cobden that:

> . . . The present men are much more honest, and they are
> certainly much more obliging than the last. . . .

and Cobden replied that:

> . . . In this I agree with you and it might have been said
> of any Tory government as compared with any Whig one
> since I have been in the political ring.   I remember when
> I came into the House in 1841, after the general election
> which gave Peel a majority of 90, I found the Tories more
> civil in the intercourse of the lobbies and the refreshment
> rooms than the Whigs.   It runs through all departments.
> —It seems as if the Whig leaders always thought it neces-
> sary to snub the radicals to satisfy the Tories they were not
> dangerous politicians. . . .[3]

Bright did not share this attitude to the same extent; he was in
practice much more connected with some of the other radical
groups advocating Parliamentary Reform and such apostasy
was harder for him.   In any event Cobden's occasional hanker-
ings after the Conservatives were only wishful thinking; both in
Parliament and in the constituencies co-operation with the

[1] 2 September 1851.   In Cobden Papers.
[2] 30 August 1852.   In Cobden Papers.
[3] Cobden/Caird, 24 March 1858.   Copy in Cobden Papers.

Whigs was the only practical policy before the various radical groups, however much they might grumble at the prospect.

It is perhaps not too surprising that the ex-Leaguers found it difficult to co-operate with the Whigs, but in addition to this they increasingly found themselves in conflict with other radical groups. Radicalism in Britain was changing, and Cobden and Bright were not the only radicals presenting an alternative foreign policy to the country. Particularly after the revolutions of 1848 focused attention on the nationalist movements on the Continent, sympathy with the oppressed nations—Poles, Hungarians, or Italians—became strong among many British radicals, some of whom were capable of dreaming up projects for intervention abroad which went far beyond anything which Palmerston ever seriously considered. This leaning became clear when the flow of distinguished refugees sought asylum and aid in Britain. Cobden and Bright sympathized with the fallen heroes, but not to the extent of advocating active intervention abroad on their behalf. Instead they clung to their fundamental faith that 'Commerce was the great Emancipator' and that with the growth of peaceful economic co-existence all would in time turn out for the best. This was not a very easy path for a radical politician to tread in these years; as Cobden put it after Bright had attended an enthusiastic meeting addressed by Kossuth in 1851:

> . . . Really a public man has hard work to give a generous welcome to a patriot and martyr, without falling into the trap laid for him by Palmerston's tools. . . .[1]

To many of their old radical associates the moderate line taken by Cobden and Bright on these issues seemed cold and unfeeling at a time when romantic conceptions of nationalism were much in evidence. In these years the sufferings of oppressed Poland, Hungary and Italy aroused more enthusiasm among British radicals than the more pedestrian claims of financial or parliamentary reform at home. However absurdly, many British radicals professed to see in the Crimean War a crusade against the arch-tyrant of Russia in the interests of the subject peoples of Europe, so that in their determined opposition to that war

[1] 13 November 1851. Copy in Cobden Papers.

Cobden and Bright faced not only Whig and Tory opposition, but also the fierce criticisms of many of the leading Parliamentary radicals. Cobden received many letters from old allies of League days denouncing his actions at this time. A comparatively mild example was that from an old York friend who declared that:

> ... I will become a convert to your peace principles after one more general war for freedom! This must come within ten years. I had hoped that a war between Russia and Turkey would give Hungary and Italy a chance to be free. ...[1]

Three months later Cobden complained of the war that:

> ... I must say that we cannot charge it upon the aristocracy, or the executive ... The so-called radicals of the old school are more to blame ... Now the radicals (I speak of those who are anything better than Whigs and yet not of the Manchester School) have continued to identify themselves with an absurd policy ...[2]

In these circumstances the leaders of the Manchester School had a hard furrow to plough, increasingly isolated in Parliament and in the country from the more powerful political groups. A despondent Cobden wrote to Bright early in 1852 that:

> ... We, the so-called Manchester party, have a sickening fate before us in the House. Hated by the old Tories, dreaded by the Whigs, suspected by the Peelites, we have no hopes from any existing party, and in any attempt, if we should be foolish enough to make it, to set up by ourselves, we shall become the objects of the envy, hatred and malice of the kid-glove democrats, the unscientific radicals of the Finsbury school, and everybody else, with the exception of about 25 earnest free traders and financial reformers. A very pretty corps to enlist in. ...[3]

As it happened, when this letter was written another moment of apparent triumph was about to come to Cobden and Bright, and with it a postponement of the demonstration of their real weakness because of the circumstances in which the general

---

[1] J. P. Thompson/Cobden, 18 August 1853. Copy in Cobden Papers.
[2] Cobden/Bright, 9 November 1853. Copy in Cobden Papers.
[3] 20 January 1852. Copy in Cobden Papers.

H

election of 1852 was fought. The fall of Russell's government saw Derby installed at the head of a minority Conservative administration which had not yet explicitly disavowed Protection. This enabled the cry of the Corn Laws to be raised again, and all the various Whig and radical groups were able to come together on this basis in a transient co-operation for the general election. At Manchester even the *Guardian* preferred Bright's re-election to a clear demonstration of liberal disunity at this crucial moment. Bright and Gibson were re-elected there with little trouble. In the West Riding things went smoothly too; all liberal groups worked together for the occasion, and since Cobden's Conservative colleague had swallowed Free Trade, it was possible there to secure the return of the sitting members without opposition. In this year too the Anti-Corn-Law League was re-created with great parade, although in fact the resurrection was more nominal than real. However, for another brief moment Cobden and Bright could believe that they stood at the centre of the political stage. The elation soon passed and disillusionment followed. As soon as the crisis passed the situation returned to normal, and despite the part played by the Corn Laws cry Cobden and Bright were ignored in the negotiations which brought about the formation of the Aberdeen ministry. The general election itself had shown some disquieting features. Corruption had been more obvious than in the preceding few elections, nor was it confined to any one side of the political spectrum. Nothing had been done to shake the hold of the aristocratic Establishment on the reality of power. Here for example is a small part of the analysis of the situation in the North Warwickshire division sent to George Wilson by the knowledgeable Joseph Parkes, showing the terms in which skilled agents saw these contests:

> . . . you are aware that Sir Geo. Chetwynd who always brought up 150 electors free of charge is dead—his son a violent Tory. Then old Sir Robert Peel gave Lord Leigh last time all help; and no mortal man knows what side young Bobby would take. Then we had Dugdale tenantry, doubtful now. Also Sir Francis Sankey who proposed for us and who had great personal influence . . .[1]

When calculations such as this were the stuff of politics in many

[1] Parkes/Wilson, 7 July 1852, in Wilson Papers.

constituencies it is clear how hard it was for a radical group, dependent on principle and persuasion rather than property and influence, to make headway. For much of the time Cobden and Bright by the very nature of the prevailing political system were working outside the realities of power. The next few years were to show that they were unable to maintain even the shaky position which they occupied in 1852, for events abroad now took a line which rapidly eroded most of the support and sympathy which they had retained till then.

The Crimean War, and the courageous and consistent opposition to it which Cobden and Bright persisted in, demonstrated without doubt that the two leaders were now deserted by most of their old allies. Many of the more prominent ex-Leaguers made it quite clear that they no longer followed their old mentor; such men as Absalom Watkin, George Hadfield, and Mark Philips carefully dissociated themselves from what the last named described as

> . . . the anti-national policy of the Members for Manchester. . . .[1]

and under the influence of these circumstances the *Guardian* and its supporters stepped up their attacks on Bright. If those who attacked Cobden and Bright because of their attitude to the war could have seen the private letters of the two men their attacks would have been even more bitter than they were. Two letters from Cobden to Bright, written in the summer of 1855, may serve as examples of their feelings in the matter; on 31 May he wrote that:

> . . . speaking in the interests of our children, I doubt whether it be desirable that our arms should have a great triumph in the Crimea—for it would only foster the war spirit and make us more eager for further intervention. . . .[2]

On 26 June he was even more explicit:

> . . . Nothing I fear short of the loss of an army by disease will break up this confederacy and turn the public mind against both government and public instructors. . . .

[1] For Watkin, Alexander Ireland/Wilson, 2 November 1854; for Hadfield, Bright/Wilson, 16 December 1854; for Philips, Philips/Wilson, 10 January 1855. All in Wilson Papers.
[2] Copies in Cobden Papers.

We have already seen that the hold of the two men on their
Parliamentary seats was shaky; in both cases the effect of the
Crimean War was to make their expulsion almost inevitable.
In the West Riding the influential Chairman of the Liberal
election committee, Carbutt, flatly declined to preside at a
meeting called to give Cobden an opportunity to explain his
policy towards the war, and indeed ceased to correspond with
Cobden for some time after this. A meeting was still held,
but with unhappy results for Cobden; Lord Stanley of Alderley
wrote to his wife that:

> . . . Cobden met with a great slap in the face at a meeting
> at Leeds where he hoped to make converts and to per-
> suade the W. Riding that his pacific views were the true
> policy, and did all he could to help the Emperor of
> Russia and to injure England. The result was a resolu-
> tion all but unanimous that the war should be prosecuted
> with the utmost vigour. . . .[1]

Similar events took place in Manchester; great public meetings
were called to demonstrate that the town was out of sympathy
with the views of its sitting members, and Bright was publicly
burnt in effigy.   Palmerston was given an enthusiastic welcome
when he visited the town, and in 1857 his name was seriously
put forward as a possible Parliamentary candidate for Manchester, though in the event he declined to stand.   There is
no reason to doubt that he could have been elected.

By this time Cobden and Bright were well aware of their
political isolation, but would not budge an inch, taking consolation in a firm belief that they were morally right while the
bulk of the nation were engaged in a bellicose aberration.
They were well aware that their following was reduced to a
tiny minority possessing very little weight in the country.
Indeed, some of their most fervent supporters were in some
ways more of a liability than an asset.   Joseph Sturge and other
Quakers associated with the Peace Movement remained loyal
to them but were generally regarded in the country as a
remarkably cranky group, an impression which was heightened
on the eve of the Crimean War when they sent emissaries to
see the Czar, and after that war's close when they collected

---

[1] *Stanleys of Alderley.   Letters 1851–65*, ed. by Nancy Mitford (London, 1939).

money to pay to Russian civilian sufferers from British naval actions in the Baltic.

Although the position of Cobden and Bright had been under-mined much earlier, disaster was delayed until 1857, and then, ironically enough, electoral defeat was precipitated by Cobden's success in bringing together a heterogeneous majority in the House of Commons behind his attack on Palmerston's Chinese policy.   Briefly Cobden was heartened into optimism by this success, but when Palmerston dissolved Parliament Cobden's illusions vanished.   The crisis came at a peculiarly inopportune moment; Cobden himself had been hit hard by the recent death of his son, and was not at his best.   A few months earlier Bright's health had broken down completely, and he was embarked upon a prolonged convalescence abroad when the general election took place; he was, however, determined to stand for Manchester again, despite the weakness of his position. It was quite clear that Cobden could not stand for the West Riding with any chance of success; all the important Liberal groups there, including Baines and the *Mercury*, had supported the Crimean War and were now hostile to Cobden.   It was not easy to find *any* constituency which he could fight with hope of success.   His old seat at Stockport was out of the question; not only had he been replaced there, but there too most of his old supporters, including Henry Coppock who had been his principal agent when Cobden sat for the town, had turned against him during the Crimean War.[1]   In addition Cobden spent a great deal of the available time fighting Bright's hopeless cause at Manchester.   Eventually a hasty decision was taken that Cobden should stand for Huddersfield.   It was of no avail; Cobden was beaten soundly there, while Bright and Gibson were rejected at Manchester in favour of two very moderate liberal candidates.   It is possible that Gibson's seat might have been saved if Bright had agreed to withdraw, for Bright was always the main target of the opposition there, but Bright would have none of this, and he and Gibson fought a joint campaign.   In the terms of the address in which Bright took his leave of the Manchester electors we can see some of the reasons for his unpopularity:

[1] J. B. Smith/Bright, 26 January 1856.   In Bright Papers, British Museum, Add. MSS 43,388.

. . . Many amongst you have abandoned the opinions you
professed to hold in the year 1847, and even so recently
as the year 1852. I believe that slander itself has not
dared to charge me with having forsaken any of the principles, on the honest support of which I offered myself
twice, and was twice accepted, as your representative.
The charge against me has rather been that I have too
warmly and too faithfully defended the political views
which found so much favour with you at the two previous
elections.

If the change in your opinion of me has arisen from my
course on the question of the war with Russia, I can only
say that . . . I would not unsay or retract any of the
speeches I have spoken, or erase from the records of
Parliament any one of the votes I have given upon it, if I
could thereby reverse the decision to which you have
come, or secure any other distinction which it is in the
power of my countrymen to confer. I am free, and will
remain free, from any share in the needless and guilty
bloodshed of that melancholy chapter in the annals of my
country. . . .[1]

Cobden might have tried to make the same point, but would
not have used such irritating terms. One feature of the 1857
General Election was that even those who had contributed to
Cobden's defeat were somewhat taken aback at the event.
Carbutt wrote[2] from Leeds, for example, to express sympathy
for Cobden, and to say one or two nasty things about the
wealthy local business man who had won the Huddersfield
seat. Yet such letters could be but slight consolation, for it
was clear that the electorate had rejected the policies and the
arguments of Cobden and Bright. Palmerston had won a
clear, if not an overwhelming victory, in the election, but the
defeat of the 'Manchester School' was clearer still. Moreover,
it was obvious why this defeat had come; resentment at their
conduct during the Crimean War was the prime factor involved. While Cobden and Bright talked about peace and
non-intervention in the abstract they could at least receive a
hearing, but when it was a question of Britain actually engaged
in war, with our soldiers fighting and dying then the way of

[1] Enclosed in Bright/Wilson, 31 March 1857, in Wilson Papers.
[2] Carbutt/Cobden, 31 March 1857, in Cobden Papers.

the pacifist was hard indeed.   Even some of those who thought
that on the single issue of the China question Palmerston and his
agents were in the wrong could not follow Cobden into his
wider policies.   During the China debate Chichester Fortescue,
a well-connected and quite sensible Whig politician, noted in
his diary that:

> . . . I was, and am still, very much provoked at Bowring's
> conduct, and at first had some inclination to vote with
> Cobden, before I heard his speech, merely to condemn
> Bowring.   But Cobden's speech, Bulwer's, and indeed
> all the speakers on that side of the question, made it more
> and more impossible for me to have anything to do with
> Cobden.   They were so un-English, so ingeniously unfair
> against ourselves and in defence of the Chinese. . . .[1]

The General Election of 1857 was not of course the end of
the story for the two radicals.   Both Cobden and Bright
returned to Parliament in the next few years, and had successes
to come.   Cobden was offered the Presidency of the Board of
Trade by Palmerston in 1859 and although his principles
proved less elastic than those of Gladstone he succeeded, to
his own and others' surprise, in establishing cordial personal
relations with Palmerston, which proved a great help during
the negotiations for the Anglo-French treaty of 1860.   Bright,
of course, was destined for a longer career as a prominent
Liberal leader.   1857, however, marked the obvious failure
of the two men and their followers to recapture the spirit and
the scale of the League for their wider policies, and in particular
the failure of their attempts to wean Britain from Palmerstonian
policies abroad.   After 1857 when Cobden and Bright returned
to Parliament they were, somewhat unwillingly, involved in
that Liberal synthesis which was to produce Gladstone's party
by the later 'sixties.   The high hopes of 1846 had proved
illusory.   The leaders of the League had not occupied a major
place in British politics; in the political drama of these years
Cobden and Bright had been extras rather than principal
players.
  It is to Cobden's credit that he assessed the situation
accurately, for the most part.   Given on rare occasion to undue

[1] . . . *and Mr Fortescue*, Diaries ed. by O. W. Hewett (London, 1958).   Entry
under 28 February 1857.

optimism, Cobden nevertheless more often saw the realities of the situation. As early as January 1853 he wrote to Bright that:

> . . . I am sick of this everlasting attempt out of doors to give the semblance of an agitation which don't exist. . . . Our meeting and talking in Manchester positively misleads people. They think there is something grand doing and it is nothing but a holiday gathering of our good friends. . . .[1]

After the catastrophe of 1857 he expressed the same view in a letter to one of his sympathizers.

> . . . year after year we met and paraded ourselves as the 'Manchester Party', but I was never myself inspired with much faith in our proceedings. I attended our annual gatherings and talked as soundly as the rest. How could I refuse our good friend Wilson's invitations? It would have been said that I had turned my back on my old friends, and so we went on until we were knocked on the head last month. . . .[2]

This contrasts with Bright's normal attitude; he was much more ebullient and confident, and in these years less realistic than his mentor Cobden. Cobden's assessment of the situation stemmed from his clearer appreciation of the ways in which British society was changing in these years, for apart from the immediate political reasons for the defeat of Cobden and Bright they were faced with more general developments which did not help their cause. One important factor in the impressive show made by the League had been the hostility felt by the industrial interests towards the preponderance of the landed aristocracy; in the years after 1846, as Britain moved into Professor W. L. Burn's 'Age of Equipoise' this hostility diminished. The middle decades of the century see the emergence of a more homogeneous upper class, with industrial magnates joining the county benches and even serving as High Sheriff on occasion, while Manchester Corporation, to the disgust of Cobden and Bright, adopted the scarlet gowns and the civic junketings of the City of London, abandoning the more

---

[1] Cobden/Bright, 8 January 1853.   Copy in Cobden Papers.
[2] Cobden/J. Vaughan, 23 May 1857.   Copy in Cobden Papers.

severely economical attitude of earlier years. This development made it more difficult to raise steam behind radical
agitation and was paralleled by a more tranquil attitude
towards their betters by lower orders of society. Even the
revelations of the Crimea did not immediately shake the
predominance of the aristocratic establishment, while in a few
years the Volunteer movement aroused enthusiasm in all
classes for warlike experiences. In the aftermath of the 1857
defeat Cobden wrote that:

> . . . During my experience the Higher classes never stood
> so high in relative social and political rank, as compared
> with the other classes, as at present. The middle class
> has been content with the very crumbs from their table.
> The more contempt a man like Palmerston (as intense
> an aristocrat at heart as any of them) heaped upon them
> the more they cheered him. . . .[1]

Nor was this perception merely the bitterness of defeat. A
few months earlier Cobden had bared to Wilson his reactions
to the events of the last ten years:

> . . . Now I must be as candid with you as I have been with
> Sturge, to whom I have said that I will never again be a
> party to the old movement, carried on in such a [way] as
> to allow everybody, *Baines* included, to join in the 'Halle-
> lujahs' for *peace*, and nine-tenths of them to run off and
> cheer any minister who will offer to make war with any
> people on earth. I must have something more definite
> and binding before I go into a partnership of that kind
> again. It is merely beating the air. But I have a similar
> feeling arising out of the late war, respecting 'Financial
> Reform'. It is a delusion to propose economy in the
> public expenditure so long as the people of this country
> as represented by almost every leading politician and
> newspaper—from Palmerston to Roebuck—from *The
> Times* to the *Despatch*—lay it down as their duty that they
> must regulate the affairs of the whole world, and protect
> Europe in particular against the encroachments of Russia
> or any other ambitious power. So long as such a policy
> is seriously professed by the country, I cannot honestly
> tell it that there should be a moderate peace establishment.
> On the contrary a nation which undertakes to sway the

[1] Cobden/Caird, 24 March 1857. Copy in Cobden Papers.

destinies of Europe by bullying one half and protecting
the other must make up its mind to bear the expense of
such an attitude.   The little that I shall have to say on
the subject of our finances will be to link together cause and
effect in this unpalatable way.   But there is no party as
yet in the country that I can see to support one in these
views. . . .   As for Parliamentary Reform, I hold that we
might as well call out for the millennium.   The Radicals
have turned more warlike than the Tories—what have
they to promise the country in the way of practical benefits
as a result of Parliamentary Reform?   Not 'peace, retrenchment and reform', which were Lord Grey's watch-
words, but the very reverse.   No, depend upon it the
Radicals have cut their throats before Sebastopol.   It
is useless to utter their old shibboleths.   So you will see
that I am desponding.   The world will I suppose come
right in the end, but we don't stand now where we did
8 years ago.   The aristocracy have gained immensely
since the people took to soldiering. . . .[1]

There is a good deal of truth in this analysis.   It is unlikely
that Cobden and Bright could have made much progress with
their policies in any event, given the realities of the existing
political system.   They were not, however, operating in a
vacuum, but in a society which was itself changing markedly,
but changing in ways which immensely increased the difficulties
of their task.   Greater social peace and prosperity at home
diminished reforming enthusiasm, but these changes were
certainly not parallelled by pacific policies abroad.   Unable
to mobilize effective political power, or to appeal successfully
to public opinion in Palmerstonian Britain the 'Manchester
School', apart from the two false dawns of 1852 and 1857,
tasted bitter defeat in the years after the repeal of the Corn
Laws.

[1] 23 September 1856.   In Wilson Papers.

5

Popular Protestantism in Victorian Britain

'YOU are a Catholic, sir!' cried the lady who saw A. W. N. Pugin cross himself in the railway compartment; 'Guard, let me out—I must get into another carriage!'[1] The state of excitement into which she was thrown by his gesture (in the early days of railway travel, no less prudent than pious) was similar to that of the Browning family's clergyman, the nonconforming Joseph Irons of Camberwell Grove Chapel, whom young Robert once heard to proclaim, 'as an undoubted fact, that Roman Catholic and midnight assassin are synonymous terms'.[2] These are strong—one might say, fighting—words and because they would, so far as I can judge, not have struck many early or mid-Victorians as being much stronger than the situation demanded, I believe it is worth inquiring seriously into the nature and effects of the common state of mind which provoked them.[3]

---

[1] Kenneth Clark, *The Gothic Revival*, ch. 7.

[2] Cited in M. St J. Packe, *John Stuart Mill* (London, 1954) p. 120.

[3] I have been campaigning for this for years, and have discussed the question with groups at Cambridge, Columbia, Leicester and Sussex Universities. On each occasion, helpful criticisms were made. To my critics, some of whom will recognize the points at which they have strengthened or corrected my argument, I am properly grateful; to those who merely recognize points at which they failed to persuade me to alter it, I also apologize.

Like most other elements in the religious and intellectual history of at any rate the first half of the century this popular protestantism was a shared concern of Britain and North America. It was, indeed, a common feature of the whole English-speaking world; Melbourne and Auckland intermittently resounded to the beat of the Orange drum no less than Liverpool and Philadelphia. But the connection between Britain and North America seems to have been particularly close. What happened on one side of the Atlantic cannot satisfactorily be studied

How much 'No Popery' continued to matter after the so-called 'Catholic Emancipation' in 1829, and in what parts of the country, on what occasions, at what periods in particular, are questions to which I can propose no firm answers. It seems worth while to offer some tentative ones, however, because too little attention has so far been given to this wide and weighty phenomenon: the ubiquitous persistence through a century allegedly of secularization, education, propriety, and class conflict, of a tight-knit cluster of avowedly religious beliefs and justifiable feelings springing from ignorance, credulity and prurience, and matched only by 'Queen and Country' for its power to unite peer and peasant. These British beliefs and feelings—the main subject of this paper—have, so far as I know, been described with tolerable adequacy in only one place: in Chapter 4 of J. E. Handley, *The Irish in Modern Scotland* (Cork, 1947). This is a kind of group-portrait of the clustered feelings which popery was sure to evoke in protestant breasts, and of the variety of troubles which followed. It is pleasantly done; yet it does not go beyond description, and being concerned solely with what notions Scottish presbyterian Protestants had about papists (usually Irish immigrants), says

in isolation from what happened on the other. The North American part of this story has been copiously covered by R. A. Billington in *The Protestant Crusade 1800–1860* (New York, 1938), which no other work in the field can match for care and completeness. (See also articles by Marsden and Griffin in the *Catholic Historical Review*, vol. XLVI (1960–1), pp. 1–21 and vol. XLVII (1961–2), pp. 325–41.) But for all the similarities of sources (puritanism, evangelicalism, and the common law) and tone (the American manifestations being merely more physically violent than the British), the social and political bottles into which this heady wine poured were so different as to make the overall contrasts no less striking than the likenesses. Whoever sets out to write the history of nineteenth-century 'No Popery' in Britain may go astray if he supposes he has merely to write a British Billington. There is, however, so far no sign of anybody attempting even that. All we have is a few studies of particular aspects of the British side. G. I. T. Machin has done justice to *The Catholic Question in English Politics 1820–1830* (Oxford, 1964), while that question's more theoretical sides have been considered in ch. 5 of U. R. Q. Henriques, *Religious Toleration in England, 1787–1833* (London, 1961) and my article 'The Protestant Constitution and its Supporters 1800–1829' in the *Transactions of the Royal Historical Society*, 5th series vol. VIII (1958), pp. 105–27. (The late eighteenth-century antecedents are well dealt with in E. C. Black, *The Association: British Extra-Parliamentary Political Organisation, 1769–1793* (Cambridge, Mass., 1963), ch. 4, and (for its Scottish branch) *Review of Politics*, vol. XXV (1963), pp. 183–211. G. A. Cahill's valuable articles in the *Catholic Historical Review*, vol. XLIII (1957), pp. 273–308 and *Review of Politics*, vol. 19 (1957), pp. 62–76, demonstrating, with tantalizing brevity, the important place of Protestantism in Tory politics during the 'thirties and 'forties, deserve to be better known; as does J. Murphy's fine close-up of popular protestantism at work during the same years in Liverpool, *The Religious Problem in English Education* (Liverpool, 1959).

nothing of English Protestants' not less colourful notions about those (hardly ever Irish) traitors within the gates whom they considered crypto-papists: Puseyites, Ritualists, Anglo-Catholics. The Kirk had its troubles during Victoria's reign, but the prospect of popish subversion was not among them. South of the border, however, it was this very readiness to see the same Roman evils at work outside the formal frontiers of popery as well as inside that gave to English anti-sacerdotalism (no lesser word will do it justice) its special vigour and enterprise, and a large degree of distinctness from those common anti-Irish attitudes with which it was often, in politics, mixed up. Once unleashed, the anti-sacerdotal hound could scent its quarry in the most unexpected and, to a less impassioned eye, improbable places: in Bishop Colenso, for example, and in Miss Havisham of Satis House.[1] The extraordinary wildness and nastiness into which even its more educated and respectable adherents readily ran are not the least curious aspects of this popular protestantism, and they no doubt require the attention as much of the psychologist as of the historian. It would indeed be helpful to have the psychologist permanently on tap. Much of the surface force and fury of anti-sacerdotalism evidently came from subconscious preoccupations at whose nature a historian with no more than the layman's smattering of psychology can only guess.

The substance of the grand anti-sacerdotalist idea was complex and variegated. It can be broken down for purposes of analysis, and it is better understood that way. But in examining it thus we must note that its separate parts rarely functioned singly. Were any of the delicate spots pressed, the whole frame would throb and jangle—though most of this might happen out of sight, and thus be easy for the unsuspecting observers to miss. When any one of the parts was touched, I believe, the others would be too; and the strength of feeling

---

[1] P. Hinchliff, *John William Colenso* (London, 1964), pp. 69–70 cites a passage from a Durban newspaper, *c.* 1855, denouncing Colenso's 'spiritual despotism. . . . skulking under a Bishop's lawn while it wields the tyrant's sword' in the language that was common to English anti-sacerdotalism and (so far as it had any appreciable distinction from it) anti-clericalism. Colenso's offence was the introduction into his lax diocese of the prayer for the Church, of an offertory, and of the use of the surplice. As for Miss Havisham, readers of pp. 127–131 below will have no difficulty in spotting in ch. 49 of *Great Expectations* the passage of popular protestant reflections on the uselessness and miseries of the conventual life.

engaged could be much stronger than was superficially expressed.

☆   ☆   ☆

At the heart of the matter were certain serious theological objections to Rome. (These seem rarely to have gone unaccompanied; the political, moral, sexual and other parts of the case were always in close attendance, however discreetly hidden, just as when they, or any one of them, stood to the fore, the theological part was never wholly uninvolved.) The objection was, in the first place, to the operations of a sacrificial priesthood: a special class of men who could alone, so they claimed, mediate between the soul and its salvation, offering on the individual's behalf a sacrifice that could be as efficacious for the dead as the living. The protestant denounced these claims as superstitious, fallacious and delusive. No mortal, he said, could come between the believer and his God, and it was positively cruel to gull men into thinking that salvation could be secured by anything but their own direct converse with their Saviour. 'That which renders Popery so dangerous,' wrote C.G.H.[1] in the Preface to *Constance Lyndsay; or, the Progress of Error* (Edinburgh, 1849), 'is that it seeks to relieve an individual of responsibility in working out his own salvation with fear and trembling.... His substitution of a father in earth for our Father in Heaven . . . and of the voice of the Serpent-Priest for the holy dove, the Comforter—this is the grand Mystery of Iniquity . . . which will continue to delude until the day of the coming of the Son of Man.' The protestant also thought the 'sacrifice of the mass' derogatory to the saving character of Christ, as in effect reduplicating again and again His sacrifice. Protestants in general could agree on the definition given in the consecration prayer of the Anglican service of Holy Communion: 'His one oblation of Himself, once offered, as a full, perfect and sufficient sacrifice for the sins of the whole world.'

The protestants saw further insults offered to Christ in the fact of 'popery'. The word 'popery', in its limited literal sense, signified the supremacy claimed by Rome over the whole

---

[1] Also author of *The Curate of Linwood*; *Margaret Waldegrave, or, the Power of Truth*; and *Amy Harrington, or a Sister's Love*.

of the Christian church. Here again was an affront to Christ, the sole head of His church. Whether that church was understood as a visible one or, as was more the evangelical way, an invisible, it made no difference to the detestation in which protestants held the notion that a foreign secular potentate had a right to interfere in the government or self-government of their national or voluntary churches.

A third and very important element of the unmixedly religious part of the case rested on the biblical prophetic books. Until the progress of biblical criticism gave them the order of release, all Christians had to try to make something of the prophecies, because it was the orthodox belief—held until at least the middle of the nineteenth century by all self-confessed believers save unitarians and deists—that the *whole* of the Bible was spiritually meaningful: that every bit of it had spiritual sense and purpose. Intelligent Christians would readily admit that the sense and purpose of some of the books was obscure, and (with an eye, perhaps, on what had happened in the days of Pym and Cromwell) that men could go very wrong by too rashly concluding that they understood them. Caution was needed. Much of the prophecies was not clearly intelligible. But one point stood clear enough within its fringe of speculations: these prophecies foretold the downfall of the Pope of Rome, and the downfall of the Pope was a necessary overture to the Second Coming. Edmund Gosse was brought up in a home where all this was taken for granted. Looking back from the lax days of the seventh Edward, he recalled the stricter views they had held of the Scarlet Woman in the 1850s. 'As a little boy, when I thought, with intense vagueness, of the Pope, I used to shut my eyes tight and clench my fists. We welcomed any social disorder in any part of Italy, as likely to be annoying to the Papacy. If there was a custom-house officer stabbed in a fracas at Sassari, we gave loud thanks that liberty and light were breaking in upon Sardinia. If there was an unsuccessful attempt to murder the Grand Duke, we lifted up our voices to celebrate the faith and sufferings of the dear persecuted Tuscans, and the record of some apocryphal monstrosity in Naples would only reveal to us a glorious opening for Gospel energy. My Father celebrated the announcement in the newspapers of a considerable emigration from the

Papal Dominions, by rejoicing at "this outcrowding of many, throughout the Harlot's domain, from her sins and her plagues".[1] The Gosses moved in quite different circles from Lord Shaftesbury, but this was a language which Lord Shaftesbury could perfectly understand.

Closely related to these specifically religious elements of popular protestantism were a clutch of mixed religious-political ones, very natural in a land with a politically established protestant church and with an all but universal determination among its public men to preserve what they understood to be their country's Christian character. Protestants saw the sacrificial powers of the priesthood and the oecumenical supremacy of Rome together as threats to liberty: the liberty of the individual, and the liberty of the nation. It is not difficult to trace the historical genealogy of this marriage of Liberty with No Popery. At the Reformation had been equally asserted the religious liberty of the Christian man, and the religious liberty of the nation or state, against the claims of a common enemy. What liberty meant then, and what it had come to mean by the nineteenth century, were clean different things, but England's social and political development was such that a connection naturally developed between the individualist, privately-judging side of the national religion and the anti-absolutist, libertarian side of the national politics. Already by the reign of Charles II this link was firm. The Whig mobs that paraded the London streets during the Exclusion crisis shouted 'No Popery' and 'No Wooden Shoes!' indifferently, to express their combined fears of spiritual and secular tyranny. In their Pope-burning processions, effigies of Queen Elizabeth I might be protected by shields representing 'Protestantism' and 'Magna Carta'.[2] That these were not mere partisan fancies soon after appeared in the all-party Declaration of Rights, recognizing that William of Orange had rescued the nation from 'Popery and arbitrary power'. From the Revolution on, this was the common language of all politicians and public men, slackening not a jot through years which made the political probabilities of coming under any

[1] *Father and Son*, ch. 4.
[2] See O. W. Furley, 'The Pope-burning Processions of the late 17th Century' in *History*, vol. XLV (1959), pp. 16–23.

sort of popish tyranny increasingly remote. Indeed, the intensity of the sentiment seems positively to have increased. An 'Invocation to the Freemen of Grimsby' urged them, in 1826, to vote for the 'No Popery' candidate, Sir Thomas Phillipps, in these terms:

> See a Phillipps nobly stand,
> Holding Freedom in his hand!
> He who loves his King and land,
> Give to him a willing voice.
> 'Gainst vile Popery he draws
> Weapons to defend your cause,
> And support Old England's laws:
> Freemen—Make him now your choice![1]

That was a year when 'Catholic Emancipation' was still being debated. The *Leicester Journal*, standing fast by the Protestant colours after Peel's 'ratting', thought it necessary to reassure its readers: 'Let what will come, we shall do our duty as men, while we have the power of speaking to our fellow-subjects. Chains may be forged for us, we may be tortured and persecuted by triumphant Popery, but we shall still put our trust in the righteous cause, and still feel that the life of man cannot be more nobly expended than in the service of freedom.'[2] So it continued. Victorian Protestants did not apparently pause to consider whether it was not entirely fanciful in them to apprehend a possibility that Popery might bring to Britain national servitude and individual martyrdom. Their theme only broadened as the years went by, until it was indistinguishably mixed up with the common cant of manly freedom-loving patriotism.

> We're the sons of sires that baffled
> Crown'd and mitred tyranny;
> They defied the fire and scaffold
> For their birthright—so will we.

That is actually a verse from a Kensitite hymn;[3] but it might equally have been sung at a Regency Whig Club on Mr Fox's

---

[1] A. N. L. Munby, *The Family Affairs of Sir Thomas Phillipps* (Cambridge, 1952), pp. 64–5.
[2] *Leicester Journal*, 13 March 1829.
[3] I regret to have to admit that I have lost track of the exact source of this verse.

I

birthday, or on the eve of the hols at Wellington or Cheltenham.

The mixed religious-political objection to Popery had at its heart a dislike of the Papist's divided allegiance. This was the main point urged against 'emancipation' before 1829. Thereafter, it had not the same commanding position in the protestant case; but it retained some importance. The question still bothered protestants, whether Roman Catholics could honestly give to their king the same undivided allegiance as Protestants. Were their loyalties not shared between Monarch and Pope?—and would not their spiritual allegiance, in the event of any conflict of claims, have to be the superior? Protestants had no doubt that, for a conscientious and virtuous Papist, the spiritual indeed should be the superior allegiance; they admired such religious seriousness, while deploring its premises. National and individual liberty could only, to their way of thinking, be secured by a bringing together of the two allegiances under a single head: as, for example, in the English situation, by means of a national church under the monarch's supremacy.[1] The Royal Supremacy over the established church did not necessarily mean Erastianism, however much it tended that way in practice. The higher sort of Anglicans were sensitive about this but the more protestant sort were driven by the logic of their argument almost to embrace it. Sir William Harcourt, strongly affirming parliament's right to put down ritualism, knew that his opinions would be denounced as Erastian ones. But he insisted that they were the doctrines on which 'the Parliamentary State Church of England' was founded, and on which alone she stood. If you did not have Erastianism, he thought, you would infallibly get its opposite —Ultramontanism.[2] Harcourt and his like had no doubt which of the two they preferred.

The next segment of the anti-sacerdotalist circle displayed what we may call the moral objections: objections made as much by secularists and humanists as by trinitarian Christians. Roman Catholicism was apprehended to be inimical to truth. There was much more to this than the simple, though perhaps passionate, objection to the principle of the Index and the

[1] The Kirk must have looked at this matter differently, but I do not know what the difference was.

[2] See especially his speeches on 31 July and 5 August 1874; 3 *Hansard*, CCXXI, 1085–90 and 1341–54.

relative unimportance, in the Roman scheme of religious
education, of Bible study. A Protestant could not but think
the road to Truth thus much obscured. But what was worse,
was the irresponsible way Papists handled Truth when they
had got it. Casuistry, for instance: ignorant of the quantity of
respectful attention paid to that science by Protestant English
divines two centuries earlier, nineteenth-century Protestants
professed to hold it in abhorrence, as blurring the distinction
between right and wrong. Then there were dispensations.
Every Protestant knew about them. Operating from the
commanding heights of the spiritual power, a priest could give
a man a dispensation to release him from an inconvenient oath,
or to enable him to commit what others would consider a crime.
Papists believed that the end justified the means. Seemingly
unconscious that they too might sometimes be thought to act
as if this was so, Protestants repeatedly brought this charge
against their foes, as a sort of summary of their different
attitude towards Truth. The word of a Roman Catholic,
and even the oath of a Roman Catholic, they proclaimed,
could not be relied on!

Out of this particular notion came one of the most celebrated
controversies of the century, and one of its most famous books.
Charles Kingsley took occasion when reviewing Froude for
Macmillan's to say, 'Truth, for its own sake, has never been a
virtue with the Roman clergy. Dr Newman informs us that
it need not, and on the whole ought not, to be; . . .' There
followed an exchange of letters, which Newman published.
Kingsley countered with *What, then, does Dr Newman mean?*,
and Newman's reply came out as his famous *Apologia*. But
isn't Mr Kingsley right after all?, asked F. Meyrick in his contribution to the subsequent melée. Our concern must not be with
that intriguing question but with other aspects of Kingsley's
argument; for Kingsley embodied with gratifying completeness
the whole spectrum of anti-sacerdotalist feelings and beliefs,
and we may conveniently use him to open up another, and
murkier, section of the moral case.[1] The cardinal passage from
his review went on thus: '. . . that cunning is the weapon which

[1] Kingsley's introduction of the theme of christian marriage in this particular
context of Truth versus Falsehood, moreover, emphasizes his place in that peculiar
tradition of allegorizing Truth as a virtuous heroine which has been brilliantly
explored by Alexander Welsh in *Victorian Studies*, vol. IX (1965), pp. 7–28.

Heaven has given to the saints wherewith to withstand the brute male force of the wicked world which marries and is given in marriage.'   Here, somewhat crudely introduced, was Kingsley's passionate subscription to the protestant belief that the sacerdotal system was unmanly, unEnglish, and unnatural; the more particularly because of its attachment to the ideal of celibacy.

This important aspect of the matter demands close scrutiny. In the first place, the apartness of the priest—the degree to which was emphasized his difference from even the holiest of laymen—went against a strong English tradition.   The close ties that joined clergy and laity were a feature of the church establishment upon which its apologists and glorifiers, in the late eighteenth and early nineteenth centuries, especially congratulated the nation.[1]   They delighted to point out how men who were in various ways to take the lead in church and state underwent the same kind of education, picked up a common code of manners, accepted the same political allegiance and imperial responsibility.   They rejoiced that ordination and ecclesiastical office in practice raised no serious barriers between ministers and their nominal flocks.   They maintained that the social state of England was sound so long as ordained and un-ordained Christians understood each other so well. The 'official' theory running on these lines, any ecclesiastical system which tended to distinguish and separate clergy from laity could not but evoke serious suspicions.   The Roman system certainly did so.   Instead of combined education to the highest possible level, it accepted separation from quite early on.   It brought priests up in a different and secluded atmosphere, to accustom them absolutely to their separateness and speciality.   It cut them off designedly from participation in the common 'natural' concerns of 'ordinary men'; by denying them matrimony, it took the most effective single step possible to keep open that gap which separate education had created. A priesthood thus reared and organized and disciplined was able to bear strains and to obey orders which any less 'unnatural' body of men would find intolerable.   When priests were stigmatized as unmanly, the word (such a favourite one

---

[1] I have written of this at greater length in my *Temporal Pillars* (Cambridge, 1964).

with the leaders of early Victorian public opinion!) was being applied in quite a strict sense; it meant not that the priest was falling short of the standards of manliness expected of a christian gentleman, but that in consequence of his education and commitments, a priest could not (unless he had gone off the rails prescribed for him—of which possibility, more presently) be expected to be as other men were. The good priests would have been dehumanized. This was deplorable. Protestants preferred that their clergy should face and tower triumphant over the lusts of the flesh and the cares of the world than that they should (if their training 'took') be simply unconscious of them. Protestant laymen liked their clergy to be morally superior versions of themselves, not a different sort of beings altogether. The idea of theological colleges, when it began to exercise the Anglican world about the 1830s, encountered much opposition on this score; and one of the most engaging testimonies to the seriousness with which clerical unmanliness was regarded comes from Samuel Wilberforce, the chief campaigner for such institutions and therefore hyper-sensitive to the danger that they would go wrong in this respect. Of Cuddesdon College, the one he himself had founded, he was soon observing that 'our men are too *peculiar*—some, at least, of our best men . . . I consider it a heavy affliction that they should wear neckcloths of peculiar construction, coats of peculiar cut, whiskers of peculiar dimensions—that they should walk with a peculiar step, carry their heads at a peculiar angle to the body, and read in a peculiar tone. I consider all this a heavy affliction. First because it implies to me a want of vigour, virility and self-expressing vitality of the religious life in the young men. It shows that they come out too much cut out by a machine and not enough endued with living influences. . . .'[1] Wilberforce did not in this passage use the word 'unnatural' but evidently that is what his 'peculiar' meant.

The most unnatural point of this extensive unnaturalness was undoubtedly its insistence on celibacy. The natural man normally wanted a wife and a family. Some men could be happy and virtuous without them but they must have the freedom to choose the single life. 'After all,' wrote the poet

[1] Cited by Owen Chadwick, *The Founding of Cuddesdon* (Oxford, 1954), p. 93.

Wordsworth, 'I reckon the constrained celibacy of the clergy the monstrous root of the greatest part of the mischiefs of Popery. If that could be got rid of, most of the other evils would gradually melt away. If we would truly spiritualize men, we must take care that we do not do so by unhumanizing them, which is the process in respect of all those who are brought up with a view to the making of that unnatural vow.'[1]   This was the case against celibacy put at its most dignified and well instructed.   It was felt no less intensely by at least one member of the great Darwin dynasty.   Charles Darwin's daughter Henrietta was, recalled her niece, 'a very fierce anti-Catholic'. One evening about the turn of this century she wrangled about Rome with her young relation until bedtime, till both went to bed with headaches.   'I was lying peacefully reading, and beginning to feel a little calmer, when the door burst open and a tiny frail figure, in a red dressing-gown and a white shawl, appeared at the end of my bed.   Fixing me with eyes burning out from the deep hollows under her shaggy brows, she began without preamble: "I could SWALLOW the Pope of Rome, but what I can NOT swallow is the Celibacy of the Clergy".'[2]   Aunt Etty could no doubt have given a rational explanation of her aversion.   At least she understood what she had the aversion to; as did not all who shared it.   The matter cannot have been well understood by the correspondent who complained to a local paper, about 1896, that their 'new Vicar was not ashamed to practise celibacy openly in the street'.[3]

Thus the protestant was led to suspect the sexual morals of the priesthood.   Of course priests would sleep with their housekeepers!   Of course nunneries were always liable to become priests' brothels!   If their perversion of human nature did not lead to the one sort of horrors—morbid asceticism, cruelty, mania—it must lead to the other.   'Fellow Britons!' declaimed the incumbent of Cleasby, in the mid-'thirties, 'keep your little daughters from the popish schools for they are nurseries out of which the handsomest may be selected for the seraglios of the Popish priests . . . freedom is the Britain's noble birthright, rescued from Popish tyranny, at the expense

[1] Letter dated 5 February 1840, in W. R. W. Stephens, *Life and Letters of W. F. Hook* (London, 1878), vol. II, p. 47.
[2] Gwen Raverat, *Period Piece: a Cambridge Childhood* (London, 1952), ch. 7.
[3] J. G. Lockhart, *Cosmo Gordon Lang* (London, 1949), p. 121.

of the heart's blood of our valiant Christian forefathers, bravely shed amidst the racks, tortures, and the fires of the bloody popish inquisition; and shall any of our lovely countrywomen be confined in nunnery prison-houses, to be the victims of licentious priests, and without one hope of escape but through the gloomy portals of death?'[1] The Rev. Michael Augustus Gathercole must have been more irritably excitable than most of his co-Protestants, and I have come across no one else of comparable respectability (it was of course a stock theme with *low* writers) who made such extreme allegations about 'those seraglios of the popish priests called nunneries'. His suspicions of their bolted doors and barred windows, however, were widely shared; and that brings us to the nastiest vein of thoughts in the Protestant's mind when he contemplated the two institutions which became, during the middle and later nineteenth century, most popularly significant of Sacerdotalism: the convent and the confessional.

There were no convents (I use the term in a loose sense, to describe all forms of religious communities of women) in Britain between the fifteen-fifties and the seventeen-nineties, although there were several convents full of British women on the continent. Only after the outbreak of the French Revolution, and as a direct result of it, did convents openly reappear on the British soil. Unable to subsist under the newly hostile revolutionary régimes, and welcome arrivals in an anti-revolutionary land, many communities moved over from France and Flanders.[2] Peaceful, unostentatious, and innocent of proselytizing, they seem for long to have attracted no hostile attentions. It was not until after 1829—not until the Catholic Emancipation Act and other less flamboyant causes had produced the aggressive and edgy revival of 'No Popery' of the 'thirties—that convents became a Protestant talking-point.

What really went on in the convent? That was the question that, from about 1830, increasingly obsessed Protestants; and not necessarily because they shared Mr Gathercole's suspicions. Their most obvious concern was that girls, like 'helpless victims adorned for sacrifice', too young to know exactly what they

[1] Gathercole's case, which ended up at the York summer assizes 1838, may be found in 2 *Lewin* C.C. 237–256, or 168 *E.R.* 1140–5.

[2] F. F. Anson, *The Call of the Cloister* (London, 1955), pp. 24–5. All the ones he lists settled in England. Did any dare to plant themselves in Scotland?

were doing, were induced to take 'that irrevocable vow which bound [them] to perpetual seclusion, and separated [them] for ever from all the social ties and endearing charities of life'.[1] Such girls simply could not tell what opportunities of happiness and usefulness they were forfeiting, what a lifetime of disappointment and frustration they might be embracing through the indulgence of their ingenuous enthusiasm. Very wicked were held to be those—surely Jesuits, for the most part—who took advantage of this girlish enthusiasm; and particularly wicked if along with the girl they were scheming to get her money. And what happened when she came, too late, to her senses (as Protestants were sure a good-hearted Protestant girl must do) and wanted to get out of it? She would be held by force. Those bars on the windows, those locks and bolts on the thick-studded door, that system of security and secrecy behind the peep-hole and the grille, were not just for ornament. The nun's vows included obedience, and obedience would be enforced. Nay, by the laws of sacerdotalism it had to be enforced, for the nun's spiritual good. Her efforts to engage outside help (father, brother, former lover) would be met by imprisonment and removal. Just as Charles II's administrations had nullified the effect of the *habeas corpus* writ by moving prisoners secretly from place to place, so would the sacerdotalist superiors thwart it by moving their victims to sister-houses on the continent. Protestants who worried about this kind of thing used to agitate for compulsory inspection of convents. Factories, prisons, mines, workhouses, madhouses, had to be open to public scrutiny; why not convents too?

Just when this particular branch of the popular protestant case opened up, I cannot be sure; but I suspect it was among the elements imported into the British movement from Ireland in the 'thirties. From the 'forties through the 'sixties were, I think, the years of its vogue, the years when no competent protestant orator (least of all, George Whalley) would neglect to bring it in somewhere, and it reached its apogee in 1864 with the case of Mary Ryan. This began with a *Daily Telegraph* report from Dover of a screaming young beauty being forced by two nuns on to the Ostend boat. A London lawyer, considering this 'so great an insult to every Englishman', sent

[1] *The School Girl in France* (London, 1840), p. 315.

the cutting to the Home Office. The Home Office instituted an inquiry. Bit by bit the girl's story came out. She was an Irish orphan who had entered the convent in 1859. Her mental derangement had become so acute that the medical superintendent of the Bethnal House Asylum had recommended her removal to Belgium where she could get proper treatment. Sir George Grey, a Home Secretary to whom Protestants never looked vainly for support, asked the Commissioners in Lunacy whether the lunacy laws had been violated. No, they said. He then asked the Crown Law Officers whether anyone should be prosecuted on any other ground. They replied that there certainly had been an illegal abduction, but that prosecution was only advisable when the motives were improper; in this case they seemed not to be so. Still the Protestants were not satisfied. They were sure that the girl's superiors, anxious to keep her under lock and key, would never admit to her being cured. Her Majesty's Ambassador in Brussels reported that the girl really could not be allowed out, but the agitation continued until at last one of the medical commissioners in lunacy went over early in 1865 and reported after examining her himself, that hers was an acute case of melancholia with suicidal tendencies.[1]

It is probably not fortuitous that another and as it would seem grosser abduction case, that of Annabella Kohrsch, had been revealed and publicized at Ghent only four years previously. H. C. Lea's account of it seems reliable enough but for one thing, which makes me slightly suspicious: 'On 16 January 1860, Richard received a letter . . . which over an unintelligible signature informed him that his lost Annabella was in the convent of Eecloo under the name of Marie Toinez, where she could be recognized on Sunday during mass behind the screen in church.'[2] I am suspicious because of that screen. That screen is a regular stage property of a regular brand of anti-sacerdotalist fiction: the 'reluctant nun' brand. Typically, this was the story of a lovely innocent warm-hearted girl, lured by friends or relations who were either aristocrats or foreigners and who had the advantage of a Jesuit's aid, to

[1] *Parliamentary Papers* 1865 (*c*. 81), XLV, pp. 265–83.
[2] See his *Minor Historical Writings*, ed. A. C. Howland (Philadelphia, 1942), pp. 292–6.

forsake her home and/or her fiancé in favour of the life of the convent; which, after the first flush of zeal subsided, she came to dislike and fear—too late! The Protestant men, sensing her plight, would try to rescue her. She would be secretly removed to foreign parts where, however, she would be glimpsed through that screen, and a hue-and-cry raised after her. The end of the tale could see her either rescued and taken back to home and husband, or tortured to death in a Calabrian convent. The screen scene is nowhere better done than in *Sister Agnes; or The Captive Nun: A Picture of Conventual Life*, by a Clergyman's Widow, (Seeleys, 1854).[1] The new nun caught sight of Colonel Hayward just in time. 'Throwing up her arms, and dashing them against the bars, she screamed wildly, "Uncle, save me!" ' In vain she clung to the grating; in a moment she was drawn back, and the curtain fell. . . .

' "My niece!" exclaimed the Colonel, at once recognizing the voice, and, turning to a priest, he said, "I wish, Sir, to speak with that young lady": . . .

' "I am sorry, Sir, that gentlemen are not permitted to speak with the sisters."

' "What!" exclaimed the Colonel, "an Uncle not permitted to speak with his niece. I *demand*," he added, imperiously, striking the grating with his cane; "I *demand* to see my niece."
. . ."I am an Englishman," said the Colonel, folding his arms, and planting one foot forward. . . .'

But the guile of the abbess was too much for Colonel Hayward; he never saw Agnes again and she died of convulsions under torture, thirty pages later. Isabel and Rosa in R. McCrindell's, *The Convent: a narrative, founded on fact* (London, Aylott and Jones, 1848), were luckier. The church in which their vow was to be taken was on the island of Malta, and it so happened that a British Admiral had come to witness the goings-on, with some of his officers. When, therefore, Fr. Giacomo put the question—' "Daughters, is it by your own free will that you now devote yourselves to God?" ' the agitated novices boldly chorused "No!". . . and, throwing

---

[1] The scene is, moreover, illustrated opp. p. 336. The frontispiece is very fine. It shows the infatuated girl leaving home by 'faint moonlight'. Behind her, closing the french windows, stands the treacherous French governess; handing her out is 'Padre Carlo . . . disguised as an Italian, with a moustache and cloak'. He looks extraordinarily villainous.

themselves on their knees, Isabel exclaimed, "Englishmen, help us, deliver us from this cruel bondage"; then, rising up, emphatically begged the interference of the British government on their behalf.'

'It is impossible to describe the scene of tumult that followed.'

Every ingredient of popular fiction can be found in these anti-sacerdotalist novels: high life (and this kept quite close to reality: Disraeli's *Lothair*, 1870, followed the course of the most recent fashionable conversion—that of the third Marquess of Bute, in 1868) love, mystery, adventure, stolen fortunes, heroism, melodrama, villainy, horror, wicked foreigners—and sex in nasty forms as well as nice. *The Female Jesuit: or, the Spy in the Family* (London, Partridge and Oakey, 1851), a 'true' tale of domestic intrigues and deceptions, is prefaced by the far more incredible story (taken from the American W. Hogan's *Auricular Confession and Popish Nunneries*) of a handsome and accomplished girl, 'a lay sister belonging to the order of Jesuits in Stonyhurst, England', who was placed by them as governess, chambermaid, etc., in one after another of Philadelphia's leading homes, and then disguised as a 'waiter at Gadsby's Hotel in Washington City', where she eavesdropped on the Senators at lunch and sent her findings to 'the General of the Jesuit Order in Rome'. Not only secrets were stolen in these stories. Family fortunes were stolen too. The naïve youngster, wax in the hands of the Jesuits, would make over his or her fortune to the community. The depth to which this suspicion could go appears in several court cases and blue books.[1] Mr Alfred Smee, M.O. to the Bank of England, complained to the Home Secretary that his ailing young relation William Hutchison had been 'decoyed' from Trinity to Birmingham where he was 'introduced to a priest without any visible means of living, of the name of Faber', who took him to the Brompton Oratory ('architecturally constructed to facilitate the concealment of young men of wealth and position from their friends') and secured his fortune of £40,000 before the lad's death and burial in the Roman Catholic cemetery at Sydenham ('it is difficult to conceive anything more

---

[1] *Parliamentary Papers* 1864 (*c.* 134) L, pp. 351–60, on the Roman Catholic Burial Ground at Sydenham; 1870 (*c.* 383) VII, pp. 1–277, and 1871 (*c.* 315) VII, pp. 181–95, the Reports of the Select Committee on Conventual and Monastic Institutions.

dangerous to the public interest than the existence of an informal burial-ground attached to a monastic establishment. . . .')[1]

Burial grounds and other ingredients of mystery and horror were not new in the 'forties and 'fifties but it sounds as if they may have attained spectacular heights in *Geralda the Demon Nun*—a work the existence of which is attested by E. S. Turner.[2] Romantic ingredients were very common, and so were sado-masochistic ones. Far too close an interest was shown in what happened to naughty nuns—the penances imposed, the chains and constrictions fastened on, the whippings inflicted—for one to doubt that these aspects of the subject had an agreeable fascination for much of the protestant public; and to these same elements, no doubt, is due the evergreen longevity of that dreary classic of popular 'pornography', *The Awful Disclosures of Maria Monk*, which has been going strong under some such title since 1836.[3] This unwholesome interest in the torture of nuns was obviously related to the appetite for stories and pictures about the Inquisition, which had been the zealous Protestant's stock-in-trade since the reign of Elizabeth I.

Not sadistic but prurient at its lowest level was the Protestant's obsession with the Confessional; a key part of the sacerdotal system, and the aspect of Anglo-Catholicism on which attention was most closely focused. What went on in the Confessional?

This concern seems to have been at its most intense pitch during the 'sixties and 'seventies, but from at any rate the 'thirties it had been growing. The spiritual dangers of auricular confession were apparently not the only ones which a protestant had to watch out for; but what exactly were the others? From hints and allusions and Latin quotations the Protestant propagandists, becoming bolder with time, bit by bit removed the veil. Some priests, it seemed, were sure to use their powers of spiritual direction and psychological suggestion in order actually to seduce their penitents; all

---

[1] Smee turns up in all the *Parliamentary Papers* just mentioned. He seems to be less than wholly reliable. For a case on this same theme, see Allcard *v*. Skinner, 1887, 36 *Ch.D.* 145.

[2] *Boys Will be Boys* (London, 1957), p. 19. *Geralda* appeared in *The Calendar of Horrors*, edited by one of the leading writers of Lloyd's Salisbury Square school, Thomas Peckett Prest, the distinguished inventor of Sweeney Todd.

[3] *Maria Monk*, like so much of the anti-sacerdotalist literature published in Britain, was an import from the U.S., and Billington devotes many excellent pages to her. This literature travelled freely and quickly across the Atlantic. It looks as if each side gave as good as it got.

priests were bound to probe pruriently into their penitents'
sexual activities, putting dirty ideas into the minds of the
innocent virgin, and questioning the blushing matron about
matters which ought to be private between herself and her
husband. At last, in 1865, an organization calling itself The
Protestant Electoral Union, alarmed by the progress of the
Anglo-Catholicism revealed in the Wagner and Scobell cases,
overcame what it called its natural repugnance and dared to
bring the question plainly into the open! It added to its list
of publications (which included several by Mr Murphy, *The
Photograph of the Great Antichrist* and *Awful Disclosures of New
Hall Convent*) the celebrated best-selling pamphlet *The Confessional Unmasked*.[1] Here at last the truth was plainly wrung
out of the indecent obscurity of the priests' manuals by St
Alphonsus Liguori, Peter Dens, Cabassutius and others, and
printed in parallel columns. Every aspect of marriage, contraception and sexual technique was minutely and unmistakably
inquired into. To a modern eye, familiar with marriage
guidance handbooks and the Kinsey report, none of this is
(the sacerdotal element apart) particularly surprising. But
such matters were not to be canvassed openly in Podsnap's
England: not for long, anyway. Henry Scott, a Wolver-
hampton metal broker and member of the Protestant association which published the pamphlet, had his copy (copies?)
seized and destroyed by order of B. Hicklin and another,
magistrates. Scott appealed to Quarter Sessions. He said his
association existed to combat 'those teachings and practices
which are un-English, immoral, and blasphemous, [and] to
maintain the Protestantism of the Bible and the liberty of
England'. The Recorder allowed his appeal, on the ground
that his object was neither to make a profit nor to prejudice
good morals, but this judgment was reversed in Queen's
Bench by Cockburn, C.J., whose insistence that obscenity was
by some objective test obscenity, whether the author intended
it or not, remained the law until 1954.[2] The other copies of the

---

[1] *The Confessional Unmasked: showing the Depravity of the Roman Priesthood, the
Iniquity of the Confessional, and the Questions put in Confession.* Published by the
Protestant Electoral Union, 3 Craven Street, Strand, price 1s. The copy in the
Cambridge University Library is one (or perhaps I should say, claims to be one)
of the '50th thousand'. It also claims: 'A copy of this pamphlet . . . was sent to
each member of both Houses of Parliament in 1865.'

[2] *Regina v.* Hicklin, 1868, *L.R.* 3 *Q.B.* 360.

pamphlet remained confiscated, and an attempt two years later to dodge the effect of the Hicklin judgment by 'reproducing the offensive publication under the guise of a [law] report' was condemned by Bovill, C.J. in *Steel v. Brannan*.[1] These most prurient of protestant fires were well stirred again in the later 'seventies, when the anti-sacerdotalists got hold of *The Priest in Absolution*, a manual circulated among members of the Anglo-Catholic Society of the Holy Cross—of which, more in a moment; but nothing comparable to the contents of *The Confessional Unmasked* came to light. Seekers after sexual sensation had to make do with the assurance given them by *Reynolds' News*, that it was really worse than the birth-control book that was currently exciting them, Knowlton's *Fruits of Philosophy*.[2]

Punch, of course, made his usual great play with priestcraft: on this occasion, a particularly unshaven, heavy-jowled priest —Tenniel's stock bad Irishman, infused with a dash of Sicilian bandit—being ejected from a disgusted Britannia's house by John Bull, who grasps a heavy stick.[3] Nor was this house representative merely of the protestant nation at large. It was, especially, John Bull's own home, and in turning the priest off the premises John Bull was only doing what every good paterfamilias was expected to do; for the priest was seen to be a menace to the family. Here we reach the most emotive element of the syndrome: the danger felt by the protestant father and husband on account of his womenfolk.

No social fear is so strong as that felt by dominant males for an idealized womankind. We are most familiar with it as an element in inter-racial situations, where it is clearly responsible for some of the most aggravating and intractable of their aspects. Such racial antagonism is not clearly visible in the Victorian situation, although there are at least two hints of its presence: the priest was understood to embody a peculiarly Latin form of wickedness, and one cannot help recall Belloc's summary of the belief of the next generation of right-thinking

---

[1] 1872, *L.R.* 7 *C.P.* 261–72. Steele, a shopkeeper of 14 Tavistock Street, had been selling a report of the trial of another member of the Protestant Electoral Union, Mackey; Winchester Quarter Sessions, 18–19 October 1870.

[2] 24 June 1877.

[3] 30 June 1877. 'Whenever you see any of these sneaking scoundrels about, Ma'am,' says Bull to Britannia, 'just send for me. *I'll* deal with 'em, never fear.'

Britons, that 'the most degraded' of all European races, the Mediterranean, inclined to be 'saucy with the girls';[1] colleagues who know more about the nineteenth century than I do have given me fragments of evidence that the Irishman, whatever his other supposed attributes, was popularly regarded as formidably virile. Whether there is anything in this or not, the British father's concern for the sanctity of his home and the purity of his women is plain enough, and there are enough non-racial explanations to account adequately for his fear of the intrusive priest. The ideal woman was intellectually weak, pliable, submissive: eager—fatally too eager—to do what was right, and anxious to be instructed in it; easy prey, therefore, to the insinuating subtle charm of

> This wily, crafty Ritualist,
>   With cope and incense strong,
> This unctuous and bearded priest
>   With cope and vestments long . . .
>
> Your wives and daughters soon will learn
>   On him their hopes to rest,
> And every feeling overturn
>   Unless by him expressed.[2]

To the natural charms of his person, and the sartorial attractions of his uniform, might be added some unscrupulous use of his spiritual authority.

> His lips bent forward near her ear,
> 'Come, cast away your foolish fear;
> Confess the sins that on you press—
> Confess to me, sweet girl, confess!'
> Save heavier sighs, no answer came.
> The vicar's breath came quicklier then;
> 'Dear Alice!'—for he knew her name—
> Burst forth that villain among men—
> 'I quite forget my own distress
> In telling you I love you well;
> So well, that all the pains of Hell
> I'd bear for one long close caress

---

[1] 'The Three Races', first published in *Ladies and Gentlemen*, 1932.
[2] Cited (from what source is unstated) by E. Wingfield-Stratford, *The Victorian Tragedy*, (London, 1930), p. 178.

I claim you, who shall dare say nay,
Or tear you from my arms away?
Come darling, we are all alone;
One hour will all past pain atone;
Come, let no longer aught divide—
Come, darling, be the Church's bride![1]

Physical seduction could seem likely only to the excitable and the vulgar; the danger of corruption was, however, apparent to everyone. Archbishop Tait admitted it in the second parliamentary debate on *The Priest in Absolution.* 'I cannot,' he said, 'imagine that any right-minded man could wish to have such questions addressed to any member of his family; and if he had any reason to suppose that any member of his family had been exposed to such an examination, I am sure it would be the duty of any father of a family to remonstrate with the clergyman who had put the questions, and to warn him never to approach his house again.'[2]

But the priest brought other than moral dangers with him. Ultimately more disturbing was his rôle as a rival father. Through the back door of the home the priest was reintroducing that same division of allegiance which Henry VIII had formally expelled from the nation in the fifteen-thirties. Sacerdotalism was a menace to family life principally because it implied a Father who could say 'Obey *me!*' on some matters; and those the very highest. They might include matters political. The ultra-protestant conservative M.P. Charles Newdegate thought they certainly would. He seemed to fear female suffrage principally because it would open to the priests a promising road to the undoing of the Reformation.[3] Not many perhaps entertained so extreme a fear. Newdegate might have meditated on the fact that Roman Catholic M.P.s were against female suffrage too. But once again, one is kept from dismissing this prejudice as entirely the possession of a hysterical sect by solid evidence that it was held also, in an apparently not

[1] This comes from 'Jon Duan in the Aisles of Rome', one of the elaborate parodies in *Weldon's 1874 Christmas Book*, a pulp production which must, one imagines, have enjoyed a large sale. It is racy, irreverent (towards Queen as well as all other bearers of authority), ribald, and clever. Mr Arthur Sale kindly lent me his copy. Such works appear to be exceedingly rare now.

[2] 3 *Hansard*, CCXXXIV, 1745ff. 14 June 1877.

[3] See R. Fulford, *Votes for Women*, ch. 8. John Bright expressed the same fear.

much weaker form, by distinguished representatives of public opinion. Just as one can produce Tait to support the ribaldry of the pulp press, so the Marquess of Salisbury's familiar figure lends respectability to the presumed neuroses of Newdegate.

Auricular confession, Salisbury once said, could not be considered as merely a religious question. 'It so happens that this practice is deeply opposed to the peculiarities and idiosyncracies which have developed among the English people ever since they became a free people. The English people are specially jealous of putting power unrestricted into the hands of a single man. More than any other system, the practice of habitual confession does put unrestricted and irresponsible power in the hands of a single man. An Englishman values and cherishes the private independence of his family life; he looks with abhorrence upon any system that introduces another power into that family life, that introduces a third person between father and daughter, between husband and wife.'[1] Allegiance could not be divided. The proper English family could only flourish under paternal supremacy. Once relax that, and what discord followed! The Victorian novel which made the most of this theme was Mrs Lynn Linton's *Under Which Lord?*, in which the religious and family allegiances were inextricably intertwined. The family's troubles really began when the old low-and-slow vicar was replaced by the Hon. and Rev. Lancelot Lascelles, 'one of the most advanced of the ritualist party'. He was clever—devilishly clever. Again and again the author remarked on his complete self-control ('entirely master of himself and his methods') as one of the worst, the most unnatural things about him. The end of it all was wreck and wretchedness, with the daughter, a nun in Rome, refusing to talk to her widowed mother. 'Was it well done?'[2]

☆   ☆   ☆

[1] Cited by the Earl of Harrowby in the 'Priest in Absolution' debate, 14 June 1877. *Hansard, loc. cit.*, 1752–3.

[2] *Under Which Lord?* was published in 1879. The memory of it was presumably still green twenty years later, when the *Daily Chronicle* used the title as a heading for its account of the Kensitite row at St Cuthbert's Philbeach Gardens, 2 February 1899. Mrs Humphry Ward made an elaborate study of the conflict between human affection and papist rigidities in *Helbeck of Bannisdale* (1898).

K

To attribute some general importance to this antisacerdotalist syndrome is one thing; to prove specific effects is another. That task must be all the more difficult if I am right in sensing, first, that its main elements (the theological, the political, the moral, and the domestic-sexual) were normally called jointly into action when any one of them was roused; and, second, that the manner and power of their combined operation would not always—perhaps not often—appear on the surface of things. Some surface phenomena are obvious enough: 'Catholic Emancipation', Maynooth, 'Papal Aggression', the Murphy riots, and thereafter an intermittent trickle of more or less small beer which can still attain a disturbing degree of strength when Rangers play Celtic. Beneath and between these and other less familiar 'No Popery' incidents evidently lay a solid persistent substratum of anti-sacerdotalism.

How persistent and how uniform was this anti-sacerdotalism? Did it much matter everywhere, and all the time? Am I trying to palm off as something like a national characteristic what was, for *most* of the time, only an obsession of religious extremists?

I don't think it did matter equally all the time. I have the impression that it was at its most intense and ubiquitous from the middle 'thirties to the later 'seventies; that classical English and Scottish 'No Popery' took on a new fierceness and hysteria in the early 'thirties, and that by the end of the 'seventies the self-appointed leaders of protestant opinion were increasingly feeling an uncongenial isolation. Not that they made less noise. Far from it. The years from the 'eighties to the First World War were great years for the Church Association and all other bodies, Anglican or Nonconformist or mixed, devoted to the preservation of protestant truth; they witnessed the publication of such classics of the anti-sacerdotalist genre as Walter Walsh's *Secret History of the Oxford Movement* and the Hiberniocentric productions of Michael J. F. McCarthy.[1] Murphy-style riots still occurred.[2] The politics of the Irish

---

[1] Walsh's masterpiece came out in 1897. He wrote at least 11 other books of similar character. McCarthy's main anti-sacerdotalist books were *Church and State in England and Wales 1829–1906* (Dublin, 1906) and *The Nonconformist Treason* (Edinburgh, 1912).

[2] One of them, proceeding characteristically from Liverpool, achieved the celebrity of a minor constitutional cause célèbre: Wise *v.* Dunning, 1902, 1 *K.B.* 167–180.

question were still incarnadined with religious feeling. And yet one senses that the sound and fury was signifying less and less. Probably this slackening of force proceeded *pari passu* with the general decline of organized religion which was a feature of the times; and it may also have been weakened by those changes in the status of women and in the constitution of the home which were also happening.

As for what happened in the 'thirties, that can best be summarized as an unforeseen consequence of 'Catholic Emancipation', as the importation into the older kingdoms of the Union of virulent Irish (mainly Ulster?) strains of Protestantism. The Act of 1829, far from quietening or confining the Irish religious conflict, in fact assisted its extension. While the flood of Irish immigrants thickened through the 'thirties, Irish protestant orators began to stump England and Scotland in hitherto unprecedented numbers. The oneness of the protestant interest on both sides of the Irish Channel was emphasized as never before; now that 'Protestant Ascendancy' was no longer constitutionally guaranteed over there, it became necessary for keen Protestants—and politically profitable for keen Tories—to keep the fires of the true faith well stoked beneath a widening range of political public. It was, as one would have expected, through Evangelical channels that this new virus principally flowed. The pages of the *Christian Observer*, the most respectable of their Anglican organs, during 1830–3 show it happening quite clearly. The establishment of the more bigoted and obsessive *Record* in 1828 was another sign of the times. By the later 'twenties the benighted Irish peasantry were a standard popular field for protestant missionary endeavour, and it was, I think, under the auspices of such Evangelical societies as the London Hibernian and the British and Irish Ladies' that the itinerant Irish orator first got his hooks into the British fleshpots. His tone at first could be simply religious, but the constitutional upheavals of 1828–33 gave him new problems and opportunities. Cahill has shown that popular protestantism contained (whether more in some parts of the country than in others, his analysis does not show) powerful protestant, anti-Irish elements from the Reform Bill time onwards. Much of its gusto came from Anglo-Irish clergymen like D. M. Perceval, Mortimer O'Sullivan, R. J.

McGhee, and Hugh McNeile.[1]   They opened the door through which William Murphy was later to enter and to disturb so remarkably the Black Country and the cotton counties between 1866 and 1872.[2]

Students who get their social history of mid-Victorian England primarily from Matthew Arnold's *Culture and Anarchy* will miss the fact that his Mr Murphy was no isolated figure.   The anti-sacerdotalist was a stock type of public orator, agreeably blending edification with entertainment.   If he were an ex-papist, so much the better.   (If he were an ex-jesuit, best of all!)   Newman's bane, 'Fr Achilli', was perhaps the best known of this species, but there were many more.   Handley came across a lot in his intensive study of the Scottish scene: Greenock's 'Angel Gabriel', Camillo Mapei, Alessandro Gavazzi (who was active on the platform circuit on both sides of the Atlantic from 1851 to the later 'sixties, and whose tone at Birmingham was so gross that his respectable sponsors disowned him), Brother Alphonsus, the Rev. Patrick McMenemy (who ended up drunk in a Liverpool brothel), Pastor Chinniquy, *et al*.[3]   These men (and women?) were a kind of religious entertainers who did it for money but were often sponsored by protestant and denominational organizations who approved it as edification.   The Murphy story suggests that such entertainments were not uncommon wherever Irish men were to be found.   Were they so all over protestant Britain?

If the full significance of anti-sacerdotalism in the social history of the nineteenth century looks likely to remain unclear for many years yet, its place in the more 'public' parts of British history is not much better charted.   Murphy (not Matthew Arnold's friend, but the Liverpool historian) has convincingly attributed to it the responsibility for the collapse of the most

---

[1] In May 1840 McGhee presented to each of the Bodleian, Trinity College Dublin and Cambridge University Libraries, a handsome glass-fronted case of books, described on a brass plate as 'Documents on the Crimes of the Papal Apostasy'.   It may still be seen at Cambridge by anyone who asks for it in the Anderson Room.

[2] An admirable account of Murphy and his techniques is given by H. J. Hanham, *Elections and Party Management* (London, 1959), pp. 304–8.

[3] Handley, *op. cit.*, pp. 95–8, 102–4, 121.   Gavazzi's 'booking agent' was James Rattray, the Glasgow bookseller.   For information about his Birmingham appearance, I am indebted to the Rev. Dr D. E. H. Mole.   E. R. Norman, *The Catholic Church and Ireland* (London, 1965), p. 44, refers to 'the infamous apostate Catholic, Gavazzi' touring western Ireland and provoking a riot in Galway in April, 1859.

promising English experiment in elementary education in the whole century. Was that its only signal intervention in the educational sphere? Its place in church history is superficially unmistakable; but how far is its true depth and irritability properly appreciated by us students of the Oxford Movement and the running battle between Church and Chapel? It was not the early course of the Oxford Movement that provoked angry protestant reactions. The angry protestantism was there already, bursting out as each opportunity offered; Charles Pourtales Golightly did not for the first time realize the sinister menaces of romanism when he detected them in Newman and Pusey; and the fixation of so much protestant attention on these alleged 'romanizing' tendencies of the Tractarians was surely because of the moral and political dangers apprehended from them, at least as much as because of the theological and disciplinary issues around which the ostensible controversy generally raged. And if the latter had really been the whole of the matter, why should Dissenters have presumed to take such an interest in it? The unrelenting passions that underlay many Dissenters' hostility towards the established church need a great deal of explaining. Much of it no doubt came from social resentment and jealousy, but some surely sprang from a peculiar irritation at the fact that the Church of England, which had until the 'thirties been, with all its faults, a bulwark of international protestantism, was no longer sound in that respect. While it retained the proud and representative title of the *established* church, it stood in some sense for the nation; and while it retained so many crypto-papists, it seemed to insult Dissenters as well as to injure them.

Politically, the significance of anti-sacerdotalism must be sought in the contexts of the Tory party and the Irish question: contexts congenitally linked. Of courts and cabinets we know, for the time being, enough; it is the organizations and ideas of voters in the constituencies that remain too largely mysterious, and the nature of their contacts with local protestant clergymen and with national or local organizations with protestant titles, of which the simply named Protestant Association of the Peel period was only the first and best known.[1]

[1] Murphy was sponsored by the Protestant Evangelical Mission and Electoral Union: presumably the same body that published *The Confessional Unmasked*. Very active just after the 1870 Education Act was a body called the Protestant

What were the social and political rôles of the Orange Lodges of Victorian Britain? Were these protestant organizations in practice limbs of the Tory party? Is the large extent of English indifference to the Irish Famine partly explicable in terms of a protestant acquiescence in Divine Justice? Did a double-barrelled hostility to the Irish and to Popery anywhere else remain as big a part of popular toryism as it seems to have done in Liverpool?[1] Had the global imperialism of Salisbury's age some roots in the old Protestant Ascendancy? Should Dicey have considered anti-sacerdotalism as one of the 'cross-currents' in Victorian public opinion? These seem to me to be questions as well worth serious consideration as they are difficult to answer.

Alliance (see V. A. McClelland's article in *Victorian Studies*, vol. VIII (1964–5)). The riots, etc., at St George's in the East were said to have been managed by the National Protestant Society and the National Anti-Puseyite League (see *Parliamentary Papers* 1860 (*c*. 58), LIII, pp. 121–58). The Evangelical Alliance had exactly the same objects. How many such bodies were there, and what literature did they put out?

[1] See S. Salvidge, *Salvidge of Liverpool* (London, 1934), Barbara Whittingham-Jones, *The Pedigree of Liverpool Politics: White, Orange and Green*, (Liverpool, 1937) —for the loan of which rare pamphlet, as for much other help, I am grateful to my friend and colleague, Professor H. J. Hanham—and George Thayer, *The British Political Fringe* (London, 1965), ch. 12 'The Protestant Party'.

6

Mid-Century Scottish Nationalism:
Romantic and Radical

I

SCOTLAND in the eighteenth century suffered from a deeply-rooted sense of inferiority and subordination. When it came to the test, the Scottish nation had not been able to hold out against the English. Economically backward and politically demoralized, the Scots had been driven to accept the Union of 1707 as the best way out of their present difficulties. The immediate consequence—the Hanoverian accession—was too much for many Scots to swallow, and they rose in arms twice in a generation. But even those Scots who accepted the Union and the House of Hanover were nagged by the fear that they had sold their birthright to the English and had received little more than a mess of porridge in return. Hence the enthusiasm with which they greeted the attempts of the Edinburgh *literati* to demonstrate that the Scotland of Hume and Adam Smith was as culturally advanced as the France of Voltaire and Rousseau (and well ahead of England), that in Ossian Scotland had a poetry of greater antiquity than anything found in England, that the Scottish peasant was better-educated than his English counterpart, and that the gibes of the *North Briton* were prompted by jealousy rather than by Scottish uncouthness. Hence, too, the enthusiasm with which a later generation greeted the exploits of Scottish sailors, soldiers, merchants and proconsuls in India and other parts of the Empire, which served to underline the personal qualities

of the Scot and to distract attention from the political subordination of Scotland to England.   Consciously or not, the educated classes of Scotland were engaged in creating a new
Scotland, based on the cult of Scottish letters and of the
Scottish personality.   And by the end of the American War
of Independence their masterpiece—Augustan Edinburgh—
was complete.   Scotland at last had a national culture and a
national capital of which to be proud.   Indeed, as a cultural
centre the Edinburgh of Adam Smith, Dugald Stewart, Sir
Walter Scott, Robert Burns and the *Edinburgh Review*, set the
tone not merely for Scotland, but for England and for most
of Europe.

The eighteenth-century Scotland of David Hume and Adam
Smith had posed as one of the great centres of the European
enlightenment: rational, international in outlook, and superior
to local fads and superstitions.   The early nineteenth-century
Scotland of Scott and Burns presented an entirely different
image, romantic, firmly rooted in the Scottish past, and prone
to dwell on the peculiarities and oddities of the Scots.   For the
first time Englishmen and Europeans became aware that
Scotland was profoundly and romantically different from
England.   And by the time of Sir Walter Scott's death in
1832 the Scotland of Adam Smith had been displaced in the
consciousness of the world by the Scotland of the Scottish
minstrels, of Rob Roy, of Gothic castles, and of *The Heart of
Midlothian*.[1]   A new Scotland had been born and Scots,
rather to their surprise, found that they were living in it.

Scots were, indeed, for a time astonishingly willing to revel
in the new opportunities for dressing up and showing off,
afforded by the fashionable interest in the Highlands.   Edinburgh in 1822 was given over to a gigantic pageant staged by
Sir Walter Scott to welcome King George IV to his Scottish
capital, and the show turned out to be quite as remarkable as
the Eglinton tournament of 1839.   New Highland outfits
were designed by David Stewart of Garth for all who could
afford them, and lairds, citizens and soldiers, Highland and
Lowland, along with Sir Walter, the King, and Sir William
Curtis, Lord Mayor of London, all appeared in a Highland

[1] See on this John Henry Raleigh, 'What Scott meant to the Victorians',
Victorian Studies, vol. VII (1963), pp. 7–34.

dress deemed appropriate to their station.[1] *Rob Roy* was given
as a royal command performance, the final royal toast
was to 'the chieftains and clans of Scotland', and the King's
letter of thanks to Sir Walter especially commended 'the
Highland chiefs and their followers, who have given to the
varied scene which we have witnessed so peculiar and romantic
a character'. Of course, there were voices of protest at the
equation of the Highlands with the whole of Scotland, but the
events of 1822 and the 'tartan frenzy' which accompanied it,
confirmed the outside world in its view that Scotland was a
land of Highland romance. The cult of 'Balmorality' had
begun.

Of course, the romantic revival in Scotland was not all of
Sir Walter Scott's making. The revival of highland dress had
been going on since the expansion of the highland regiments
in the eighteenth century. Gothick architecture was so much
a part of Scottish life that even classical Edinburgh mixed
Grecian and Gothick styles on Calton Hill. Burns did his
best to keep alive the folk tradition of Wallace and Bruce.
And there was a good deal of romantic medievalism, expressing itself sometimes in literature and sometimes in
painting, which drew its inspiration from the same sources as
Scott's own work. As early as 1818 there was a proposal for
a national monument to Sir William Wallace, and there were
a variety of schemes for commemorating Scottish heroes, few
of which got beyond the first stages. This romanticism drew
on the works of Sir Walter Scott, but did not owe its existence
to him. Indeed, it owed its nourishment as much to English
writers and painters as to Scottish. Its culmination was that
greatest of all Gothick adventures, the Eglinton tournament,
at which the thirteenth Earl of Eglinton endeavoured to stage
a full-scale medieval tournament. There was nothing
peculiarly Scottish about the tournament. The participants
were mostly English and Irish; and so were the planners;
while the models for the tournament were English or continental, like the sources for *Ivanhoe*. The main Scottish

---

[1] There is a good account of the visit in J. G. Lockhart, *Narrative of the Life of Sir Walter Scott, Bart.* John Telfer Dunbar, *History of Highland Dress* (Edinburgh, 1962), gives the background to the sartorial experiments of the occasion. The 'Glengarry' bonnet dates from this visit. The fullest account is Robert Mudie, *A Historical Account of His Majesty's Visit to Scotland* (Edinburgh, 1822).

contribution was indirect—through the illustrations of the
Waverley novels, many of which bear a close family resemblance to Henry Nixon's well-known drawing of the Eglinton
tournament.[1]

After Scott's death the literary floodgates were opened and
romantic novels, poems and book-illustrations poured out by
the thousand. In Bulwer Lytton, Harrison Ainsworth and
their imitators one finds that degeneration of romanticism into
emotion for the sake of emotion to which Dr Kitson Clark has
drawn attention.[2] Indeed, one sometimes wonders whether
Bulwer Lytton was not parodying himself when he followed
The Last Days of Pompeii with *Rienzi, the Last of the Roman
Tribunes, The Last of the Barons,* and *Harold, the Last of the
Saxons.* None the less, Bulwer Lytton exercised a great deal
of influence, in spite of the hostility of reviewers. His works
sold widely, and he made a special appeal to those with a taste
for romantic national heroes. His *Rienzi* occupies an honoured
place in the literature of nineteenth-century nationalism alongside the myth-making popular biographies of William Tell,
George Washington, Kossuth, Mazzini and Garibaldi. And
he was particularly highly regarded in Scotland. He was
twice elected Lord Rector of Glasgow University (1856 and
1858) at the instance of Sir Archibald Alison, and he was
also a favourite among the students of Edinburgh.

The cult of the national hero was naturally strong in Scotland. We read in the reminiscences of Principal Donaldson
that in the 1840s 'When we gathered round the fireside in the
long wintry evenings to hear stories of adventure, the exploits
of Wallace and Bruce were sure to be rehearsed, and our
elders would tell us of the strange disguises and escapades of
James V.'[3] Similarly, Charles Rogers, the antiquarian,
recollected that as a child he 'wept at the fate of Wallace and
hated the race that slew him'.[4] The novels of the day were
full of stories of Mary Queen of Scots and of Bonny Prince
Charlie, of the Scottish soldiers of fortune, and of the wars

[1] Reproduced in Ian Anstruther, *The Knight and the Umbrella: an Account of the
Eglinton Tournament, 1839* (London, 1963), p. 198.
[2] 'The Romantic Element—1830 to 1850' in J. H. Plumb, ed., *Studies in Social
History: a Tribute to G. M. Trevelyan* (London, 1955), pp. 209–39.
[3] D. A. Millar, ed., *George Buchanan: a Memorial, 1506–1906* (St Andrews, 1907),
p. 463.
[4] Charles Rogers, *Leaves from my Autobiography* (Grampian Club, 1876), p. 44.

of the seventeenth century. But there was very little that was political in all this. Scots thought there was nothing odd about Queen Victoria at Balmoral cherishing a romantic affection for Jacobites and Highland clans, because the independent political life of the clans had been destroyed. Scottish nationalism consisted of an outpouring of emotions about the past rather than of political aspirations for the future. There were, it is true, a pair of Jacobite pretenders, John Sobieski Stolberg Stuart and Charles Edward Stuart, who styled themselves successively Count D'Albanie. But even their friends found it difficult to take them seriously. In a small country too many people remembered them under their former guise as the Allen or Hay Allan brothers. Their literary work— notably *The Tales of the Century* (1847), *The Costume of the Clans* (1845), *Vestiarium Scotium* (1842), and *Lays of the Deer Forest* (1848)—was regarded as a typical outcome of heated romantic imaginations. It amused those who read it, and was ridiculed by the reviewers.[1]

Because Sir Walter Scott and the romantic movement had resurrected the Scottish past, any movement for the redress of Scottish grievances tended to take on an antiquarian tinge. During the early 'fifties the most effective statements of the Scottish case for a better deal from England were the work of James Grant, one of Sir Walter's second cousins, who earned his living by writing romantic historical novels and historical sketches. The chief exponent of the Scottish cause in Edinburgh was W. E. Aytoun, professor of rhetoric, author of *Lays of the Scottish Cavaliers*, and romantic Jacobite. In Glasgow, William Burns, leader of all patriotic causes, immersed himself in the past in order to justify Scotland's claims to independent national status, and ultimately produced a two-volume account of *The Scottish War of Independence: its Antecedents and Effects* (Glasgow, 1874), which still has a certain interest. In Parliament the Scottish spokesman was that romantic Earl of Eglinton who had staged the Eglinton Tournament in 1839 and had subsequently taken up a political

---

[1] Notably in the *Quarterly Review*, for June 1847. Sir Walter Scott also attributed the Sobieski Stuarts' claims to 'warm imaginations' (*The Journal of Sir Walter Scott* (Edinburgh, 1950), p. 649). A new account of the Sobieski Stuarts would be welcome. There is some account of them in Dunbar, *History of Highland Dress*, pp. 103–43, and in Hugh Beveridge, *The Sobieski Stuarts. . .* (Inverness, 1909).

career which culminated in his appointment as Lord Lieutenant of Ireland in 1852. Indeed, at almost every gathering of
those devoted to the Scottish cause, there were sure to be men
with antiquarian interests like Professor George Skene of
Glasgow, the Reverend Charles Rogers of Stirling, and a host
of other antiquaries, whose names are associated with the
Scottish antiquarian publishing societies—the Roxburghe
Club, the Bannatyne Club, the Abbotsford Club, and their
imitators.

Scots were slow, however, to put their antiquarian
enthusiasms to practical use. Patriotic societies, which were
a feature of nationalist movements in other countries, got
off to a late start. The first of them were formed in London,
not in Scotland. The pioneer St Andrews Society of Glasgow goes back only to 1854, when it sprang naturally from the
patriotic interests of William Burns. Most Burns Clubs and
Caledonian Clubs in Scotland also date from about the
same period. So do the great Highland festivals. The
Braemar Gathering, founded in 1832, took on its modern
shape after Queen Victoria's visit in 1848. Games Day at
Aboyne was instituted in 1867, although it claims to be a
revival of a pre-1745 gathering. The clan societies were even
later. Most were not formed until the 1890s,[1] when the cult
of Scottishness had been a feature of Scottish life for generations. Scots abroad were naturally more ready to organize
themselves, and it seems likely that Scots at home picked up
much of the now well-established habit of holding convivial
social gatherings for the commemoration of Scottish heroes
from returning *émigré* Scots, as much as from the little bands
of Highlanders who met together in the West of Scotland or
the dining clubs of Edinburgh.

II

What must be styled the cult of Scottishness began to
acquire a basis of organization in the early 1850s. By then
Scots had begun to realize that Scottish romanticism by itself
was not enough. The old Scottish culture, enshrined by Scott,
was rapidly being swamped by urbanization. Many of the

---

[1] R. W. Munro, 'The Rise of Clan Societies', *Scottish Genealogist*, Nos. 2–3,
pp. 14–20.

new industrial towns were virtually indistinguishable from their English counterparts and were largely populated by immigrant Irish Catholics to whom the Scottish Presbyterian tradition was alien. If the Scotland of Wallace and Bruce and Scott and Burns was to survive it must be actively preserved. As a result there appeared all over Scotland little knots of men who set themselves the task of preserving the Scottish heritage from destruction alike by English power and industrial society.

Like Sir Walter Scott, the new generation of Scottish patriots thought well of the consequences of the Union. Industry and trade were flourishing—perhaps flourishing too much; the Scottish legal, educational and local government systems remained intact after the alarms and excursions of the reforming 'thirties; there was no hindrance to the employment of Scots in England or the Empire—rather the Scottish education system gave Scots an advantage; and in Parliament Scotland was represented by solid middle-of-the-road Scottish worthies whose ideas were well attuned to those of their countrymen. Even the one major source of conflict in Scotland itself—the disruption of the Scottish church—had not involved any serious attack on the Union. Both Church and Free Church leaders supported the union, and the Free Church *North British Review* was one of the leading advocates of the view that the Union had led Scotland from barbarism to the pinnacle of civilization; or to put the matter in rather a different way, Scotland, once 'the poorest country in Christendom' had become 'one of the richest countries in the world'.[1]

Free Churchmen, far from suffering from a sense of inferiority, felt that they were on top of the world, with God firmly behind them; ready to rule the Empire in partnership with the English and to carry Christianity to the far corners of the earth. For them the Union was, indeed, the very foundation of modern Scotland.

> Increased quiet, increased commerce and wealth, increased liberty, increased civilisation—these have been the consequences to Scotland of the once detested Union. That Scotland, if left to pursue her separate career, would still have made progress in these respects, need not be doubted;

[1] *Memoirs and Portraits of One Hundred Glasgow Men* ... (Glasgow, 1886), vol. I, p. xi.

but that the degree and the kind of the progress she *has* made are traceable to the fact of the Union, admits of historical proof. . . . since the Union, Scottish talent and Scottish energy have had a wider and richer field to expatiate in than they would otherwise have possessed. There can be no doubt that, in the general field of British activity, in all its departments, Scotchmen have, during the last century and a half, done a disproportionate share of the work, and earned a disproportionate share of the recompense.   There have been Scottish Prime Ministers of Britain; Scottish Chief Justices of England; Scottish Lord Chancellors; Scottish Generals of British armies, and Admirals of British fleets; Scottish Governors of India, and other colonial dependencies of Britain.   England is full of Scottish merchants and manufacturers.   London is full of Scottish literary men, and Scottish editors of newspapers.[1]

None the less, even in the Free Church there was a good deal of uneasiness about the relations between Scotland and England.   The English government was blamed for the disruption: the English church was suspected of Romanism because of the Oxford Movement; and the growing numbers of Scots who visited England as a result of the opening of the railways found much that distressed them.   Hugh Miller, the remarkably influential editor of the Free Church *Witness*, gave a very cool account of England when he returned from his first visit in 1845, even though he was an ardent admirer of English literature and believed the Scots incapable of producing writers of the calibre of Shakespeare and Milton.   He had little good to say of English religion (a Puseyite service reminded him of 'maggots developed into flies by artificial heat amid the chills of winter')[2] and he came to the conclusion that the Scots were as a whole superior to the English because whereas Scottish religion was 'a serious intellectual exercise' English religion had 'no tendency to exercise the thinking faculties'.[3] England for him was a friendly foreign country, whose habits and ways of thought were essentially un-Scottish, and he wanted his fellow-Scots to recognize that this was the case.

---

[1] *North British Review*, vol. XXI (1854), p. 82.
[2] Hugh Miller, *First Impressions of England and its People* (Edinburgh, 1857), p. 216.
[3] *Ibid.*, p. 339.

Miller, as a result, was confirmed in his predilection for the Scottish character, and gave every encouragement to those who wrote about the peculiar virtues and features of the national personality—an essential concern for any national movement. Soon Miller and *The Witness* became identified with the statement of national grievances against England, and Miller's assistant Patrick Edward Dove became one of the leading figures in the Scottish Rights Association.

For generations there had been a tendency to grumble about the consequences of the Union, even amongst its strongest supporters. Given a good cause, the press could whip up an agitation remarkably quickly, and enlist behind it a host of grumblers in all walks of life. The best-known of these agitations occurred in the mid-twenties when the Scots feared that their currency was endangered. Sir Walter Scott leapt to its defence and his *Thoughts on the Proposed Change of Currency: Three Letters to the Editor of the Edinburgh Weekly Journal from Malachi Malagrowther, Esqr.* (1826) became a model for subsequent controversies. By the middle of 1849 a great many Scots were ready for a new Malagrowther agitation, although they were by no means agreed as to the form it should take. A new generation had grown up since 1826, which was anxious to win its spurs in the traditional battle against English hegemony. The immediate occasion for the mobilization of Scottish opinion was the failure of the government to carry important Scottish legislation through the House of Commons during the 1849 parliamentary session. Two important measures, a Marriage and Registration Bill and a Public Health Bill, were abandoned by the government amidst intense Scottish indignation. English ministers, preoccupied with other matters, clearly thought that Scottish legislation could wait, just as they thought that Irish legislation could wait. They did not seem to realize that the disruption had caused in Scotland quite as much of a stir as the famine in Ireland, and that the Scots like the Irish were impatient for legislative changes. As a result movements for the redress of national grievances sprang up almost simultaneously in both Scotland and Ireland.[1]

---

[1] The Irish, of course, went further than the Scots, but there was a distinct parallel between events in Scotland and those in Ireland, which led to the formation of the so-called Irish Brigade, on which see J. H. Whyte, *The Independent Irish Party, 1850–9* (London, 1958).

In Scotland the statement of national grievances was at first largely a matter for the newspapers. The newspapers were full of complaints against English neglect, English domination, and English rudeness. In most papers English rudeness attracted most attention. At the time of the disruption, the English had made it plain that they despaired of ever understanding Scottish religion, or Scottish customs. While the Scots were preoccupied with the consequences of the disruption, the English were losing patience at the way the Scots allowed runaway English couples to marry at Gretna. Moreover, the opening of the railways made it possible for English tourists to make short excursions into Scotland, just as it made it possible for Hugh Miller to visit England. The first reaction of most of these English tourists, as of their predecessors over the previous two centuries, was to contrast the grandeur of the Highlands with what they considered the squalor of the Lowlands. When the Scottish press complained about English rudeness there was, therefore, a background of irritation which gave force to their complaints.

There was, moreover, a lurking fear lest the English were applying to Scotland the old imperial maxim, divide and rule. Like subject peoples all over the world, the Scots feared that in some ill-defined way they were being deliberately manipulated by their rulers. As *The Witness* was to put it in 1853:

> It has been the tendency of English misgovernment and aggression to render us a divided people. The encroachments which ought to have led us to band together, have had an entirely opposite effect. Every great aggression has acted like a wedge, and broken up into fragmentary parties, necessarily weak from their state of division, a people which, had they held together as a united whole, might have succeeded in getting the wrong redressed.[1]

At the practical level the most common Scottish complaint was that English ministers would not set aside parliamentary time for dealing with Scottish business and that when they did, they made the Scottish M.P.s sit up all night because English business was always taken before Scottish. The Scottish press also complained about the way English M.P.s voted down

---

[1] *The Witness*, 5 November 1853.

Scottish proposals, and the off-hand manner in which English
ministers received Scottish delegations. They were shocked when
Englishmen described the Scottish marriage laws as barbarous
and an encouragement to immorality, and demanded that they
should be assimilated to those of England.[1]   And they resented
the English habit of referring to the Scottish lowlands as dirty
and drunken. Indeed, some years later William Burns
attributed the national movement which arose in 1850 to the

> . . . revival of the old scurrilous spirit towards Scotland
> that prevailed in the South more than a century ago. . . .
> Scotland—her institutions, her manners, and customs—
> were railed at in every imaginable shape and form, until
> the Thistle could stand it no longer. . . . [and there was]
> a powerful reaction among Scotsmen in favour of the
> preservation of old memories and feelings, and against a
> spirit that, at one time, seemed to prevail in the direction
> of anglicizing our whole system of social life.[2]

In all this there is a clear parallel with events in Wales as
well as in Ireland. The Welsh, too, were accused by the
English of being dirty and immoral, and reacted in much the
same way. When the predominantly anglican education
commissioners of 1846 demanded the rapid anglicization of
Wales, Welsh nonconformity was shocked and dismayed. The
English were not as contemptuous about Scottish culture as
they were about Welsh (the 1846 Commission had remarked
that 'there is no Welsh literature worthy of the name'), but the
Scottish reaction was perhaps even stronger, for the Scots had
to hand in the Free Church a reforming movement of major
dimensions. Free Churchmen were already engaged in the
business of putting the affairs of Scotland to rights, and they
felt no compunction about taking a few swipes at the English
now and then.

The first clear statement of the Scottish national case was
made by a Free Church minister, the brilliant, flamboyant

---

[1] Even in 1862 Scots were extremely angry when a speaker at a meeting in
London of the Society for the Amendment of the Law said 'I attribute a great
deal of the immorality in Scotland, at which I was so horrified, when I was in
Glasgow, to irregular marriages and the law by which they are sanctioned.'
North British Daily Mail, 1 February 1862.

[2] From a speech by Burns to the Glasgow St Andrews' Society in 1858, preserved
in the Mitchell Library, Glasgow, B. 115063/4.

L

and erratic James Begg, in January 1850. Begg is best known to history as the leading Free Church champion of national education and social reform. But he also had a wider objective. For him one of the consequences of the disruption was that Scots could think for the first time of launching a national movement for rejuvenating Scottish life and for giving Scottish culture a new foundation. He called for nothing less than a national revival to remedy a host of Scottish ills:

> We are sinking in our national position every year, and simply living on the credit of the past. . . . A people that might match the world for energy, and who have heretofore stood in the first rank of nations, sinking under a combination of increasing evils—the efforts of ministers paralysed—our universities locked up, dwarfed, and comparatively inefficient—crime increasing—drunkenness and Sabbath-breaking making progress—Christianity languishing—pauperism threatening to swallow up the whole property of the country—hundreds of our best people flying from our shores under the pressure of want, or at the command of tyranny—the great natural resources of our whole country locked up in the iron embrace of feudal despotism—little intelligence amongst the people to understand this, far less to battle with it—the very passes of our mountains interdicted—the fishings of our rivers monopolized—our public grounds and gardens shut up—the Parliament of England despising us, our natural guardians joining in the oppression.[1]

These ills Dr Begg attributed as much to English as to Scottish influences. For a generation he was to argue that the Scots were not capable of dealing with the education question and other social problems because of ecclesiastical divisions; that these divisions were 'mainly caused by a deliberate violation of the Treaty of Union on the part of England';[2] and that this violation was part of a wider scheme to subordinate Scotland to Whitehall. Hence the Scots must strive to assert themselves if they were to preserve the main feature of the Union: 'That Scotland must be regarded not as a conquered province of

---

[1] James Begg, *National Education for Scotland practically considered* . . . (Edinburgh, 1850), pp. 35–6.

[2] James Begg, *A Violation of the Treaty of Union the Main Origin of our Ecclesiastical Divisions and other Evils* (Edinburgh, 1871), p. 4.

England, but a distinct independent kingdom, which has united with England on equal terms, and under a clear and solemn treaty.'[1]

Following the logic of this argument, Dr Begg was prepared to go further. In a speech to a United Presbyterian Church in Edinburgh on 10 January 1850, he boldly stated the case for a measure of Scottish home rule

> . . . the state of Scotland would never be very materially improved until some better plan was fallen upon by which to govern it. At this moment Scotland was treated not merely as a petty province, but just as if it were an additional county of England. . . . Scotland had only fifty-three members in the House of Commons; and her affairs were taken up there always after twelve o'clock at night as a general rule, they were taken up when most of the members had gone away to bed, as if matters relating to Scotland were not worthy of a moment's serious consideration. . . .
>
> Scotland must take up her own questions, and bring her own intellect to bear on them. He thought that at the very least they ought to get that justice in Scotland which was dealt out to every colony of the British empire. When he was travelling in those petty dependencies of the British empire—Nova Scotia and New Brunswick—he found that they had their own Parliament and their own Government. . . .
>
> They had . . . reached times which required very wise and careful statesmanship; and if no attention were to be paid to their affairs,—if a Secretary of State were not appointed for Scotland, with a Council of Scotchmen,—if some effectual plan were not fallen upon, he was not sure but they must endeavour to get such a change in the existing system as would secure them some legislative body in their own country to dispose of purely Scottish questions.[2]

It is significant that James Begg's speech was delivered in a United Presbyterian Church, for members of that dissenting church were even more ready than Radical Free Churchmen to accept Begg's main lines of argument. The U.P. Church,

[1] *Ibid.*, p. 3.
[2] Thomas Smith, *Memoirs of James Begg, D.D.* (Edinburgh, 1888), vol. II, pp. 148–50, reprinted from *The Witness*, 12 January 1850.

formed in 1847 by the amalgamation of the United Secession and Relief Churches, was strong in personalities, in theologians and in Radical politicians, and was in no way tied to the traditional Scottish polity in Church and state. Essentially the U.P.s were dissenters in matters of church and state, with many of the characteristics of the more rigorous English non-conformists. Like the English nonconformists the Scots dissenters had a political wing, represented by the Scottish Central Board for Vindicating the Rights of Dissenters (1834), whose first Chairman was Duncan McLaren and whose secretary was James Peddie. The U.P.s went into politics on a nonconformist platform ('viewing with alarm the recent encroachments on their civil rights'),[1] and naturally established close links with their English nonconformist counterparts. But their leading characteristic was their championing of specifically Scottish grievances. Hence the U.P.s, along with a small group of Free Churchmen headed by James Begg, were usually to be found backing any Radical Scottish movement, and it is no surprise to find Duncan McLaren, Lord Provost of Edinburgh, 1851–4, M.P. for Edinburgh 1865–81, the friend and brother-in-law of John Bright, as one of the leading lights of the National Association for the Vindication of Scottish Rights founded in 1853. The title was clearly borrowed from the earlier dissenting organization, and the objects of the two bodies were in many ways very similar.

The Radical nationalism of James Begg and the Scottish dissenters closely resembled the Radical nationalism of the Welsh nonconformists. Sir Reginald Coupland was therefore wrong when he commented that 'It was not a Scottish *bràd* that roused the nationalists of 1853. They were agitated only by a dry and practical question—the machinery of government.'[2] He was also wrong in a much wider sense, in that he failed to recognize that in Scotland the national movement inaugurated in 1850, had an astonishingly high romantic content.

The romantics joined in the campaign for the redress of Scottish grievances early in 1852, prompted no doubt by the

[1] J. B. Mackie, *The Life and Work of Duncan McLaren* (Edinburgh, 1888), vol. I, p. 175.
[2] Sir Reginald Coupland, *Welsh and Scottish Nationalism: a study* (London, 1954), p. 281.

hope that they might find in the statement of national grievances a popular basis for Scottish Toryism. The opening
salvo was fired by James Grant, already a successful historical
novelist, in a series of letters and articles published in two very
old-fashioned papers, the *Edinburgh Advertiser* and the *Caledonian
Mercury*. His theme was 'Justice to Scotland', and the growth
of what he styled 'Centralization'.[1] He began by going back
over all the major Scottish grievances since the Union, emphasizing that what mattered was not so much the violation
of the terms of the Union, but the violation of its 'essential
spirit' and the neglect of Scottish interests. England had
eight dockyards and six arsenals: Scotland had none what-
soever; nor were government vessels ordered from shipyards
north of the Tweed. Retrenchment in government offices
had hit Scotland hard without giving any advantage in return;
rather it had threatened Edinburgh's position as a seat of
government. Scottish talent was being drawn off to London
in every sphere of life. Above all there was neglect:

> A shamefully partial system of government, which lavishes
> all on the sister kingdom, and nothing, absolutely nothing,
> on Scotland; a cold neglect of our most vital interests, and
> a steady, crushing, iron-handed system of absorption and
> Scottish retrenchment, which, in open defiance of our
> ancient laws and hereditary rights, of chartered liberties,
> and old immunities, abolishes every officer of state, and
> all which our ancestors secured to us by their energy and
> valour; and which was also further secured to us by the
> Articles of Union.

The worst feature of this system of government was the under-
representation of Scotland in the House of Commons, but to
remedy this alone would not be enough. What was needed was:

 I. A complete reorganization of our present system of
  representation in Scotland
 II. A Secretary of State and a local Privy Council, for the
  greater despatch of public business
 III. The restoration of the Board of Excise, the Exchequer,
  and other Courts which have been so scandalously
  abolished.

---

[1] Grant's articles were preserved by his brother John and are now in the National
Library of Scotland along with many other articles by James and John Grant
and a collection of Nationalist pamphlets. N.E.20. f. 13–14.

Essentially this was an old programme, echoing the disputes of the early years of the century. But it was also, it should be noted, very much the same programme as James Begg had put forward two years before.

Once in his stride James Grant hit at another evil of the day —absentee landlords and capitalists who drew away the wealth of Scotland to London:

> In search of health or amusement, the idle and dissipated man of pleasure comes casually among us, to shoot or to travel; but in London he spends the rents of his Scottish estates—that hard-won rent which our able farmers and moral peasantry, by frugality and parsimony, scrape together with toil and care; but from their poor pockets it all goes south, to the aggrandizement of England.

so too:

> vast numbers of respectable and well-educated young men pining for lack of employment, are forced to emigrate to become private soldiers in India, while their unmarried sisters (as Belhaven prophesied of old) must resort to the most humble means for subsistence—to labour with their hands, or become poor dependents, teachers and governesses amongst that very English people, into whose pockets and Exchequer *nine millions* of our Scottish money are annually poured.

In all this the voice of the impoverished and dispossessed Highland laird[1] speaks as loudly as that of the novelist and political economist, and Grant ends his appeal by drawing attention specifically to the fate of the Highlanders 'driven from their humble houses and beautiful glens' by 'the acrimony and villainy of Lowland factors, the tyranny and intrigues of English proprietors and holiday Celtic chiefs' who 'more sure and deadly than the butcheries of Cumberland . . . have destroyed the clans for ever.'

During the remainder of the campaign that preceded the general election of 1852 James Grant and his brother John turned to more pressing themes, and it was not until late

---

[1] Grant's father was head of the Grants of Corrimony in Glen Urquhart, which had been sold in 1830.

in 1852 that they figured again as 'nationalists'. Then they took up a typical theme of the gothic revival already suggested at the head of James Grant's letter on centralization quoted above by an extract from an unidentified work of Louis Reybaud: ' "Our heraldic thistle," said the old gentleman, "is no longer fit for anything but food for asses." ' The object was now to bring to bear on the national question the extraordinary contemporary interest in heraldry and genealogy. James Grant had always had an interest in heraldry; John Grant was an accomplished heraldic connoisseur; and both would have liked to turn professional. James Grant, indeed, tried unsuccessfully to become Lord Lyon King of Arms in 1866 (he was supported incongruously by the London *Morning Post*) and John Grant late in life served successively as Carrick Pursuivant and Marchmont Herald.[1] Their uncle Stewart Watson, an historical painter, encouraged them in their interests and late in 1852 the two Grants, Stewart Watson, James MacNab, a solicitor, and Hugh Miller's assistant Patrick Dove, hit the headlines with an appeal to the Lord Lyon to suppress the irregularly quartered royal arms which appeared on various flags, the curious exercise in heraldry which figured on the new florin coins, and also to deal with certain other examples of heraldic irregularity.

The English press was dumbfounded. *The Scotsman* and the *Edinburgh Courant* denounced the agitation as puerile. The comic papers had a field day (one paper inquired why the Welsh rabbit did not feature in the arms of Great Britain). And Lyon Depute hastily ruled that he had no jurisdiction in cases of public as distinct from private arms. Whereupon the five protesters got up a public petition to the Queen, which was circulated all over Scotland, notably to town councils and other public bodies, placarded on hoardings, and advertised in the newspapers. On paper at least the protesters had a good case. The new florins (first minted in 1849) were badly designed, with the arms of England, Scotland, Wales and Ireland set out on shields on the spokes of a wheel, and it was

---

[1] In everyday life, James Grant was first a regular soldier, in the 62nd regiment, then an architect, and finally a full-time novelist and writer, and John Grant was an accountant. John Grant's son, Sir Francis Grant, actually became Lord Lyon King of Arms (1929-45). James Grant got into the *Dictionary of National Biography*; John did not.

by no means clear whether the Scottish arms should have been on the right of those of England, where the Mint had placed them, or somewhere else. The royal standard flown at Edinburgh Castle and on other Scottish official buildings did undoubtedly have the Scottish lion in the wrong place (the second quarter instead of the first). And the Union flag used in Scotland was undoubtedly the English version rather than the Scottish version used on Scottish seals. The weak point of the petitioners' case lay in their attempt to treat on all fours with these major heraldic issues, the absence of the traditional crown from the head of the Scottish Unicorn on the arms printed on a number of official documents. None the less, the petition caused an extraordinary stir in Scotland, and was no doubt responsible for the care with which government departments subsequently handled Scottish heraldic matters, and ultimately, perhaps, for the minting of the current 'Scottish' shillings.

The heraldic petition demonstrated how easy it was to mobilize support in the local authorities for the statement of a national grievance. Petitions to the Queen (duly presented to the Home Secretary by that most heraldic nobleman Lord Eglinton[1]) were sent in by the Convention of Royal Burghs, the town councils of all the chief towns—Edinburgh, Glasgow, Aberdeen, Dundee, Inverness, Perth, Ayr, Falkirk and Kirkcaldy—and a goodly number of smaller towns. The Grant brothers, realizing that they had stumbled on a splendid propaganda device, determined to use it as the basis for a new national movement. This was duly announced in an unsigned article on 'The Scottish Movement' by John Grant in the *Morning Post*:

> Insignificant as at first sight this question of precedence may appear, the principle which the present [heraldic] movement is intended to show forth is pregnant with most important consequences to Scotland, and we are led to understand it is the precursor of a general movement

---

[1] Nothing came of the petitions. The Home Office passed them to Lyon Depute, who sat on them until he thought the storm had died down, when he again said that the matter was nothing to do with him, quoting a variety of documents in support. The dispute dragged on in the press for years, partly no doubt because the Home Office at first sent the Brechin petition to the English College of Heralds by mistake.

for obtaining a greater share of the attention of Government to the interests of Scotland than has hitherto been accorded, and also the re-institution of certain offices of state, and other officials, which the better government and increasing importance of Scotland render it absolutely necessary she should possess.[1]

In due course Grant's 'general movement' took shape as the National Association for the Vindication of Scottish Rights with James Grant as one of its two joint secretaries.

The heraldic agitation had put the Grant brothers in touch with like-minded men all over Scotland. Among them was William Burns, already widely known for a series of letters in the newspapers on Scottish grievances, published over the name 'A North Briton'. William Burns (1809–76) was in many ways a characteristic figure in the Victorian romantic movement. By profession a solicitor, he was one of the best-known businessmen in Glasgow. He himself acted for over twenty years as adviser to the West of Scotland mine owners and ironmasters, he was one of the leading Liberals in the west of Scotland, and the firm of which he was ultimately the head had one of the biggest legal practices in Glasgow, particularly in parliamentary business. His friendly temperament was commented on by many contemporaries, and at the end of his life, when his firm practically ran itself, he was described as 'a pleasant, portly, man, with a happy-looking Scottish face—through which shines the general disposition within', and 'a general favourite'.[2] How, one wonders, can this be the same William Burns whose devotion to the Scottish national cause was a passion, and whose letters to the press tend to be not merely forceful, but sometimes shrill and cantankerous? How can this be the same man whom the Reverend Charles Rogers describes[3] as a vindictive monster? Admittedly Rogers suffered from persecution mania, but his denunciations cannot be dismissed out of hand: Burns was clearly a difficult man to deal with. Why? The answer appears to be that Burns had

---

[1] Newspaper clipping in National Library of Scotland, N.E. 20. f. 13.

[2] *The Bailie*, 14 January 1874. Most of the Glasgow papers carried obituary notices when he died. See, for instance, *Glasgow Herald*, 3 August 1876.

[3] Rogers' *The Serpent's Track: a Narrative of Twenty-Two Years Persecution* (London, 1880), and *Leaves from my Autobiography* (London, 1876), both consist largely of attacks on Burns.

assigned to himself the unexpected rôle of advocate for Scotland. He was prepared to fight for Scotland as he fought for his firm's clients, and nobody was to be allowed to get in his way.   The principal on the other side was of course England, with the English newspapers as her advocates, and it was Burns' policy not merely to answer every attack by these advocates against his client, Scotland, but to hit back at the character of the other side.   This is why Burns was always in danger of being accused, as Rogers accused him, of fomenting racial disharmony between England and Scotland, of hating England, and of developing a theory of Scottish racial superiority.

Burns became involved in the national question as one of the leading members of the Society of Procurators in Glasgow. The Procurators were much exercised by the need for reform of the Scottish law and the Scottish courts, but found it hard to proceed because English ministers were prone to argue that the easy way out of their difficulties was by assimilating the law of Scotland to that of England.   The threat of English aggression against the Scottish law put Burns on his mettle, and he began looking round for other signs of English attack. These he found in the language commonly used with reference to Scotland.   Statesmen from Lord Palmerston downwards, and historians—even Sir Archibald Alison, Sheriff of Lanark- shire—were found to be using the word 'England' when they meant 'Great Britain' and 'English' when they meant 'British'. Burns resolved to cure them of the habit.   In a series of pamphlets published over a long period of years[1] and in a stream of letters he badgered and cajoled the offenders, until his name became a joke among those who did not understand his purpose.   But in time Burns' very persistence was rewarded: the use of 'England' for 'Britain' or even 'Scotland' quickly died out in Scotland itself, and gradually decayed in England too.   Burns also deserves credit for his war against the use of 'Scotch' for 'Scottish', against which he seems first to have protested in the *North British Daily Mail* in 1858, asking 'by what literary authority, the modern, and, as I opine, vulgar, form of expression, "Scotch", as applied to the people of

---

[1] The best are *Scottish Rights and Honour Vindicated by A North Briton* (Glasgow, 1854); *What's in a name?* (Glasgow, 1861); *'England' versus 'Great Britain'* (Glasgow, 1865); and *Address by William Burns to the Glasgow St Andrew's Society* (Glasgow, 1869).

Scotland, was introduced and sanctioned among men of letters'.[1] The *North British Daily Mail* promptly started to use 'Scotsmen' and 'Scottish' instead of 'Scotchmen' and 'Scotch', and the *Glasgow Herald* followed suit, condemning 'Scotch' as 'a horrid vulgarism, and as barbarous as vulgar, being sometimes used as a substantive, and sometimes as an adjective. . . . No correct writer ever uses it.'

The Grant brothers and William Burns could not hope to start a national movement alone. They needed links with a much wider circle and set out to find them. Lord Eglinton, who had presented the heraldic petition, was an obvious figurehead for the movement, and readily agreed to become its president, but he had little real influence in political circles either in England or in Scotland. Patrick Dove who had signed the heraldic petition during a chance visit to the Grants, became their go-between with Hugh Miller and the Free Churchmen, although not with any great success. Hugh Miller joined, but most of the Free Church clergy preferred to devote their energies to the National Education Association and other specifically religious campaigns. McLaren, Lord Provost of Edinburgh, and his U.P. friends, along with Charles Cowan, M.P. for Edinburgh, came in of their own accord, because they were already fighting for Scottish reforms. The chief recruit was William Edmonstoune Aytoun, advocate, man of letters, and professor of rhetoric in the University of Edinburgh. Aytoun was tireless in the cause in its early stages, and whipped up the support of a number of north of Scotland local authorities.[2] Probably it was he who also brought in the Edinburgh medical world (in the persons of the presidents of the Royal Colleges of Physicians and Surgeons, the Queen's Physician and Surgeon, and other medical men) which was smarting at the English refusal to recognize Scottish medical degrees. The Grants themselves were apparently responsible for recruiting a number of Edinburgh notables, like Charles Halkett Inglis, laird of Cramond, and David Buchanan, editor of the *Caledonian Mercury*. Burns contributed a few

---

[1] This is one of the many letters and other newspaper clippings preserved by Burns, and now in the Mitchell Library, Glasgow, B.115063/4. Where no other source is given for Burns' writings it is this collection.

[2] Theodore Martin, *Memoir of William Edmonstoune Aytoun* (Edinburgh, 1867), pp. 139–42.

businessmen, who were afterwards useful as organisers, but remained in the background.

The National Association for the Vindication of Scottish Rights was launched in May 1853 in an *Address to the People of Scotland*, which was advertised in the press at the beginning of July along with a long list of sponsors. A revised edition published in November subsequently included the names of a considerable number of additional sponsors, including the Marquis of Ailsa, the Earls of Errol, Caithness, Buchan, and Dundonald, Lords Gray, Colville, Elibank, Berriedale, and Cochrane, Sir Thomas Gladstone, Sir Archibald Alison, James Baird of Gartsherrie, M.P., the Rev. Dr James Begg, and a considerable number of businessmen, medical men, accountants and lawyers. Apart from McLaren and Cowan no prominent Liberal politicians joined, but there were many Whigs and Radicals on a list ultimately said to include 3,000 names.

The *Address* was a composite effort. It began with a short statement of aims by Patrick Dove, but the bulk of the document consisted of a 'Statement of Certain Scottish Grievances' put together by James and John Grant under 31 headings.[1] The topics covered varied greatly in importance and may be summarized under eight heads.

(1) *Revenue*. The Scottish Revenue was largely spent in England, although Scottish institutions badly needed help. Scottish hospitals and other public charities, the Scottish Society of Antiquaries, and the arts and sciences generally received no help comparable with that given to the London and Dublin hospitals, the British Museum and the National Gallery. There was no Scottish geological museum, no Scottish military academy, no Scottish equivalent of the English and Irish institutions for the education of the children of soldiers and sailors, or for the maintenance of decayed soldiers and sailors, and no adequate system of parliamentary grants to the Scottish universities. In defence expenditure Scotland suffered particularly badly because there were no royal dockyards or arsenals, and relatively few military establishments. The Scottish police did not receive the subsidies to which they were entitled. There were no harbours

---

[1] John Grant's annotated copy is in the National Library of Scotland, NE. 20. f. 14 (1).

of refuge, although many had been built farther south and the Scottish coasts were exceptionally dangerous. Even in the case of the royal revenues, there was an abuse, since the revenues of the Scottish woods and forests were used for the upkeep of the English palaces instead of for preventing Holyroodhouse from decaying.

(2) *Centralization.* A large number of Scottish offices had been abolished and nothing had been put in their place: these included the Boards of Customs and Excise, the Scottish Mint (abolished in violation of Article 16 of the Union), the Scottish Household and a large number of honorary offices. Other cases of centralization had recently come to notice: the separate revenue returns for Scotland were abolished in 1851; the Stamp Office had been centralized in London so that documents had now to be forwarded to London for stamping; the post office establishments in London and Glasgow were being run down; the Commissioners for Northern Lights were to hand over their functions to Trinity House; even the Ordnance Survey (published in England) neglected Scotland.

(3) *Heraldic.* 'The Heraldic emblems of Scotland . . . have been degraded.'

(4) *Income Tax.* Scots landlords paid income tax on the gross rent of their properties, English landlords only upon the net income.

(5) *Parliamentary Representation.* Scotland was under-represented in both the House of Commons and the House of Lords. In addition the Scottish universities lacked M.P.s although the English and Irish universities had them.

(6) *Legislation.* The Scottish burghs lacked the power to provide free libraries, museums, baths and washhouses. The Scottish patent laws were unsatisfactory.

(7) *Ministerial.* Scotland needed its own Secretary of State to promote Scottish business.

(8) *Medical.* Scottish medical degrees were not recognized in England, yet on Scottish medical degrees a tax of £10 was levied, whereas English medical degrees were exempt. The Public Health arrangements for Scotland were quite inadequate.

The tone of the *Address* was deliberately set rather low, to avoid scaring anyone. Indeed, Dove inserted a long passage

to prove that the Scottish Rights Association was to be nothing
like the Irish Repeal movement and rather overdid the appeal
to Unionist sympathy.

> Self government and self administration are not . . .
> incompatible with union. The more union the better,
> provided it be based on true principles, and the rights of
> all parties be respected. Union obviates war, encourages
> commerce, permits of free transit, abolishes national
> antipathy. Union—provided it be union and not domina-
> tion—brings equals together for common benefit, enlarges
> human sympathies, throws down the barriers to brother-
> hood, stimulates to honourable competition, and teaches
> each nation that it is only one phase or development of
> social humanity, by exhibiting the virtues and peculiarities
> of another possessing peculiar merits of its own.[1]

What was asked for was simply the recognition that the union
'was a legislative Union, but not an Administrative Union'.[2]
Scotland must be allowed her own institutions and 'a national
existence . . . quite distinct from that of the Southern portion
of the Island . . .'.[3] As if to underline the point *The Witness*
remarked that there was not a single sane Scotsman, in the
Association or outside it, 'who entertained . . . the question of
repeal'.[4] What *The Witness* wanted was not a Scottish
parliament, but the machinery for providing and encouraging
specifically Scottish measures like the Forbes Mackenzie Act
of August 1853, which closed Scottish public houses on Sunday
because the Scots who went abroad on a Sunday made a
disgraceful exhibition of themselves.

The reason for the Grants' caution was speedily demonstrated. *The Times* denounced the new movement with quite
unexpected venom, and *The Scotsman* attacked 'The Imbecile
Address' as the work of a 'few unknowns constituting themselves an aggrieved and indignant nation',[5] and suggested

---

[1] *Address to the People of Scotland and Statement of Grievances by the National Association
for the Vindication of Scottish Rights* (Edinburgh, 1853), p. 3.
[2] *Ibid.*, p. 6.
[3] *Ibid.*, p. 7.
[4] *The Witness*, 16 July 1853.
[5] *The Scotsman*, 6 July 1853. The Scots Whigs were equally hostile. Lord
Cockburn admitted that there were genuine grievances, but thought the Association was worthless as a means of redressing them: *Journal of Henry Cockburn . . .
1831–1854* (Edinburgh, 1874), vol. II, pp. 291–6.

that it was merely the prelude to a demand for repeal of the union. The rest of the press, apart from the papers already committed to the cause, anxiously waited to see whether the combination of *The Times* and *The Scotsman* would kill the movement stone dead. For a time there was a real danger that this might happen, but in September an anonymous article by Aytoun in *Blackwood's* tipped the scale.[1] Aytoun gave his support to all the main points in the *Address*, and argued that the combination of grievances was such that something was seriously wrong:

> We must look to the system in order to ascertain why Scotland should have been exposed so long to so much injustice; and, believing as we do, that there was no deliberate intention to slight her interests, we are driven to the conclusion that the fault has arisen from the utterly inadequate provision made by the State for the administration of her internal affairs.[2]

Aytoun's solution of the problem was simply the appointment of a Secretary of State for Scotland, a proposal which fell a good way below James Begg's demands, and did little to meet the grievances of William Burns against the English press. For the moment, however, it sufficed. The Conservative papers fell into line behind *Blackwood's* and were followed by most of the rest of the press after the first public meeting of the Association at the beginning of November.[3]

The November meeting, described by *The Witness* as 'one of the greatest and most enthusiastic ever held in Edinburgh',[4] was intended to bring together representatives of every section of Scottish opinion. Hugh Miller, indeed, spoke in *The Witness* of the need to create a 'Scottish party' which would replace the older parties in Scotland.

> In truth, the present period is, from a curious combination of circumstances, a more favourable one for the formation

---

[1] 'Scotland since the Union', *Blackwood's Edinburgh Magazine*, vol. LXXIV (September, 1853), pp. 263–83.

[2] *Ibid.*, p. 281.

[3] R. M. W. Cowan, *The Newspaper in Scotland: a Study of its First Expansion, 1815–1860* (Glasgow, 1946), p. 326, reports that of thirty papers examined twenty supported the movement in November (although four of these dropped out later), five were neutral and five were hostile.

[4] *The Witness*, 5 November 1853.

of a Scottish party, than any other in the history of our
country . . .   The coalition Ministry of the present time
is significantly indicative of that decay of the old political
parties which has been going on so steadily during the last
fifteen years . . .   Whiggism and Toryism are alike
passing to extinction; and the only other *ism* that has any
general claim to be set in their place, is . . . worthy, old,
time-honoured Patriot*ism*.[1]

Parties, however, need some homogeneity, and this the
Edinburgh meeting and its subsequent Glasgow counterpart,
notably failed to achieve.   The dominant tone was set by the
old-fashioned Tories—the picturesque Lord Eglinton, Sir
Archibald Alison, the Tory historian, W. E. Aytoun, the
Jacobite literateur, and Alexander Baillie Cochrane (afterwards Lord Lamington), one of Disraeli's 'Young England'
associates, who claimed descent from Sir William Wallace.
That fierce Radical Duncan McLaren seemed singularly out
of place as a leading speaker, and so did Patrick Dove.   Sir
Henry Wellwood Moncreiff, one of the leading Free Church
ministers, said so in so many words.   In a letter to McLaren
(which in passing told Dove to stop pretending to be a sort of
Cromwell) Moncreiff argued that although he agreed with all
the main points made in the *Address*, he could not see how any
Reformer could join in a movement which included Alison,
Eglinton and Aytoun on the one hand, and William Burns
('whose future is an attempted restoration of the past') on the
other.[2]   These men were irrevocably opposed to all that
Radicals stood for—progress, parliamentary reform, free trade,
the abolition of the laws of primogeniture and entail, the
separation of church and state, unsectarian education, temperance, and peace—and supported a system of 'Functionaryism'
on French lines, which was sure to result in the destruction of
freedom.

Hugh Miller, although he recognized that the November
meeting was

a most strange specimen of heterogeneous coalition.   The
Voluntary and the Establishment-man stand side by

---

[1] *The Witness*, 16 July 1853.

[2] [Sir H. W. Moncreiff Bt.], *Scottish Rights and Grievances: Reasons for Declining to
join the National Association for the Vindication of Scottish Rights*, by a Scotchman
(Edinburgh, 1854).

side,—the Whig and the Conservative,—the Presbyterian and the Episcopalian,—nay, even the Jacobite and the Free Churchman.[1]

was none the less inclined to argue that this might still be a source of strength. He felt that what was wanted was simply a band of honest Scots ready to defend their country. A member of the Scottish Rights Association should, he felt, be as free 'to entertain his wonted views and opinions, as if he were called to defend his country, not from legislative aggression on the part of our neighbours, but from foreign invasion on the part of some Continental power'. But this last was an ominous remark. Already the Turks and Russians were at war; on 12 March 1854 Britain and France became allies of Turkey; and a fortnight later Englishmen and Scotsmen alike found themselves at war with Russia.

The 'heterogeneous coalition' held together surprisingly well at first, although it never again attracted the attention it secured in November and December 1853. The *Glasgow Herald* said firmly that 'Any man calling himself a Scotchman should enrol in the National Association.'[2] Lord Eglinton presented the great array of petitions that came in from the local authorities and staged a debate in the House of Lords on 6 April.[3] There were occasional meetings outside Edinburgh and Glasgow. There was a steady flow of pamphlets.[4] There was a certain amount of free publicity in the press, notably a long article in the *North British Review*.[5] And William Burns got up a Glasgow Young Men's Association for the Vindication of Scottish Rights. But by 4 October 1854 when Lord Eglinton's services were commemorated in Glasgow at a great banquet, with the Duke of Montrose in the

[1] *The Witness*, 5 November 1853.

[2] *Glasgow Herald*, 4 November 1853.

[3] *3 Hansard* CXXXII, 496–522. Bulwer Lytton agreed to present petitions to the Commons (*The Witness*, 18 February 1854) but was not active in the movement. Lytton was Honorary President of the Associated Societies of the University of Edinburgh, in which office he was installed in January 1854.

[4] The Association itself published six anonymous (and free) Tracts, five of them by William Burns. Other pamphlets included Alexander Baillie Cochrane, *Justice to Scotland* (Edinburgh, 1854); 'A Citizen of Edinburgh', *A Vindication of Scottish Rights* (Edinburgh, 1854); Hugh Scott of Gala, *The Progress of the Scottish National Movement* (Edinburgh, 1854); and Robert Christie, *Injustice to Scotland Exposed* (Edinburgh, 1854).

[5] *North British Review*, vol. XXI (February–August 1854), pp. 69–100.

M

chair, the Scottish Rights Association was on its last legs.   A pamphlet by John Steill which demanded the repeal of the Union,[1] William Burns's persistence in attacking politicians for equating 'England' with 'Britain', the Grant brothers' continued heraldic campaigns, and the tendency for speakers to make extreme statements at country meetings, had already alarmed both Eglinton and Aytoun.   Duncan McLaren had other campaigns to fight.   And even *The Witness* had become preoccupied with the education question and the spread of Popery, so that it gave much more attention to the meetings of the National Education Association and to the great protest movements against 'the endowment of Romish chaplains' than to the Scottish cause.   As a last flutter John Grant in January 1855 composed a petition to the House of Commons, but by early 1856 even the Grant brothers had given up.   To all intents and purposes the Scottish Rights Association was dead, killed by a mixture of pre-occupation with the war, the growing willingness of government to listen to Scottish complaints, and the instability inherent in any organization with a heterogeneous membership.

Frustrated in the attempt to achieve their main objective— the creation of a permanent Scottish national movement—the original promoters of the Scottish Rights Association turned to other activities.   In Edinburgh they made little progress, but in Glasgow they had a base for operations in the St Andrew's Society formed by William Burns in 1854.[2]   Burns set out 'by degrees to give the Society such a character as would . . . lead to the general establishment of similar societies at home, and the affiliation of these with kindred associations among Scotsmen abroad, and especially in the British colonies'. But he also made use of the name of the Scottish Rights Association.   In October 1858, four of the 'leading spirits of the Scottish Rights Association', Councillor David Dreghorn, William Burns, George Wink, and Patrick Dove, now editor of the *Commonwealth* published under Burns' auspices, issued an appeal to Scots of all parties to join together to press for

---

[1] *Scotland and her Union with England* (Edinburgh, 1854).
[2] Burns also got up a celebration for the Robert Burns centenary and may well have been responsible for the strongly nationalist tone of some of the placards used at Glasgow University during rectorial elections right down to 1862.   These included whole passages from the publications of the Scottish Rights Association.

increased Scottish representation in parliament. 'It has been demonstrated, again and again, that whether population, revenue, or intelligence be taken as the basis of representation, Scotland has not had her proper share. . . .' Burns suggested that the best way to get this increased representation was to make use of the 'still existing' Scottish Rights Association, which had been put into cold storage during 'the Russian war' and 'the Great Indian war'. But the political temperature in Glasgow was low (even a meeting addressed by Kossuth in November was poorly attended), no politician joined the promoters, and the attempt to revive the association had to be abandoned. Subsequently, in 1864, when he got up a 'Protestation contre l'attribution du nom d'Angleterre donné au Royaume—Uni de la Grande Bretagne' directed to the people of France[1] which was signed by 3,565 people, Burns did not bother to use the name of the Association. By then he was sure that his ideas would be carried on by his successors. Indeed, William Burns' favourite theme continued to be aired after his death, and the Scottish Home Rule Association, in the 'eighties, included among its lists of grievances: 'Depriving Scotland of the fame derived from the deeds and genius of her own people by encouraging the practice of calling the United Kingdom England.'[2] But the meeting in October 1858 was to all intents and purposes the end of the resurrected Scottish Rights Association.

III

The decay of the Scottish Rights Association did not leave Scottish nationalists without a cause. In its place came the movement for erecting a National Wallace Monument, which was ultimately to lead to the erection of an enormous stone tower on Abbey Craig just outside Stirling. When Sir Walter Scott's influence was at its peak there had been a good deal of talk of national monuments—a Wallace monument was discussed in 1818 and the National Monument on Calton Hill was started in 1822—but on the whole contemporary taste preferred monuments to the recently dead. It was another twenty years before monuments to national heroes came into

---

[1] National Library of Scotland, N.E. 20. f. 13.
[2] *Home Rule for Scotland*, National Library of Scotland, 3.2820* (12).

favour, perhaps as a result of the erection of the Scott monument in Edinburgh in 1844. At first the public taste ran to memorials for heroes of the Protestant religion—one of the earliest being the Knox monument erected at Edinburgh in 1846, which occupied a position in Scotland rather similar to that of the Oxford Martyrs' Memorial (1841) in England. But it soon turned to popular historical figures and to statuary of all sorts. The most remarkable instance occurred at Stirling where, under the auspices of the Reverend Charles Rogers, a remarkable series of statues was erected in a rush.[1] Rogers soon found that a number of young Scottish sculptors were making historical statues as a speculation, and on two occasions he was offered enormous ready-made statues of Wallace.

The proposal to erect a national Wallace monument was first put forward in March 1856 in the columns of the Glasgow *Daily Bulletin*. The suggestion came from a number of quarters, but the real originators of the subsequent campaign were John Steill of Edinburgh, William Burns of Glasgow, and Charles Rogers of Stirling. Steill was a wayward figure, chiefly notable in Scotland as an isolated champion of Young Ireland and an advocate of the repeal of the Union of 1707.[2] Burns we have already encountered. Rogers, the Stirling monumentalist, and Burn's most vociferous opponent, was chaplain to the Stirling castle garrison, an antiquarian of some note, and ultimately founder of the Royal Historical Society. The attitude of the three differed in emphasis. Steill was steeped in the romantic nationalism of Ireland. For him England was the old enemy.

> England took care not to let the people of Scotland have amongst them the sacred ashes of Wallace to kneel over; for when she could not subdue, she got the patriot by treachery into her hands, and hewed his body to pieces.[3]

To honour Wallace was to honour the greatest of the Scots

---

[1] James Guthrie, executed in 1661, was commemorated in 1857; then Ebenezer Erskine, John Knox, Andrew Melville, Alexander Henderson, James Renwick (the last of the Scottish Martyrs), Margaret Wilson (another martyr) and Sir William Wallace were all commemorated in rapid succession. Rogers, *Leaves*, pp. 105-10.

[2] He published in 1846 *A Word in Vindication of Young Ireland*, a letter reprinted from the *Scottish Herald*, and in 1848 the satirical *Scotland for the Scotch: or Reasons for Irish Repeal*, a letter reprinted from the *Glasgow Reformers' Gazette*.

[3] *Daily Bulletin*, 9 April 1856.

patriots who stood out against the English. He called on the Scottish people to put aside 'the chief idols of their worship, in the monumental way', men of 'English birth and English ideas', and to honour Wallace in the same way as Switzerland had honoured William Tell, the Tyrol had honoured Hofer, and America had honoured Washington. William Burns, although in many ways anti-English, was more interested in using the Wallace monument as the focus of a national movement, than in honouring Wallace. He argued that Wallace was the 'greatest name' in Scottish history, but he did not much care where the Wallace monument was or what it looked like. Not for him Steill's plea for a monument which might 'be the last object that the emigrant may set his eyes on when he leaves Scotia's shore, and the first that he welcomes when it is his lot again to return to his native land'. By contrast Rogers, who secured the site of the monument on Abbey Craig, was interested in Wallace almost entirely for antiquarian reasons, and shared none of the broader enthusiasms of his colleagues, with whom he soon quarrelled. He was primarily concerned to promote an historical revival and his own interests (his income came to depend on his connection with the monument).

The Wallace Monument project became a national concern when a giant meeting was held at Stirling on 24 June 1856 to celebrate the opening of the fund-raising campaign. Few notables were present, but the chief speaker and chairman was the Earl of Elgin, and one report has it that 20,000 people visited Stirling for the occasion. Subsequently a long list of peers, M.P.s, and other distinguished people agreed to serve on the committee, with the Duke of Montrose and Lord Elgin as Presidents, Sir John Maxwell of Pollok and Sir Archibald Alison as Vice-Presidents, and Charles Baillie (later Lord Jerviswoode) as Convener. The Scottish press generally was sympathetic, although doubts were expressed whether the necessary funds could be raised. And, as before, *The Witness* offered its support, and indeed gave the best summary of the promoters' case.

> Either Scotland has no history at all, or that history finds its centre in Wallace. Either it is not desirable that the nation should understand its history at all, or it is desirable

that it should understand the historical place and significance of Wallace. Either Scotland contributes nothing distinctive to the philosophy of history, offers nothing remarkable to the student of man or of nation, or her contribution is all summed up in the name and in the work of Wallace.[1]

Once again, there was an immediate onslaught on the promoters by the English press, headed by *The Times*, which maintained that 'the Wallace himself . . . is the merest myth'. *The Times*, indeed, excelled itself on this occasion, and launched a full-scale attack on the whole pattern of Scottish life, under the heading 'Scotland . . . in Want of a Grievance.'

There is a widespread feeling that Scotland has not within the present generation quite upheld her own past reputation. Edinburgh, indeed, continues to affect literary airs, and a coterie of writers live together on terms of mutual admiration. Numbers of young Scotchmen, as of yore, come south, and reap the reward of energy and ability, but on the whole, Scotland has lost way. She remains motionless, relying on past achievements, boasting of great men that are dead and gone, repeating maxims which were discoveries once, but are mere platitudes now, and showing few signs of intellectual or moral vigour. Past generations gave the country good primary schools, and the present has added nothing. The Universities are inferior, the schools for the middle and higher classes are inferior, professional education and professional spirit are not what they are in England. The clergy are comparatively an unlettered class of men. Hardly a single idea on political or social subjects comes in the present day from Scotland. Literature is merely a faint and worthless imitation of old models. Poems in the style of Burns, which can be written by any human being who can write at all, are actually still produced in incredible quantities. The old metaphysics, the old divinity, are quite worn out with the discussions of cliques, who cannot get beyond them. Scotchmen, in fact, seem to do nothing but masquerade in the garments of their grandfathers.

Now, it seems to us that this general poverty of thought is the cause why Scotch Lords and professors and men of letters are continually harping on their nationality and

[1] *The Witness*, 13 March 1858.

their historical renown. When there really was a national mind the world heard nothing about the Abbey Craig, the Royal arms, and the rights of the Scottish heralds. Now, by their exclusiveness, and what we will make bold to call their provincialism, the Scotch have not only kept out English influences which might have done them good, but they have driven the best of their own countrymen to England. There can be no doubt that we get nearly all the talents that the northern kingdom produces, and the cause is not difficult to ascertain. It is not merely because Parliament sits in London that England draws away the best brains from the other two kingdoms, but because Englishmen have thrown away those confined notions of nationality which still prevail in Scotland and Ireland. We south of the Tweed have risen to the conception of a United Kingdom; nay, more, of a British Empire, and every subject of the Queen finds here a career in which he may advance without fear of jealousy or prejudice. But in Edinburgh the cry, or at least the feeling still is, Scotland for the Scotch. Yet the more Scotland has striven to be a nation, the more she has sunk to be a province.[1]

The attack by *The Times* of course made it a matter of national pride that the monument should be finished. Once again, as in 1853, Scotland was confronted with an all-out attack on Scottish values, and must defend herself. This time, however, there was less Scottish reaction. The Crimean War was about to be followed by the Indian Mutiny and there was not much incentive to fratricide. Indeed it was hard to raise money and the raising of funds was to drag on for over a decade before the monument was eventually completed in 1869.[2] And James Begg was almost certainly not alone when in a speech in connection with the Radical and strongly nationalist Forty Shilling Freehold movement, of which he and Duncan McLaren were leaders, he called upon the people of Scotland to remember that even in 1856 there was still need for political action as well as for monuments to past heroes.

[1] *The Times*, 4 December 1856.
[2] Details are to be found in William Burns's newspaper clippings in the Mitchell Library, in Rogers' *Leaves*, and in the many editions of the guide to the monument. The 220 foot tower includes a 'Hall of Heroes' stuffed with busts of Scottish heroes. There are also busts of William Burns and Charles Rogers. The massive statue of Wallace was added in 1887.

Build your monument to Wallace by all means; let it be raised as high as Ben Lomond if you have the means; but still, if from its top on Ben Lomond you can look far and wide over an enslaved country, over a prostrate and politically dead people, blush for shame, that with a monument to the fame of a great patriot, your country is in such a state of vassalage six hundred years after he died as a martyr for her liberty. And let no man ever lay a stone on that noble cairn who is not prepared to assist us in following out this movement, by which to make our country free.[1]

During the long campaign for the Wallace monument public attention slowly shifted to more practical ways of preserving the Scottish national heritage. The Scottishness of Scottish education, under fire from England, attracted a new school of defenders, whose latest representative is Dr George Davie, author of that significantly titled work *The Democratic Intellect*.[2] For contemporaries, Professor John Stuart Blackie, eccentric and celtophile, defender of the Scottish pronunciation of Greek, and denouncer of the Scottish section of H. T. Buckle's *History of Civilization in England*, became the central figure in newspaper controversies. Like Professor James Lorimer and the Association for the Extension of the Scottish Universities, Blackie was attacked in the English press in the same way as the promoters of the Wallace Monument had been attacked.[3] As a result he became one of the symbols of the Scottish protest against anglicization, a rôle in which he revelled, adopting a curious rustic form of dress and indulging in highland fantasies. Scottish education also found defenders of many different types in the various Presbyterian denominations. None of them was as avowedly patriotic or radical as James Begg, who wanted a purely Scottish system governed entirely by popularly elected

[1] Smith, *Memoirs of James Begg*, vol. II, p. 233. There is a different version in Begg's *Scotland's Demand for Electoral Justice* . . . . (Edinburgh, 1857), p. 33.

[2] G. E. Davie, *The Democratic Intellect: Scotland and her Universities in the Nineteenth Century* (2nd edn., Edinburgh, 1964). This remarkable book is both a work of scholarship and an attempt to keep alive a peculiarly Scottish approach to Scottish education. Inevitably Dr Davie is a myth-maker as well as an expounder of an once almost-forgotten tradition.

[3] The most important attack was in the *Saturday Review*, 6 July 1861, vol. XII, pp. 12–13, with Blackie's response in the *Glasgow Citizen*, 11 January 1862. It is significant that on 8 December 1864, the *Stirling Observer*, anxious for the future of the Wallace monument, tried to dissociate it from 'the wild talk of such men as Professor Blackie and Mr Burns.'

authorities free of all control from England.[1] But there were
plenty of patriotic speeches. Scottish nationalism in the
'sixties was as alive as it had been in the 'fifties, but it had
largely turned into educational channels. It was not again
to turn to politics until the 'eighties, when the campaign for a
Scottish minister was at last successfully concluded (the first
Secretary for Scotland was appointed in 1885), and a Scottish
Home Rule Association came into being with Professor Blackie
as Chairman of its General Committee. Then once again,
Liberal and Conservative, Unionist and repealer, joined
together to present a common front against England, taking this
time as their starting point a demand for Scottish Home Rule
on the lines suggested by James Begg in 1850.

IV

European national movements in the nineteenth century
took many different forms. Most of them—those in Ireland,
Poland, Hungary, Bohemia and the Balkans—involved a
subject nation striving for independence from an occupying
power. But there were others. In Norway, the union with
Sweden had not destroyed the national political system, and
the national movement was both a political and cultural one.
When the Norwegians were ready, they simply announced
their independence from Sweden. In Switzerland there was
a federation of national groups, each of which strove to keep
alive its distinctive characteristics, so that Swiss nationalism
was the nationalism of a number of cantonal pressure groups.
In Wales and in Brittany a small nation incorporated in a big
one had perforce to fight not for independence but for the
national language, and the national culture—chiefly a matter
of religion. In Scotland, the main function of the national
movement was to remind the nation that Scotland was a
cultural and political entity, and to fight against the more
blatant forms of assimilation with England. There was no
direct challenge to the Union with England—merely a
reminder that prosperity is not everything.

The mid-nineteenth-century Scottish national movement
none the less laid the foundations on which a Hungarian or
Bohemian-style national movement could have been built.

[1] Smith, *Memoir of James Begg*, vol. II, p. 473.

William Burns was following the example of the Hungarian and Polish patriots he admired, when he directed his attentions to the War of Independence and heroic struggle of Wallace and Bruce against the English. At the time, this theme appealed rather to the imagination of those with a taste for romantic fiction than to scholars or statesmen. But the theme was kept alive, and today a great many Scots learn at school that the Declaration of Arbroath was as important as Magna Carta—something that even William Burns was not disposed to claim. Burns also won his battle against the words 'English' and 'Scotch' as applied to Scotland—although there is today some sign that the tide is beginning to turn the other way.

More important, Scottish propagandists succeeded in establishing in the Scottish consciousness the myth of what Dr George Davie calls the 'democratic intellect'. Here, the writings of Hugh Miller were more influential than those of the academics whom Dr Davie commemorates. Hugh Miller, the stone-mason turned geologist and writer, personified the humble Scot who makes good, and even today his birthplace at Cromarty is preserved by the National Trust for Scotland as a national shrine. His preoccupation with the Scottish national character and the national mission—his presbyterian high seriousness—became part of the Scottish tradition. His underlying theme that the Scot is fundamentally different from the Englishman, reinforced the national predilection for the 'Here's to us wha's like us' of the little Scotlanders of the villages, painted so vividly in George Douglas Brown's *The House with the Green Shutters*. The campaign for a distinctively Scottish system of education, whether sponsored by Dr Begg or James Lorimer or John Stuart Blackie, was no more than an extension of Hugh Miller's cult of the Scottish personality.

The weakness of mid-nineteenth-century nationalism was that it failed to produce a nationalist literature. James Grant was a good historical novelist, and his *The Scottish Cavalier* was much admired by Thomas Hardy;[1] his best heroes were Jacobites and his themes were generally Scottish; but his works were essentially adventure stories making their greatest appeal to schoolboys. Mrs Oliphant, who also wrote Scottish

[1] S. M. Ellis, *Mainly Victorian* (London, 1924), pp. 108–12.

novels and contributed regularly to *Blackwood's*, was out of sympathy with the Grants and their friends. W. E. Aytoun was best as a writer of short stories and verses and lacked the temperament for a national myth-maker. Only John Stuart Blackie had the required combination of personal flamboyance and high earnestness which could have made him the creator of a national literature. But he preferred to devote himself to the Celtic revival rather than to the lowlands. Scotland had a culture of her own, but until the 1920s lacked a school of writers burning with the desire to commemorate Scottishness for its own sake above the level of the 'Kailyard' school.

Without a nationalist literature to fortify them, it was hard for the Scottish people to go the whole way with the nationalists. Scots could never quite make up their minds whether or not John Stuart Mill was right when he commented that 'free constitutions are next to impossible in a country made up of different nationalities' and that 'the boundaries of governments should coincide in the main with those of nationalities'. They were quite willing to apply the doctrine to the continent of Europe, but they drew the line at applying it to relations between Scotland and England. As always they wanted the advantages of the Union without its disadvantages.

7

The Uses of Philology in Victorian England

WHEN Alton Locke, 'tailor and poet', was considering what kind of education could raise his social station and provide a career more profitable than poetry, he had, according to his mentor the Dean of D——, two courses open to him. 'Philology is one. But before you could arrive at those depths in it which connect with ethnology, history, and geography, you would require a lifetime of study. There remains yet another. I see you stealing glances at those natural curiosities.'[1] The alternatives, in fact, are natural history and 'philology', the former being, according to Kingsley's cleric, both the superior discipline and, since it required less prior knowledge, the softer option.

Crudely, the distinction is between science and arts, and no one familiar with the mid-nineteenth-century intellectual scene will be surprised that it is natural history, rather than physics or chemistry, which is recommended, or even that it is preferred to the humanities. After all, at a time when the application of German critical 'philology' to the Bible probably still outranked geology or the theory of evolution as the chief cause of religious doubt, science was not necessarily even the more spiritually dangerous, and in any case the Dean of D—— was a fairly broadminded clergyman.

What he means by 'philology', however, may require some interpretation for the twentieth-century reader, and may not

---

[1] Charles Kingsley, *Alton Locke, Tailor and Poet* (1850), ch. xv.

have been altogether unambiguous even to the book's first readers. In its primary sense, in the first half of the nineteenth century it still tended to mean the general study of classical literature—scholarship *tout court*. It derives, no doubt, from the wide sense of *logos*, but it is also aptly symptomatic of the heavily linguistic emphasis of classical scholarship, especially in England, the country of Bentley and Porson, and also of the fact that comparative linguistics had barely, as yet, emerged in England as a scholarly discipline to contest with classics the title of philology.[1]

By the mid-century, however, the meaning of philology, and hence, in a sense, men's notions of the humanities in general, and of the place in them of the study of language, was changing rapidly, and Kingsley and his fictitious cleric were, as one would expect, aware of it: hence the reference to ethnology, history, and geography. Essentially, this essay is an attempt to gloss those words, and to trace, rather sketchily, the changes in attitude to scholarship and language which underlie them. This may seem a pedantic exercise; a better criticism would be that it is too ambitious, for it touches on some of the central intellectual preoccupations of mid-nineteenth-century Englishmen: ethnology, philosophy, the philosophy of history, comparative religion and mythology, and the study of classical antiquity.

Chronologically, it is the last which forms the point of departure. It requires some effort fully to appreciate the classical domination of the educated world in the early nineteenth century, a world in which bishops could grow heated over the digamma and Francis Horner felt out of place in the highest Whig circles because the modernity of his Edinburgh education had left him deficient in Greek.[2] Ecclesiastical preferment could be the reward of a well edited text of a classical poet and two Prime Ministers, Derby and Gladstone, spent part of their leisure working on Homer. In such a world

---

[1] The ethnologist J. C. Prichard, noting the ambiguity to which the development of comparative philology (Linguistics) gave rise, suggested 'glottology' as an alternative name. J. C. Prichard, 'On the various methods of Research which contribute to the Advancement of Ethnology', *Report of the British Association* (1848), p. 239. The German philologist, August Schleicher (1821–68) called linguistics 'Glottik'. O. Jespersen, *Language, its Nature, Development and Origin* (London, 1922), p. 71.

[2] M. L. Clarke, *Greek Studies in England, 1700–1830* (Cambridge, 1945), p. 7.

it implied a significant shift in intellectual inclination when Thucydides and Plato began to supplant Horace in esteem and when ancient history and even philosophy began to appear, though tentatively, in the curricula of some of the leading Public Schools.[1] The change—in so far as there was one— from an educational ideal based on the correct reproduction of metrical forms, the study of classical authors as stylistic models, and, at the highest level of scholarship, the skilful editing of texts, to one which emphasized the study of the ancient world as a complete and distinct civilization, derived, like so much else in nineteenth-century intellectual history, largely from Germany. It involved an attempt to supplement classical philology in the narrower sense by *Altertumswissenschaft*, the study of antiquity in every aspect, historical, philosophical and archaeological, as well as literary and linguistic,[2] though as in Germany the term 'philology' was not abandoned. The journal founded by Julius Hare and Connop Thirlwall in 1831, in a deliberate attempt to broaden classical studies, was called the *Philological Museum*.

The growth of *Altertumswissenschaft* in late eighteenth- and early nineteenth-century Germany was intimately connected with some of the central enthusiasms of the Romantic movement, reflected in a desire not merely to write correct Greek and Latin, or to have a cultivated taste in classical literature, but to recapture the inner spirit of Greek antiquity in particular;[3] it was associated, above all, with an enthusiasm for Greek art and for Homer, now seen as the greatest of all folk poetry. A passion for Homer combined readily with an almost equal passion for Ossian, and an absorbing concern with the folk song and legend of one's native land. Under the influence of Winckelmann, Lessing and Herder, a generation of classical scholars grew up with a new interest in classical art and archaeology, and in the classical myths, seen, not in isolation, but as part of an interest in mythology in

---

[1] R. M. Ogilvie, *Latin & Greek. A history of the influence of the Classics on English life from 1600 to 1918* (London, 1964), p. 91ff.

[2] Clarke, *Greek Studies in England*, pp. 39, 101. See also Duncan Forbes, *The Liberal Anglican Idea of History* (Cambridge, 1950) and Klaus Dockhorn, *Der Deutsche Historismus in England* (Göttingen, 1950), *passim*.

[3] Sir John Sandys, *A Short History of Classical Scholarship* (Cambridge, 1915), pp. 286–315, and E. M. Butler, *The Tyranny of Greece over Germany* (Cambridge, 1935), chs. ii, iii.

general, Teutonic and Hindu[1] as well as Greek. Just as the new German Biblical Criticism treated the Bible as an historical work,[2] whose character had been decisively influenced by the times at which its various books had been written and by the people whose sacred writings they were, so classical literature was to be seen in the context of the world's history, as the expression of the life experience and genius of the Greek and Roman peoples.

The German affiliations and inspiration of Julius Hare, Thirlwall and Thomas Arnold, the leading English advocates of *Altertumswissenschaft* as well as the upholders of an essentially Romantic and Providential theory of history, have been thoroughly established[3] and there is therefore no need to labour the point here. Their view of history is essentially religious; though it involved subjecting the sacred writings and traditions of Christianity to the historical criticism which, to the orthodox appeared so destructive, it did so in order ultimately to fit them into the wider designs of Providence, as a vital part of human history, not something detached from it. History and myth must be clearly distinguished, in sacred history just as Niebuhr had distinguished them in his *History of Rome*,[4] but myth was not to be regarded simply as error but as the natural expression of a people's consciousness at a certain stage of development.

In its simplest form, this view of myth was fitted into a conception of history founded on the so-called 'genetic analogy'. The history of a people followed a sequence similar to that of the life of a man: childhood, manhood and old age.[5] Knowledge of the divine in childhood could not be expected to take the same form as in subsequent ages, but it was not to be despised on that account. Each end of the process had its peculiar strength and its weakness: on the one hand a naïve concreteness of religious imagery and a disposition to credulity, on the other desiccation and barren abstraction. As Jowett

---

[1] Especially F. Schlegel, *Über die Sprache und Weisheit der Indier* (Heidelberg, 1808).

[2] 'as far as theology is interpretation or exposition it is but a branch of philology'. J. W. Donaldson, *The New Cratylus* (Cambridge, 1839), p. 13.

[3] Forbes, *op. cit.*, Dockhorn, *op. cit.*

[4] Which Hare and Thirlwall translated into English.

[5] A simplified form of it is put forward in Frederick Temple's contribution to *Essays and Reviews* (London, 1860), 'The Education of the World'.

put it, 'There is a time when the freshness of early literature is lost; mankind have turned rhetoricians'.[1] One almost expects a reference to the dissociation of sensibility.

Obviously there was a strain of Romantic primitivism and tenderness to the mythopoeic in this attitude, though it was controlled within the framework of a providential, teleological view of history.   At the very least, however, it allowed one to enjoy poetry with a clear conscience, to appreciate the primitive elements in Greek literature without denigrating them, and to find continuing religious inspiration in the Bible, even though as a conscientious historian one might have reservations about the evidence for miracles and doubt whether Moses could have written the account of his own death.

It is not, however, with this conception of history, about which a good deal has already been written, that this essay is directly concerned, but with a particular aspect of it, and of the German influence on nineteenth-century English intellectual life, which has received less attention, the development of comparative philology. We shall see how comparative philology, starting from the same intellectual roots as the change in classical philology and the interpretation of ancient history we have just been considering, takes, in a sense, the opposite path, in that while classical scholarship was becoming less purely linguistic, comparative philology took up the study of language for its own sake, as an object of attention in its own right.   Yet the divergence was never complete, for the inspiration of the two types of philology remained essentially the same, each continuing to bear the marks of its German Romantic origin, while the same scholars were sometimes involved in both.

Both, in fact, were interpreted in the light of a Romantic, anti-materialist theory of knowledge, and comparative philology was placed in the service of a providential theory of history.   To show how, in mid- and later nineteenth-century England, the study of language came, particularly in the hands of those two anglicized Germans, Baron Bunsen and his protégé Max Müller, to provide a basis for such a version of history, a kind of sub-species of the Liberal Anglican view, will be the object

[1] Benjamin Jowett, 'On the Interpretation of Scripture', *Essays and Reviews*, p. 332; cf. Temple, 'We never find again that universal radiance', *Ibid.*, p. 27.

of the rest of this essay. It is a theme worth attention because it became, in the later nineteenth century, the only real rival to the better known, positivistic, Victorian philosophy of history —history as 'the March of Mind', or, later, a kind of analogue of biological evolution: history as 'social evolution'.

Comparative philology derived originally from the work of the eighteenth-century English orientalist Sir William Jones.[1] His perception of the relationship between Sanscrit and the classical languages[2] was the original insight on which the study of comparative philology was built. Until then, much effort had been uselessly expended on trying to relate Latin and Greek to Hebrew. With the revelation that Sanscrit was the elder sister of the classical and Romance languages, and, as it later appeared, the Teutonic as well, the classification and derivation of languages could be put on a systematic footing and linguistic change could be studied on a comparative basis.

Jones himself did not follow up his insight. It was left for the German scholars of the early nineteenth century, particularly Franz Bopp, the Schlegel brothers, Jacob Grimm and Wilhelm von Humboldt, to derive from it a disciplined comparative linguistics which, by taking grammar rather than etymology as the basis of comparison, did away with much of the wild speculativeness of the older attempts at tracing the genealogies and affinities of languages. It was not, however, the mere fact of the foundation of comparative philology which was important for general nineteenth-century intellectual history, though the belief in an 'Aryan' race, with its momentous consequences, was derived from the notion of an 'Indo-European' or 'Aryan' family of languages, but also the philosophy of language by which, in early nineteenth-century Germany it was generally inspired.[3] Language could be endowed with almost all the Romantic virtues. It was the paradigm of something not made but growing, the

---

[1] For a general history of comparative philology, see Jespersen, *op. cit.*, and H. Pedersen, *Linguistic Science in the Nineteenth Century*. Translated from the Danish by J. W. Spargo (Harvard, 1931). Also Donaldson *op. cit.* chapter i, and F. Max Müller, *Lectures on the Science of Language*, 1st Series (London, 1861), 2nd Series (London, 1864).

[2] Sir William Jones, 'On the Origin and Families of Nations' *Asiatic Researches*, vol. III (1799).

[3] Not invariably. See P. A. Verburg. 'The Background to the Linguistic Conceptions of Bopp'. *Lingua*, vol. II, no. 4 (1949–50).

N

spontaneously created accompaniment and medium of the manifold activities of the folk.   Its appeal was often linked, as with Jacob Grimm, with that of myth and folk tales.   No king or legislator had made it; it was the unique achievement of a people, the supreme, spontaneous expression of its particular genius, and to be respected as such.[1]   The tools of comparative philology could take one back to the dawn of civilization, and perhaps beyond.   Nor did it appear that the languages of more primitive peoples were necessarily impoverished or crude; if anything, there seemed to be an antagonism between the richness and grammatical subtlety of language and the advance of civilization.   For Grimm the historical path of language was on the whole one of decline.[2]   The nature of language itself, even apart from the atmosphere of enthusiasm for the primitive and tenderness to the uniqueness of each folk spirit with which the study of comparative philology was early associated, seemed to encourage an attitude to history very different from the rationalist philosophy of progress of the Enlightenment.

The study of comparative philology was thus closely linked at the outset with the central doctrines of German Romanticism. Even the concentration on grammar rather than on etymology alone can be related to the Romantic concern with grasping phenomena as wholes rather than analysing them into discrete parts.[3]   It was also, though perhaps more distantly, related to German Idealist epistemology.   Among the thinkers of the Enlightenment an empiricist epistemology had often been connected—notably in Condillac and Horne Tooke—with a view of the origin of language which saw it as a kind of reflex response to men's surroundings: the first words were onomatopoeic or ejaculatory.   This obviously fitted well with an epistemology which regarded knowledge as the result of an automatic compounding of sensations.   In both cases, man was the more or less passive recipient of stimuli.   For the German Romantics, however, following the lead of Herder's essay on the origin of language,[4] language was neither a reflex

---

[1] Jespersen, *Language*, pp. 41, 57.

[2] *Ibid.*, 62.

[3] W. Haas, 'Of Living Things'.   *German Life and Letters* X. (Oxford, 1956–7), p. 86.

[4] J. G. Herder, *Über den Ursprung der Sprache* (1772).

response nor, as the still older view had held, the gift of a divine revelation,[1] but sprang from an inner, creative necessity of man's nature. Man was not the passive recipient of sensation —or revelation—and language was the interpretative medium through which men necessarily experienced and moulded the raw stuff of the world. There is obviously an analogy here with the Kantian categories as the necessary presuppositions of knowledge, and in fact in England, as we shall see, Kantianism and comparative philology were closely associated. In its extreme form, however, the notion that experience was shaped and moulded by language, combined with the assertion of the uniqueness of the genius of each language, could lead, as it appears to have done with Herder,[2] to a virtual assimilation of philosophy to philology. Thus, logic was not the supreme arbiter of all languages, but simply the logic of this or that actual language. Even if they did not go to these lengths, the idea that philology held the key to philosophical problems, and especially to the refutation of materialist doctrines, was to tantalize the advocates of comparative philology in England; the identity of philosophy with philology is an idea which can be traced from Herder at the end of the eighteenth century to Max Müller at the end of the nineteenth.

It was sometimes suggested that nothing was known of comparative philology in England until Max Müller's lectures at the Royal Institution in 1861.[3] This may be true of the general public—the lectures attracted wide attention—but it is certainly not true of scholars.[4] Comparative philology entered English intellectual life in a number of guises, as a model for different kinds of inquiry into the remote past, as an ethnological tool—a means of classifying racial families and perhaps even showing the single (or diverse) origin of the human race, and a clue to the connections between ancient civilizations, and as a means of revitalizing the study of the classics.

Comparative philology, as the maturest and apparently

---

[1] This idea was still current in the nineteenth century; it appears, for example, to have been the view of Thomas Arnold. Forbes, *op. cit.*, p. 72.

[2] See the article on Herder by Sir Isaiah Berlin, *Encounter* vol. XXV, no. 1. (July, 1965).

[3] E.g., *Life & Letters of Friedrich Max Müller*, ed. by his wife. (2 vols London, 1902), vol. I, pp. 242, 248.

[4] E.g., W. B. Winning, *A Manual of Comparative Philology* (London, 1839).

most precise of the disciplines by which, in the nineteenth century, men were attempting to trace modern phenomena in an unbroken line to a remote or prehistoric past, naturally appealed as an example to scholars working along these lines in biology, in legal and social history, and in folk lore. Even Darwin found comparative philology a useful analogue.[1] Sir Henry Maine, in his attempts to trace the primitive origins of legal institutions, seems to have modelled his method directly on what he took to be that of comparative philology, and to have thought of his work as revealing the legal and institutional history, not of mankind, but of the Aryan race which he thought had been revealed by philology.[2] This was a point of considerable importance, since it set him apart from the social evolutionists such as J. F. McLennan and Sir John Lubbock, who refused to be limited, in their conjectural reconstructions of the early history of mankind, to comparisons between people which could be shown |by philology to be racially, or at any rate culturally, connected.

This in fact was the aspect of comparative philology first made use of by English scholars.[3] Ethnologists like J. C. Prichard and R. G. Latham saw in philology a means of tracing the prehistory of the races of mankind. The possibility of a scientific classification of races had been raised by the development of physical anthropology based on comparative anatomy and particularly on the work of J. F. Blumenbach in the late eighteenth century.[4] Now, philology seemed to supply an additional means of classification,[5] which might also help to reveal the cultural relations of different peoples in prehistoric times. It is, of course, to be remembered that before the late eighteen-fifties human prehistory was still thought of only as

[1] C. Darwin, *The Descent of Man*, 2nd ed. (London, 1874), pp. 90–1.

[2] Sir Henry Maine, *The Effects of Observation of India on Modern European Thought* (The Rede Lecture. Cambridge, 1875). A fuller discussion of Maine's debt to comparative philology is given in my book *Evolution and Society* (Cambridge, 1966), Ch. iv.

[3] Apart from works mentioned below, see also J. Crawfurd, *History of the Indian Archipelago*, (3 vols Edinburgh, 1820), and Vans Kennedy, *Researches into the Origin and Affinity of the Principal Languages of Asia and Europe* (London, 1828).

[4] A. C. Haddon, *History of Anthropology* (London, 1934), chs. i and ii.

[5] There was also considerable opposition to the incautious equation of linguistic and racial affinities. Max Müller, though prone to speak of 'the Aryan race', consistently protested against the confusion of ethnological and philological categories, cf. J. Crawfurd. 'Language as a Test of the Races of Man'. *Transactions of the Ethnological Society*, vol. III (1865).

a few thousand years. Bunsen is clearly conscious of some daring in claiming 'that the race of man cannot be older than 25,000 years, nor younger than 20,000'.[1] It was even thought possible that if all languages could be shown to be related, one could establish the single origin of the human race—an *Ur-Volk* speaking an *Ursprache* from which all the families of mankind were descended. After the dramatic and wholly unexpected revelation that the languages of India and Europe shared a common origin, nothing seemed impossible, and philology was to be the Ariadne's thread into prehistory.

To Latham, for example, in ethnology 'as elements of classification the *non*-philological moral characters are of less value than the philological; since common conditions develop common habits; whereas nothing but imitation determines the use of similar combinations of articulate sounds in different languages'.[2] Latham also believed that the question of the antiquity of man was 'most likely to be solved through philology'.[3] Prichard, the leading English ethnologist of the period, was of the same opinion. Speaking at the British Association in 1847, he said: 'The analytic comparison of languages furnishes more important aids to the cultivation of ethnology than any other part of what may be termed historical research.'[4] It is more important, according to Prichard, than archaeology; 'the history of mankind is not destined like the fundamental facts of geology, to be dug out of the bowels of the earth'.[5] It was an unfortunate guess, only a dozen years before the revelation of the antiquity of man based on the work of Pengelly and Boucher de Perthes.

Ethnology could hardly, at a time when the Bible was still regarded by the orthodox as an exact record of the early history of mankind, escape entanglement with religion. For Prichard, one of the objects of ethnology, aided by philology, was to disprove the theory of polygenesis and to show that 'the

---

[1] Frances, Baroness Bunsen, *A Memoir of Baron Bunsen*, (2 vols London, 1868), vol. II, p. 377.

[2] R. G. Latham, *The Natural History of the Varieties of Man* (London, 1850), p. 562.

[3] *Ibid.*, p. 565. Latham was also the author of *Elements of Comparative Philology* (London, 1862).

[4] J. C. Prichard, 'On the various methods of Research which Contribute to the Advancement of Ethnology', *Report of the British Association* (1848), pp. 238-9.

[5] *Ibid.*, p. 236.

various tribes of men are of one origin'.[1]   Another was to show, by comparing the religions of the ancient East, that a pure monotheism had been the earliest religion of mankind, and that this could only be explained by a primeval revelation.[2] Prichard upheld what was then the orthodox view[3] that primitive and non-Christian religions represented corruptions of the original divine revelation.   His attempt to link Hindu with ancient Egyptian religion was based on the assumption that comparative philology showed a cultural link between the two civilizations.   He tried to trace their religions to a common source, an elevated monotheism, and, given what was then accepted as the approximate date of man's appearance on earth, it was reasonable to assume that this took one very close to the primeval religion of mankind.

This belief, and the concomitant assumption that the earliest state of man could not have been one of low savagery, and that modern savages must be literally degenerates, became highly vulnerable as the time-scale of human prehistory was enormously extended at the end of the 'fifties by the findings of prehistoric archaeology.   In the work of another advocate of comparative philology as the clue to prehistory, F. W. Farrar, the future Dean of Canterbury, one can actually observe the orthodox view crumbling.   In his *Essay on the Origin of Language* (London, 1860), he wrote scornfully of 'the error of man's slow and toilsome development from an almost bestial condition',[4] and announced rhapsodically, in the manner of Temple and Jowett, that 'the dawn of language took place in the bright infancy, in the joyous boyhood of the world'.[5]   As usual, we are given a kind of profit and loss account.   Civilized men are said to 'sacrifice the magnificence of mystery to the light of distinct comprehension'.[6]   Farrar also shows a certain caution: philology cannot prove the single origin of the human race.   He also disclaims, probably with one eye on Darwin,

---

[1] 'Remarks on the Application of Philological and Physical Researches to the History of the Human Species', *Report of the British Association* (1833), p. 544.
[2] J. C. Prichard, *An Analysis of Egyptian Mythology* (London, 1819), p. 296.
[3] Vernon Storr, *The Development of English Theology in the Nineteenth Century* (London, 1913), p. 179.
[4] Farrar, *op. cit.*, p. 15.
[5] *Ibid.*, p. 140.   The author of *Eric, or Little by Little* perhaps regarded himself as an authority on joyous boyhood.
[6] *Ibid.*, p. 176.

whose work he admired, knowledge of 'the original appearance of the fathers of mankind'.[1] Nevertheless, the stylistic exuberance of *Eric* and *St Winifreds* was not altogether suppressed. Even if one allowed that comparative philology might throw light on an early Aryan civilization, when 'the ancestors of the Celts, the Germans, the Danes, the Greeks, the Italians, the Persians, and Hindus were all living beneath the same roof', it is difficult to see how any philological evidence could assure us that they were (despite their apparently cramped living conditions) 'austere patriarchs . . . in the midst of their chaste and obedient families'.[2]

In Farrar's later work, *Chapters on Language* (London, 1865), however, while reiterating that language is the key to prehistory,[3] he admits that men may originally have been savages, quoting the recent work in prehistoric archaeology,[4] and attacks man's refusal 'to see in his far off ancestors what he *must* see in his living congeners, a miserable population . . . forced to dispute their cave-dwellings with the hyena and the wolf'.[5] In a *volte face* like this one can feel, as it were, the quickening pulse of intellectual history in the early eighteen-sixties.

Farrar was a liberal churchman, a friend of F. D. Maurice and familiar with German theology.[6] His *Origin of Language*, although avowedly based on the work of Renan, is clearly influenced by the German Romantic attitude to language. Language is said to be 'An immediate emanation of human nature . . . a living monument on which is written the genesis of human thought',[7] and there are approving references to Herder and Bunsen.[8] Farrar's use of philology goes beyond Prichard's purely enthnographic use of it; he calls on it also to refute a materialist view of human nature and development, and particularly the doctrine that language is in origin a kind of reflex. His chief adversary is Horne Tooke, who had tried

[1] *Ibid.*, p. 201. Farrar was to be a moving spirit in getting Darwin buried in Westminster Abbey.
[2] *Ibid.*, pp. 192, 201.
[3] *Chapters on Language*, p. 296.
[4] *Ibid.*, pp. 42, 55–6.
[5] *Ibid.*, p. 49.
[6] Dockhorn, *Der Deutsche Historismus in England*, p. 108.
[7] *Origin of Language*, p. 4.
[8] *Ibid.*, pp. 22, 106, 165n.

to base a philosophical nominalism on etymology, deriving all abstract terms from concrete ones.[1] Farrar objects that a language is not a mere collection of words, and draws attention to the importance placed by comparative philology on grammar: 'no system of materialism will account for grammar, that *form* of language which is due to the pure reason'.[2] Essentially this is an attempt to put philology at the service of a Kantian theory of knowledge.

Farrar's book had no pretensions to originality, and in so far as this view of language was not taken simply from the standard Continental authorities it seems likely that his arguments are derived from a much more original book, which he cites freely, J. W. Donaldson's *The New Cratylus* (1839).   Donaldson was a Fellow of Trinity, Cambridge, and a member of the Hare-Thirlwall circle there.[3]   The Liberal Anglican historians were as enthusiastic in adopting the characteristic German attitudes in the study of language as in other fields.[4]   Donaldson's book represented an attempt to broaden and revitalize the study of the classics in England by studying Greek and Latin in the context of comparative philology, an object which Farrar also had at heart.   Both, incidentally, were schoolmasters, and Farrar's *Greek Syntax and Hints on Accidence* (1867) was an attempt to produce a Greek grammar for school use guided by the general principles of comparative philology.[5]

Donaldson's book was a vigorous attack on the narrowness of English classical scholarship in the tradition of Bentley and Porson, and he noted with approval that London University gave a rôle to comparative philology in its classical teaching.[6] But it also had a wider purpose: to proclaim the identity of philology and philosophy. Language is thought, and the history of language is the history of thought. This view of

---

[1] Horne Tooke, *The Diversions of Purley* (1829. First part published 1786) on Horne Tooke, see Leslie Stephen, *The English Utilitarians*, (3 vols London, 1900), vol. I, ch. iv.

[2] *Origin of Language*, p. 162.

[3] Dockhorn, *op. cit.*, 23.

[4] Especially Hare. See Dockhorn, pp. 46–7. Forbes, *Liberal Anglican Idea of History*, pp. 138, 189.

[5] Reginald Farrar, *The Life of Frederick William Farrar, Dean of Canterbury* (London, 1904), p. 92. Cf. Farrar's review of Max Müller, *Fortnightly Review*, N.S. Vol. iv. (1868), p. 347.

[6] Donaldson, *op. cit.*, p. 30. Latham was Professor of English at University College.

language has the usual concomitants: an admiration for the primitive, a partial denial of the doctrine of progress,[1] and a kind of philological endorsement of Kant as an antidote to materialism. Language 'was as perfect at the beginning, indeed much more so, than it is now', for 'The effect of increased use upon the structure of inflected language is rather to weaken and corrupt than to improve'. Primitive man was a natural poet, and Donaldson refers to 'the careful but barren elegances of logical prose'.[2] Where philology touches on philosophy, Horne Tooke is the enemy, and Donaldson even says that the chief object of his own book is the refutation of Tooke and 'the support of religion and morality'.[3] He is taken as the type of sophist against whom Plato had written his *Cratylus*—hence the title of Donaldson's book.[4] The argument against him is very much the same as Farrar was to use, with similar references to Kant.[5]

Men like Donaldson had to carry on a war on two fronts; on the one hand, as we have seen, to refute a materialist explanation of language and, generally, to deny the evolution of civilization and religion from a state of savagery, and, secondly, to oppose those who put all their faith in revelation, to win acceptance for a genuinely historical approach to the classics and—with infinitely more difficulty—the Bible, so that revelation could be seen not as a single act of God, outside the ordinary course of history, but as a continuing process, a relation between men—all men—and God. Donaldson in fact lost his headmastership of Bury St Edmunds Grammar School for his unorthodox views on the lost Hebrew book of Jasher. Probably the most elaborate exposition of the doctrine of continuous revelation in mid-Victorian England, however, as well as the point at which comparative philology and Biblical research met most significantly, was in the work of Baron Bunsen.

There is nothing arbitrary in including Bunsen in an essay

---

[1] See his review of Bunsen's 'Egypt's Place in World History', *Quarterly Review* no. CLV. (1846), p. 157, where he endorses the view of a primeval monotheism, later corrupted.

[2] *The New Cratylus*, pp. 52, 54.

[3] *Ibid.*, p. 73. Tooke, among other arguments, had tried to demonstrate the relativity of truth by deriving the word from 'troweth'—thinks.

[4] *Ibid.*

[5] *Ibid.*, p. 7, n. 1.

on the intellectual climate of mid-Victorian England. He did not, it is true, hold an English academic post like Max Müller, but he was an anglophile, married to an English wife, who lived in England as Prussian Minister in London, from 1841 to 1854. More important, he was a member of the Liberal Anglican circle, being a close friend of Hare and Thirlwall, whom he had met in Rome, where he was secretary to the Prussian Legation and later Minister, as a young man. He was also extremely intimate with Thomas Arnold, whose Broad Church views were so very like his own.[1] Incidentally, Kingsley introduced Bunsen into *Alton Locke*—the character is unmistakable—to speak a few encouraging words to the hero; some consolation, perhaps for being warned off 'philology'. The appearances of Bunsen's books were events in English intellectual life, and one of the most controversial contributions to *Essays and Reviews* was based entirely on Bunsen's work. Among other points the author, Rowland Williams, pointed out that the linguistic changes traced by philology, no less than geological changes, required a lapse of time far greater than Biblical orthodoxy allowed.[2] But 'He [Bunsen] could not have vindicated the unity of mankind [i.e. by linguistic relations] if he had not asked for a vast extension of time, whether his petition of twenty thousand years be granted or not. The mention of such a term may appear monstrous to those who regard six thousand years as part of Revelation.'[3]

It is not surprising that Bunsen got on so well with the Liberal Anglicans; the background to his thought was very similar to theirs. Niebuhr, in particular, was an immense influence on both.[4] It was under Niebuhr that Bunsen worked as a young man at the Prussian Legation in Rome. Even before that, it had been to Niebuhr that he had submitted an elaborate plan of his life's work, a plan to prepare himself to write a universal history, by becoming master of the languages and cultures of the three great ages of the world's history: the

---

[1] Chief sources for Bunsen's life are Frances, Baroness Bunsen, *A Memoir of Baron Bunsen*, (2 vols London, 1868), and Wilma Hocker, *Der Gesandte Bunsen als Vermittler zwischen Deutschland und England* (Göttingen, 1951).

[2] Rowland Williams, 'Bunsen's Biblical Researches', *Essays and Reviews* (1860), pp. 54–5. Williams was one of the two contributors tried for heresy.

[3] *Ibid.*, p. 54.

[4] Bunsen, *Memoir*, vol. I, pp. 84ff. For the Liberal Anglicans, Forbes, *op. cit.*, p. 12 *et seq.*

'Medean-Persian-Indian', the classical and the Germanic.[1] The guiding purpose was religious. As he wrote to his sister in 1817, when he was twenty-six: 'The consciousness of God in the mind of man, and that which in and through that consciousness, He has accomplished, especially in language and religion, this was from the earliest point before my mind.'[2] It was to remain so with unusual consistency, even the bracketing together of language and religion.

The central theme of Bunsen's history of mankind is the continuity of Christianity with the ancient religions of India and Egypt. Christianity in his own time seemed to have reached a crisis, its sacred books challenged, its outward forms decayed.[3] The crisis could only be overcome by men's grasping the spirit behind the letter and the form. The spirit of a thing is identical with its development—a favourite doctrine of German historicism—and recovery of the spirit of religion must therefore be through an understanding of its history conceived as a continuous unfolding process.[4] God reveals himself in the history of the world, and the essence of personal religion is 'our consciousness of the Divine activity in the History of Mankind'.[5]

Bunsen's version of history is inspired by religion and guided by a characteristically German philosophy of history of a type most familiar to us through Hegel, but its foundation is philology. Partly, of course, he used it in the familiar, ethnological fashion, to show, or at least to speculate on, the connections of various peoples of antiquity, and he refers to 'the ethnological development of mankind made known to us by language'.[6] Philology is also the key to the history of religion since it unlocks the sacred books of the world.[7] But language for Bunsen is far more than a simple tool. 'All history of the religious consciousness must repose upon language, not only because it is the historical record, but also because it is the

---

[1] *Memoir*, vol. I, p. 88.

[2] *Ibid.*, p. 137.

[3] One of Bunsen's other interests was the reconstruction of Protestant liturgy.

[4] *Memoir*, vol. I, p. 394.

[5] Bunsen, *God in History, or the Progress of Man's Faith in the Moral Order of the World*, trans. S. Winkworth, (3 vols London, 1868) vol. I, pp. 7, 18.

[6] *Ibid.*, vol. III, p. 294.

[7] Bunsen, *Outlines of the Philosophy of Universal History applied to Language and Religion*, (2 vols London, 1854), vol. II, pp. 5ff.

primordial work of the human intellect.'[1]   Philology becomes, in fact, not merely a guide to prehistory, but in a sense a substitute for it.   Language is to Bunsen what contemporary savages were to the social evolutionists—the evidence of man's earliest states of consciousness.   Philology is a kind of substitute for archaeology and anthropology.   'The structure of thought revealed by its deposits in language precedes all other coinage of the human intelligence.'[2]

Bunsen's view of the history of mankind has very much the same kind of ambivalence towards the primitive state of man that we have seen in Donaldson, Farrar, and in *Essays and Reviews*.   Certainly modern savages are not, according to him, the living exemplars of the natural original man, 'for linguistic inquiry shows that the languages of savages are degraded, decaying fragments of nobler formations'.[3]   Language is the crucial difference between men and animals, and hence the refutation of the theory of biological evolution.[4]   Language being in origin not a response to stimuli but a creative act of the human mind, Bunsen thinks that evolution has been proved an impossibility by—of all people—Kant![5]   Nevertheless, he sees the history of mankind as the development of self consciousness in man, which has, significantly, perils as well as rewards. Bunsen uses the metaphor of Paradise lost and Paradise regained, a return, through sophistication, to an original, unclouded vision.[6]

Language and religion are linked, in Bunsen's philosophy of History because they are the twin, primordial expressions of human consciousness, and they develop along parallel lines: 'The power of the mind which enables us to see the genus in the individual, the whole in the many, and to form a word by connecting a subject with a predicate, is essentially the same which leads man to find God in the Universe and the Universe in God.   Language and religion are the two poles of our consciousness, mutually presupposing each other.'[7]   Bunsen, it appears, can see eternity in a grammatical construction and

---

[1] *God in History*, vol. III, p. 294.
[2] *Ibid.*, p. 305, cf. *Outlines*, vol. ii, pp. x–xi.
[3] *Outlines*, vol. II, p. 78.
[4] *Ibid.*, pp. 75–7.
[5] *Ibid.*, p. 77.   Bunsen also attacks Horne Tooke.   *Ibid.*, pp. 136–8.
[6] *Ibid.*, pp. 186–8.
[7] *Ibid.*, p. 78.

heaven in a copula. The uses of Philology could hardly be pushed further.

Bunsen's historical categories are derived from the comparative philology of his day; they are, in fact, philological. Thus, the most primitive form of language, and hence of thought, is said to be Chinese, because it is a monosyllabic, uninflected language, i.e. all its words are roots. Hence Chinese 'is in itself the oldest conceivable form of the intellectual denotation of things, because it bears a thoroughly substantive character'. This is said to correspond—for some reason—to a conception of the universe as 'a vast, ordered Whole'.[1] The next language group, the Turanian,[2] belongs to the 'agglutinative' stage of language and thought; an agglutinative language being one in which roots are combined. Bunsen finds this stage one in which there is a lack of sense of individuality, and 'it is precisely the absence of the sober intellect which characterizes the Turanian sense of the Divine presence'.[3]

It would be unnecessarily tedious to illustrate Bunsen's attempts to relate the condition of language and religion in the ensuing stages of the development of man's consciousness: the Khamitic (Egyptian), the Semitic and the Aryan. Its deficiencies are obvious, even apart from the fact that the philological basis itself was highly speculative and unsound. It does, however, represent a remarkable attempt to base a philosophy of history, not merely on the cultural affinities revealed by comparative philology, but actually on philological categories taken as the stages of man's intellectual and spiritual development.

Bunsen's work does not seem to have exercised much direct influence. Even apart from its intellectual and scholarly deficiencies, it was handicapped by being scattered through a number of heterogeneous volumes and expressed uninhibitedly in the language of German Idealism. It was left to Bunsen's protégé Max Müller to win wide, though never undisputed, enthusiasm for the interpretation of history through comparative philology. Bunsen encouraged Max Müller when he first came to England as a young student of Sanscrit, lent him

[1] *God in History*, vol. III, p. 296.
[2] A kind of residual category, intended to include all languages which could not be found a place in the established families of languages—later discredited.
[3] *Ibid.*, p. 297.

money and managed his intellectual debut at the British Association in 1847.[1] Max Müller's writing was generally lucid and his style persuasive—everything that Bunsen's was not. Nevertheless, the coincidences in their work and in the general direction of their ideas are so striking that it is tempting to assume that Max Müller must have owed his 'much honoured friend, master and benefactor' a heavy intellectual as well as personal debt. This is not necessarily so. Despite the difference in their ages, the thought of both of them was deeply rooted in the German philosophical, philological, historical and religious thought of the early nineteenth century. Schelling appears to have been a particular influence on both.[2] It would be rash to claim any of Max Müller's ideas as a case of direct influence from Bunsen without a detailed examination of their common sources.

Max Müller's work falls essentially into four categories: his edition of the Hindu sacred books of the *Rig-Veda*, which he began as a young man and which brought him to England, the country with the richest collection of Indian manuscripts, in 1846. It was on this that his scholarly reputation was founded. Secondly, his popularization of comparative philology in his Royal Institution Lectures in 1861 and 1863.[3] He became first Professor of Comparative Philology at Oxford in 1868, having failed to obtain the Chair of Sanscrit in 1860 owing to suspicions of his religious orthodoxy. He lived in England until his death in 1900, marrying, like Bunsen, an English wife —a niece of Kingsley. Thirdly, there was his work on comparative mythology and religion, whose chief monuments are his four series of Gifford Lectures[4] and his *Contributions to the Science of Mythology* (London, 1897). Lastly, there were his philosophical pretensions, based on the belief that thought

[1] Bunsen, *Memoir*, vol. II, p. 76. F. Max Müller, *My Autobiography. A Fragment* (London, 1901), p. 13. *The Life and Letters of F. Max Müller*, ed. by his wife, (2 vols London, 1902), vol. I, pp. 29, 54, 55, 58–9, 61, 64.

[2] Bunsen, *Memoir*, vol. I, p. 488. Max Müller, *My Autobiography*, p. 188, *Life*, vol. I, p. 29.

[3] Published as *Lectures on the Science of Language*, 1st Series (London, 1861) and 2nd Series (London, 1864).

[4] *Natural Religion* (London, 1889); *Physical Religion* (London, 1891). *Anthropological Religion* (London, 1892) and *Theosophy, or Psychological Religion* (London, 1893). Note also his Hibbert Lectures: *Lectures on the Origin and Growth of Religion as illustrated by the Religions of India* (London, 1878), subsequently cited as *Origin of Religion*, and *Introduction to the Science of Religion* (London, 1873).

and language were the same, and embodied in his book *The Science of Thought* (London, 1887).

His thought is more coherent, however, than this summary might suggest. He is also repetitious, and in many cases one reference to his work may stand for a good many others as well. He himself referred to 'the thread that connects all my labours . . . namely, the thread that connects the origin of thought and languages with the origin of mythology and religion.'[1] He admitted that he studied the *Veda* as a means to an end, 'namely, a philosophy of mythology and religion',[2] while the ultimate object was, as he wrote elsewhere, 'to recognize in history the realisation of, a rational purpose . . . a Divine drama'[3]—the central inspiration of German historicism from Herder onwards.

His attitude to language as the clue to history is very much the same as Bunsen's. Language itself contains a record of the earliest thoughts of mankind, and the rôle of philology in giving access to that record is even more important than the deciphering of the earliest written religious records.[4] We are again assured that Chinese reflects 'the earliest workings of the human mind'.[5] The identity of language and thought means that 'what, as the grammarian tells us, happened in language, should, as the psychologist tells us, have happened likewise in thought'.[6] And comparative philology is 'the final consummation of all that has ever claimed the name of philosophy'.[7] Modern philosophy has sometimes been accused of trying to turn itself into linguistics. According to Max Müller, it had already done so.

Max Müller's remarks on philosophy sometimes sound strikingly modern, notably his assertion that philosophical problems are generated by language. His elaboration of them, however, is crude and equivocal. By saying that philosophical problems are generated by language he means merely that they arise because people use words in different

[1] *My Autobiography*, p. 3.
[2] *Natural Religion*, p. 20.
[3] *Life*, vol. II, p. 290.
[4] *Natural Religion*, p. 281.
[5] *Selected Essays on Language, Mythology and Religion*, (2 vols London, 1881), vol. I, p. 110.
[6] *Natural Religion*, p. 406.
[7] *Ibid.*, p. 423. *Science of Thought* (London, 1887), pp. 44-5.

senses and hence cannot agree. He toys with the idea of a perfectly unambiguous language of precisely defined terms, but he is sharply aware of the difference between artificial and natural languages and makes no attempt to follow this up. Nor does it seem, at least at first, that philology has anything to offer, for language being in constant flux the search for original meanings does not help either. Eventually, he seems to have sought an answer, not in contemporary usage, which he would have thought an evasion, since he was interested not in alleviating metaphysical 'cramps' but in establishing an unambiguous meaning for each word, but in the notion that the meaning of a word was equivalent to its whole etymological history[1]— though he admits that this does not help the practical problem of communication much either.[2] This identification of the unique essence of a thing with its historical development reminds one, in another context, of Bunsen's equation of the spirit of religion with its history—a doctrine which Max Müller shared.[3]

It is probably significant that he had first turned to philology in despair at his inability to understand the Hegelian philosophy he was taught at university,[4] and he held the common nineteenth century belief that 'History, if properly understood, can take the place of philosophy'.[5] It was this belief which lay behind his insistence on the etymological approach to meaning, and also behind his confidence in 'the historical proof of the existence of God, which is supplied to us by the history of the religions of the world'.[6]

Max Müller's interpretation of history, and particularly the history of religion, was, like Bunsen's, based on philology. In the first place, language provided a serious obstacle to the theory of evolution; 'the Science of Language will yet enable us to withstand the extreme theories of the evolutionists, and to draw a hard and fast line between spirit and matter, between man and brute'.[7] Max Müller gave three lectures at the

---

[1] 'Biographies of words are perhaps the most useful definitions which it is in our power to give.' *Natural Religion*, p. 32.

[2] *Ibid.*, p. 44.

[3] *Ibid.*, p. 198. Cf. *Anthropological Religion*, p. 92.

[4] *My Autobiography*, pp. 134, 139.

[5] *Life* vol. i, p. 203. For a brief discussion of similar views among positivistic mid-nineteenth century thinkers, see my 'Evolution and Anthropology in the 1860s', *Victorian Studies*, vol. VII (1963).

[6] *Anthropological Religion*, p. 92.

[7] *Selected Essays*, vol. I, p. 199.

Royal Institution in 1873 attacking 'Mr Darwin's philosophy of Language'.[1] He doubted the development of civilization from a state analogous to that of contemporary savages for the same reason as many philologists: the high art and complexity to be found in the languages of these peoples, which suggested to him that they had degenerated from a higher state of which their languages were relics.[2] During the latter part of his life Max Müller fought a running battle with the social evolutionists[3] and though his language was sometimes equivocal his views gave considerable support to those who clung to a 'degenerationist' view of savagery. Man was 'noble and pure from the very beginning',[4] and fetishism, which most evolutionary anthropologists regarded as the earliest form of religion, Max Müller held to be merely a corruption of it.[5]

It comes as no surprise to discover that Max Müller continued to think highly, as Bunsen had done, of the now unfashionable work of Prichard.[6] Prichard, however, had given no coherent account of the causes of degeneration, though he had referred to 'sensuality' and 'the figments of philosophy'.[7] Bunsen had been rather more systematic. Degeneration in religion occurred when the symbol or the rite of the sacred revelation became an end in itself, taking the place of what it symbolized or revealed.[8] Max Müller's famous theory that myth was a disease of language was another attempt to explain, this time in philological terms, an aspect of religious degeneration; mythical characters were personifications of the forces of nature, predicates changed by linguistic usage into proper nouns, while the attribution of sex to these nature gods and goddesses was at least partly the consequence of grammatical gender.[9]

Of course, there had been progress, too, in man's ways of expressing his intuition of the infinite, which is for Max Müller,

[1] *Published in Fraser's Magazine.* For Max Müller's correspondence with Darwin over this, see *Life*, vol. I, p. 452.
[2] *Last Essays*, 1st Series (London, 1901), p. 159. *Science of Mythology*, vol. I, pp. 24–6.
[3] Max Müller's chief antagonist was Andrew Lang, whose *Modern Mythology* (London, 1897), was a protracted attack on his theories.
[4] Max Müller, 'Comparative Mythology', *Oxford Essays* (1856), p. 5.
[5] *Origin of Religion*, Lecture ii.
[6] *My Autobiography*, p. 205. Bunsen, *Memoir*, vol. I. pp. 475–7, 482. *Outlines*, vol. II, p. 100.
[7] Prichard, *Egyptian Mythology*, p. 297.
[8] Bunsen, *Outlines*, vol. II, pp. 180–1.
[9] *Oxford Essays, Science of Mythology*, passim.

as for Bunsen, the essential core of all religion.[1] All modes
of expressing the infinite were in a sense valid, as they were all
imperfect, but there had been a development from a more to a
less concrete form of expression, and this represented a kind of
progress. But this was not a field in which one could speak
unequivocally of progress. The last word of Comparative
Religion appeared to be a paradox. Only in maturity could
one learn the wisdom of a childlike faith: 'There is the same
glow about the setting sun as there is about the rising sun: but
there lies between the two a whole world, a journey through
the whole sky, over the whole earth.'[2] One is reminded,
obliquely, of *The Four Quartets*, though it would doubtless be
difficult to establish any real affinity between Max Müller's
rotund eloquence and Eliot's more pregnant paradoxes.[3]

Mr Duncan Forbes, in the conclusion to his book on the
Liberal Anglican historians, raises the question to what extent,
in the latter part of the nineteenth century, their ideas 'perished
amidst the spears of triumphant positivism'.[4] In so far as
Max Müller's work is representative of the later phases of the
view of history which both he and the Liberal Anglicans
derived from late eighteenth- and early nineteenth-century
Germany, we may now be in a position to hazard at least some
part of the answer. And it appears that although Darwin
was a major obstacle—Max Müller could never quite emulate
the airiness with which Bunsen had assumed that the doctrine
of evolution had been demolished by Kant[5]—a more direct
challenge was provided by the findings of prehistoric archaeology. It was the evidence that primitive men had hunted and
cooked their food in Devon and the Dordogne, much as they
did along the upper Amazon and in the Australian bush in the
nineteenth century, many thousands of years before any period
of language which could be reconstructed by even the most
speculative uses of comparative philology, which discredited,

[1] Probably they both derived the idea from Schleiermacher. See *Natural
Religion*, pp. 48, 57, 68, 141.
[2] *Origin of Religion*, pp. 367, 374–5.
[3] But perhaps not. After all, presumably Max Müller really did know what
Krishna meant.
[4] Forbes, *Liberal Anglican Idea of History*, p. 152.
[5] For whom, however, Max Müller shared the customary enthusiasm. He
translated the *Critique of Pure Reason* into English, and referred to Kant in his Preface as his constant inspiration.

as we have seen in the case of Farrar, the Romantic 'bright morning of the world' doctrine. Philology could no longer plausibly claim to be the clue to the remotest period of man's history, and archaeology seemed to go far to justify the assumption of the evolutionary anthropologists, the purveyors of a rival, positivistic theory of history, that modern savages could be taken as a fair guide to the condition of the prehistoric ancestors of civilized men.

The *Veda* had at one time, as Max Müller admitted, when it was almost unknown, been looked to for a picture of the most primitive ideas of mankind.[1] But the sacred writings of the Brahmins might be almost *parvenu* compared with the contents of a Danish kitchen-midden, while the Andaman islanders came to seem a better guide to the origins of civilization than the doubtless noble but all too hypothetical Aryans. Philology had seemed the clue to prehistory so long as prehistory was thought, as Bunsen had claimed—and even that was venturesome—to extend back some ten or twenty thousand years. There is something almost pathetic in Max Müller's appeals to his readers to be content with what philology could offer.[2] At least its findings, he claimed, were truly historical, not speculative like those of the social evolutionists, and he wrote bitterly of 'the ignorant attempts at explaining classical myths from Melanesian tattle, the wild comparisons of Hebrew customs with the outrages of modern cannibals'.[3]

Time has brought some redress. Most of Max Müller's objections to speculative evolutionary anthropology would now be echoed by anthropologists themselves. There is irony also, however, for if anthropology has turned away from hypothetical reconstructions of prehistory, much the same has occurred in linguistics. Similarly, though the boundaries between philosophy and linguistics may have become blurred in places, this is certainly not because philosophy has become more historical—whatever that may mean.[4] Apart from his

[1] *My Autobiography*, pp. 187–8. Bunsen, when Max Müller showed him his transcripts, said, 'I am glad to have lived to see the *Veda*'. *Ibid.*
[2] *Last Essays*, 1st Series, p. 170.
[3] *Ibid.*, p. 55.
[4] It would not have seemed puzzling in the nineteenth century. The Westminster reviewer (possibly Max Müller) of Bopp's *Comparative Grammar* was uttering a common sentiment when he remarked that: 'Whoever would appreciate a system of philosophy, should engage it to write a *history*.' *Westminster Review*, N.S. vol. VI (1854), p. 557.

pioneering work on the *Rig-Veda*, however, there is perhaps one aspect of Max Müller's work which has left some permanent deposit: his contribution to comparative religion. Possibly the beliefs which inspired it were no more than a well-meaning syncretism; W. H. Mallock's parody of Jowett as Dr Jenkinson in *The New Republic*, could well have applied also to Jowett's friend Max Müller, though at least he was not a Church of England clergyman. Enthusiasm for Oriental religions had its bizarre side; Max Müller was obliged to disavow Madame Blavatsky[1] and to protest with obvious irritation that 'it should be known once and for all that one can call oneself a theosophist without . . . believing in any occult sciences and black arts'.[2]   Nevertheless, it was undeniably an improvement on the view of non-Christian religions which had seen in them only benighted ignorance and wickedness.

Comparative religion was an aspect of the enlargement of nineteenth-century European intellectual horizons, and in that enlargement Max Müller, and the tradition of German Romantic historiography and philology to which he belonged, played a significant part, emphasizing the unique value of every language and culture. Comparative philology provides another example of the same intellectual expansion. Not only Latin, Greek and Hebrew, but Hottentot and Tasmanian were now of interest to the philologist. One of the most influential philological essays of the nineteenth century, Wilhelm von Humboldt's *On the Variety of Human Speech*, appeared as a preface to his three volume work on the ancient language of Java.[3]

Twentieth-century historians have found much that was ominous in early nineteenth-century German Romanticism. Even its specific interest in philology can be made to have a baleful aspect; it is scarcely an exaggeration to say that in Eastern Europe and the Balkans the first act of awakening nationalism was often a scholar compiling a dictionary. It is worth remembering therefore, that there is another side to the story, and the history of the reception of comparative philology in nineteenth-century England is part of it.

---

[1] *Life*, vol. II, p. 297.
[2] *Theosophy, or Psychological Religon*, p. xvi.
[3] W. von Humboldt, *Über die Kawi Sprache auf der Insel Java*, (3 vols Berlin, 1836–9).

8

The Atheist Mission
1840–1900

THE atheist campaign in the nineteenth century found its most thorough expression in the mission to the working classes. In Charles Southwell, the Holyoakes, Bradlaugh and their allies, the cause found apostles as self-sacrificing and implacable as any of their evangelical Christian contemporaries. They preached atheism in the market place, suffered the hostility of mobs and endured imprisonment as common felons. What is more, unlike sceptics among the upper classes, they never dissembled and never doubted the righteousness of pressing the attack. Their example and programme made a distinctive contribution to that culture, now vestigial, of ardent hopes and fears, inexhaustible fact-hoarding, dogmatic speculation, excitement in disputation, and taut morality which shaped the thoughts of aspiring working people in the Victorian Age.

The first avowedly atheist periodical, Southwell's *Oracle of Reason*, appeared in 1841, surprisingly late, in view of the scepticism of Biblical authority and anti-clericalism prevalent in radical literature since the 1790s. The format and style of the *Oracle* derived from such publications as Carlile's *Republican* and the *New Moral World*, but the matter was new. For the first time in British history a journal arose which was devoted to the denial of all supernatural agency, and preaching that man's concerns lay only with the world around him. Rather than advocating reform of the churches and the purification of Christian principle, the *Oracle* called for the demolition of religion. Southwell and his coadjutors, and Bradlaugh after them, did not deny that a Divine Being could conceivably exist; they simply claimed that there was no evidence of the existence of such a Being and that belief in a supernatural order was the prime obstacle to human betterment.

The mission was precipitated by the Owenite movement and its Paineite Deism. The split arose when Owen equivocated before the attacks of the Bishop of Exeter and the Vice Society. He had his Halls of Science declared chapels and ordered his lecturers, including Southwell and Holyoake, to swear when necessary the dissenting preachers' oath.[1] Both young men rebelled. Holyoake has told his story; but Southwell, who instigated the revolt, is now forgotten. He had cause to be angry.

Charles Southwell was born in 1814, the youngest of thirty-three children to the same father. He was good at his lessons and was the best reciter in the school at Bristol, but he was removed early to follow his father's trade as cabinet maker. Charles hated manual labour. One day in the shop he disparaged orthodox Christianity, whereupon a pious fellow workman lent him Dwight's *Theology* . . . and Paley's *Evidences* . . . . Reading Dwight he came upon the argument that belief was God-given: an 'electric shock struck through his frame' as he found relief in the thought that man could not be responsible for his doubts. In 1834 he finally broke with his family and journeyed to London to become a Shakespearean actor; but he found his lowly origins made him unacceptable as a 'grand actor' and he was reduced to giving open-air recitals for pennies. These he varied with attacks on social exclusiveness, the blasphemy laws and the taxes on newspapers. The following year, on the death of his wife, he joined the British Legion to fight for Isabella II of Spain, but his spell of soldiering was brief, for he disliked mingling with 'the sweepings of the large towns'. Upon his return to London he discovered Owenism. His 'mind was awakened' to the promise of brotherhood and the improvement of every individual through education and social reorganization and in 1838 he became a salaried lecturer at Leicester. Southwell loved lecturing. He was eloquent, irreverent and widely read in the standard radical and Deistical writers: he could talk for hours, becoming ever more hortatory as the audience warmed to him. When, in

[1] Frank Podmore, *Robert Owen*, (2 vols London, 1906), vol. II, pp. 518–26.

1839, Robert Owen forbade the discussion of theological subjects in the Halls of Science, Southwell ignored his instructions. His dismissal in the following year seemed to him proof positive that the dragon of persecution had to be slain. Southwell induced a young gentleman, Malthus Q. Ryall, to put up money, and a former bricklayer and self-taught compositor, William Chilton, to set the type for the *Oracle of Reason*, eight pages, price, one penny. Within weeks it was selling 4,000 copies.[1]

The concerns and arguments of the *Oracle* were to remain typical of atheist propaganda for a century, but since the enemy hardly altered its repertoire in the same period, this immobility is understandable. The editors' positive concern was the improvement of man through education and the increase of liberty; but their immediate quarry was religion. Religion was immoral: it was destructive of personal happiness, intellectually false, anachronistic and in general socially pernicious.

The mission took over the arguments of Voltaire, Paine, Godwin, Owen and Carlile and pressed them to their logical conclusion in total scepticism. Faith in the supernatural became immoral because it made human virtue dependent upon external, unverifiable sanctions enforced by terror. Morality in Southwell's and G. J. Holyoake's, and later Bradlaugh's, view was 'practical' in that it arose from man's own desires after the good, aroused by objective appraisal of his needs and the needs of others. Man could only be 'strictly moral' if he desired good for its own sake, that is, if he became 'a practical atheist'. To do good in the hope of future reward or fear of future punishment was to make man servile like the brutes or meanly self-interested. Man had no innate idea of the nature of morality: he accumulated such notions by experience of his environment; it was therefore vitally important to cleanse his environment of falsities and distorted precepts so that he might attain to a purer view of his aspirations and duties.[2]

In themselves, these ideas are indistinguishable from those of any philosopher of the Enlightenment, but the tone of their propagation is unmistakably evangelical. The atheists' onerous

[1] 'Charles Southwell', J. P. Adams, *National Reformer*, 12 January 1861; 'Trial of Southwell', *Ibid.*, 15 January 1865; and reminiscences by W. H. Harris, *Secular Chronicle*, 28 October, 1877.
[2] *Oracle of Reason*, 27 November 1841; 17 June 1843.

pursuit of the good and the abolition of the devil gave the movement an earnestness of demeanour that is altogether lacking in the deft and deadly sallies of a Voltaire. Their adherence to a regimen of prudery and indurate seriousness put them at one with their enemies, Bishop Phillpotts and the Anti-Infidel Society, in the mainstream of nineteenth-century moral endeavour.

It was incredible, the atheists asserted, that the mere eating of an apple should have produced an irremediable set-back in the progress of mankind, and monstrous that succeeding generations should have been visited with its penalties. No creature could be so evil as to deserve eternal torment.[1] Likewise, the doctrine of the Atonement was 'a shock to all justice and common sense': why did God wait 4,000 years before sending a Redeemer? What was the fate of the generations who lived in the interval? And why should Jesus have had to suffer for the errors of others? Why did the Omnipotent Being not save the world without the sacrifice? Beyond these objections, why did God condone the pain of His creation? Why, even worse, had He ordained it?[2]

These traditional criticisms led to an onslaught on the argument from design, as popularized by Paley. *A View of the Evidences of Christianity*, as a university text and subject of sermons and as intellectual pabulum for Wordsworth, Shelley, Tennyson and Darwin, was one of the major formative influences of the English imagination in the earlier nineteenth century. Paley's use of the natural order to prove the existence of a Heavenly Father, his genial illustrations, his simple argument and basic fatuity, made him the ideal chopping block for the atheists. His work remained the only set Christian text for part III of the National Secular Society's Diploma of Lecturing until the 1890s.[3] The Doctor's complacent assertion that the world and its working existed for the best, if most inscrutable, of reasons offered endless exercise for the artisan who liked to sharpen his logic. G. J. Holyoake, for example, remarked that the same watch that warned the

[1] G. J. Holyoake, in *Movement*, 23 December 1843.
[2] Robert Cooper, in *London Investigator*, November 1854; Charles Watts, *The Christian Scheme of Redemption* (London, n.d.), pp. 9–11.
[3] *National Secular Society's Almanack*, 1884. The other texts were *The Freethinkers' Text-Book*; *Supernatural Religion* and W. K. Clifford's *Lectures and Essays*.

victim when to escape instructed the murderer when to strike, and the fire that warmed the traveller also burnt the martyr. By fastening the Creator to His world Paley also fastened on Him the wanton distribution of pain. Paley's blandness in counting his blessings made the atheists enumerate the evils. 'Why should animals be created in excess; only that the required portion should live in terror, and the excess die in convulsive agony? . . . Why should the shoal fish dread the . . . shark? . . . Why should so many poor men be the helpless prey of destitution? If pain be good for man, then medicine is blasphemy'.[1]

The atheists, armed by Hume, struck at the argument from a First Cause. There could be none, according to Holyoake, for 'all cause is bifold', as part of an observed sequence of antecedent causes and effects. Paley offered no reason why the chain of cause and effect should suddenly stop with a 'creation' and gave no proof that it had done so. But the unexamined assumptions and logical slides in the atheists' own apologetic show how completely they were under the Doctor's spell. The Creator had never demonstrated to men that there *was* a First Cause: had He done so there would be no difficulty about believing it. Paley said that God was both a person and a Power; but if God was a person He could not also be a Power because power was an attribute of matter, and matter was ever impersonal. The believer's claim to know God as Spirit was equally faulty, because spirit was the negation of matter and therefore was unknowable. As an infinite Being God could not be defined as Intelligence, for intelligence was the use of accumulated sense data and was therefore subject to measurable growth. Paley argued that the design of the world proved that God, as the Designer, possessed consciousness; but, Holyoake argued, God, as a supernatural Being, could not share a human attribute that was subject to the natural laws of sleep, sickness and death. Similarly, if God were universal, He could not be Love, for love was a human reaction called forth by external and relative objects.[2] Like the more respectable 'agnostics' later in the century, the atheists were careful never to declare the impossibility of God.

[1] G. J. Holyoake, *The Trial of Theism* (London, 1857), pp. 32-44.
[2] *Ibid.*, pp. 11-13, 44-53. Cf. Southwell in *Oracle of Reason*, 4 December 1841.

They took the view that the onus of proving God's existence lay with those who asserted it and they delighted in eliminating the inferential arguments. Given the fixed, Newtonian universe, they were content to rest in awe: 'Who can conceive the beginning of a universe, or imagine its annihilation?'[1]

It followed that in a newly enlightened, progressive world Paley's claim in defence of the Book of Genesis, that animal and plant species were distinct, static creations, came into question. Chilton, the former labourer and Owenite science lecturer, contributed a remarkable series of papers foreshadowing both Chambers's *Vestiges* and Darwin's views on the transformation of birds under domesticity. He postulated that variation of species was a 'purely natural . . . reaction to environment' and that gulls, if domesticated and trained to eat grain instead of fish 'would present every appearance of having been *designed* by infinite wisdom'. While Sedgwick and Lyell were still referring to 'secondary causes' to link God's will with the formation of land forms and species, Chilton had already plumped for a system of change within a self-acting environment. Still, despite his pleasure in the grandeur of his speculations, Chilton never forgot their immediate purpose, which was to prove the falsity of the Book of Genesis.[2]

The deliquescence of Christian dogma in this century makes it hard to recover that ambience of ideas in which the Scriptures and creeds were looked upon as the inspired, literal words of God. Many churchmen in the early nineteenth century regarded the Scriptures as poetic myth and primitive history, but amongst the Methodists, Baptists, Independents and other scriptural communions, literalism was the core of belief until at least the 1870s. In the same fashion, literalism made the Bible prey to atheists, sleuthing for immoralities and inconsistencies. Thomas Paine provided the technique and some references for beginners, and the subsequent discoveries of Lyell and Strauss helped to fill in the clues. Once he had undergone conversion to atheism the sceptic began an untiring search among the Scriptures and creeds for 'untruths' which would justify his opinions. The cruelties and immoralities

---

[1] Southwell, *Oracle of Reason*, 8 January 1842.
[2] *Oracle of Reason*, 10 December 1842; *Movement*, 6 November 1844, 8 January 1845; *Reasoner*, 3 June 1846.

of the Old Testament, often the same episodes which first aroused his doubts, were used to titillate an audience or to embarrass Christian opponents. Southwell, Bradlaugh and Charles Watts delighted in challenging enemy debaters to read aloud the 'obscene' verses about Lot and his daughters, Solomon and his concubines, or the taking of virgins into slavery. The Book never ceased to shock: confronted with a lull in a debate Bradlaugh could excite an audience to cheers with a sudden reference to concubines or fornication.[1] How could so filthy and disgusting a book, which twice approved slavery and prostitution (Deut. xxi, 11–14; Levit. xxv, 44–6), be a moral guide? The keen student could assemble immoralities and discrepancies for himself.[2] The *Reasoner* and *National Reformer* regularly published lists submitted by readers. 'Search the Scriptures', enjoined the motto on Independent Sunday School Certificates; those who became atheists commonly had their certificate re-framed and hung above the desk at which they read their Bibles.[3] There were also logical gaps to be worked: 'Who was Cain's wife? Why did he build a city when there were only his wife and son to occupy it?' And there was the favourite puzzle in the New Testament: How could the body of Jesus have lain three days in the tomb if Joseph of Arimathea had collected it on the Sabbath, which must have been a Saturday?[4]

The Deluge story, as a problem in practical mechanics, became a major controversy. The lecturer for the Anti-Infidel Society, the Rev. Brewin Grant, B.A., upheld the reality of the Flood and the Ark by quoting the wealth of corroborative detail about Noah's family and the animals. Dr Cumming declared in 1851 that the perfect construction of the Ark would have earned it an Admiralty certificate, thus proving God's inspiration to Noah, for how else in the infancy of the world could he have made a ship to measure up to the

[1] *Is The Bible Divine? A Six Nights' Discussion between Mr Charles Bradlaugh . . . and Mr Robert Roberts of Birmingham (Editor of* The Christadelphian) . . . , (London and Birmingham 1876), pp. 107, 110. *Christianity versus Secularism. Report of a Public Discussion between David King . . . editor of the British Harbinger . . . and Charles Brad-laugh . . . at Bury* (Birmingham, 1870), p. 41.

[2] E.g. I Chron. ii, 22 recorded Jair as having 23 cities in Gilead, but Judges x, 4 said 30; 2 Sam. xxiii, 8 stated that Jashobeam slew 800 men at one time, but I Chron. xi, 11 gave the figure as only 300. *Secular Chronicle*, 1 March 1873.

[3] *Secular Chronicle*, 14 July 1878.

[4] *Reasoner*, 8 February 1857; *Christianity versus Secularism*, Bradlaugh, pp. 50–1.

standards of the nineteenth century? In 1875 Dwight Moody was still marvelling at the way the insect lay down with the elephant. All of which kept the atheists on their mettle: How could Noah have collected the animals? How did he gather the insects? How did he find two duckbilled platypuses when Australia was unknown? How did he gather food for the animals? How did he keep the meat fresh for the carnivores? How did he provide the required temperatures for the lions and polar bears? How did the animals and Noah's family manage to scramble 17,000 feet down Mt Ararat and then disperse themselves to their respective habitats? The platypuses, for example, could not have swum through salt water.[1] The atheists were on to a good thing and they knew it: sternly they deprecated attempts 'to be wise above what is written', by twisting or giving a poetical signification to 'language that could only have had one meaning when originally used'. They welcomed Bishop Colenso as an honest ally, but were suspicious of *Essays and Reviews*.[2]

The other miracles, especially the Resurrection, received the same treatment as the Deluge. Following Hume and Paine, the atheists teased at the divergences between the gospel accounts: Luke wrote that Peter looked into the sepulchre but did not enter, while John described Peter as entering and another disciple with him.[3] Thomas Cooper, W. R. Bradlaugh, Charles' shiftless younger brother and organizer of the Anti-Infidel Society, Dr King and others, tried in debates to make a virtue of necessity by claiming that the discrepancies proved the human frailty and honesty of the evangelists, but it was a comfortless rejoinder before an audience bent upon the perfect truth.[4]

Atheists could always flatter their hearers' common sense. If Christ's miracles, like the multiplication of the loaves and fishes, were performed before so many people, why did so few

---

[1] *Investigator*, 1 July 1858; *Reasoner*, vol. X, No. 13, 1857, p. 242, [undated number], 4 March 1855; *Secular Chronicle*, 14 February 1875; *London Investigator*, November 1856.

[2] 'A London Zulu' [G. J. Holyoake] *The Colenso Controversy: A Reply to Dr Cumming's 'Moses right, Colenso wrong'* (London, 1863). *Secular Chronicle*, 11 February 1877.

[3] Robert Cooper, *The Immortality of the Soul* (London, 1852), pp. 32–3.

[4] Thomas Cooper, *The Verity of Christ's Resurrection From the Dead* (London, 1875), pp. 40–3; W. R. Bradlaugh, *One Hundred Answers to Infidel Objections* (London, 1897).

believe in Him? If God chose to break His natural law He must have known He would do so from the Creation, yet why did He cause needless suffering before He intervened? Why let people be hungry on the shores of Galilee, or allow Lazarus to die so miserably? The whole of modern life proceeded on the assumption that miracles did not happen and that effects regularly followed observed causes. There were no miracles in modern times, why then should it have been different in the past? New wonders in nature were being discovered, but these could be accommodated within the realm of scientific law; whereas, to assign an extraordinary happening positively to Divine Agency predicated knowledge of the full limits of natural law, when this knowledge was incomplete.[1] When Christians replied by pointing to their church as the living miracle and proof of Daniel's and Christ's prophetic power, the atheists asked if tithes and ill-tempered clerical magistrates were among the institutions Christ left behind as proof of His benevolence? Moreover, the Koran and Book of Mormon were not proved true by the fact that Mohammedanism had spread faster than Christianity and that Mormonism was increasing rapidly.[2]

As people whose prayers had seemingly gone unanswered and who now found themselves unable to pray, the atheists were determined to show the inutility of supplication. Emma Martin, the converted former editress of the *Baptist Magazine*, argued that, as God was immutable and had foreordained every part of every life, prayer could not alter events. 'The palsy of effort' which resulted from doctrines accustoming believers to wait upon Providence destroyed their independence and made them 'slaves of the priests'.[3] As Holyoake remarked, orphans were not fed by prayer but by the assurance money bequeathed by thrifty parents. And if God were moved by prayer He must necessarily be deficient in the wisdom of His original creation. Like much else in religion, prayer was a legacy of old fears and propitiatory practices.[4]

[1] *Can Miracles Be Proved Possible?* . . . *Report of two nights' debate between Charles Bradlaugh and W. R. Browne* . . . *of* . . . *the Christian Evidence Society* . . . *in the Leeds Mechanics' Institute* (Leeds, 1876); *Freethinkers' Magazine*, May 1851.
[2] *Can Miracles Be Proved Possible?* Bradlaugh, p. 17.
[3] 'Emma Martin on Prayer', *National Secular Society's Almanack*, 1880, p. 56.
[4] *Reasoner*, 31 August 1853.

This view of prayer as a barter nexus was not a creation of atheist over-simplification. The city missionary of Burslem, during a debate with an atheist in 1853, held his audience spellbound by instancing three cases of the efficacy of prayer. He had prayed when 'tempted in a bad position' and had been relieved; he had prayed when desperately sick and had recovered; and he had once been in want of a situation, when, after praying, he had found one, though 'not as good . . . as that which he had left', which showed that God had reprimanded him for valuing his former employment too lightly.[1]

The Manichean flavour of popular Christianity dwelt more upon the omnipresence of evil supernatural agencies than on that of God and His angels. Children of the artisan and lower middle classes were exposed to threats of Hell and the Devil from their cradles. The endless tortures of heat, cold and thirst, devils with claws and red-hot tongs feature *ad nauseam* in revival sermons and hymns, catechisms, the *Pilgrim's Progress*, and penny tracts. H. G. Wells' mother was noted as unusual for trying to shield her child by pasting stamp-paper over the pictures of the Devil in Sturm's *Reflections*.[2] None the less, Wells, like others who became atheists, was possessed by residual fear and sought to requite the orthodoxy that had caused him so much misery, long after he had convinced himself that hell did not exist. There was comfort in the thought that Christianity was a primitive anachronism. The atheists were indefatigable in tracing primitive survivals in Christian dogma and rites. The discovery of parallels to the Garden of Eden and the Deluge narrative, the anthropological explanations of baptism and communion, the similarities between the life stories of Buddha and Jesus Christ, helped to strengthen the conviction that the Scriptures could not be true because they were not unique: and that their barbaric content made them irrelevant to a progressive, industrial society.[3]

There was also comfort in travellers' tales showing that religious intuitions were not innate in human beings. These proved both that God had been remiss at the Creation, and that unbelievers need not fear damnation or being classed as

[1] T. M. Smith, reported in *Potteries Telegraph*, 13 August 1853, quoted *Reasoner*, 14 September 1853.
[2] H. G. Wells, in *George Whale 1849–1925* (London, 1926), pp. 40–1.
[3] *English Leader*, 12 October 1867.

unnatural for not possessing faith. The religionless natives
were brilliant examples of practical atheism. According to
Robert Cooper, reports agreed that the noble inhabitants of
the Arru Islands had 'no notion of rewards or fears after death,
but live at peace with each other'. Similarly, the 'Bechuanas,
an intelligent tribe, [had] not the slightest idea of immortality'.[1]

The proofs that man had no innate tendency to religion
increased the atheists' difficulty in explaining why men did
believe in supernatural forces. The conspiracy theory,
popular in the bishop-baiting days of Carlile and Wooler,
clearly did not cover devoted Christians and worthy men such
as Dr Livingstone and Mr Bright. By the 1850s the notion
of a gang of cynical priests holding the peasantry in subjection
by the terrors of hell and the spies of the Inquisition had been
superseded (at least for Britain—the concept held good for
Catholic Austria, Italy and Spain) by the anthropomorphic
explanation given in Volney's *Ruins of Empires*. Accounts of
primitive peoples confirmed the view that gods were pro-
jections of human beings, conceived to propitiate natural
forces and strangers. Christians were more to be pitied than
feared.[2]

The acceptance of this more sophisticated explanation
coincided with a gradual acknowledgement that religious
faith might in certain cases be the expression of a natural and
honest inclination. As the tensions of the 1840s lessened at
the end of the decade, 'priestcraft' fell into desuetude, and
Holyoake replaced 'atheism' with 'secularism', to indicate that
the atheists' concerns should lie more with creating an objective
morality than with attacking religion.[3] Secularism did enter
the language as the generic term for atheist activities, but the
secularists remained preoccupied with denying religion. In
1850 Southwell admitted 'the reality of religious instincts' and
incidentally signalled his first step back to Christianity.[4] Still,
to men who trusted fervently in the innate rationality of every
human being, the religious instinct was a puzzle. 'Conrad'
described himself as having a large 'development of the organ

[1] Cooper, *Immortality of the Soul*, p. 74 Charles Watts, *Secularism and Christianity*
(London, 1867), p. 10; *Reasoner*, 3 August 1856.
[2] *Reasoner*, 17 May 1857.
[3] *Reasoner*, 4 August 1852.
[4] Charles Southwell, *Impossibility of Atheism Demonstrated* (London, 1850).

of veneration', yet he had abandoned religion three years before. The organ must relate to some alternative quality: 'Perhaps', he suggested hopefully, 'respect for superior merit?' Another poetical young man who, it appears, had just been crossed in love, concluded that it was impossible to reason with believers, especially female Christians, who were 'hopelessly illogical'.[1] Towards the end of the century, after twenty years of universal elementary education and the rise of psychology, the *Agnostic Annual* ascribed the persistence of belief to that reverence for the supernatural 'imposed by authority and early teaching' and the clothing of this scheme with 'natural human goodness'.[2] But Holyoake, perceptive, humane and immovable as ever in 1905, cut deeper than any when he remarked that, although Christianity was a 'silly business', poor people valued it because they could not conceive of help from any other quarter. This, he added, was what made religion so bad; it justified the rich, taught submission to the poor and diverted them from working for their independence.[3]

The atheists' antipathy to religion and the ever-present threat of prosecution necessarily involved them in politics. The first fetter to be smashed was clerical control of education. The atheists remained thoroughgoing exponents of Owen's educational theories. Firm in their belief that man was born without prejudices and acquired ideas of his environment through his *sensorium*, they envisaged the infinite improvement of the human race if the world were simultaneously improved.[4] The process was cumulative, for, as a creature possessed of memory and foresight, man was a 'reacting force' and as his rationality increased he would in turn work to improve his environment. The major difficulty was to develop the initial impetus and here the atheists had a crucial rôle, for they had the task of beginning the purge of superstition and of opening men's eyes to the truths that accrued from the objective study of nature. Once launched, education and a fearless knowledge of duty would make human progress inevitable. Science showed how cats could be taught to live peaceably with rats,

---

[1] *Reasoner*, vol. IV, no. 90, 1848, p. 167; 'L. H. Holdreth', *Ibid.*, 24 May 1857.
[2] R. Furneaux Jordan, 'The Religious Propensity', *Agnostic Annual*, 1894, pp. 62–4.
[3] G. J. Holyoake, *Bygones Worth Remembering* (2 vols London, 1905), vol. II, p. 226.
[4] Harold Silver, *The Concept of Popular Education* (London, 1965), ch. i.

and men of different temperaments could similarly be educated
to live easily together.[1] The requirement was free, secular,
mass education. The atheists strove to liberalize Graham's
Bill of 1843 and supported W. J. Fox's Bill of 1850. They
were staunch members of the National Public Schools
Association, the Secular Education Association and the
National Education League. They petitioned against the
Cowper-Temple clause in the Act of 1870 and later campaigned
strongly and won seats on local School Boards in London and
the Northern towns.[2] From the 1850s onwards they maintained Sunday schools and improvement classes in competition
with the churches, teaching grammar, chemistry, geology,
astronomy, political economy and, of course, Biblical history.[3]
The classes were hard-working and conducted without con-
descension. There is repeated testimony in the *Reasoner* and
National Reformer that the secular Sunday schools enabled
artisans to become articulate and to formulate their interests
in the rocks and stars. Holyoake's 'Freethinkers' Library'
offered cheap selections from Voltaire, Paine, Milton, Godwin,
Bacon, Southey, Pope and Chaucer; he also, in the *Freethinkers'
Magazine*, serialized chapter XV and the other sections
excluded from Bowdler's *Family Gibbon*, and later paraphrased
and serialized the *Origin of Species*. Another atheist publisher
brought out Hume's *Complete Essays* in penny numbers. The
projected first issue of the *Secular Juvenile Magazine* contained
articles on physiology and reproduction by the celebrated
Dr Drysdale, the 'history and contents of caves', astronomy,
law, and Scandinavian mythology.[4] No effort was too
tedious, no information too esoteric, if the working classes
were to comprehend their environment and liberate themselves.

It is significant that Southwell, Chilton and Holyoake
rebelled against Owen just when the Queenwood community
was beginning. They realized that the capital requirements
of Harmony Hall were overriding its equalitarian purpose.
Labouring men paying 1*s.* a week could never become full

---

[1] *Report of a public discussion between the Rev. Brewin Grant . . . and George Jacob
Holyoake* . . . (Glasgow, 1853), pp. 104–6; Southwell, *Investigator*, no. 5, 1843.

[2] W. F. Connell, *The Educational Thought and Influence of Matthew Arnold* (London,
1950), pp. 48, 56; *Secularism versus Christianity. Report of discussion between Dr
Sexton and F. W. Foote,* . . . (London, 1877), pp. 17–18.

[3] *Reasoner*, 24 March 1852.

[4] *Reasoner*, 6 May 1860; *Secular Chronicle*, 10 March 1878.

P

members of the Home Colonization Society and would always remain at hire. After the break came, the atheists discerned Owen as a paternalist. He preached unity and liberty, but he took for granted 'passive obedience' and admitted that he had no faith in the 'directing' powers of the working class.[1] But the atheists' opposition did not mean they favoured 'levelling down', particularly when it involved the intervention of the state. Equality was 'prospective'—to be achieved by levelling up—and the immediately practicable work was to liberalize the conditions under which individuals could better themselves, materially and morally. The economy had to be freed of undue regulation and protection and the working classes disabused of their reliance on providence.[2] Like many of their contemporaries, the atheists ultimately hoped for the withering away of the state. As they knew from unhappy personal experience, the state was the embodiment of traditional authority and the ally of religion. Its corn laws, oaths requirements, blasphemy laws and newspaper taxes showed that it never intervened but to curtail liberty on behalf of reactionary interests. So far as industrial questions were concerned, the only fruitful rôle for government was to equalize the respective bargaining strengths of capital and labour by withdrawing the protection given to capital through the Master and Servant Law.[3]

Capitalism itself was not evil: the increase of liberty coincident with its growth in the nineteenth century testified to that. 'I have no antipathy to rich men,' Holyoake wrote, 'I wish we were all rich.'[4] Property, except in land, was the reward of enterprise and created employment and general prosperity. Extremists who demanded that it be redistributed were therefore foolish: moreover, the redistribution could only be carried out by force, and so would augment the coercive power of the state. The burden of taxation had to be re-arranged to allow the rewards for work to remain more equitably with their begetters, but even this intervention could go too far: in 1896

---

[1] *Movement*, 13 April 1844; G. J. Holyoake, *A Visit to Harmony Hall!* (London, 1844).

[2] G. J. Holyoake, *Rationalism* (London, 1845), p. 36; A. C. Cuddon, in *Reasoner*, 2 November 1856.

[3] [Charles Southwell], 'An Apology for Atheism', *Reasoner*, 24 June 1846; Charles Bradlaugh, *Some Objections To Socialism* (London, 1884), p. 103.

[4] Holyoake, *Rationalism*, p. 36.

the National Secular Society opposed the introduction of Old Age Pensions.[1] Bradlaugh had earlier specifically rejected the theory of surplus value as the cause of low wages. These, in his view, reflected poor rates of output and the small margins on hand-produced goods. There was no remedy in destroying capitalism, for capital made materials, machinery and markets available to workers.[2] The atheists worked to correct the excesses in competition, not to abolish the process itself. As Southwell remarked: 'It never ought and never could be eradicated.' Competition lay at the root of earnestness and improvement, and the way to improvement, Holyoake, Southwell, and Bradlaugh insisted, lay through self-help—the phrase which Holyoake proudly claimed to have invented two years before Samuel Smiles popularized it.[3] The co-operative movement, with its emphasis on independent household economy and education, and its fundamental ambiguity about the profit motive, was the typical product of secularist principles. Holyoake is remembered as one of its most devoted advocates.

The agency of improvement that by-passed the difficulties of state intervention and taught self-discipline was Malthusianism. The atheists became its most courageous publicists. Their adoption of the cause rendered them liable to prosecution, and defenceless before the indecent abuse of Christians. The sale under atheist auspices of birth-control literature and contraceptive devices killed any faint chance the mission had of becoming popular. Hypocrisy bred hatred. At a time when the use of contraceptives was spreading rapidly, spokesmen of the middle classes declared themselves aghast at the atheists' shamelessness and working men delighted in ribald interjections at meetings. Some apostles faltered and wanted to renounce the publicity, but the majority stood firm: no other agitation illustrates so well their pertinacity and heroism. Emma Martin pioneered lectures to women on 'physiological subjects', Holyoake advertised and sold contraceptive appliances in his shop and later Bradlaugh and Annie Besant were vilified and Edward Truelove was gaoled for their defence

---

[1] *Secular Work*, October 1896.
[2] Bradlaugh, *Some Objections to Socialism*, p. 110.
[3] Southwell, *Movement*, 25 September 1844; Holyoake, *Reasoner*, 17 May 1857. Carlyle had published the term in *Sartor Resartus* in 1834.

of the liberty to spread information about family limitation.[1]

The apostles' Malthusian campaign was intended both to relieve the distress of working-class families, and to liberate the lower classes from acquiescence in the hardships sent by providence. Control of procreation was the most intimate and telling way of inculcating in the lower classes the belief that power over life itself lay in science and material forces. Contraception offered, too, the best long-term chance of mitigating competition: it was the key to effective adjustment of the economy and social relations. In Bradlaugh's view, there could be 'no permanent civil and religious liberty, no permanent and enduring equality amongst men and women, no permanent and enduring fraternity, until the subject on which Malthus wrote . . . is thoroughly examined, and until the working men make that of which he was so able an exponent, the science of their everyday life'.[2]

The atheists' repudiation of Divine sanctions for the social hierarchy sometimes led them to socialism. Herbert Burrows, John Burns, and Annie Besant came to the S.D.F. and the Fabian Society through the National Secular Society. But, as the subsequent careers of all three illustrate, the old faith in self-help and competition ran deep. Atheism, far from opening the floodgates to socialism, reinforced the working classes' fears of state and municipal control. The mission helped perpetuate Gladstonian liberalism among radical working class groups and so played a part in transmitting those humane, puritan values which still distinguish modern British left wing parties.

The revolutionary import of their programme could have made the apostles into political firebrands, but like their spiritual ancestors in the Enlightenment, they show a marked contrast between their aims and their behaviour. They were determined to prove that reason bred composure: violence, on the other hand, was a product of religious fanaticism. Southwell and Holyoake were outspoken 'moral force' men in the Chartist period; they always damped the occasional threats of violence among their followers. Holyoake and Bradlaugh

[1] Hypatia Bradlaugh Bonner and J. M. Robertson, *Charles Bradlaugh* . . . (2 vols London, 1895), vol. II, pp. 12–29; F. Amphlett Micklewright, 'Neo-Malthusianism', *Population Studies*, vol. XV, 1961–2.
[2] *National Reformer*, 14 June 1862.

were leading advocates of proportional representation in the parliamentary reform movements of the 1860s, and courageous anti-Jingoes in the 1870s and 1880s (Holyoake invented the pejorative usage of the word).[1] Their most notorious political aim was the ending of the monarchy and hereditary aristocracy and the introduction of a republic. The mission continued to preach that militant republicanism current during the Regency long after other radicals had given up before the irreproachable domesticity of the Royal Family. The old attacks on the Hanoverians' immorality and avarice were endlessly rehearsed, while the charge that the Crown interfered too much in politics was, during the 1850s, altered to the claim that the monarchy had become a useless constitutional anachronism. As the embodiment of past theological and hierarchical traditions and the prop of the aristocracy, the monarchy also nourished that superstitious deference which prevented the lower classes from aspiring to independence.[2] Abolish the monarchy and secular virtue and brotherhood would reign: 'That true liberty, which infringes not the freedom of my brother; that equality which recognizes no noblemen but the men of noble thoughts and noble deeds; that fraternity which links the weak arm-in-arm with the strong, and, teaching human-kind that union is strength, compels them to fraternize and links them in . . . true brotherhood.'[3] Nevertheless, the path to the republic lay through Parliament and the constitution. Parliament had put the Brunswicks on the throne and it had the power to ensure, upon the death of the Queen, that she was not succeeded. The abolition of primogeniture and state pensions, together with the transformation of the House of Lords into an elective body, would be sufficient to break the grip of the aristocracy; and this too could be achieved through legislation by a reformed House of Commons. Although the atheists were staunch supporters of Continental republican movements, and reluctantly agreed that assassinations and bombs might be necessary against

---

[1] Bradlaugh Bonner and Robertson, *Charles Bradlaugh*, vol. II, pp. 82–5; Joseph McCabe, *Life and Letters of George Jacob Holyoake* (2 vols London, 1908), vol. II, p. 281.
[2] Austin Holyoake, *Would a Republican Form of Government be suitable for England?* (1873), pp. 2–3.
[3] Bradlaugh, in *London Investigator*, 1 November 1858, quoted in Crane Brinton, *English Political Thought in the Nineteenth Century* (New York, 1962), p. 245.

Tsarist police and Neapolitan spies, they firmly believed that such methods were wrong in Britain. Confident that British voters were rational, they never lost faith that Parliament could be used to further progress.[1]

The apostles' involvement in politics remained a diversion rather than a central concern. Politics too often tarnished principles by compromise. A setback or squabble in their chosen agitation was often sufficient to plunge them back into their Bethels without God. J. C. Farns, successively an Owenite, atheist lecturer and trade union official, became disillusioned with strikes after a severe defeat for his union in 1857. He re-dedicated himself to atheist proselytism, explaining that unions wasted their means upon useless contests while the mission brought real mental independence to the workers. Similarly, Henry Tyrrell decided that the parliamentary reform movement of the late 1850s was too weak to educate the workers to their duties, and returned to the 'living cause' of atheism. Both rationalized their desertion by arguing that there were plenty of others to carry on the political fight, whilst the battle against religion was understaffed and more important. The cases of the United States after the War of Independence and France after 1848 showed how newly won 'freedom in each was strangled by peasants led by priests'.[2] Some purists even regarded participation in agitation to amend the oaths laws as compromising the essentially educational rôle of the mission. Southwell refused to become an active Chartist because the movement was led by Irish papists and Wesleyan preachers and remained well-disposed to Christianity, and later in the century G. W. Foote and Charles Watts refused to join radical or socialist agitations, ostensibly because they were neutral to religion.[3]

This temptation to withdrawal was inevitable in a movement based on such esoteric standards. Intent upon their personal quest for certainty, atheists often looked beyond their unregenerate fellows. By sad irony, that moral austerity and

---

[1] Charles Bradlaugh, *The Impeachment of The House of Brunswick* (London, 1881), pp. 3–4.
[2] *Reasoner*, 30 September, 2 December 1857; *London Investigator*, March 1855; *Investigator*, 15 June 1858.
[3] *Reasoner*, 19 December 1849; *Secular Work*, June 1896; *Investigator*, No. 6, 1843 [undated]; *Reasoner*, 5 June 1850; *Secular Work*, May 1896.

'honourable perseverance' in saving a competence which the atheists strove to implant in their lower class fellows were precisely the things which kept them apart. The masses' want of earnestness was linked with their lack of Christian knowledge. Atheism, with its experiential morality and its panoply of Biblical exegesis, depended upon a prior Christian allegiance and this the poor did not have. What they did have, Mayhew, Dickens and the Scripture readers reported, was a crude awe of future punishment and a vague idea of a Jesus who was kind to poor folk. These notions, at least among the men, seem to have co-existed with a neglect of religion that amounted to contempt. Working men flocked to debates and cheered at the merest hint of a salacious Bible story, or an account of orgies in a convent; but they drooped whenever the atheist champion expatiated on Biblical etymology or 'practical atheism'. Their poverty and shiftlessness made them unrewarding supporters. They did not join the atheist societies and they apparently spent their pennies on more lurid prints than the *Reasoner*.[1]

The missionaries never bridged the gap between their respectability and the brutishness of the men they were trying to save. One wing, represented by Southwell, Thomas Paterson, Robert Cooper, G. W. Foote and Joseph Symes, sought to meet the working men half-way with crude onslaughts on the 'Jew Book' and nasty asides about the Immaculate Conception. The other wing, containing Holyoake, Bradlaugh and Mrs Besant, sought to impress the masses by their high tone and punctilious politeness. But Southwell and his successors were right about the popular temper. Under his editorship the *Oracle of Reason* sold 4,000 copies, reaching its highest circulation in the week he published his grotesque article on 'The Jew Book'. When the paper became more refined under Holyoake and Chilton, its circulation fell to 900.[2] Thereafter, the *Investigator*, Holyoake's *Movement*, and the earlier volumes of his *Reasoner*, all of which were sedate, never sold more than 1,500 copies. This was a tremendous decline

---

[1] *Daily News*, 2 November 1847; *Theological Review*, 1 May 1865, quoted *National Reformer*, 14 May 1865; *English Leader*, 22 December 1866; 'The Religious Heresies of the Working Classes', *Westminster Review*, January 1862, p. 68; R. K. Webb, *English Working Class Reader 1790–1848*, (London, 1955), pp. 111–22.

[2] *Reasoner*, 13 August 1846; *National Secular Society's Almanack*, 1881, p. 26.

from the 15,000 circulation which twenty years earlier Carlile had achieved for his *Republican*, and the estimated 16,000 circulation of Hetherington's *Poor Man's Guardian* in 1833.[1] Through the 1850s sales of the *Reasoner* rose from 3,000 in 1852 to about 5,000 at the end of the decade, but at no time did it pay its way. In 1853 the mission could only secure 4,000 signatures to its petitions to amend the Evidence Acts.[2]

Had Southwell, Paterson, Matilda Roalfe and others not been subdued by their harsh sentences for blasphemy (Southwell served 13 months and was fined £100) the mission would doubtless have held more of the old anti-episcopal, priest-baiting audience, and had greater impact among the lower classes. But even Southwell's and Cooper's *London Investigator*, which sugared its atheism with 'tales of the Inquisition', sold only 2,000 copies.[3] In positing the simple irrelevance of super-naturalism to the everyday getting, spending and enjoying of the English lower classes, the atheists spoke truer than they knew; for their high-flown sermons on atheist duty proved equally remote. The mission never captured more than a tiny minority of the 5,000,000 'unconscious secularists' who stayed away from public worship on census Sunday in 1851. Their well-written, earnest little papers were lost among the flood of 'vicious infidel' publications which were alleged to have sold 10,000,000 copies in Great Britain in that year.[4] Holyoake liked to believe that his message was received by that increasing class of artisans, 'who, in the awakening conscious-ness of their own intelligence [were] disposed to deny the authority of tradition'. But in 1847, when replying to a charge that he catered for the 'lowest infidels', Holyoake half-proudly admitted that 'more than a third of the *Reasoner's* supporters [were] of the middle and educated classes'.[5]

After the foundation of the National Secular Society in 1862 Holyoake and Bradlaugh briefly combined their activities. The circulation of the *National Reformer* rose to 8,000 and the

[1] William H. Wickwar, *The Struggle for The Freedom of the Press, 1819–1832* (London, 1928), p. 94; Webb, *Working-Class Reader*, p. 61.

[2] *Reasoner*, 23 June 1852; 30 November 1853; 1 July 1857; Charles Watts, *Freethinkers' Text-Book*, Part III (London, 1876), p. 753.

[3] *London Investigator*, November 1857.

[4] *Reasoner*, 9 April 1854; *Annual Report* of Religious Tract Society, quoted in *Freethinkers' Magazine and Review*, 1851.

[5] *Reasoner*, No. 76, 1847 [undated], p. 61.

small groups of secularists in London and the northern towns expanded their meetings.[1] But the movement still grew very slowly: in 1876, before the split occasioned by Bradlaugh's and Mrs Besant's stand on the Knowlton pamphlet, the N.S.S. had under 2,000 members, of whom a clear majority were in the North. London had 96 members in 1875, while 140 attended a N.S.S. Secular Tea in Huddersfield.[2] Particularly after the split, both the N.S.S. and the rival Foote-Watts faction claimed that ten times the number of enrolled atheists remained outside the movement for fear of public hostility, but this probably is exaggeration. A strong campaign by the N.S.S. in 1879 secured only 4,800 signatures for the repeal of the blasphemy laws.[3] In 1880 the list of branches and activities shows a sharp increase, as radicals became involved with Bradlaugh's parliamentary battle, but by 1884 the impetus seems to have died.[4] After 1885 the movement fragmented further into the Bradlaugh, Foote and Holyoake factions, the Malthusians, and the various cliques of socialists. Upon Bradlaugh's final illness and death in 1891 the mission became virtually quiescent until its revival with the pro-Boer and schools agitations at the turn of the century.

The removal, by death and senility, of the old, implacable, working-class leadership persuaded agnostics of the educated class to join the movement and assume its direction. The formation of the Rationalist Press Association in 1899, with Adam Gowans Whyte and Charles Hooper among its founders and Leslie Stephen among its 'Honorary Associates', signalled the emergence of a new style of austere educational work and academic debate that distinguished the movement in the twentieth century.[5]

The factious history of the atheists highlights one paradoxical weakness in their situation, for they lacked that stimulating social turmoil and pervasive clerical interference in affairs

---

[1] *National Reformer*, 4 January 1862; Bradlaugh Bonner and Robertson, *Charles Bradlaugh*, vol. I, p. 128.

[2] *Christianity versus Secularism . . . Foote versus Sexton*, Sexton, p. 22; *Secular Review*, 30 November 1878; *Secular Chronicle*, 21 February 1875.

[3] *Christianity versus Secularism . . . Foote versus Sexton*, Foote, p. 261; *National Secular Society's Almanack*, 1879, p. 15.

[4] *National Reformer*, 23 November 1884.

[5] A. Gowans Whyte, *The Story of the R.P.A. 1899–1949* (London, 1949), pp. 24–50.

which united their colleagues on the Continent and commended them to their audiences. The apostles had hopes
of Church rates as a source of disaffection, but they failed to
make them a popular issue, probably because so many working
people evaded payment.[1] The atheist journals diligently
reported cases of clergymen tried for theft or indecent assault,
and publicized cruel judgments by clerical magistrates (Holyoake did notable service when he was instrumental in securing
the release of Pooley, the lunatic convicted of blasphemy in
deepest Cornwall in 1857), but, perhaps because Anglican
priests were 'gentlemen' and benignly distant with their
parishioners, the apostles never succeeded in developing that
virulent anti-clericalism which flourished in countries with a
peasant priesthood. Moreover, disaffected persons could
always shift into militant dissent and thereby have their faith
refreshed. The pattern of Sunday marketing and drinking
and the Sunday Trading Riots showed that the English working classes had never conformed to the Sabbath taboos, but
the atheists' own puritanism inhibited them from exploiting
the situation. Subsequent to the Sunday Trading Riots a
National Sunday League was established, with the purpose of
providing music in the parks on Sabbath evenings and securing
the opening of national museums and art galleries. The
committee was headed by radical M.P.s and the atheists did
the work of selling programmes, marshalling the crowds and
organizing petitions. In this manner music was provided in
the major London parks, and in Manchester, Sheffield, Halifax,
Northampton, Rochdale and other industrial towns. There
were enormous numbers of people ready to eschew the gloom
of the Sabbath: on a sunny day an estimated 150,000 people
attended the concerts in Regent's Park. Still, the managing
committees refused to break with the ritual aspect of the day.
The music was almost entirely 'serious', usually oratorios by
Handel and Haydn. Dancing was forbidden and smoking
discouraged, because 'a smoking crowd' was apt to be mistaken
for a 'public-house' crowd.[2] The audiences became famous
for their respectability and it is not surprising that by the

[1] *Movement*, 16 December 1843; *Propagandist*, 4 October 1862; Holyoake, *Bygones
Worth Remembering*, vol. II, p. 197.
[2] *Reasoner*, 15 June, 10 August, 5 October 1856.

mid 1860s, long after the working classes had returned to their old enjoyments, the committees should have become lethargic and the attendances fallen off. The committee members sadly agreed that concerts did not make converts.[1] A desultory agitation for the opening of the British Museum and National Gallery was kept up through the next generation, but it was not until 1896, when the N.S.S. had virtually suspended work, that these institutions quietly opened on the Sabbath.[2]

The mission did not fail for want of diligence. Holyoake, in addition to delivering about three lectures a week over a period of sixty years, wrote about 5,000 words a week and single-handedly published at least one weekly during most of that period. Bradlaugh, in a typical year, gave 171 lectures and Charles Watts, 200.[3] All travelled hundreds of miles every year, often speaking twice a day, staying at cheap hotels or the dreary cottages of supporters. Unremitting preachers and journalists as they were, the missionaries died poorer than they would have done if they had devoted their talents to conventional occupations. And even at its best in the early 1880s the mission never had more than about six full-time lecturers. Perhaps the real achievement is to have reached as many as they did. Yet their effort was minute beside the enormous reserves of manpower, money and official approval which sustained the great Christian revivals and building campaigns of the century.

For the chosen few the atheists provided exhortation, ritual and fellowship. On Sabbath mornings at the 'Halls of Science' there were sermons, science lectures and hymns, and in the evenings, sermons, teas and musical items. Occasionally beribboned groups of atheist families set off on picnics to Epping Forest, or the moors, in omnibuses festooned with leaves, and Tom Paine's and Bradlaugh's names stitched in banners. The party sang freethought hymns as they jogged through the streets:

> Take the spade of perseverance;
> Dig the fields of progress wide;

[1] *National Reformer*, 21 May 1865.
[2] *Secular Work*, June 1896.
[3] *National Secular Society's Almanack*, 1872, p. 23 [1870].

Every rotten root of faction
Hurry out and cast aside.

Every stubborn root of error
Every weed that hurts the soil
Tares, whose every growth is terror
Dig them out, what 'er the toil!

Give the stream of education
Broader channel, bolder force;
Hurl the stones of persecution
Out, where'er they block its course.[1]

Sometimes the trips received a deliciously exciting send off
when the city missionary ran alongside pelting the vans with
tracts: 'My friends and countrymen, consider your ways . . .
allow me kindly but faithfully, to remind you that in breaking
the Sabbath *you openly insult God.* . . . But that's not all—*you
corrupt the neighbourhood in which you live!* . . .'.[2] At their rendez-
vous, before they dispersed, they heard lectures on the botany
and geology of the area, and upon gathering for supper, they
began discussions on the Bible and land reform which lasted
until the vans drew up to carry them home.

But, despite the hymns and shared emancipation, the mission
never developed that network of class meetings and lecture
circuits which so many of its ex-Wesleyan converts hoped to
build. The atheists talked much of 'fellowship', but often
concluded by lamenting its absence in the movement.
Embittered, proud souls that they were, they vied with each
other in projecting their 'independence', and never hesitated
to defy their leaders in the local groups and the N.S.S. That
'sober coolness' which the mission approved in its adherents
was reflected in their meagre contribution to its upkeep. Most
of them had little to spare, but the patchy filling of subscription
lists bears out Holyoake's plaint that atheists were mean as
compared with chapel-folk.[3] But for the self-sacrifice of the
lecturers and the small subventions from a handful of wealthy
eccentrics, notably Arthur Trevelyan, W. J. Birch and W. D.
Saull, the mission would have disappeared.

The atheist rank-and-file were remarkably consistent in their

---

[1] *National Reformer*, 26 August 1886; *English Leader*, 27 July 1867; Annie Besant,
ed., *The Secular Song and Hymn Book*, second ed. no. xxvii, by C. Swain.

[2] *Reasoner*, 29 June 1856.

[3] *Reasoner*, 23 June 1852.

social origins and pattern of conversion. Commonly they were sons of pious artisan fathers, from whom they early became estranged. Nearly all were precocious readers, 'athirst for knowledge'. They read obsessively and often defied parental authority in doing so. All reported themselves to have been deeply devotional in their Methodist, evangelical Anglican or Baptist faiths, and many, at an age younger than that of their fellows, became leaders in their Sabbath schools. Frequently they aspired to become lay preachers but found their way blocked by their poverty and the exclusiveness of their chapel leaders. Almost uniformly they confess that their thoughts were oppressed by fear of sin and terror of hell. Joseph Symes, for one, identified Satan with his father. Another recalled that he cried himself to sleep every Sunday, in horror that he and his classmates were damned in the fires their teacher had depicted to them.[1] Fear accumulated during adolescence and led them to doubt their own salvation, to brood upon the evils of the world, and thence to question the benevolence of the Creator. Once doubt began, the immoralities and errors of the Bible became of consuming interest as they heightened the discovery of God's imperfection. During this anxious period, which often continued two or three years, they began to study atheist and radical propaganda and to frequent radical meetings. Then, sometimes immediately after a brush with the preacher to whom they had revealed their doubts, they underwent a conversion, similar, many reported, to that sense of grace they had striven to experience in their chapels. 'With conversion came unspeakable... relief' and 'tears of joy at being released from sectarian prejudice and fears of torment'.[2] The renegade refused to attend chapel or family prayers, often broke with his family and, if he were old enough or out of his apprenticeship, removed to another town. This migration, as it must have done for thousands of 'unconscious secularists', completed his release from the tutelege of his parents, the local preacher and chapel committee, and the Scripture readers. In his new environment he felt free to join in atheist activities, his intelligence and trade skill enabled him to prosper, and

---

[1] *Liberator* (Melbourne) 1 June 1884; William Wadman, *Reasoner*, 12 October 1856; B. Scarth, *National Reformer*, 3 September 1865.
[2] 'S.R.H.', *Reasoner*, vol. XIII, no. 7, p. 108.

he became an independent, hard-reading head of a family, in some cases allowing his 'strong power of Reason . . . [to lead] him to undervalue those who had only feeling to give in place of evidence'.[1] His abilities found expression in public speaking, leadership of local temperance movements, Mechanics' Institutes, and reform agitations. He arranged visits by atheist missionaries and his literary bent found outlet in anti-theological essays and hymns. Like John Horner, a porter of Wakefield, he was 'always hammering away at theology, and never so happy as when puzzling the pious with metaphysical abstraction'.[2] Others spent Sundays when there was no atheist meeting in sampling Christian services; if opportunity arose, they challenged the preacher on the difficulties in his sermon text. In a typical foray Joseph Firth, of Keighley, went to a Wesleyan revival meeting in his town. The exhortation, testimony and singing continued for three hours, during which time Firth remained standing in the middle of the chapel. The preacher led the congregation in prayer for 'Joe Firth the infidel', and then demanded of him if he believed. Midst the hushed congregation, Firth roared back that he 'believed in love and truth and everything that was founded on reason'.[3]

Their truculence became even more harsh on their death beds. The atheist had dared to redefine his 'soul' as an 'aspiration to duty'; and in place of immortality and the resurrection of the body he looked to an endless sleep, and the bequest of enlightened children. His last judgement, according to Holyoake's *Logic of Death*, came as he looked back upon his efforts to seek the truth and diminish superstition. He had no need to fear Hell and, as an honest man, there was the comfort that he would be received into heaven if it existed. Parties of secular friends watched at the bedside, reading from the *Logic of Death* (it sold 7,000 copies within two years of publication and was reprinted till the end of the century), and ensuring that the local clergy were repulsed.[4] Towards the end they got their pens ready, in the hope that the last message would

[1] G. J. Holyoake, *Secular Prospects in Death* [obituary of Josiah Gimson] (London, 1883), p. 15.
[2] *National Reformer*, 13 January 1863.
[3] *Reasoner*, 2 June 1852.
[4] G. J. Holyoake, *The Logic of Death* (London, 1850); *Freethinkers' Magazine*, 1851, p. 27; *National Reformer*, 5 May 1867.

be the usual one, as it was with Joseph Hirst: 'Tell Huddersfield I died a Secularist.' There was need to protect the dying from the clergy. One Wesleyan parson broke into the cottage of a dying atheist in Rochdale, struggled past the man's wife to the bedside, 'for he [had] come *purposely* to *disturb* him, for he had better be disturbed now than damned hereafter'. Upon the man's death the town was convulsed for weeks with argument as to whether the deceased had been re-converted to Christianity. Another man suffered whole days of exhortation from relays of Scripture readers, and had his bed covered with tracts on the deaths of infidels. His wife pleaded with them to desist, as 'Mr Jackson was too feeble to receive any more theological visits'.[1] The tracts were commonly headed with pictures of coffins licked by flames and engravings of beaky devils with forks hovering about the atheist's death-bed. Tom Paine's terrors of Hell and his last minute repentance were still being recounted in the 1880s. Thousands of narratives of Thomas Paterson's and Emma Martin's death-bed fears and conversions were distributed while they were still alive. The story of the boy struck blind in Brighton while playing tip-cat on the Sabbath featured in the daily and religious press for weeks, long after it had been proved false.[2]

Occasionally the apostles found their spiritual isolation too great to bear, and a succession of them, notably Joseph Barker, Thomas Cooper, J. B. Bebbington, Dr Sexton, Towneley and J. H. Gordon, publicly recanted and threw themselves into lecturing on Christian evidences and writing for the *British Banner* and the *Liberator*. Joseph Symes, the former Wesleyan parson, often concluded his atheist sermons by defying God to send him a sign, that he might again have faith. Even Southwell came to believe that the world could only progress under the governance of God and that the Bible *was* a moral book; he ended his career editing a newspaper under Wesleyan auspices in New Zealand.[3]

[1] John Ashworth, *Sanderson and Little Alice* (Rochdale, 1865); *Reasoner*, 6 August 1854.
[2] *A Roman Catholic Canard* (New York, 1884); *Reasoner*, 8 July 1846; *National Reformer*, 8 March 1862; *English Leader*, 19 May 1866.
[3] *Reasoner*, 7 July 1852 [Henry Knight's recantation], 28 July 1852 [Towneley], 31 December 1876 [Southwell]; *National Reformer*, 22 August 1863 [Bebbington]; *Secular Chronicle*, 31 December 1876 [J. H. Gordon]; *Liberator* (Melbourne) 22 November 1885 [Symes].

There might have been more recantations if persecution of atheists had been less common. Vicars ordered their flocks to boycott booksellers who stocked atheist publications, with the result that booksellers often hawked their pamphlets in the streets and at the railway stations and probably found a wider market. Sunday school teachers warned their pupils not to associate with the children of atheists. In 1850 the proctors banned the *Reasoner* and *Logic of Death* in Oxford and thereby lifted sales. Printers lost their Christian customers if they were discovered accepting atheist jobs; Southwell's *Lancashire Banner* ceased publication after the Wesleyans learned of his printer and duly threatened him.[1] Until they secured their own halls in the provinces in the late 1860s the apostles frequently were locked out by trustees and sometimes were subjected to violence. A visit from a vicar or Wesleyan parson was sufficient to persuade trustees to refuse their hall, even after it had been booked and the meeting advertised, as happened in Bury, Derby and Finsbury. Towns with Irish populations were especially dangerous. In Whitehaven, where the local Methodists egged on the Irish miners, the hall was wrecked and Holyoake barely escaped alive. Matilda Roalfe was stoned in the street in Edinburgh; the cottage in Northampton in which John Watts stayed was smashed after his lecture. Bradlaugh's meeting at Wigan was brutally broken up, this time at the instigation of the vicar.[2]

Rarely, though notoriously enough to give men pause, an artisan who showed his unbelief was dismissed by his employer. Two engine makers of Middlesbrough were sacked by their Quaker masters after they had been seen applauding a lecture by Holyoake. Another unbeliever, a locomotive driver for the Great Western Railway, was dismissed for forwarding to the *Reasoner* a report of an unusually stupid sermon by a vicar in Swindon. The vicar wrote under a pseudonym to Holyoake for the name of his correspondent: Holyoake supplied it, whereupon the clergyman and a director of the railway, who was also a churchwarden, waited upon the manager and saw

---

[1] *Reasoner*, 23 January, 25 June, 10 July 1850; 7 September 1853.

[2] *Movement*, 23 December 1843; *Utilitarian Record*, 10 February 1847; *Reasoner*, 10 September 1851, 22 June 1853, 9 March 1856; G. J. Holyoake, *Thomas Cooper Delineated* . . . [1856], p. 3; Bradlaugh Bonner and Robertson, *Charles Bradlaugh*, vol. I, pp. 158–93.

to it that the driver received two hours' notice. The ex-driver set up as an itinerant vendor of atheist prints.[1]

The unbelievers were also tried by their refusal to swear oaths. Men who had property stolen were unable to begin proceedings for its recovery. Holyoake was prevented by his scruples from swearing a writ against the cabby who drunkenly ran over and mortally injured his son. Not surprisingly, Bradlaugh's offer to take the parliamentary oath in 1880 caused as much distress in the atheist camp as it did among Christians.[2] Although none of the ameliorative Acts (Common Law Procedure Act and its subsequent extensions, which permitted witnesses in civil cases to affirm, the Juror Affirmation Acts of the mid-1860s, and the Evidence Further Amendment Act of 1869, which allowed affirmation in the lower courts) arose directly from atheist pressure, all included clauses to remedy a situation made notorious by the unflinching demeanour of atheists in the courts.[3] Each was an important step in breaking ancient ties between state authority and religion and in forwarding the view that citizenship was independent of religious forms. Bradlaugh's more famous victory only served to confirm the process.

Reform of oaths required simple innovations in procedure, but the blasphemy laws involved questions of taste, and the atheists had little success in sapping them. Local magistrates were shorn of their jurisdiction in such cases as a result of Holyoake's harsh prosecution and imprisonment in Cheltenham in 1842, but the laws remained and judges continued to inflict savage sentences. The worst bouts occurred during the desperate 1840s and 1880s, but throughout the period each missionary in turn, and several booksellers and local advocates suffered prosecution by informers, fines and imprisonment. Each suffered legal costs he could hardly afford, loss of income from lecturing and publishing, and, worst of all, the debility that resulted from imprisonment. Southwell, after thirteen months in Bristol gaol, emerged sick and with 5s. Holyoake was virtually penniless before he even went to gaol; his daughter died of malnutrition while he was there. Thomas

---

[1] *Reasoner*, 8 December 1852, 7 December 1853.
[2] *Movement*, 23 March 1844; *Reasoner*, 31 May, 2 September 1857; Holyoake, *Bygones Worth Remembering*, vol. I, pp. 28–32.
[3] *Ibid.*, vol. II, pp. 209–10.

Paterson's imprisonment cost him his bookselling business and caused him to emigrate. Bradlaugh's legal battles drained his energy and money. Some, like Southwell, Paterson and Annie Besant, welcomed martyrdom, but it almost broke Holyoake and it shortened Bradlaugh's life.

The uncertain tone that enters the apostles' utterances during the 1870s makes their sufferings all the more poignant. In increasing numbers they confess that their faith in inevitable progress and the rationality of man was shaken by the Franco-Prussian War, the spread of jingoism, and Darwin's demonstration of man's continuity with the brute creation. Far from liberating them from Paley and the argument from design, Darwin trapped them in a hateful system of blind, inexorable pain.[1] Some, like Watts, Symes and Bradlaugh himself, became deeply anxious at the resurgence of violence; Symes, especially, during his recurrent states of depression, doubted whether it was right to hasten the decay of religious obligation while 'democratic discipline', that is, self-help among the masses and respect for other classes, remained so weak.[2] They consoled themselves with the reminder that man was 'a progressive being', but increasingly they admitted that liberty was 'not the offshoot of a day'.[3]

The foundations of their anti-theological position had also crumbled. The churchmens' concessions on eternal torment, Biblical inspiration, the immanence of Providence and the reality of miracles, left the atheists with no real dogmas to fight, at least in British Protestantism. The last generation of the nineteenth century, midst the economic and political stresses of their age, inattentively witnessed the abandonment of doctrines and taboos that had ruled the British imagination through nearly two millennia. Consumed in the revolution of which they were the harbingers, the atheists' onslaughts on the Pentateuch became irrelevant; none the less, stalwarts such as Hypatia Bradlaugh Bonner and Charles Albert Watts continued to chip at the fallen bastions until well into the twentieth century. But the younger people in the movement, especially after the accession of Joseph McCabe, concentrated

[1] *National Reformer*, 18 January 1862; *Secular Chronicle*, 24 March 1878; Charles Cockbill Cattell, *Is Darwinism Atheistic?* (London, 1889).
[2] *Liberator*, (Melbourne) 19 October 1889; Bradlaugh, *Some Objections To Socialism*.
[3] Charles Watts, *Freethought and Modern Progress* (new edition, 1889), pp. 1, 5.

their fire on the Roman Catholic Church, as the last great engine of superstition. Although the blasphemy laws remained, affirmation was yet suspect, inheritance of property by atheists continued insecure, the Church of England was still Established and the state yet embellished its occasions with religious ritual, the clerically dominated society which Southwell and Holyoake had challenged in 1841 had passed for ever. The transition had been arranged by their betters among the agnostics and liberal churchmen, but the working class atheists by their energy and inflexible common sense had created a situation that impelled their betters to act.

By its own admission, the movement largely failed to indoctrinate the British lower classes with its notions of secular duty. The view that duty had precedence of happiness apparently had little appeal to people whose lives had already too much of the one and too little of the other. Moreover, the atheist idea of duty for its own sake made little sense to workingmen whose everyday existence was controlled by a system of goads, rewards and punishments.

The apostolate's central aim of liberating the working classes from religion was, however, congruent with the movement of society. The shrinkage of religious adherence in the suburbs resulted, not so much from the exertions of the atheists or the agnostics, as from that mass urbanization which so many of them feared. The break with the soil and the seasons, the decline of clerical tutelage and the growth of an anonymous mass society geared to machinery and the pursuit of pleasure devitalized British Protestantism (and atheist duty) more effectively than the missionaries could have dreamed.

☆ **9** ☆

John Robert Seeley and the Idea of a National Church

A study in Churchmanship, Historiography, and Politics

THE importance of the school of Churchmanship known as 'Broad' or 'Liberal' in the religious and, to a great extent also, the general intellectual and social life of England in the nineteenth century needs no urging here, though one might suggest that a good deal of useful study is yet to be made of it. The purpose of this essay is to draw attention to a neglected aspect of the Broad tradition, and to point to certain important influences derived from it. This aspect has its origins in one of the most characteristic features of the outlook of the Broad school: the idea of a National Church Establishment co-extensive with the nation at large, liberal and comprehensive in doctrine, tolerant and inclusive in its formularies, rooted in the nation's past and expressive of its historic continuity, a spiritual image of the State, the organ of national conscience, national culture, national unity and cohesiveness.

The major documents of this tradition are in themselves well enough known and appreciated. Coleridge's *On the Constitution of the Church and State According to the Idea of Each* (1830) and Thomas Arnold's *Principles of Church Reform* (1833), *Fragment on the Church* (1844), and *Fragments on the Church and State* (1845), and his son Matthew's religious and social writings, especially *Culture and Anarchy* (1869), form a central core of doctrine, with a clear line of descent and development. Further characteristic expressions of various aspects of the

National Church idea are to be found in Stanley's *Essays Chiefly on Questions of Church and State* (1870), Westcott's *Christian Aspects of Life* (1897), and Mandell Creighton's *The Church and the Nation* (1901). The notorious *Essays and Reviews* (1860) contained an essay on 'The National Church' by its editor, Henry Bristow Wilson. Perhaps the most representative single specimen of the genre is *Essays in Church Policy* (1868), edited by W. L. Clay with the specific purpose of discussing 'the principles upon which the Church of England may be sustained as a National Church, and the modes of action by which her national character may be further developed'. One of the seven contributors to this volume was John Robert Seeley, the Professor of Latin at University College, London, soon to be made Kingsley's successor as Regius Professor of Modern History at Cambridge by Gladstone.

Identification of Church and State to the closest possible degree is the constant basic principle of the Broad school's National Church idea. Thomas Arnold pressed the ideal further than most of his followers would have considered practicable; but in one form or another the ideal abided. In this concept, neither theocratic nor Erastian, Church and State are not merely two parties to a contract or treaty; they are to be two attributes or functions, spiritual and civil, of the one organic national society. In the realization of some such ideal the Broad Church school saw the solution to many, if not all, the political and social problems racking England in the nineteenth century. Faction in politics would be at an end. Sectarianism in religion would fade away; and particularly the Broad school hoped for an end to the breach between the existing unreformed Establishment and Nonconformity, which they looked upon as the single most important divisive influence in English society, the evil which more than any other poisoned and debilitated the body politic. They saw a truly National Church mediating in the conflict between the classes and the masses, ameliorating the social dislocation consequent upon industrialism, resisting and overcoming the socially dissolvent propaganda of Benthamism, rendering harmless the *laissez-faire* theories of Herbert Spencer, absorbing the shock of the onrush of vulgar democracy and preserving the high culture of the traditional ruling class, and at the same time educating the lower orders for their coming wider share of the new and fuller national life.

One immediate implication of the National Church idea is, therefore, a marked disposition towards an 'idealization' of the State as the civil function or attribute of the organic nationality. The essential significance of *Culture and Anarchy* is that it is the the great literary monument of this disposition. But it is important to document such a tendency by reference also to other, and in a sense more 'representative', Churchmen as an indication of how widely and deeply the implications of the National Church idea were beginning to ramify.

The *Essays on Church Policy* of 1868 is an excellent source of such documentation: the Rev. T. W. Fowle's essay on 'The Church and the Working Classes', the Rev. W. L. Clay's essay on 'The Church and the Education of the People', and Seeley's essay on 'The Church as a Teacher of Morality' are all contributions towards an ideal of a positive, Christianizing State. The Rev. J. Llewelyn Davies's essay, 'The Voluntary Principle', a critique of Nonconformity in what may be described as the classic Broad manner, contains the following characteristic passage:

> The sons of a National Church are taught that their nation, of which God has made them citizens, is entitled to the same kind of reverent service that the Church in which God planted them may claim . . .   At the present time there is a hope stirring in many loyal hearts that our national life may be made wider, stronger, and higher in tone and aspiration.   The theory that none but ignoble functions should be reserved to the State does not satisfy them.   They think that a great people may aspire to act nobly and wisely as a people, and not only through casual voluntary combinations.   The idea of a National Church is strictly in harmony with such hopes and aims, implying as it does that a Christian nation should publicly confess its Christianity.[1]

Another case in point is Brooke Foss Westcott, Bishop of Durham. The argument of his *The National Church as the Spiritual Organ of the Nation* (1893) may be compressed as follows: The demand for disestablishment has forced a

[1] *Essays in Church Policy*, ed. W. L. Clay (London, 1868), p. 84.

reconsideration of what is the 'idea of a National Church, what is the idea of a Nation'. The progress of thought in the past fifty years has helped this reconsideration. Ideas are no longer dominated by the narrow individualism which formerly played down the rôle of the State. We now see the necessity of the idea of corporate life. The national idea is now seen as necessary to the full development and fulfilment of human powers. 'We are coming to grasp the truth which was fore-shadowed in the old dream that the Nation is a greater Man, a living, a divine whole, through which mankind reaches out to the full expression of its God-given endowments in obedience to a God-given law.' We must have a National Church through which the corporate nation can declare its faith and uphold the divine nature of its life at a time when the duties of the State are being more and more enlarged. There must be a witness: 'the continued unforced natural acknowledgement of the sacred destiny of things by the State exercises silently a subtle and penetrating moral influence. It adds a confirmation of a Divine sanction to the sense of duty.' 'Thus the National Church brings all the great crises of national life into connection with the unseen and the eternal.' 'Completeness' and 'invigorating discipline' are thereby given to the national life. 'The National Church should recognize the duty of facing the problems of English society and English private life, with all their consequences.'[1]

It is perhaps worth while, at this point, following Westcott seven years later into one of the 'great crises of national life' to which he referred in 1893 to see what application of the National Church idea he makes to a new situation. The occasion is a critical phase in the war in South Africa, in 1900. The main purpose of his sermon on *The Obligations of Empire* was to defend the policy which led up to the war and to refute its critics who wanted a settlement by compromise by insisting that it was 'impossible for us to submit to arbitration the fulfil-ment of our imperial obligations'. The destiny of empire imposes its own conditions, its own logic.

> It is not only our paramount authority in South Africa which is at stake, but, as involved in that, our dominion

[1] B. F. Westcott, *Christian Aspects of Life* (London, 1897), pp. 59–138 *passim*.

in India, and our fitness to inspire and guide the life of Greater Britain. We have to show that we are still worthy to hold, both by might and by counsel, the Empire which has been entrusted to us, to protect those who rightly look to us for help, and to bear patiently the thankless burden of the white man and train uncivilised races to a nobler life.

For Westcott, the great glory of the South African War was that it had given Englishmen a chance to show clearly what was meant by the 'idea of Empire'. Materialism had not dulled the nobler and spiritual side of the national life. 'An imperial call has been met by an imperial temper.' 'God has called us to reign, who welcome the conditions of royalty and reign in Him who reigned from the Cross.' 'We hold our Empire in the name of Christ.'[1]

Westcott's attitude to imperialism generally is, in fact, a very illuminating insight into the way in which, as with many other Broad Churchmen who espoused the National Church idea, the 'national idea' becomes by natural extension the 'imperial idea'. If, Westcott argued, history is the revelation of the will of God, and if history shows the making of empires in the modern world, what then is England's part in this 'august drama' following on the Divine counsel when 'the Most High gave to the nations their inheritance' (*Deut.* xxxii, 8) 'having determined their appointed seasons and the bounds of their habitation' (*Acts* xvii, 26)? The National Church, as the spiritual organ of the nation, must become part of the 'mission' of Empire. In Kipling's *Recessional* 'our whole people found . . . the secret voice of their own hearts. Never, as far as I know, has a national confession of faith been more deep or more universal.' For Westcott there could be no doubt about England's destiny in the 'august drama' of history: there had been Greater Spain, Greater Portugal, and Greater Holland, but now Greater Britain alone remained. 'The experience of England is unique. Expansion is the essential characteristic of English national life.' This fact, Westcott observes, was 'brought out most impressively in Seeley's *Expansion of England*'.[2]

And it is precisely the case of Seeley, as a typical Broad

[1] B. F. Westcott, *The Obligations of Empire* (London, 1900), pp. 6–14.
[2] B. F. Westcott, *Lessons from Work* (London, 1901), pp. 372, 373, 381, 413–14.

Churchman, which best exhibits the implications inherent in the idea of a National Church.[1] In Seeley is established a coherence of thinking in which the Broad Churchman, the historian, and the imperialist are one. Seeley was a man of deliberately direct intellect. He is never subtle, obscure, surprising, or wayward. His conclusions are almost invariably discernible from his premises; a quality, as one of his pupils remarked, very flattering to his hearers or readers, for they very easily assumed that they had known all along things which in fact they had never thought of. Everything he wrote or said had a forceful simplicity about it and an unmistakable argument which came from utter clarity of ideas. Seeley was never perplexed, and the great aim of his life was to remove the perplexities of others. The science of history, for him, consisted in relieving people of perplexity about what had happened in the past, and why. As a Churchman he wrote to relieve people of perplexity about the shifting currents of religious belief and disbelief. As an imperialist, he wrote to relieve Englishmen of perplexity about the future.

Ecce Homo, a life of Jesus from the viewpoint of natural as opposed to supernatural or revealed religion, published anonymously in 1865,[2] is deservedly the most famous of Seeley's religious writings. It was a success both of scandal and esteem, but it is not, as it happens, the best means of understanding Seeley's application of liberal religious principles to politics. For this purpose the following articles are essential: 'The Church as a Teacher of Morality', first published in the *Essays in Church Policy* of 1868, already referred to, and later republished in *Lectures and Essays* (1870); 'Natural Religion and the State', which is Chapter IV of Part II of *Natural Religion* (1882); and 'Ethics and Religion', an address to the Cambridge Ethical Society, published posthumously in *Ethics and Religion* (1900).

---

[1] The literature on Seeley (1834–95) is meagre. The only substantial study is by the Hamburg professor and enthusiast for German colonial expansion, G. A. Rein, *Sir John Robert Seeley, Eine Studie über den Historiker* (Langensalza, 1912). It is thin on the English background. There is a useful bibliography. The most perceptive discussion of Seeley that I am aware of is by the Rev. R. H. Murray, in *Studies in the English Social and Political Thinkers of the Nineteenth Century* (Cambridge, 1929). He does not, however, deal with the National Church aspect. C. A. Bodelsen, *Studies in Mid-Victorian Imperialism* (Copenhagen, 1924), gives a complete inventory of biographical sources.

[2] To spare Seeley's father, a pious Evangelical publisher, from pain. Seeley's authorship, however, was an open secret.

The province of religion, Seeley maintains as a basic principle, is 'much more national and political, much less personal, than is commonly supposed'. The vulgar assumption that religion, whether based on reason or on revelation, is a man's private philosophy, is a misconception, caused mainly by the 'exceptional circumstances' which have prevailed since the Reformation. Men have been under a prepossession which has caused them to 'overlook the leading part which *nationalities* have played in the great religious revolutions and to attribute everything to persons and individual opinions'. Likewise, men have tended to confuse religion with tradition, dogma, and the naïveties of literal inspiration. True, or 'natural' religion, by which men instinctively teach themselves to be pure, generous, and humane, far from being unable to hold a Church together, is in fact the essential basis of a truly Christian and ethical society, for it is the only kind of religion that can effectively weld Church and State together, for it is the only kind of religion that can embrace wholeheartedly the idea of nationality. 'For State and Church belong together, and the link between them is nationality.'[1] The one without the other is feeble. Secularity is feeble—indeed, in the long run it is impossible as the foundation of a State. 'Secularity', for Seeley, means a 'lower life' of materialism and 'machinery'; and secular education is essentially unethical education. The new State educational system about to be established in England must not be allowed to be merely secular. The 'good cause of the world' is the 'higher life', which means, at least in its negative sense, resistance to secularity.

'Supernatural' or revealed religion, in Seeley's opinion, by its dogmas and its untenable claims flung in the face of the intelligent and scientific nineteenth century, does the cause of anti-secularism much harm. In England the High Church's worship of tradition and the Low Church's bibliolatry and Calvinistic fatalism drive 'many patriotic men who are not hostile to religion into active hostility to all religious bodies.' Worse, the insistence of both parties of the Church that the teaching of morality is possible only if the inward spirit is already received, results simply in the fact that 'the people of England are not taught morality at all', and therein lies the

[1] *Natural Religion*, pp. 186–90.

fundamental weakness of the English political and social system, for true ethical principles are the indispensable basis of good politics. The great bulk of the clergy are neglecting to perform what is, in fact, their most important function, which is a social, political, national, and educative function.[1]

Seeley sees hope for the future in the emergence of a new school in the Church which avoids the faults of exclusiveness and narrow partisanship of the Catholics and Evangelicals. 'The Broad Church party . . . aspires to guide, not a small section of the community, but the community itself.' With Broad Churchmen there is no shrinking from the affairs of the world as with 'sectarian Christianity'; and the Broad school has the further immense advantage that it is, unlike Roman Catholicism or the High Church party, not conservative in politics. 'The Broad Church party is thoroughly liberal.' Hence it is the only school in the Church capable of adjusting to the needs of the modern age. 'Before this party, then,' Seeley wrote in 1868, 'there evidently lies a task to which the older parties were not equal. No conservative prejudices, no theological despair, need hinder them from giving the people a Christian morality suited to the age.'[2]

What, in Seeley's view, are the elements of this task facing the Broad Church? First, politics must be rescued from their present state of degradation. 'Morals cannot be severed from politics any more than the individual can be severed from society.' Morality makes religion, not the other way around. Therefore morality must be *taught*. The clergy are better positioned than any other profession for such a duty: 'the Church furnishes an organization by which the presence of at least one man of cultivation is secured even in the most secluded districts'.[3] And as morality must be political, it must also be national. Examples for the teaching of morality should accordingly be taken from our own English history, not from such traditional and irrelevant sources as the Old Testament. Seeley suggests, therefore,

> that the clergy should draw largely upon English history and biography for illustrations of their moral teaching.

---

[1] 'The Church as a Teacher of Morality', *Essays on Church Policy*, pp. 247–9.
[2] *Op. cit.*, pp. 250ff.
[3] *Op. cit.*, p. 281.

Carlyle has said that every nation's true Bible is its history. If the Hebrew history be a cosmopolitan Bible, or rather the first part of one, I think there should be national Bibles also, and I can imagine no more proper and nobler task for a clergy than the perpetual shaping and elaborating of such a national monument.

Again: 'We should form, as it were, a national calendar, consecrate our ancestors—keep their images near us,—and so reap the inestimable advantage of living always *coram Lepidis*.'[1] The history of England, in a word, must be moralized. Seeley insists that he by no means under-estimates the obvious dangers involved in resorting habitually to English history for moral examples.

> However many mistakes might be made in the estimate of character, however many false idols set up, however much exaggerated declamation delivered, however often the truth of history might be warped to gain a moral, the continual application of a large number of minds to the work of sifting our history for the purpose of preserving in memory whatever in it was memorable, would, I believe, result in nothing less than this [national monument]. The clergy themselves would have a task to perform which would demand some reading and thought; they would have to make their Bible, instead of merely citing it by rote. The people would listen to matter intrinsically interesting to them, and hardly capable of being made dull by any feebleness in the preacher; and in the end there would spring up an idealized history, which would become familiar to every imagination and give a new sureness and continuousness to the progress of the national mind, and a new elevation to individual character.[2]

The absence of such a diffused political education, in which the integral relationship of morals and politics is constantly underlined and brought out, means that the more general moral education via 'generally understood political principles' is impossible, and hence, according to Seeley, political matters are decided as a result of factionalized and 'senseless bickering'.[3]

Seeley sees this deplorable state of affairs as a consequence of

---

[1] *Op. cit.*, pp. 266-7.
[2] *Op. cit.*, pp. 267-8.
[3] *Op. cit.*, p. 277.

the general decay of the English national character since the days of the Revolution and Napoleon. With the weakening of the 'old principles' of 'solid English discipline, a narrow but effective code of duty, a rule of life which was scarcely called into question', when Church and State were still 'irresistibly strong' and the old constitution was venerated, has declined also the quality and character of English politics. We had formerly, Seeley alleges, 'what I may call a national discipline, which formed a firm, strongly marked national character'. Now, instead of this 'massive strength approaching to brutality', a 'strong individuality', a 'masculine grasp of reality', a 'cool contempt for sentimentalism and fine phrases', Englishmen have acquired all the contrary qualities: 'loquacity, sentimentalism, helpless confusion and inaccuracy of thought, hysterical weakness, and the habit of thinking in crowds'.[1]   The primary condition of 'national health' must be free and abundant contact between the most advanced culture and the masses, with due pains being taken to 'marshal well the ranks behind', and 'keep the whole army together'.   The remedy against the danger of a vast, undisciplined social residuum of ignorance and stupidity must be constant insistence on the principle that a very important part of the moral duty of the individual is to the State. 'Patriotism should be inculcated, national history closely connected with morality, and civil duties carefully explained.'[2]

Seeley is careful to insist that he does not disparage the need for a universal morality grounded on the New Testament: 'But as the race rose to the universal morality through the national [i.e. the Old Testament], so, it seems to me, must the individual.' Here is where the moralization and idealization of the State is so important. 'The abuse of patriotism is not to be cured by destroying patriotism itself; but patriotism is to to be strengthened and purified, by being deprived of its exclusiveness and ultimateness.' The Christian unity of mankind can only be taught as a final lesson, 'which will be easiest learnt, or rather will only be learnt, by those who have already realized the unity of the State'.[3]   Seeley cites Coleridge in

---

[1] *Ethics and Religion*, pp. 11–13.
[2] *Essays on Church Policy*, pp. 276–8.
[3] *Op. cit.*, pp. 278–9.

support: 'Cosmopolitanism is not possible but by antecedence of patriotism.'[1] 'Universal patriotism', taken in itself, Seeley regards with special contempt as 'not Christianity but Jacobinism'.[2]

Nor is the unity of the State merely to be a matter of moral discipline. One of the especially important rôles of the clergy of the future must be that of mediating in the 'perpetual warfare between class and class'. This class war is a 'fundamental political fact', and the great need is for an influential and pervasive educative and missionary force, independent of parties and not acting as an instrument of the ruling class, to 'moderate' it. Hence the Church becomes an engine of national unity from the economic as well as the moral aspect. For this purpose the clergy must be specially trained in social and economic science. 'Politics then', Seeley emphasizes, 'should be a part, and a principal part, of the studies of the clergy. To discover and popularize the lessons that may be drawn from our history, to idealize the nation and familiarize it in its unity to the minds of its members, is a most vital part of the moral teaching of the community.' But if morality cannot properly be taught without entering into political issues, neither can it be separated from social science. There is an enormous amount a properly trained clergy could do. Occasional philanthropy is not good enough. 'Is their province limited to the pointing out of social evils and the application of remedies? Should not rather cure give place to prevention? Is not the removal of the causes of social disease more important than the alleviation of its effects? An immediate start could be made, Seeley suggests, on the problem of the agricultural poor; more Kingsleys and more Girdlestones must soon be heard of.[3]

There are clear and constant links between Seeley's application of the National Church idea and the central Broad Church tradition. The contemporary parallel with Matthew Arnold is especially noteworthy. Seeley's morality answers, in all

---

[1] *Op. cit.*, p. 266.
[2] *Ecce Homo* (Everyman ed.), p. 121.
[3] *Essays in Church Policy*, pp. 280–2.

essentials, to Arnold's culture. The parallel is close also in
relation to specific political events. The franchise agitation
of the 1860s and the manner in which the Second Reform Act
was passed in 1867 provoked strikingly similar responses. It
presented to both Arnold and Seeley a spectacle of political
demoralization, symptomatic of a profound national malaise.
Gladstone's later development as a spokesman of 'sentimentalism' and as a leader of 'mobs' in the Eastern Question
crisis of 1876–8 and in the Midlothian campaigns of 1879–80
and as a crusader for Home Rule provoked equally similar
responses.

But Seeley transcended the existing Broad Church tradition.
With Matthew Arnold it was faltering. Arnold had not
enough confidence and stiffening of faith left in him to save
himself from lapsing into a delicately ironic and self-deprecating
pessimism. Delicacy, irony, self-deprecation and pessimism
were qualities totally absent from Seeley's character. Seeley's
self-confidence enabled him to offer much more than Arnold:
not only a diagnosis of the national malaise but also a remedy
'practical' to the point of crudity, though not lacking in engaging audacity. Furthermore, and equally if not more important, Seeley had other practical lessons to offer. Gladstone,
impressed by Seeley's clear-sightedly Christian conception of
what the teaching of history was about (and disregarding the
fact that Seeley had published no history except a couple of
articles on Rome), had made him one of the two academic
heads of the historical profession in England. As a historian
officially accredited by the State Seeley could present historical
examples of the actual moralization of a national idea; he could
show that the thing had been done. He could, further, offer
a specific programme for the English case. For it is clear that,
in Seeley's view, the 'clergy' were by no means to be alone as
social moralizers; and particularly, of course, with regard
to the scientific study of history, as opposed to its dissemination
in his scheme of national idealization. The historian must
necessarily become a vital part of the great process. Indeed,
since history is to be made into the scriptures of the National
Bible, historians, as a profession, become a species of State
priesthood.

This is really the point of Seeley's *chef d'œuvre* as a professional historian, the *Life and Times of Stein, or Germany and Prussia in the Napoleonic Age*, published in three volumes by the Cambridge University Press in 1878.   In *Stein* Seeley provides Englishmen with an example of the way in which a foreign country, defeated and demoralized, won its way back to greatness by means of a deliberate policy of discipline, education, 'masculine grasp of reality', harsh but salutary social and political reconstruction, all within a clearly recognizable framework of a national idea and an idealized State.

Stein is indeed a very revealing work, providing one looks at it from the correct angle.   It is much more important, in fact, for the light it throws on Seeley and his ideas than for its historical value as an original study of Stein and Prussia. From the latter point of view it has, one might perhaps say, been justly neglected; but from the former point of view it represents an asset too long left to waste.

Seeley himself took a very high—indeed, almost blasphemously high—view of the significance and standing of *Stein*.   At no point does Seeley's conception of what must be called the priesthood of the historian emerge with more clarity than on the occasion of a remark he made to Jebb, the classical scholar, as related by Lady Caroline Jebb in her biography of her husband.   Seeley was staying with the Jebbs at Glasgow some years after the publication of *Ecce Homo*, and Jebb, who had hoped that Seeley might complement his study of the human life of Christ with a divine counterpart, asked Seeley if he intended to bring out another study of Christ.   'The answer, most unexpected, was to the effect that he had fulfilled this intention already.   On being pressed for an explanation, he said that he meant his Life of Stein!   His questioner's comment on this . . . was that if he had heard this statement attributed to Seeley, he would have scouted it as incredible.'[1]

There is, of course, from the viewpoint of Seeley taken in this essay, nothing at all incredible about such a statement.   It reveals, certainly, that Seeley had no sense of humour; but that is neither here nor there.   Stein, in his plans and his achievement, embodied a divine principle, for in him was manifest the working of God's providence.   Seeley was as clear on this

[1] C. Jebb, *Life and Letters of Sir Richard Claverhouse Jebb* (Cambridge, 1907), pp. 85–6.

point as Westcott. His ideas about history were, as he once pointed out, 'fundamentally *Biblical*', not in the ordinary sense, but in the sense of seeing the Bible 'as a whole, its great plan and unity', and principally the 'grand poetic interpretation' he found in it 'of modern views concerning history'.[1] Naturally one must assume that such modern views concerning history are to be equated with Seeley's own. Stein embodied and made manifest to the world at the beginning of the nineteenth century the idea of nationality; and in Seeley's interpretation of modern history, the nineteenth century was the beginning of the epoch in which the national idea was to become the basis of a certain—though not necessarily ultimate —historical and divine dispensation to mankind.

There is thus no problem as to why Seeley should have chosen Stein as the vehicle for the propagation of his gospel. Matthew Arnold, in *Friendship's Garland*, had already made Stein a minor but by no means negligible issue in England and Ireland, especially with regard to land reform. And there was, simply, no one else available. This was a great pity, for in truth Stein was of a narrow and unsympathetic personality, and though unquestionably, to use Seeley's own words on the earlier English character, of a 'strong individuality', with a 'massive strength approaching to brutality', and so on, he was by no means a great enough man to bear gracefully the divine burden Seeley was obliged to load on him. Seeley was forced, moreover, by the logic of his scheme, to make Goethe into an angel of the satanic Bonaparte. No wonder *Stein* has never had much appeal. On the other hand, it should be stressed, in fairness to Seeley in this matter, that he never liked the 'biographical approach', and used it only for 'educative purposes', because people simply could not be got to read 'philosophical history'.[2]

There were other contributory motives also. German culture in the early nineteenth century had always had an obvious attraction to the Broad school and the intellectual circles associated with it. To a man like Seeley the attraction of Germany as the home of liberal theology was doubled by the

---

[1] *Natural Religion* (3rd ed., 1891), p. viii.
[2] See Seeley's preface to the English edition of *The Life and Adventures of Ernst Moritz Arndt, the Singer of the German Fatherland* (London, 1879), pp. iv, v.

R

additional attraction of Germany as the home of scientific history: the Prussian historical school he revered, especially Ranke. 'Most good books,' he was fond of saying, 'are in German.' Seeley shared, in a general way, the Prussophilia of the era in which the illustrious Bunsen had for so long adorned the Prussian embassy in London. But, for Seeley especially, the fundamental and irresistible attraction of Prussia was in its providential rôle as the State-evangelist of the national idea, triumphantly vindicated by force of arms in 1866 and 1870–1. Seeley undoubtedly went much further than his like-minded contemporaries in his scorn for the 'immortal ideas of 1789' and his insistence that the truly 'immortal ideas of 1808 and 1813' were really far more important, and ought to have much more attention paid to them than they had so far received.[1]

The theme of *Stein*, then, is a struggle between a moral conception of the State—Stein's Prussia—and an immoral conception—the Napoleonic Empire, embodiment of the universal monarchy principle. To be moral, a State must be national, for the coincidence of the Nation and the State alone permits the utmost level of 'idealization', the service of the State, the service of the community, the service of the citizen. Only thus can there be a 'living organic community'.[2] Prussia, as the State most closely approximating to this idea, represented, for Seeley, both 'Europe' and international law; for Napoleon's Empire meant the destruction of the only valid Europe, the Europe of nations; and, in Seeley's view, 'international law ceases where universal monarchy begins'.[3]

The essential moral virtue inherent in the Prussian State Seeley accepts, as it were, retrospectively. It justified Frederick the Great's aggressions and bad faith, though Seeley is perfectly aware that Frederick himself had no idea of a German nation. Seeley is critical enough, to be sure, of the fraud and violence of Frederick; but he never questions its necessity. It was part of a process of historical destiny. Frederick had to establish a mindless militarism, for otherwise Prussia could not have grown great—perhaps might not have

---

[1] *Loc. cit.*
[2] J. R. Seeley, *The Growth of English Policy* (Cambridge, 1895), vol. I, p. 365.
[3] *Stein,* vol. I., p. 349.

survived. Hence there can be no question of any fundamental moral criticism. Stein's historical mission was, essentially, to preside over the transformation of the Frederician military despotism into a moralized nation-state.

To Spain fell the honour of first teaching Europe, as it languished under Napoleon's 'monstrous lawlessness', that neither democracy nor liberty was the answer, but 'the one thing needful', nationality, 'the idea of the nation as distinguished from the state'. From Spain the inspiration passed, after characteristically fumbling failure in the hands of the Habsburgs in 1809, to Prussia. Fichte, the religious refugee from Saxony, provided Prussia, in his *Addresses to the German Nation*, with the ideology of the new national idea, 'the prophetical and canonical book which announces and explains a great transition in modern Europe'.[1] For this new doctrine did not cease to be important with the peace. 'The middle part of this century has been principally devoted to the remodelling of Italy and Germany on the basis of nationality, and to reducing to system the *levée en masse* of Spain, and at this moment [1878] the doctrine is causing the re-arrangement of the east of Europe.'[2]

And as Prussia represented the moral State, so her wars were necessarily moral wars. They but fulfilled Fichte's canonical prophecies of a 'more natural system' of Europe.

> The three principal wars of Prussia since her great disaster [of 1806], those of 1813, 1866, and 1870, have a character of greatness such as no other modern wars have; the objects of them, and the spirit in which they were waged, were as high as the intelligence with which they were guided. They have in a manner reconciled the modern world to war, for they have exhibited it as a civilizing agent and a kind of teacher of morals.[3]

Even the most patently aggressive of these wars, the attack on Austria in 1866, did not merely on that account forfeit its moral quality; for it had 'a motive so great and powerful that it did not seem unreasonable to call on the whole nation to take part in it'. It was the decisive beginning of the train of events which by 1871 had 'virtually solved' the German question.

[1] *Stein*, vol. II, p. 41.
[2] *Op. cit.*, p. 25.
[3] *Op. cit.*, p. 96.

Seeley's attitude to the particular institutional elements of Prussian moral superiority are illuminating. Even on the level of eighteenth-century absolutism he was very ready to argue that the Frederician despotism was more 'moral' than the monarchy of Louis XV. In parliamentarianism the French still cannot win: Prussia was right and France was wrong, Seeley argues, despite appearances to the contrary in the early nineteenth century. The French started from the top, and failed; the Prussians started from the bottom, and succeeded, if slowly. The basis of Prussian success was Stein's policy of municipal reform. This reform made one of the two great points of difference between the French Revolution and the 'great European or anti-Napoleonic Revolution, which began in 1808': respect for the principle of nationality was, of course, the first; but second only to this was respect for local and municipal liberties. 'In the one it followed the lead of Spain; in the other it took its lesson from England.'[1]

Naturally the religious situation in Prussia would present itself to Seeley as a decisive factor. Prussia had the 'incalculable advantage', as Seeley saw it, of being a Protestant country, despite the annexation of the Rhenish provinces in 1814. This meant that, in a very significant sense, Prussia was 'self-contained'.[2] Seeley, of course, regarded the Roman Catholic Church, the greatest institution both of supranationalism and supernaturalism, with intense hostility; and the fact that he was writing *Stein* when the *Kulturkampf* was at its height would do nothing to weaken his conviction, which he did not hesitate to assert even in the bland and cool pages of the *English Historical Review*, that the Papacy was the 'burning heart of all human discord'.[3] Roman Catholicism had the same disintegrating effect on the German national fabric as did the antinational cosmopolitanism of bad patriots like Goethe, Herder, and Dalberg. Being thus religiously 'self-contained', Lutheran Prussia had at her disposal what amounted virtually to a national State Church; which is the indispensable foundation for the full development of the national idea. Seeley does not, however, explicitly claim for the Lutheran clergy of Prussia

[1] *Op. cit.*, pp. 224–8.
[2] *Op. cit.*, pp. 181–2.
[3] *English Historical Review*, vol. III (1888), p. 298.

the same kind of positive, creative function that he sketched for the future Broad Church school in England. Rather, he stressed the 'State priesthood' aspect, the great rôle of Humboldt's University of Berlin, and the new national system of education inspired by it, in reconciling nationality and literature.[1] Seeley's views on university reform in England were aimed, of course, at exactly the same end. In any case, Seeley regarded the educative rôle of a national clergy and the educative rôle of the universities as merely two aspects of the one function.

At no point in his thesis of the essential moral superiority of the Prussian State is Seeley so lyrical and enthusiastic as in his treatment of the system of compulsory national military conscription instituted by Stein's colleagues Scharnhorst and Gneisenau. Here, for Seeley, is the making of a new 'noble style of war' through a truly 'national army' composed of the whole youth of the nation. This system ensured 'war in its fairest aspect', for it necessitates an intelligent code of discipline, a raising of standards of treatment of recruits, no longer mere peasants to be flogged into battle. Most important, besides providing a simple and comprehensive method of inculcating a sense of social discipline in its widest aspect, it necessitates a moral cause to fight for, since the educated classes will not fight for anything less. The morality of such a system shone even more brightly when contrasted with the wholly professional system (such as the British), composed necessarily of the scum of society, enlisted for pay or drink, or, even worse, the monstrously unfair system of selective conscription practised (naturally enough, in Seeley's view) by the Austrian and French services, until salutary defeat at the hands of the Prussians taught them wisdom. Instead of uniting all social orders in a common enthusiasm for the service of the State, selective conscription, by allowing the wealthy in effect to purchase themselves out, was a socially divisive influence. Universal military obligation is, in itself, a noble morality; 'voluntaryism' is, at bottom, the negation of morality.[2]

It is interesting to note that Seeley is aware of certain regrettable, or potentially regrettable, consequences of the

---

[1] *Stein*, vol. II, pp. 434–5.
[2] *Op. cit.*, pp. 97–9.

success of the Prussian military system. The development of this system 'turned all Germany into a camp'. But now, thanks to the Prussian example, all Europe is a vast series of rival camps. Seeley appears to betray a twinge of doubt: 'And now, when at a distance of half a century we see the principle then laid down in full operation, and Germany, Russia, France competing with each other in the creation of armies such as the world never saw before, there must be few who can rest satisfied with such a state of affairs considered as final or normal.'[1] Seeley is, also, willing to admit that the old theory of the unity of Europe is, in some respects, 'higher', as a theory, than the national theory. The important point, however, for our understanding of Seeley's position, is to note his unwillingness to countenance any radical criticism of the validity of the existing European system, deeply divided and dangerously armed though it might be. The theory of Europe, if noble as a theory, is, however, Seeley argues, impossible to put into practice, certainly in the nineteenth century. Granting this, nothing could be more mischievous than the naïve assumption that it may be supposed to be possible. This kind of naïvety led people like Goethe and Dalberg to their equivocal relationship with Bonaparte, who simply exploited them cynically. On the whole, Seeley concludes, it was and is better for Europe that nationalism should have revived 'even in too extreme and narrow a form, than that it should remain in the condition of a discredited and obsolete virtue'.[2]

This attitude Seeley makes more explicit in an address to the English Peace Society, published in *Macmillan's Magazine* as 'The United States of Europe'. The Peace Society, it is clear, stands in Seeley's eyes in much the same position as Goethe and Dalberg. Their response to the problems of power and the relations between States is, in the same sense, 'equivocal'. Seeley's argument to them is that war can never be abolished in Europe unless there is a complete and full federal system as in the United States. (He interprets the Civil War between the States as having, in effect, abolished war: had the Union not been preserved there would be now two rival armies facing one another, as in Europe.) The Peace Society proposed to

---

[1] *Op. cit.*, p. 387.
[2] *Loc. cit.*

abolish war by a limited federation of the European States, along the lines of the defunct Germanic Confederation. This, Seeley told them, would be a waste of time. A common citizenship, a common legislature and executive, are *sine qua non*. Seeley begs the Peace Society not to think him cynical; but it is better to face the facts. A true federated Europe would take a very long time to achieve, and it would need a vast popular movement of opinion in support of it, of which present indications give but little promise. One must be practical; and for the foreseeable future, one must reconcile oneself to the existing situation—which, Seeley leaves no doubt, will involve wars, and he is quite clear that the democratic wars of the future will be much more bloody than the wars of kings in the past.[1]

This is, in fact, the most important conclusion to be drawn from Seeley's handling of Stein and Prussia as an exposition of a historical moralization of a national idea. An inescapable consequence, for Seeley, in such a process, must be the moralization of war. Prussia had, in his own words, 'in a manner reconciled the modern world to war'. The Prussian State, in its external aspect, was simply the most efficient machine for the exertion of power in Europe. In other words, regardless of such twinges of regret as he may have had, Seeley does accept the power factor as the dominant reality in the world. And this acceptance is the basic datum of the historical moralization of the English State which he prepared after the publication of *Stein*.

☆   ☆   ☆

It would certainly have been strange if Seeley had neglected to complete the course on which his bent of mind was leading him. In one way or another, everything he had hitherto published led up naturally to *The Expansion of England*, a course of lectures delivered in Cambridge and published in 1883, and his *Growth of English Policy*, published posthumously in 1895. Of the national idea of England he offered an imperial interpretation. As Westcott was to point out, Seeley revealed the providential dispensation, through history, for England. For Englishmen he pointed a grand moral: the key to their history

[1] *Macmillan's Magazine*, vol. XXIII (1870–1), pp. 436–48.

and thus to their present politics was a certain unique pattern and relationship of events in the past; with this key they had the means of unlocking the future—providing they had the will and the discipline necessary to unite in agreement as to what needed to be done, and the perseverance to see the great affair through to its logical end, which was the survival and security of England as a Great Power in the world, in spite of many disadvantageous circumstances. Seeley had already made quite clear his views on the kind of religious moralization and social reconstruction necessary in England to secure the vital strength of national will, discipline, and perseverance. He had already given elaborate historical demonstration that the thing could be done, had been done. He had shown that a man of affairs who had grasped the needful idea, who had taken the leadership of the movement of the idea, who was enabled by his 'knightly breeding without affectation to think, speak, and act patriotically', nor ever suffered his 'clear national feeling to be clouded either by the sophistries which made patriotism an empty name . . . or by . . . blind party passions',[1] could achieve the seemingly impossible. In his *Expansion* Seeley in effect offered a programme for the future English Stein.

Seeley started from the proposition that 'the history of England ought to end with something that might be called a moral. Some large conclusion ought to arise out of it; it ought to exhibit the general tendency of English affairs in such a way as to set us thinking about the future and divining the destiny which is reserved for us.'[2] The present state of historical studies in England was profoundly unsatisfactory. It did none of these things. Obsessed with the domestic and now in any case obsolete theme of the growth of constitutional government, of 'Wilkes and General Warrants', in Seeley's notorious sneer, it was irrelevant to present needs and present problems.[3] And hence it was useless for the present and coming generations of statesman responsible for the guidance of national affairs. These statesmen were bred in the universities; and the teachers in universities must become a 'clerisy' of the future ruling class

---

[1] *Stein*, vol. III, p. 566.

[2] *Expansion of England*, p. 1.

[3] For an expression of resentment by Acton, the most solemn of the priests before the Whig Ark, at Seeley's cavalier attitude to it, see *Letters of Lord Acton to Mary Gladstone*, ed. H. Paul (London, 1904), pp. 6–8.

in the same way that the clergy at large must become a 'clerisy' for the mass of the lower classes. Historians obviously must lead the way. They must cease to treat English history as if it had come to an 'end'. This was good enough for Dutch or Swedish historians; but if English statesmen of the future were to be educated on a basis of a false estimate of priorities—if they were to be taught, for example, that the 'liberties' (in the Arnoldian sense) of individual Englishmen are more important than the security of the English State—then England will very soon decline to the level of a State like Sweden, whose history is indeed 'wound up', and for whom there can be no visions of a great destiny. England, above all, must build up a didactic school of historical studies comparable in quality and educative function with the Prussians, especially Ranke and Droysen, in their grasp of the problems of foreign relations, for this was precisely where English inadequacy was most conspicuous and most dangerous.

The key Seeley accordingly offered for the unlocking of the future was a total reinterpretation of English history in which the traditional 'Whig' theme of the growth of constitutional liberties was deposed in favour of a new theme, the growth of the English State as a world Power, the 'simple, obvious fact of the extension of the English name into the other countries of the globe, the foundation of Greater Britain'.[1] The power factor is fundamental: England as a State in relation to other States. 'By England', Seeley emphasizes, 'I mean solely the state or political community which has its seat in England.' Again: 'I have argued . . . that history is concerned, not mainly with the interesting things which may have been done by Englishmen or in England, but with England herself considered as a nation and as a state.'[2]

The Growth of English Policy traced the emergence of England as a world power up to the beginning of the eighteenth century. *The Expansion of England* carried the story up to Seeley's own time. Up to this point, in Seeley's interpretation, England had managed well enough on the strength of a rather crude and blind instinct—the foundation of an empire in a fit of absence of mind, in his famous phrase. The power competition of the

---

[1] *Expansion of England*, p. 8.
[2] *Op. cit.*, pp. 7, 307.

Spanish, the Dutch, the Portuguese and the French had been, in the long run, unequal to English strength and English natural advantages. But in the later nineteenth century the situation was transformed. From about 1830 the future Great Powers of the world were discernible as those essentially European States in command of a vast, continuous continental land-mass: the United States and Russia. The only possible way a State not in command of such a land-mass could maintain a comparable power-status was by means of a sea-based empire, by making itself into a 'world-Venice'.[1] Of all the European States England alone was in a position to do this. This was the great opportunity and the great challenge. Seeley had in fact already adumbrated this theme in *Stein*: 'England, Russia and the United States are now all alike Powers belonging to a higher scale of magnitude than the greatest purely European states.'[2]

In the face of competition by such 'gigantic neighbours in the West and in the East', England could no longer afford to muddle along in the old style. While the United States and Russia are developing by a natural process of increase, England is living on her capital as a Power. England must become much more nationally efficient. She must organize her resources, and above all the human resources of her great imperial colonies of settlement in Canada, South Africa, and Australasia. There must be a United States of Greater Britain. The golden moment of historical opportunity for England is the later nineteenth century, while Russia and the United States are as yet relatively undeveloped. If England waits until the threat of relegation to minor power-status is actual, it will by then be too late to do anything about it.

Thus Seeley's thesis of the imperial destiny of England has nothing ostensibly deterministic about it. It was a thesis essentially of opportunities and possibilities. He offered the English public a choice between two alternatives: they could go ahead and accept the challenge, or they could renounce. 'Is not this a serious consideration,' Seeley asked, 'and is it not especially so for a state like England, which has at the present moment the choice in its hands between two courses of action,

---

[1] *Op. cit.*, p. 288.
[2] *Stein*, vol. II, p. 5.

the one of which may set it in that future age on a level with
the greatest of those great states of the future, while the other
will reduce it to the level of a purely European Power looking
back, as Spain does now, to the great days when she pretended
to be a world-state?"[1]

Yet, while Seeley presented his arguments against the
renouncers, the 'pessimists', victims of loose thinking and
timidity, and pressed his case for acceptance on every ground
of rational advantage, it is also clear that permeating the whole
of the *Expansion* is a sense of destiny on a more exalted level
than the purely human and mundane. Renunciation, Seeley
somehow suggests, would be an act of human perversity,
perhaps almost of deliberate sin, in the face of the manifest
desires of a Higher Power. If there is a Divine plan for the
world and mankind (which Seeley could not doubt), and if
England is a truly Christian State, or at least well on the way to
becoming one by means of a National Church, then a Christian
Englishman must surely take the view that a national destiny
offered by Providence could not be renounced in good faith and
good conscience.

One has come, then, with Seeley, full circle: the imperial
destiny offered in the *Expansion* could be wholeheartedly
accepted and satisfactorily accomplished only by the idealized
Christian State sketched in *Essays on Church Policy*. And at the
centre of Seeley's circle of thinking lay a beautiful irony. The
validity of his historical thesis about the shape of the future
(and it obviously had considerable validity) was flawed fatally,
for England, by one omission: Seeley forgot Prussia. Such
hope as there may have been for the achievements of an English
Stein were wrecked by Stein's own successors in Germany.
The irony is compound and even deeper: in Seeley's own terms,
Prussia was a State more likely to benefit from his teaching
than England. Prussia, after all, had had her Stein; England
had not. In Seeley's own day, Prussia had Bismarck; England
suffered Gladstone. Prussia-Germany, however imperfectly
realized, was an idealized nation-state in a sense England had
never been, and never would be.

Seeley did not foresee in the early 1880s—could not, perhaps,
have been expected, by the time of his death in 1895, to have

[1] *Expansion of England*, p. 301.

foreseen—that the Germans would apply the doctrines of imperialism and navalism in a much more serious way than the English. This is not to suggest that Seeley was a particularly important direct influence on German colonialist and navalist thinking. They had a large literature of their own on the subject, supplemented by other outside influences such as Mahan; and in any case Seeley's highly anglocentric approach would not in itself be congenial.[1] He functioned rather as a stimulant to German rivalry and emulation. Still, the only substantial study of Seeley is, after all, in German. Seeley could not have foreseen that the Germans would refuse to accept their non-imperial destiny, their 'natural' rôle as a purely European Power, and hence of second-class power-status at best, with good grace and fatalistic resignation. The Germans defied Seeley's basic analysis, while attempting to put into operation his doctrines on the necessity of 'world-power' based on sea-power. Their failure may possibly be ascribable to this contradiction; but in any case, in the process they forced what Seeley would have regarded as a European civil war on England, with consequences disastrous to the twentieth-century prospects of both countries.

☆   ☆   ☆

This essay would end fittingly on a Seeleyan note. It should finish 'with something that might be called a moral'; some 'large conclusion ought to arise out of it'. One ought, perhaps, to apply such findings as emerge from a consideration of Seeley's thinking as a contribution towards formulating a general and tolerably coherent view of the relationship between politics and the self-consciously public intellectuals—the intelligentsia, the *clercs*, in Benda's phrase—in nineteenth-century England. Seeley himself would have regarded such a formulation as not merely desirable, but mandatory on a historian, whose business he held to be to elucidate, to make simple and significant the patterns of the past.

Moreover, Seeley himself has a place in the pattern of the political thinking of the English intelligentsia of the nineteenth

---

[1] There was no German edition of *The Expansion of England*, for instance, until 1928 (*Die Ausbreitung Englands*, edited with an introduction by K. A. von Müller, Stuttgart, 1928).

century which is much more important than he has hitherto been given credit for. His reputation has suffered unduly in the general deflation of 'imperialism' in the twentieth century. Nor, any more than his own hero Stein, did Seeley have a personality attractive or sympathetic to the world at large. Alone of the great English historians of the later nineteenth century, as Rein observed rather sadly in 1912,[1] he has had no biography or collection of letters to commemorate him. Even in his own time he was never appreciated in a balanced, undistorted manner; his reputation was made quite lopsided by the huge public success of *The Expansion of England*. This has been extremely unfortunate. The essential value of Seeley's thinking, as this essay, it is hoped, has demonstrated, lies in its unity as a whole. His contributions on the Broad Church in relation to the national idea are not in themselves indispensable; his contribution of a philosophy of imperialism was not in itself unique. His unique and indispensable rôle was to link the two through the process of historical moralization: to make the idealized State also the power State. To the 'old Liberal' reaction against 'Mill-Gladstonism' associated particularly with Fitzjames Stephen, Maine, Dicey, and Lecky,[2] Seeley, though differing in many respects from them, added the missing element. With Seeley's theory of a historical destiny went logically and necessarily an acceptance of the determinant quality inherent in the possession of power by governments. In certain circumstances a Great Power has no choice consistent with the security of what is conceived to be its vital interests but to exercise its power in certain directions. The State visualized by Matthew Arnold becomes, through Seeley, the State that prosecuted the South African War, that concluded the *ententes* with France and Russia, that declared war on Germany in 1914. It was altogether appropriate that John Morley, one of Seeley's sharpest critics,[3] should have resigned office in 1914 rather than associate himself with acceptance of such a power determinant.

[1] G. A. Rein, *Sir John Robert Seeley*, p. vi.
[2] See on this aspect generally the excellent article by John Roach, 'Liberalism and the Victorian Intelligentsia', *Cambridge Historical Journal*, vol. XIII (1957), pp. 58–81.
[3] See his review, 'The Expansion of England', *Macmillan's Magazine*, vol. XLIX (1883–4), pp. 241–58.

In thus introducing, more distinctly and effectively than any other publicist, the power factor into the intellectual debate on the politics of the later nineteenth-century England, Seeley performed a much-needed function of revision and realignment. The established tradition of intellectual debate, bred in insular security and centred around the 'condition of England' question, was almost totally innocent of any awareness of this factor. Freeman's attack on Seeley in his inaugural lecture as Regius Professor at Oxford in 1884, in the course of a eulogy on another of Seeley's bitterest critics, Goldwin Smith, is as good an example of this as may be found. It was thus quite inadequate to the task of coping with the problems consequent on the increasing deterioration of England's international position, especially from the 1870s onwards. That tradition was, by its nature, essentially domestic in scope, though it did relate to the general European background of 'liberalism' *versus* 'conservatism', the issues of 1848. It was, in its attitude to the problem of the external relations of the State, 'ideological' in a relatively pure sense, that is, in that it had very little consciousness of the existence of a problem of power as such, distinct from the 'moral' considerations arising out of the rightness or wrongness of the system of Europe established in 1815. The Crimean war brings this point out very well. It was fought, by the English, essentially as a projection of the ideological attitudes of 1848–9, much to the confusion of the Russians, who were trying, legitimately, to restore the proper power-equilibrium of 1841 at the Straits, upset by the unwarranted encroachment of English influence during the 1840s and early 50s. The 'Crimean System' erected by the English against the Russians after 1856 was the only attempt between 1815 and 1919 to institutionalize on an international level a conviction that righteousness had triumphed over evil. By the 1860s the English assumption that their foreign policy was uniquely grounded on principles of freedom, justice, and high morality, and that foreign Powers would have to take it seriously as such, had ceased to be impressive. The critical turning-point was Bismarck's brushing aside of Palmerston and Russell at the time of the war with Denmark over Schleswig-Holstein.

The established 'condition of England' tradition had

developed in a context not only of insular but also of international security after the Napoleonic Wars, which left
England in the unchallenged position of being virtually the
only world Power. This security was, in fact, a luxury, a dividend or bonus earned in special circumstances, unlikely to last
very long, and even more unlikely to be repeated. But a
general assumption grew up in England that this situation was
'normal', that it was a reflection of a permanent improvement
in the intellectual equipment of Europe, expressed in such
concepts as the Concert of Europe and the ideal of Free Trade.
'We become unable', as Seeley himself put it in one of his
strictures against English insularity, 'to conceive the possibility
of England being in danger.'[1] Neither of the two great
opposed strains of the established English intellectual tradition,
the Coleridgian and the Benthamite, had anything material to
offer for guidance in a new international context in which the
'ideological' presuppositions had ceased to be relevant.
Neither Carlyle, nor Mill, nor Cobden, nor Arnold, nor
Bagehot, nor Spencer, nor Sidgwick had an adequate theory
of England's rôle as a Great Power in a world becoming
ordered in a manner increasingly inconvenient for English
interests.

The first major opportunity for fruitful new debate was the
Eastern Question crisis of 1875–8. This crisis represented, for
England, the fact that her existing world-system was discredited. The security of the Near East, in the guise of the
'independence and integrity of the Ottoman Empire', had begun
to crumble away. Africa and the Far East would soon follow.
There was obviously scope for serious re-thinking. But the
opportunity was wasted. The 'Bulgarian atrocities', of course,
particularly in the way they aroused the Nonconformists, were
especially unfortunate in the effect they had of pushing the
debate off the rails. Apart from a minority, of whom Seeley
—by no means an admirer of Beaconsfield and his pro-Turkish
policy—was one,[2] the intelligentsia as a whole missed the

---

[1] 'Our Insular Ignorance', *The Nineteenth Century*, vol. XVIII (1885), p. 868.
[2] Seeley's attitude at this period is observable in two pieces in *Macmillan's
Magazine*: 'Political Education of the Working Classes' (vol. XXXVI, 1877,
pp. 143–5), and 'Political Somnambulism' (vol. XLIII, 1880–1, pp. 28–44).
See also R. T. Shannon, *Gladstone and the Bulgarian Agitation, 1876* (London, 1963),
p. 223.

point by confusing a fundamental revision of policy with a desire to go contrary to Beaconsfield because Beaconsfield's policy was 'immoral'. There was, in fact, much to be said for a policy of working with, rather than against, the Russians, as long as it was based on new thinking, not old thinking turned upside-down. But with Carlyle and Freeman in the lead, there was little chance of constructive new thinking; and the indignant intelligentsia followed Gladstone in inverting the old ideological presuppositions, this time in favour of the Russians against the Turks.

Instead of interpreting rightly the lesson of the rebuff of Palmerston and Russell in 1864, that 'normality' was no longer a relevant assumption, the moral agitators of 1876 looked back to Mill's campaign to prosecute Governor Eyre of Jamaica as their model. In the long run nothing was gained; and Gladstone's foreign policy in the 1880s ended up just as bankrupt as Palmerston's in the 1860s.

Much might perhaps have been hoped for in this respect from the new Hegelian line of thinking represented by T. H. Green. But Green never carried his idealist philosophy beyond a theory of society. The State, as such, he never really idealized, and the Church certainly not at all. The focus of his religious admiration was, in fact, the 'conscience' of Nonconformity. He thus had no disposition whatever to take a view similar to Seeley's; rather he resolutely followed Gladstone in refusing to accept the reality of a power problem and insisted that the 'imagined' 'competition of interests between states' is bred solely as a result of the 'imperfect realization of civil equality in the full sense of the term' within states not yet thoroughly organized into political life.[1] This was not, in fact, an attitude which advanced in any essentials beyond Cobden. Even Green's pupil Bosanquet, though much abused as the philosopher of imperialism,[2] was innocent of any radical departure from Green's 'power-rejecting' standpoint. Indeed, when attacked during the First World War for propagating dangerous 'German' idealism about the ethically self-sufficient State, Bosanquet was able to refute his critics by citing Green's

[1] T. H. Green, *Lectures on the Principles of Political Obligation* (London, 1882), Sects. 166ff.

[2] J. A. Hobson, *Imperialism* (London, 1902), p. 175. See also L. T. Hobhouse, *The Metaphysical Theory of the State: a Criticism* (London, 1918), *passim*.

treatment of the problem of the external relations of the idealist State, arguing that this represented 'a very great merit in our philosophy'.[1] Moreover, Bosanquet went on to explain the 'root of the venom in the present conflict' in terms of, first, the 'medieval condition of the Prussian franchise', and second, the deplorable influence of the 'false political economy' of protective tariffs, themselves the results of 'internal distraction', 'which is the principal source of war'.[2]

The inadequacy, to put it no more strongly than that, of such attitudes does put Seeley's contribution to the debate in a fairly flattering light. Perhaps too flattering, because it must be emphasized that Seeley's position as a pioneer of the argument for 'power acceptance' was by no means uncompromised by distorting pressures. In the first place, he did not entirely rid himself of assumptions about the 'normality' of a world-situation which happened to be convenient for English interests. Indeed, to a considerable extent some such assumption was built in to his system of thinking, for his theory of a 'destiny' for England certainly implied a moral sanction for English interests as being, in some manner, on a higher plane than the interests of powers whose history could not provide them with the same divinely-issued credentials. And in the second place, his appreciation of the European power-situation in the early 1880s, while by no means complacent, certainly did not excel in predictive foreboding. As has been indicated, he had no inkling of a German problem.

He accepted Russian enmity as a constant factor, but judged that no immediate danger was apparent from that quarter. The only Power capable of invading England was France; but the old rivalry between the two countries had long ago ceased.[3] Though *The Expansion of England* could not have been better timed from the point of view of providing a doctrine of imperialism, as its public reception makes clear, it would probably have been an even more effective book if it had been delayed sufficiently to comprehend the situation, just beginning to emerge by the mid-1880s, of a Franco-Russian combination so harassing to English interests as to force the Admiralty by the 1890s to

[1] B. Bosanquet, *Social and International Ideals* (London, 1917), p. 278.
[2] *Op. cit.*, pp. 278, 295.
[3] *The Expansion of England*, p. 289.

S

adopt a policy of 'scuttle' in the Mediterranean in the event of war.

Nevertheless, the value of Seeley's contribution is not substantially compromised by these cautionary considerations. The ambivalence of his idea of destiny did not invalidate the point that for practical purposes it was a destiny of opportunity. Except for mystics like W. T. Stead and Rhodes it was not taken seriously for anything else. And certainly in any case Seeley's opinions on particular political issues, from his opposition to Gladstone over the Eastern Question crisis of 1875–8, his opposition to Home Rule for Ireland, and such things as his presidency of a movement for 'groups of Lecturers on National Unity' in the early 1890s, as an offshoot of the Imperial Federation League,[1] give an unmistakable insight into a general political view which went far beyond that made explicit in *The Expansion of England*. It may be doubted whether Seeley's rather austere temperament would have permitted him to share the Bishop of Durham's feelings about Kipling's *Recessional*; nor can it be assumed that Seeley would have entered into the spirit of the scheme concocted by Rhodes and W. T. Stead to make him the head of a college to 'train people in the English-speaking idea', as a part of a great imperial secret Society of the Elect, modelled on the Order of Jesus.[2] It is quite possible that he would not have approved unreservedly the South African policy of his disciples Chamberlain and Milner.

But in any case Seeley had done the important thing. By insisting on the necessity of reinterpreting both English history and English politics in terms of the State and its power relationships, Seeley provided the basis necessary for a revised agenda of national debate. And it is upon this revised agenda that the general pattern of intellectual responses to the politics of England from the 1870's to the First World War is most properly to be considered. If he did not provide the answers to the great problems of English society, Seeley indicated the kind of questions which that society needed very urgently to ask. These were questions about national efficiency, and the social and economic reforms necessary to achieve the maximum

[1] See *Cambridge Review*, vol. XVI (1894–5), p. 197.
[2] F. Whyte, *The Life of W. T. Stead* (London, 1925), vol. II, pp. 209–10. The Rhodes Scholarships system was the only practical thing to emerge from these schemes.

possible degree of it. They were questions about the feasibility or otherwise of developing the imperial system towards this end. Above all they were questions about the new course the English State should pursue in the face of unprecedentedly challenging external circumstances.

☆ IO ☆

The Parliamentary Foundations of the Hotel Cecil

THE persistent hold of the landed classes on the highest offices of state, long after their economic predominance had passed, has been frequently remarked upon and extensively analysed.[1] Explanation, however, has lagged behind analysis. The commonplace and all embracing one is that of 'the charmed circle'. This explanation has appealed to successive generations of critics both conservative and radical, and was put nowhere more forcefully than in a letter to the third Marquess of Salisbury by a disgruntled supporter who wrote that it 'becomes clearer after every appointment that though men may work their hearts out and make every sacrifice financial and otherwise when the Conservative party is in opposition and in difficulties yet in prosperous times all is forgotten and all honours, emoluments and places are reserved for the friends and relations of the favoured few, many of whom were in the nursery, while some of us were fighting up hill battles for the party'.[2]

The views of disappointed men are not necessarily conclusive evidence, but the administrations formed by Lord Salisbury and A. J. Balfour between 1885 and 1905 provide the test case

---

[1] Most recently and exhaustively by W. L. Guttsman in *The British Political Elite* (London, 1963).

[2] G. C. T. Bartley to Salisbury 22 October, 1898. Salisbury MSS. Bartley was M.P. for Islington North 1885–1906, and had been Conservative party agent from 1882–5, and before that a Civil Servant in the Science and Art Department for twenty years. A vigorous propagandist for popular education and working class institutions for self-help, he was a founder of the National Penny bank.

by which to judge the truth of their theory. These administrations occupy a central point in the transition from aristocratic mid-Victorian government, and their character goes a
long way to explain the strength of aristocratic representation
in Mr Guttsman's tables. For while the party underwent a
profound change in its methods of organization and in its social
and electoral base, these administrations were undoubtedly
led by aristocrats and a high proportion of their offices was
filled by members of the landed classes. The 'charmed circle'
existed to the extent at least that these men came from the
hereditary ruling class, that they took it for granted that they
would play a pre-eminent part in politics, and that almost
everyone else did too.

The advantages of belonging to the hereditary ruling class
were in fact cumulative. A young patrician grew up in the
world of the great houses where the intimate affairs of state
were dinner table gossip; he went into parliament as a young
man, became private secretary to father, uncle or cousin, and
gained the parliamentary and administrative experience
prerequisite to high office, if he was willing to learn. The
charmed circle in fact provided opportunity, which the
favoured few might exploit if they cared to but which many did
not, since it was put upon them willy nilly as the concomitant
of their rank. Lord Ernest Hamilton for instance found
himself in 1885 'thrust an unwilling victim' into the family
seat of North Tyrone, because three elder brothers were
pledged to English constituencies. He found himself 'a mere
brick in a buttress whose sole purpose was to maintain a number
of paid officials in their billets. . . . . Nobody wanted me except
as a voter in divisions.' The only consolations he found for the
ordeal of listening to 'childish recrimination and insincere
criticism' were the oratory of Gladstone and races with the
youngest of his brothers along the terraces of the House on
tricycles borrowed from the dining room attendants.[1] He
retired gratefully after one full parliament. Other younger
sons with more stomach for parliamentary life (his own brother
George was a notable example), since they had to make a
career of some sort made a career of politics and became the

[1] Lord Frederic Hamilton, *The Days Before Yesterday* (London, 1937 ed.), p. 208.
Lord Ernest Hamilton, *Forty Years on* (London, n.d.), pp. 203, 222–3.

steady professional backbone of successive administrations, men of business in the tradition of Liverpool and Peel, if they could not aspire to the first place. For whatever the opportunities and advantages of rank, leadership went to the ablest. With the exception of Chamberlain, who was ruled out by his antecedents, and Randolph Churchill, who ruled himself out by want of judgement and self-control, there was no politician in the Unionist ranks between 1885 and 1905 who could hold a candle to Salisbury; and the succession was assured not by any ties of blood, but by Balfour's astonishing performance as Irish Secretary in the parliament of 1886. The ability of the Cecils, however, decided only which aristocrats should dominate the party.

It would be absurd to deny the advantages of possession enjoyed by the landed classes, but it may be instructive to examine how these advantages were exploited, if only as an example of the slow and complex reaction of political institutions to social change. To do this we have, first, to consider the character of the parliamentary party that accepted aristocratic leadership and, secondly, to consider what criteria were applied by this leadership in promoting its followers to office. Finally, we may consider briefly the important question which is so often ignored—what advantages beyond a tidy income and a lot of hard work office bestowed upon the holder. Aristocratic monopoly of the sweets of office may be the burden of the Conservative critic's complaint, but for the radical there is a more general significance. All studies of the personnel of Cabinets and parliaments share the underlying assumption that who takes decisions affects the content of these decisions; and, moreover, that it is the social rather than the personal or representative character of the decision makers that matters. This will be true only to the extent that in the first place social background determines political opinions and in the second to the extent that those holding office are able to translate their own opinions into policy. Thus we shall have first to consider the character of the Parliamentary party, the strength of its various sections, and the implications in terms of political opinion, influence, and access to office. Secondly, we must examine the office holders themselves, the considerations that governed the formation of ministries and promotions to office, especially as regards those claimants, both successful and unsuccessful, who came from outside the traditional ruling class. And finally we must consider, however briefly, the extent of freedom in policy making of those who held the formal positions of power, and the nature of the constraints under which they acted.

I

For the purposes of analysis the parliamentary party which provided the foundations of the Hotel Cecil has to be somewhat arbitrarily defined as consisting of all those Conservative members who sat in the House of Commons between 1885 and 1905. Furthermore, since we are concerned with the internal character of the party, no attempt will be made to compare its characteristics with those of other parties, or those of the electorate or of the population as a whole. Many of its members were titled, many were related to each other, many were educated at the same schools and universities, and many were rich. But rather than measure the distribution of these characteristics separately in order to compare them, either in fact or by implication, with those of some other group, as has been done by other analysts,[1] an attempt has been made to identify a number of social types among the members.[2] This may give a spurious precision to what is necessarily imprecise, but the aim is not statistical exactness, but some idea of the orders of magnitude involved. There are no measures of those things that can be measured precisely, such as education, occupation or interest, not only because we are not concerned with comparison, but also because these measurements have a much greater drawback—they are uninformative, they do not correspond to real social distinctions. Their significance lies in certain assumed connections between the characteristics they measure and the behaviour of individuals, such that men educated at the same school will tend to think alike, which cannot be assumed but must be demonstrated. This is not to

[1] I.e. Guttsman, *The British Political Elite*, J. F. S. Ross, *Parliamentary Representation* (revised edition, London, 1948) and most effectively Simon Haxey, *Tory M.P.* (London, 1939).

[2] Biographical information has been found in the *D.N.B.*, and various editions of *Dod's Parliamentary Companion* and a plethora of other biographical dictionaries, guides and directories, as well as the fourth edition of John Bateman's *The Great Landowners of Great Britain and Ireland* (London 1883), and the official returns of owners of lands in England and Wales, Scotland, and Ireland.

deny the importance of education, but only its value as an independent variable. There are no lists of how many men went to Eton, because whether it matters or not that a man went to Eton depends on the man. A Stanley might be educated or not, and wherever he pleased, without it affecting his social standing or political opportunities. On the other hand for a man like R. A. Cross the fact that he was at school and college with a Stanley might make all the difference in the world. Education may be a key to individual careers, and it may also be a key to wider social changes such as the fusion of the landed with the commercial and industrial élites, but for the present purpose it is useful only as one factor in distinguishing ideal types.

For the same reasons family connections within the party are not spelled out. Of course there were extensive family ramifications, and these might be of great importance especially in getting a first foot on the ladder to office. But only a study of individual cases will show whether a family connection was important or not. At least three prominent politicians of the period, Harcourt, Campbell-Bannerman and Edward Stanhope, had brothers on the opposite side of the House. From one point of view this is evidence of the parliamentary conspiracy. It helps to explain the wide areas of agreement and common assumption that underlay parliamentary conflict; but within the limits of that conflict, which was real enough to the participants, it shows that family relationships necessarily entailed neither harmony nor collaboration.

Again there are no calculations of the 'interests' of M.P.s in the manner of J. A. Thomas.[1] Useful as his method may be in tracing long term changes, it has limitations as a way of describing the character of a party at any given moment. As Thomas has shown, each M.P. may have a variety of interests and to aggregate these interests gives us no clue to the weight given them either collectively in policy decisions or in the priorities of individuals. How their interests affected policy-making can only be determined by the study of particular policies and decisions.[2]

[1] *The House of Commons, 1832–1901. A Study of its Economic and Functional Character* (Cardiff, 1939), and *The House of Commons 1906–11. An Analysis of its Economic and Social Character* (Cardiff, 1958).

[2] This is especially important for a party characterized by loose coalitions which change composition from issue to issue. See for instance S. C. Ghosh, 'Decision Making and Power in the British Conservative Party. A Case Study of the Indian Problem 1929–34', *Political Studies*, vol. XIII, June 1965, no. 2.

The question of how decisions are actually made raises two commonplace considerations: the pressures besides personal interest on those in a position to influence decisions, and the personal weight of these men. It appears frequently to be forgotten that the parliamentary system is and was a representative one and that M.P.s often press the interests of their constituents with far more vigour and persistence than their own. The importunities of dock yard M.P.s at this time were notorious,[1] and F. M. L. Thompson has demonstrated the point very well by showing how much attention to the interests of their constituents had to be paid by the Fitzwilliams as patrons of the nomination borough of Malton, as well as by the landed interest in the industrial areas to the 'feelings and interests of the trading part of the country'.[2] The character of a parliamentary party may be as much a function of the constituencies that support it as of the men who compose it. Thus it is important to observe not only changes in the social composition of the Conservative party but also the effect of the shift in electoral preponderance from rural and small town England to the urban and industrial areas.

While the parliamentary party as defined is limited to those Conservative members who sat in the Commons between 1885 and 1905, the analysis is not limited to this period in the sense that it takes into account the whole of the members' parliamentary careers. Something of the spread that this entails is conveyed by the fact that two of them, Lord John Manners and A. J. B. Beresford Hope were first returned in 1841, while the last survivor, Sir Winston Churchill, left the Commons in 1964. The structure of the Parliamentary party may be looked at in two ways: as a series of parliamentary groups or generations, the first of which consists of all members returned at the general elections of 1885 and 1886 who had sat in previous parliaments. This group represents the survivors of the Derby–Disraeli party. The other five groups consist of the members returned for the first time in the parliaments of 1885, 1886, 1892, 1895 and 1900. The second way in which the structure of the parliamentary party may be analysed is by reference to the social background of the members. As indicated above this

---

[1] A. L. Lowell, *The Government of England* (New York, 1928), vol. I, p. 149.
[2] *English Landed Society in the Nineteenth Century* (London, 1963), pp. 274–5.

has been done by the device of social types, not based on any single criterion such as occupation, education or interest, but intended to reflect general social status or prestige. While from one point of view the owners of means of production, distribution and exchange may constitute a single class, there exist distinctions that are real enough in their own eyes to create barriers between them. It is these distinctions that ideal types try to reflect and though they do some violence to the complexities of late Victorian society, it is hoped that they would be recognized as having some reality by the men themselves. This does not mean that the types are precise or that there has not been considerable difficulty in deciding which one a member best fits. But this may be an argument in their favour. The fluidity of English social distinctions is a commonplace reiterated by each editor of the successive editions of *Burke's Landed Gentry*. Nor is it asserted that men with similar backgrounds necessarily acted as cohesive political groups, showed similar concerns or held common political ideas. One may be able in fact to distinguish quite clearly between social and political types.

The first two social types, then, constitute the landed aristocracy, the traditional ruling class. It is divided between peers and their offspring and the landed gentry, partly on grounds of the greater wealth and prestige of the peers, and partly because the likelihood of eldest sons leaving the Commons abruptly suggested that there might be some difference in the parliamentary careers typical of the two groups.[1] Both peers and gentry to a lesser extent had other interests than land, but land was what gave them their social and political position, and gave it also to their brothers and cousins who did not hold land themselves and might follow a full time career in the services, at the bar, in railways, banking and even stock broking. If there is a difference in terms of parliamentary career between the two, it lies between the ducal families and the mere gentry. In the parliament of 1885 the Conservative benches were graced by four sons of the Duke of Abercorn,

---

[1] There were old established families of squires like the Chaplins whose wealth matched that of the peerage, but generally speaking the peers had not only broader acres but were more likely to have other sources of wealth such as urban or mineral property. The minimum qualification used for the category of landed gentry is 1,000 acres where no other source of income is apparent.

but it was unusual for anyone but the head or eldest son of a gentry family to enter politics.

The third type of member was drawn from what might be called the commercial and industrial dynasties, the Barings, Bairds, Hoares, Fieldens, Allsopps and Hambros, families which had made their money and been in politics in an earlier generation. Members of such families had acquired land and titles and there are good grounds for including the longer established of them in the landed aristocracy. In some cases where members have clearly become country gentlemen or followed a typically aristocractic career this has been done. But where the family has remained active in business, members belong to this distinct type. Whether a family merged with the landed aristocracy appears largely to have been a matter of taste, though the pattern of fusion seems to have changed in the course of the century. Where in the first half of the century a banker or brewer would become a landed proprietor, at the end when the value of land both as an economic and a political asset had declined, it became more common for the landed aristocrat to pursue a career in commerce or industry, while bankers, brewers and industrialists less often invested in land.[1]

The fourth type is more transitional still, since it covers members of commercial and industrial families which had been wealthy for at least a generation, but which had not previously taken any part in politics at the national level. To separate these from men of first generation wealth as well as politics has been to some extent a matter of guesswork. One means of discrimination has been the kind of education that a member was given, being some indication of the prosperity and the aspirations of his parents. It was often a matter of choice rather than means whether a boy was sent to a local grammar school or to public school and university.[2] And even public

[1] For the decline in land sales and the changing pattern of recruitment to the peerage see the excellent discussion in Thompson, *English Landed Society*, pp. 292–9, 318–20. In this as in so many other things W. H. Smith was thoroughly old fashioned. He acquired property in Suffolk and Devon to the tune of half a million: Viscount Chilston, *W. H. Smith* (London, 1965), p. 156.

[2] As in the case of Bonar Law. Unfortunately we have few such excellent accounts for these men as Robert Blake provides in *The Unknown Prime Minister* (London, 1955), especially pp. 24–8 where he describes the gulf between the world of the prosperous Glasgow merchant family and that of landed society. Their provincialism and absence of desire for social acceptance, as well as his own family background, have led me to regard Bonar Law as a 'self-made man' despite the wealth of Kidstons.

school and university might not signify any desire for social acceptance. The merchant patriciate of Manchester sent their sons to Rugby and a safe middle class college at Oxford only to draw them back into a society that had as little to do with the landed aristocracy as the Burgertum of Hamburg had with the Junkers.[1] So the distinctions are hard to draw. But by and large the fifth type represents those who had made their own money or most of it, whose business interests were generally concentrated in a single locality, and who had not yet risen on the ladder of social acceptance or had not desired to do so.

The next type is more easily isolated; professional men, chiefly barristers, with some solicitors, and a handful of doctors, architects, academics, surveyors and such like. There were considerable differences of status among these men. Several of the barristers had more or less distant relations with gentry families and one or two with the peerage, while several were entirely self made having worked their way up from a clerkship or what they described as 'commercial pursuits'. A few of the solicitors were also well connected and several had extensive interests outside their legal practices. Most of the academics and doctors sat for university seats, and perhaps should be regarded separately. But all these men, despite other connections, interests and the possession of private means, appear to have worked full time at their professions, at least before entering politics, and to have depended to some extent on earning their living by their services. This distinguishes them both from landed proprietors and from commercial and industrial capitalists.

The last four types are relatively unimportant and the last two hardly more than residual. The seventh covers those employed in the public service, whether the home civil service, the diplomatic or the I.C.S. The eighth covers the armed services, but in both these cases any member with close connections with the landed aristocracy or gentry has been judged a member of the landed classes. The ninth covers all those whom it has been difficult to place socially, such as journalists and newspaper proprietors, stockbrokers, men with colonial fortunes, authors, political organizers, and such social curiosities

[1] See Katharine Chorley, *Manchester Made Them* (London, 1950).

as Coningsby Disraeli or H. L. B. McCalmont, whose father
was a barrister, who spent eight years in the army, and then
inherited £4 million from a stock-broking great uncle.   Finally,
there are those about whom too little information has been
found to come to any decision.   The number is small, but
several spent some time in Parliament and more extensive
searches in local directories might eliminate them altogether.

THE LANDED CLASSES	1. Peerage	99 (14%)
	2. Gentry	179 (25%)
INDUSTRY AND COMMERCE	3. Dynasties	57 (8%)
	4. Second generation	102 (14%)
	5. Self made	62 (9%)
PROFESSIONAL AND	6. Professional men	121 (17%)
PUBLIC SERVICE	7. Public servants	11 (2%)
	8. Armed services	24 (3.5%)
OTHERS	9. Unclassifiable	33 ⎫ (7%)
	10. Unidentified	13 ⎭
TOTAL		701 (100%)

Thus the landed classes supplied about 40 per cent of the total,
industry and commerce 31 per cent, professional and public
services roughtly 22 per cent and the remainder 7 per cent.
Over the whole period 1885–1905 the landed classes supplied
the largest number but not a majority of the members.   But
if we break the total down into parliamentary groups (Table A,
p. 310) some modification of this overall pattern can be seen in the
recruitment of successive parliamentary generations.   In the
first group, those members who had sat before 1885, the landed
classes held a clear majority of the whole, providing nearly
twice as many members as the next largest group, Industry
and Commerce.   In the succeeding groups the landed classes
play a considerably smaller part, dropping below a third of the
new generation of 1900, while the industry and commerce
group fluctuates around a third until the sharp rise in 1900.
This rise can probably be explained, along with the fluctuations
in the size of the professional and public service groups, by the
relative success of the party in each general election.   The
new parliamentary group of 1885 reflected the change in the
nature of the constituencies and the kind of constituencies
Conservatives were winning.   Hence the increase of urban
members from the industrial and professional groups.   The
1886 group reflects the success of the party in winning county
divisions which the Liberals had taken in 1885; the candidates

came largely from the landed classes. The party also won less promising urban constituencies, for which carpet-bagging barristers were likely to stand. In 1892 when the party lost ground at the general election, fewer new members were returned and most of these came in as replacements in Conservative seats rather than by winning seats from Liberals. This meant more county members, chiefly landed, a few more businessmen from safe industrial seats, and fewer lawyers. 1895 saw a sweeping election victory, with a large number of gains from the Liberals and a corresponding increase in the proportion from the professional and public service groups, again chiefly lawyers, and a modest influx of journalists and other unclassifiables. The election of 1900 saw a small net loss of seats, but a substantial change through replacements, in which the industrial and commercial group gained at the expense both of the landed classes and of the professional and public service group.

The differences in the balance of recruitment of new parliamentary groups between gains and replacements is indicated by the following figures, which show the number of members dropping out from each parliament, either through death, defeat or retirement, and the number of gains or losses at the subsequent general election, as compared with the last:

	1885–1886	1886–1892	1892–1895	1895–1900	1900–1905
Drop-outs	20	153	53	107	225
Net gains or losses	+66	−48	+73	−7	−200

This shows that the new parliamentary groups of 1892 and 1900 were largely recruited by replacement, while those of 1886 and 1895 had substantial numbers from formerly Liberal seats. But the fluctuations of recruitment in the parliamentary groups are rather faintly reflected in the actual social composition of the party in each parliament. This can be seen in Table B (p. 310), where the proportions in the three main groups are fairly constant. The decline in the strength of the landed classes particularly is less than that in their share of recruitment. To understand this we have to examine the patterns of continuity and turnover in both the parliamentary and the social groups.

In the first place there was a steady turnover of parliamentary generations.[1] The first group, of course, includes members who first entered the Commons at every general election from 1841 and is therefore already a composite group. The numbers dropping out are affected both by the length of time elapsing between general elections and by the election results themselves. Thus there is little falling off between 1885 and 1886, a sharp fall between 1886 and 1892 and so on, until 1906 which in a dramatic way marks the end of a parliamentary era. Not only did electoral defeat cut off many careers, but internal dissension and disunity appear to have led to an unusual number of retirements before the election. What the table does not reveal is the relative strength of the different social groups within the parliamentary groups, and this is particularly important in view of the experience, influence and access to office which tended to accompany a long parliamentary career. An attempt to demonstrate the relative continuity of the social groups, without producing a mass of detailed figures, only served to show that the point could be better made by reference to the different patterns of career in the different social groups.

The ages of entry (Table D, p. 311) follow a fairly clear pattern. It was traditional for the eldest sons of peers to enter the Commons in their 'twenties (46 per cent of 'the peerage' did so) or early 'thirties, before ascending to higher things. The gentry tended to come in a bit later, though 30 per cent of them did so before the age of thirty. The parliamentary round and the life of the landed classes were geared to each other in a way that was not true for other sections of the community. The commercial and industrial classes did not enjoy the same leisure and they tended to enter parliament later in their careers and less as a matter of course. By and large the differences in their ages of entry reflect both the nature of their business and

---

[1] Table C (p. 310) shows the turnover of parliamentary groups from parliament to parliament. The total numbers for each parliament are not an indication of the actual strength of the party at any given moment in a parliament, since they include every member who sat in each parliament. Members with gaps in their parliamentary careers and those returned at by-elections, and those who retired or died between elections are included for the whole of any parliament in which they sat. Nor is the table an index of the political activity of the parliamentary groups. A number of members succeeded to titles or were elevated to the peerage and remained active in politics. A number of defeated members continued to contest elections long after their final departure from the Commons. And finally half a dozen who sat after 1906 did so as Liberals.

the degree to which it was established. The offspring of the dynasties, members of large going concerns, were able to enter relatively early (19 per cent did so before the age of thirty), as were bankers, merchants and others whose business was in London. For those with their business in the provinces, and especially for men who were building up their own firms, parliamentary ambitions had to wait for a later stage in their careers. In fact nearly 60 per cent of the self-made men came in after the age of fifty: membership of Parliament was the crowning glory of a successful lifetime in local business and politics, not a career in itself.

Professional men, particularly barristers, followed a rather different pattern. The majority of them came in between the ages of thirty-five and forty-five, when their professional careers were established. It appears that for many of the barristers a parliamentary career was regarded not so much in a political as in a professional light, as a claim to promotion to the Bench.

Age of entry naturally affected the chances of a long parliamentary career, and those who came in relatively late were not only more likely to retire through death or incapacity, but were also more likely to have their careers cut off by electoral vicissitudes. Election defeats in 1892 and 1906 caused large dropouts among the older members of the new groups in the previous parliaments: of the new groups in the parliaments of 1885 and 1886, 58 per cent and 49 per cent respectively had dropped out by the end of the 1892 parliament, and nearly half of the 1895 and 1900 new entries were finished by the defeat of 1906. This helps to explain the relative brevity of parliamentary careers in the industrial and commercial group, as does the readiness of lawyers to accept legal preferment that of the professional group. But the striking disparity between the pre-1885 group and the others, and between the landed classes and the rest remains to be accounted for. As far as the parliamentary groups are concerned, the fact that the pre-1885 group is a composite one from former parliaments means that it necessarily has more long serving members than the new groups. But the disparity is striking nevertheless. The pre-1885 group had more members serving over twenty-one years in the Commons than all the other groups put together (79 to 70), and this cannot be explained entirely by differences of social composition. In fact there was an important change in the career pattern of the group with the greatest number of long servers, the gentry. Of the fifty-four gentry in the pre-1885 group no fewer than thirty sat in the Commons for more than twenty-six years. Of the hundred and twenty-five elected for the first time between 1885 and 1905, only twelve did so. Thus a period which was marked by a small decline in the proportion of the landed classes recruited, and by a still smaller decline in their parliamentary strength, saw the withering of the main trunk of the old Tory party.

This conclusion is reinforced if we look at the fortunes of the country gentlemen proper. The ideal-type of the Tory county member might be defined as a baronet of well-established family living on his estates, with an interest in a local bank or railway, active in county government, a magistrate and deputy lieutenant, possibly Chairman of Quarter Sessions if he had had some legal training or High Sheriff if his acres were broad enough, seldom if ever Lord Lieutenant, but often a county councillor or county alderman after 1888. As a member of Parliament he would be tied to his constituency by residence, family connection, property and his involvement in local affairs. To isolate the country gentlemen proper from the gentry as a whole this ideal type was used as a syndrome, most but not all of whose characteristics a member must share in order to be counted. Two characteristics were judged absolutely necessary: that the member should sit for a county constituency, and that some at least of his property should be situated in that county. The first qualification excluded a number of landowners, notably Balfour, W. H. Long and Hicks Beach, who sat for urban constituencies, and the second a number who sat for counties in which they had no property nor any apparent personal connection. By and large the first qualification excluded what one might call professional politicians and Irish landowners, while only two or three members were excluded by the second. To these qualifications a third was added, that members should have served at least a dozen years in the Commons, in order to demonstrate not only the passing of one political generation, but the failure of a comparable body of county members of a younger generation to survive the election of 1906.

T

By these criteria thirty of the pre-1885 group qualified as
country gentlemen proper with the required length of service
and by a less strict interpretation twenty-nine of the new
parliamentary groups. Not only was there a far higher
proportion of long service members in the pre-1885 group,
but there was also a considerable disparity in the length of
service. The pre-1885 country gentlemen averaged twenty-
eight years as against eighteen years for the newcomers. The
pre-1885 group began to drop out in the parliament of 1886,
but the great exodus came in 1906; and the two survivors of
1910, Akers-Douglas and Squire Chaplin himself, retired to the
Lords in 1911 and 1916. Not many of the country gentlemen
elected for the first time between 1885 and 1905 outlasted
Chaplin. Four had gone by 1900, another fourteen by 1906,
three more by 1910. Sir John Dickson Poynder defected to
the Liberals over Free Trade in 1906, and Sir Alex Acland-
Hood went to the Lords after the row over party organization
in 1911. Colonel Mark Lockwood and F. A. Newdigate
retired in 1917, leaving only three of the old county members
among the hard faced men who had done well out of the war.
This is not to say that their species had passed from the face
of the earth. It is with us yet, and it has been too narrowly
defined to conclude that all that it stood for was lost. Their
interests and prejudices remained well represented in the higher
circles of the party and especially in the Lords. But for the
character of the parliamentary party, the eclipse of the squires
was important. For even if others of similar social background
took their places, they had not shared the same experiences and
they lived in a different political world. When the parliament
of 1900 was dissolved Disraeli had passed into the realms of
myth, Salisbury was dead, Balfour's ascendancy in the Commons was over, and the initiation of policy lay in the grasp of
Chamberlain. And however numerous the country gentlemen
might have become again, for years after 1906 they could not
but have lacked the weight and influence which parliamentary
longevity had given their predecessors.

In fact after 1906 and more clearly after 1918 the long-term
changes in the economic and social structure were reflected in
the structure of the Conservative party. But before 1906
though the process of erosion had begun, the landed classes,

and the country gentlemen in particular, provided the largest, the most homogeneous, the most stable element in the parliamentary party and the cornerstone of the Hotel Cecil.

The stability and continuity of the landed interest in the parliamentary party owed a good deal to the comparative security of its electoral base. Despite the bitter struggle of the early 1880s over the adoption of a formal mass organization, it only became a reality after 1885 where it suited the local conditions. While in Liverpool a popular organization grew up—one in which the prejudices of the rank and file were strong enough to unseat a Cabinet minister[1]—in the rural areas and county towns the old style politics continued. This was demonstrated by the introduction of elected local government in the counties after 1888: in almost all of the rural areas the majority of the former members of quarter sessions, the old appointed county government, were returned to the new county councils at the first elections, often without opposition. Subsequent county council elections were of so little interest that *The Times* failed to record them after 1892, and always meant the L.C.C. when it spoke of 'the County Council'.[2] The absence of effective opposition and the ability to conduct politics without the apparatus of popular organization reflected the continued social and economic dominance of the landed classes in those areas. Dominance is the right word, since the 'deference' of which we hear so much in discussions of British politics, was something exacted. Effective opposition in the agricultural counties was limited to those areas which had either a large population of small independent proprietors or where the larger size of farming units had produced something like a rural proletariat with its own institutions, notably the Primitive Methodist chapels. Even in these areas the landed classes were able to use their economic power and control of local institutions to disrupt opposition. The history of the agricultural workers' movement from the 1870s, when it first emerged from sporadic rioting to organized political action, is a procession of anecdotes of eviction,

---

[1] Walter Long was refused readoption in 1900 in the West Derby division because of his failure to satisfy his constituents' demands on the Clergy Discipline Bill. S. Salvidge, *Salvidge of Liverpool* (London, 1934), pp. 32–3.

[2] See J. P. D. Dunbabin, 'Expectations of the New County Councils, and their Realisation', *Historical Journal*, vol. 8, no. 3, 1965, pp. 353–79.

blacklisting, the difficulties of securing places for meetings and so forth.

The power of the gentry lay in their close personal involvement through residence, family connection, and property in the affairs of their locality. But such involvement was not of course confined to the gentry, nor to the landed classes generally, nor to county members. Of the whole parliamentary party almost half lived in their constituencies or in the parliamentary borough of which it formed a part. Almost half (but not necessarily the same members) had some property or interest, and roughly 20 per cent had some family tie. Around a third had no apparent personal connection with their constituencies. These proportions held good with very little variation for all of the parliamentary groups. The small variations in the number with no personal connections tie in closely with the relative numbers of professional men in the new groups of 1885, 1886 and 1895, which we previously related to the new constituencies in 1885 and the electoral successes of 1886 and 1895. The real differences are to be found, as one would expect, between the different social groups. The division here lies between the first five, comprising the landed classes and industry and commerce, and the remainder. None of the first five groups had more than a quarter of its members sitting for constituencies with which they had no connection, but about half the members in professional, public service and the other categories did so. Again well over half of the landed classes and business men had some property or interest in their constituency, while for the remainder the proportion was below 20 per cent. But it may be as well to point out that even among the lawyers, there were quite a few with personal connections, some of them minor landowners who resembled country gentlemen more than barristers who sat for urban constituencies, while carpet-bagging members of the landed classes often followed a parliamentary career much like that of a barrister.

It is apparent too that in certain respects the landed nobility differed from the gentry, and the commercial and industrial dynasties from other businessmen. Members of the landed nobility and the dynasties were less likely to live in their constituencies than either the gentry or the other businessmen. The landed nobility, with its many interests outside land and its social life oriented to London, was much more easily in touch with the business dynasties than were the gentry. They shared what one might call a metropolitan outlook, whereas the gentry and the other businessmen were more provincial and rooted in one locality. Members from the business dynasties had fewer ties with their constituencies than either the landed or the other business groups. Less than half of them had property or interest in their constituencies, as against nearly three-quarters of the smaller manufacturers and self-made men. In respect both of property and residence in fact these last are the urban equivalents of the country gentlemen. They too were local notables, owing their political influence to their economic position in their constituencies, even if that position was gained by hard work rather than by inheritance. But the fact that they had to spend most of their working lives achieving this position meant, as we have seen, that they entered Parliament comparatively late and were for that reason less likely to become parliamentary notables as well as local ones.

But if in this respect the landed classes retained an advantage, one consequence of the redistribution of 1885 was a change in the pattern of safe seats. Before 1885, the strength of the party had been in the counties and smaller boroughs, of which the landed classes had the pick. After redistribution the balance was somewhat altered. It is difficult to arrive at an acceptable definition of a safe seat for a period of over twenty years: seats that were safe at the beginning become marginal or are lost altogether by the end. But one can adopt what might be called a minimum definition, that is seats won at every election from 1885 to December 1910. Of these 93 seats, 55 were county divisions, 15 were in London, 14 in the larger cities, 7 were county towns, with the total made up by Gravesend and Dover. Altogether 211 of our members sat for these seats at some time between 1885 and 1910. The great majority of the members for the county divisions had local connections, and more than half of them belonged to the landed classes, though the suburban divisions round Liverpool and London returned members of all types. In the urban seats outside London the landed classes supplied less than a third of the members, and the proportion with no personal

connections was nearly 40 per cent.   In London a quarter of
the members were from the landed classes, and no less than 70
per cent had no personal connection with their constituencies.
Thus while the landed classes still had nearly half the members
for safe seats, there were now quite a number available not
only to other groups but also to men with no personal stake in
the constituency.   There was in fact a greater possibility for
others of a parliamentary career similar to that of the traditional
country gentlemen: the suburban knights like Sir Frederick
Banbury, member for Peckham 1892–1906, Sir John Blundell
Maple, Dulwich 1887–1903 or Sir Henry Kimber, Wandsworth
1885–1913, became as familiar about the House as the knights
of the shires.

Neither in the safe seats nor in the others, however, was there
any exact correspondence between the type of constituency
and the social background of the members: and it is by reference
to the differences in relation between types of constituency and
member that we can distinguish between the social and the
political configurations of the parliamentary party.   In the
first place there were those members, country gentlemen,
suburban knights or city bankers whose social character and
interest coincided or was identified with that of their constituencies.   The political position of the gentry was an extension
of their social and economic position, and in a rather different
way the merchants and bankers who sat for the City, the stockbrokers, barristers and solicitors who sat for the inner ring of
suburbs, and the bankers, brewers, merchants and manufacturers in the outer ring, reflected the dominant social
character of their constituencies in their own persons.   These
two groups held most of the party's safe seats and provided the
core of the parliamentary party.   Their attitudes and interests
were by no means identical, but neither were they incompatible.
The gentry's overriding concern to shore up the landed interest
only fell foul of the economic orthodoxy of bankers and
merchants when it involved flirting with protection.   On
social questions the traditional paternalism of the landed class
did not take the form of pressure for the kind of state action
abhorrent to political economy, while in their other dominant
concern, the protection of the Established Church, they often
enjoyed the enthusiastic support of other sections of the party.

The members for the industrial areas differed markedly from the 'natural' representatives of field and suburb. Many of them did represent in their own persons the major industries of the area—the shipowners from Liverpool, shipbuilders from Belfast, ironmasters from Glasgow, and worsted manufacturers from Leeds and so forth—and it was certainly part even of the outsider's job to represent these interests. Nobody could have been more assiduous than the members for Sheffield, C. B. Stuart Wortley, Ellis Ashmead Bartlett and Sir Howard Vincent, in pressing the claims of their adopted city for armaments contracts. But they had also to be responsive to their constituencies in another way, by paying attention to the sentiments and problems of their predominantly working-class constituents. In Belfast and Liverpool members had to conform to the demands of a virulent brand of protestantism and in Lancashire generally to come to terms with the peculiarities of local working class Conservatism. As compared with those engaged in finance or commerce, manufacturers sitting for industrial constituencies had much more direct contact with working class problems, more awareness and even sympathy with working class aspirations, and were much more conscious of the need to find positive solutions to the problems of poverty and unemployment, and of the political dangers of inaction. These attitudes varied from industry to industry, and from those who were merely owners to those actually engaged in the management of their businesses, from whose ranks came those willing to advocate unorthodox measures without much regard for the Holy Writ of political economy. It was these men who provided the support from within the party for such policies as old age pensions and protection, pressed on their leaders from outside by Chamberlain.

This group found allies among members whose presence in the House was dictated more by devotion to causes than by the representation of interests. There was first the small but vocal band of retired generals, colonial merchants, civil servants and journalists who preached the need for Imperial federation and the strengthening of the armed services to anybody who would listen and to many who would have preferred not to. Their fears for the security of the Empire matched those of the manufacturers for their markets. Imperial preference and the disasters of the Boer war cemented an existing bond. Then there were the Tory philanthropists, whose interest in social problems had led them into politics through charitable institutions, school boards and local councils. London in particular boasted a good many of this type, who collaborated with the Progressives in the early years of the L.C.C. and sat for East End constituencies. They were drawn mainly from the landed and professional classes: Harry Cust is one example, a landowner and county member, who edited the *Pall Mall Gazette* as a Conservative paper but supported the Progressives and later sat for Bermondsey. Another is Arthur Morton, a Cambridge don and headmaster, governor of various schools, institutions and settlements in London, vice-chairman of the L.C.C. committee on working class housing, and member for Deptford from 1897 to 1906.

The variety of parliamentary types was of course much greater than this. In particular there were the individualists who concentrated their fire on some special target: Sir Albert Rollit, solicitor, steamship owner, newspaper proprietor and mayor of Hull, who spent his time, energy and skill in steering through unobtrusive but useful private bills; or John Henniker Heaton who, by constant attendance, scrupulous orthodoxy on all other subjects and genial persistence on his own, brought in single handed the Imperial Penny Postage. What distinguished these men from many of their fellow members was the amount of time they were prepared to devote to their parliamentary duties. 'Boardroom' members, as railway directors were sometimes called, had more pressing claims upon their attention. Barristers carried on their practice. Country gentlemen were often away about their local business and seldom spoke save on their special interests. This did not necessarily mean that they were without influence. W. W. B. Beach, father of the House in the 'nineties and a member for Hampshire since 1857, was unknown to Sir Henry Lucy after twenty years of reporting the Commons, but a fellow backbencher who had never heard him speak in seventeen years said that his views and opinions privately expressed carried considerable weight.[1] While sporadic attendance and scant

[1] H. W. Lucy, *Peeps at Parliament* (London, 1903), p. 14, and Mrs Adrian Porter, *The Life and Letters of Sir John Henniker Heaton, Bart.* (London, 1916), pp. 26–7.

speaking did not necessarily mean lack of influence, they certainly did mean lack of ambition for office. Many, perhaps a majority, of the parliamentary party never aspired to office and did not regard themselves as full time or professional politicians. To an aristocrat, politics, besides being a natural pursuit, might be the most convenient way to augment an assured income by personal exertion. To a barrister it might be the quickest way to the Bench. But for anyone else it was an uncertain and expensive career. Men without private means who launched on a full-time political career were liable to financial embarrassment and tended to become a burden to their party. A good deal of the bitterness about promotion probably arose from unacknowledged dependence on office to make ends meet. Businessmen did better to give their attention to business at least until they had made their pile, and even if they did that relatively early it might still seem too late or too irksome to start another career. Bonar Law, who was only forty-two when he retired from business and went into politics, found the change acutely depressing and told Austen Chamberlain that it was all very well for those who came into it young, but that if he had known what it was going to be like he would never have stood for parliament.[1]

Office was traditionally the reward of a long parliamentary apprenticeship and the factors we have discussed—age of entry into politics, uncertainty of seats, distractions from parliamentary duty, the lack of attractions in a parliamentary career —all provide reasons other than the 'charmed circle' for the conspicuous differences in the contributions of different social groups.[2] While it may be easily understood that young Lords were alone able and willing to undertake the arduous and unrewarding tasks of junior whips, and while the other factors mentioned above can be seen to have limited the numbers of middle-aged professional and businessmen zealous for less

[1] Blake, *The Unknown Prime Minister*, p. 44.
[2] Table E (p. 311) shows these contributions for the parliamentary party as defined: it does not show the overall distribution of office in the Unionist administrations since it excludes peers, who held a good many offices when the minor posts in the Household are considered, and Liberal Unionists. But it does show that the aristocratic predominance in the Cabinet rested on an almost equally great predominance among those who achieved office only outside the Cabinet. If one bars the law offices which were a professional preserve, the landed classes provided a majority of office holders at every level.

menial office, we have still to consider why, among those who
were ready to devote themselves to official life, some got on and
some did not.

II

'Ministries to a great extent make themselves: that is,
one or two appointments, exacted by some external
circumstance, have a long chain of quite inevitable
consequences.'

Lord Salisbury to the Earl of Harrowby
August 1, 1886[1]

'. . . from what I have seen during the last few days I
should say the most difficult and detestable position in life
is having to form a Government.'

W. H. Smith to the Hon. Robert Bourke
August 1, 1886[2]

These quotations indicate very well the two levels at which the
problems of forming a government presented themselves. On
the first level were the problems of forming an administration
capable of coping with whatever emergencies confronted it by
commanding the allegiance of a parliamentary majority.
Though it was probably true that when Salisbury set out to
form his first ministry he enjoyed the trust and respect of a
larger section of his party than any possible rival and thereafter
became the 'natural' Prime Minister, the leadership did not
absolve him from the task of conciliating all the elements in
the party and therefore of attaching to his ministry men who
represented different political views and were in fact potential
rivals. Randolph Churchill he had to suffer for a time,
because as Hicks Beach told him 'whatever objections may
exist to the formation of a Conservative Government in any
case, would I think, be rendered insuperable if such a Government had to be formed without the man who is far and away
the most popular Conservative in the House of Commons'.[3]
Because of the overriding importance of maintaining the Union
and therefore of keeping Gladstone out of office, Churchill's
position in the House and in the country not only required
that he be given important office, contrary to the rules of

[1] Salisbury MSS quoted in L. P. Curtis jun., *Coercion and Conciliation in Ireland
1880–1892. A Study in Conservative Unionism* (London, 1963). p. 120.
[2] Hambleden MSS quoted in Chilston, *W. H. Smith*, p. 215.
[3] Beach to Salisbury, 10 June 1885. Salisbury MSS.

seniority and administrative experience, but also enabled him, until he overreached himself, to hold the Cabinet to ransom on other issues.[1] The same considerations applied to Chamberlain and to a lesser extent to Goschen. They were brought into the Cabinet because they represented important sections of opinion whose adherence was necessary if the Union was to be preserved.

These strategical considerations, while enormously important and possibly difficult to put into effect, were, as Salisbury said, clear, compelling, and relatively uncomplicated when compared with the tactical problems at the second level. At this level the problem was to maintain the reputation of the ministry and the good humour of the party by routine administrative competence and parliamentary skill. The great crises of a ministry might turn on such strategic issues as Churchill's resignation, and its fate hang in the balance of a potential realignment of political forces. But ministries were also liable to a less dramatic declension: ineptitude on the front bench, the disaffection of the disappointed, the general wear and tear of a hard session, could sap the morale of the parliamentary party to the point where the majority became unreliable and the ability of the ministers to get through their programme was severely hampered.[2] Thus even a minor appointment deserved care and attention, and often created a great deal of trouble: the business of dealing with the claimants was what most irked Salisbury and disgusted Smith.

Even in the distribution of minor offices and honours strategic considerations could not be neglected. Here is Churchill putting on the screws in 1885 on behalf of his allies:

> I do feel very uneasy indeed about Wolff and Gorst and I cannot think that I have submitted to you their position as regards myself with the urgency which they are entitled to expect from me. If it were possible for you to consider

[1] As Salisbury told his private secretary Henry Manners during a row in the Cabinet over local government: 'The problem is a difficult one— for the state of the Union question makes it unusually difficult for us to resign: and the fact that (Beach having refused) there seems no possible leader in the Commons but Randolph: these two facts taken together involve the consequence that Randolph can always put before us the dilemma of accepting his views or endangering the Union with Ireland: and this gives him a strong position.' November 28 1886. Salisbury MSS quoted in Curtis, *Coercion and Conciliation*, p. 153.

[2] The parlous condition of the Unionist majority in 1890 is well described in Curtis, *Coercion and Conciliation*, pp. 301–8.

whether it might not be in your power to recommend
Wolff for the High Dignity of Privy Councillor I should
be easy in my mind about him, and I venture to press
this desire of mine upon you.

Gorst's disappointment is intense. He knows his
powers, his position in the House, his hitherto barely
recognized claims and it makes me perfectly wretched to
feel that it must occur to his mind that his failure to obtain
that for which so many persons of knowledge consider
he is fitted in every way, is due to lukewarmness on my part.

[If things stay as they were this morning] . . . I shall
be considered to have failed my friends, and my powers
whatever they may be, of being useful to your Government
will be impaired.[1]

If Churchill's claims had to be met, as they were in 1885 and
1886, then others had to be sent empty away, which did not
conduce to harmony within the party. Robert Bourke, for
instance, who had been an under-secretary for Foreign Affairs
from 1874 to 1880 and again in 1885, wrote to Smith to ask:

What sin it is that I have committed, which has induced
Lord Salisbury to inflict so great an injury upon me as to
leave me out now, after so many years of service with my
old colleagues, with whom I was on such cordial and
intimate terms.

You know what my work in office was, from 1874 to
1880 and subsequently, and how entirely I possessed the
confidence, and received the approbation of Lord Beaconsfield, and I have fought five contested elections. I hear
that all who are not *persona gratissima* to Ld. Randolph
Churchill may in future look forward to nothing but political effacement so long as they belong to the Conservative
Party. If this is so, the sooner we place ourselves under the
allegiance of some other leaders in the House of Commons,
the better for our own self respect and consistency.[2]

The Unionist alliance presented the same problem. The

---

[1] Churchill to Salisbury, 16 June 1885. Salisbury MSS.
[2] Bourke to Smith, August 1886. Hambleden MSS, Ser. 1. M. Smith tried
to console him with his impression 'that Salisbury has a most friendly disposition
towards you, that there is really no foundation for the suspicions as to Randolph
Churchill which you appear to entertain and that sooner or later some proposals
will be made to you in recognition of your long services'. 1 August 1886, *ibid.*
Bourke in fact was given a peerage and made Governor of Madras, but forfeited
his political position by his involvement in a notorious private scandal.

Liberal Unionists appeared to Conservatives to be indecently anxious for honours and after 1895 the followers of the Duke of Devonshire and Chamberlain had also to be accommodated with office. This aggravated the sense of frustration at the lower levels of the Administration: Conservative aspirants did not take kindly to making way for Jesse Collings.

While it is difficult to separate the strategic from the tactical considerations governing appointments, it must be clear that it is only at the tactical level that the explanation of the 'charmed circle' will serve: that is to say that the leaders would only be free to discriminate between their followers on grounds of family connection and social background in situations where the political exigencies of maintaining a parliamentary majority or alliance did not obtain. Different patterns of parliamentary career have already been advanced to account for differences in availability and willingness to take office among members from different social backgrounds, with the effect of magnifying the aristocracy's share of the pool of 'official' members. But in facing its tactical problem of maintaining the reputation of the ministry, the leadership had, besides availability and willingness, to consider suitability. In the Unionist administrations formed between 1885 and 1905, there were reasons why this criterion should favour the aristocracy also. Apart from the politicians whose inclusion in the Cabinet was forced by strategic considerations, there were at any time only a handful of members with the requisite parliamentary standing and administrative experience to fill the great offices. The character of this group was more likely to reflect the dominant character of the past than the present parliamentary party, because of the ten- to twenty-year time-lag between entering the Commons and entering the Cabinet. Only three members elected to the Commons in 1885 or later sat in the Cabinet before 1905, none before 1903. Given the character of the Derby–Disraeli party, it was not surprising that a good many of those equipped for high office under Salisbury were peers. Some of the offices even seemed to require that they should be. Salisbury, when asking the Duke of Richmond to become the first Secretary for Scotland, said of the status required that 'measured by the expectations of the people of Scotland it is approaching to Arch-angelic. We want a big man to float

it—especially as there is so much sentiment about it.   I think
you seem pointed out by nature to be the man.   Lothian's health
would not be up to it—and Balfour of Burleigh or Dalrymple
are too insignificant.   The Scotch people would declare we
were despising Scotland—and treating her as if she was a West
Indian colony.   It really is a matter where the effulgence of two
Dukedoms and the best salmon river in Scotland will go a long
way . . .'[1]   Partly because of the shortage of Scottish Conservative M.P.s it remained true down to 1905 that the strongest
candidates for the secretaryship were peers.   The effulgence
of dukedoms as a criterion of suitability may suggest merely
the confidence of the aristocracy in their inherent right to
govern and a belief, probably correct, that many others
accepted the propriety of their view.   Gladstone did for one.[2]
But this by no means implied that personal fitness for office
could be or was ignored because of social background or family
connection.   Gladstone himself demanded in his appointments
a high standard of devotion to the ideals of public service which
had governed the administrations of the mid-century.[3]   While
Conservatives were apt to take a less austere line, especially in
matters of patronage, promotions to office, where not dictated
by political exigencies, were governed to a large extent by the
need for the efficient conduct of public business.   This can
be seen by observing the senior members of the government at
work filling up the inevitable gaps in the ranks between 1886
and 1892.   The problem of fitting in Beach, on his return to
active politics in 1887, prompted this comment from Salisbury:

> Holland makes a very good and popular Colonial
> Secretary—and I should be sorry to have to move him.   I

[1] 7 August 1885, Goodwood MS 871 quoted in H. J. Hanham, 'The Creation of
the Scottish Office 1881–1887', *The Juridical Review*, Part 3, 1965, pp. 228–9.

[2] ' The natural condition of a healthy society is that governing functions should
be discharged in the main by a leisured class.   In matters where the narrow
interests of that class seemed to be concerned, it has its besetting sins and dangers.
But for the general business of government it has peculiar capacities: and whatever
control a good system may impose, by popular suffrage, by gathering representation from all classes, by tradition, or opinion, or the press, yet, when the leisured
class is depressed, that fact indicates that a rot has found its way into the structure
of society.'   Quoted in G. M. Young, *Victorian Essays*, ed. W. D. Handcock
(Oxford, 1962), p. 106.

[3] See H. J. Hanham, 'Political Patronage at the Treasury 1870–1912', *Historical
Journal*, vol. 3, no. 1, 1960, and for the administrative creed of the public men of
the Liberal party, John Vincent, *The Formation of the Liberal Party 1857–1868*
(London, 1966), pp. 11–20.

doubt his making a good Home Secretary. He is so amiable, he would hang nobody.

On the other hand Beach was not a very good Colonial Secretary. His one fault is his manners—and that is an office where manner is specially important: and his record as Colonial Secretary is not quite irreproachable. On the other hand he would make a very good Home Secretary: and would hang everybody.[1]

Occasion for a more comprehensive review of the virtues of their subordinates, and hence for revealing the factors that weighed in the minds of the ministers, was provided by the death of H. C. Raikes the Postmaster General in 1891. The vacancy caused by Raikes' death was an embarrassment to the Government coming as it did towards the end of the parliament and involving a reshuffle which was bound to offend some among the numerous aspirants for promotion. The position was complicated by the fact that there were objections to the two candidates whom Salisbury thought to have the strongest claims. Of Ashmead-Bartlett,[2] a Civil Lord of the Admiralty and strenuous worker for the party organization in the provinces, Salisbury wrote: 'He has really worked so hard for the party, and that in the most disagreeable way, and I believe has done so much service, that I do not like not rewarding him: but ... he is entirely without authority in the House of Commons.'[3] To which Balfour added that 'it is a place which requires some administrative tact and capacity.... This seems to me of itself sufficient to exclude A. Bartlett.'[4] Balfour went on to point out that the Postmaster Generalship had in the past been held by Cabinet Ministers, and that it was in any case an independent office just below cabinet rank and anybody promoted to it would assume 'he was next on the rota for admission to the Cabinet'. And he asked if it would not be 'a pity to choke up the avenues of advancement by putting in any man who could under no circumstances be moved to a higher place? Does

[1] Salisbury to Smith, 19 September 1887. Hambleden MSS Ser. II. 8.

[2] E. Ashmead-Bartlett, M.P. for Eye, 1880–5, Sheffield Eccleshall, 1885–1902. Civil Servant in Education Department, 1877–80. Source of income thereafter uncertain, probably journalism and public speaking. Civil Lord of Admiralty 1885 and 1886–92.

[3] Salisbury to Balfour 25 August 1891, Balfour MSS B.M. Add MSS. 49689/118.

[4] Balfour to Salisbury 27 August 1891, Salisbury MSS.

not this exclude Dyke[1] and Fergusson[2] who have not the ability, and Plunkett[3] who has not the health, for a big department?' Balfour felt therefore that they had no alternative but to offer the post either to Sir John Gorst,[4] the Under Secretary for India, or W. L. Jackson,[5] the Financial Secretary to the Treasury. The objections to Gorst were the insecurity of his seat at Chatham and his 'disloyalty to the party' as Balfour put it or his 'independence' as he would have put it himself. Jackson on the other hand, whose services Salisbury regarded as so pre-eminent that he must have the job if he wanted it, met with Balfour's condescending approval:

> He is a man whom it would be very desirable ultimately to have in the Cabinet and who in the meanwhile would do the Post Office to perfection. He has great tact and judgement—middle-class tact and judgement I admit, but good of their kind. He justly inspires great confidence in business men; and he is that *rara avis*, a successful manufacturer who is fit for something besides manufacturing. A cabinet of Jacksons would [be] rather a serious order, no doubt: but one or even two would be a considerable addition to any cabinet.

But if Jackson were given the post, further problems would

---

[1] Sir William Hart Dyke, M.P. West Kent, 1865–8, Mid Kent, 1869–85, Dartford Div. of Kent, 1885–1906. 1874–80 Patronage Secretary to the Treasury (Chief Whip). 1885–6 Chief Secretary for Ireland. 1887–92 Vice President of the Committee of the Council. Large Landowner in Kent.

[2] Sir James Fergusson Bt., M.P. Ayrshire, 1854–7, 1857–73, Manchester N.E., 1885–1906. 1866–7 Under Secretary for India. 1867 Under Secretary Home Office. 1868–73 Governor and Commander in Chief South Australia. 1873–5 Governor of New Zealand. 1880–5 Governor of Bombay. 1885 Member of the Committee of the Council of Education for Scotland. 1886–91 Under Secretary for Foreign Affairs. 1891–2 Postmaster General. Scottish landowner, financially embarrassed, with a large number of directorships in City (which worried Goschen).

[3] David Plunkett, M.P. Dublin University, 1870–95. 1875–7 Solicitor General for Ireland; 1880 Paymaster General; 1885–6 and 1886–92 First Commissioner of Works. Raised to the peerage 1895. Irish landed and legal family. Called to the Irish Bar 1862; Q.C. 1868.

[4] John Eldon Gorst, M.P. Cambridge, 1866–8, Chatham, 1875–92, Cambridge University, 1892–1906. 1885 Solicitor General. 1886–91 Under Secretary for India. 1891–2 Financial Secretary to the Treasury. 1895–1902 Vice-president of the Committee of the Council. Inspector of Schools and Civil Commissioner in New Zealand 1861–3. Called to the Bar 1865. Q.C. 1875. Retired with pension in 1902, but later resigned pension and stood as a Liberal.

[5] William Lawies Jackson, M.P. Leeds, 1880–5, Leeds North, 1885–1902. 1886–91 Financial Secretary to the Treasury. 1891–2 Chief Secretary for Ireland. Raised to the peerage 1902. Made his fortune in worsted; leather merchant and tanner and director of Great Northern Railway Co.

then arise: first of all finding his successor at the Treasury. Balfour was inclined to think that 'the man with in some respects the handiest business head among the subordinates of the Government is Forward[1] [sic]: but he is unpopular, and deficient in powers of conciliation:—a serious defect in the mouth piece of a department whose chief function is to refuse'. Moreover, the prospect of finding a replacement for Jackson at the Treasury involved the Chancellor of the Exchequer, Goschen, and Goschen would not consider Forwood and did not want to lose Jackson. While he considered that the Post Office, with its hundred thousand employees and labour troubles, needed a strong and able man to run it 'with all its importance, it is not more important than that of Financial Secretary to the Treasury with its double set of duties, the Treasury duties, and the very difficult duty of assisting in arranging the business of the House. Jackson is so essentially "persona grata" in this latter respect, he is so popular and so handy, that it would be extremely difficult to replace him.'[2] Balfour had the further objection that if for any reason he himself had to leave the Irish office 'Jackson is the man, I think the only man, who ought to succeed me. He could not easily do so if now promoted to the P. Office:—at least such rapid changes would be highly inconvenient.'[3]

The other prominent contender was Gorst, whom Balfour found exceedingly irritating and Goschen thought dangerous for the Post Office because of his views on the labour question: 'He has the ability, but he is rather deeply pledged to take the side of wage earners on every possible occasion.'[4] Gorst had also been in trouble over India in the previous session, but Smith told Salisbury that he was inclined to favour him for the Postmaster Generalship 'notwithstanding all that has passed and if you sent for him and speak firmly "like a Father" you will judge whether or not you can or are disposed to appoint him. He is eccentric... but he has more ability as a debater on

---

[1] Arthur Bower Forwood, M.P. Lancashire South West, Ormskirk Div., 1885–98. 1886–92 Parliamentary Secretary to Admiralty. Merchant and shipowner in Liverpool. Mayor of Liverpool and leader of the Conservative party there. Tory democrat and supporter of Lord Randolph Churchill.

[2] Goschen to Salisbury, 25 August 1891. Salisbury MSS.

[3] Balfour to Salisbury, 27 August 1891. Salisbury MSS.

[4] Goschen to Salisbury, 25 August 1891. Salisbury MSS.

our Bench than any one excepting Arthur and Goschen.'[1] But
Smith agreed that the last session 'destroyed any *claim* he might
have had if you think it right to take it so'.

The same considerations of experience, of ability, of temperament, of reputation with colleagues, with the party and with
the House, and of claims upon the party for past services were
applied to all the candidates. In addition the few promotions
that had occurred in the previous four years ruled out men who
had not borne the burden of office, and the necessity for the
P.M.G. to sit in the Commons ruled out the one serious
contender from the Lords. Salisbury, Balfour, Goschen and
Smith were all agreed that Jackson would make a first rate
P.M.G. and had earned promotion, and despite the fact that
they also thought he would be more useful where he was,
Salisbury felt bound to offer him the first refusal.[2] Jackson,
accepting the view that he was more useful at the Treasury,
declined, and Salisbury after an unsatisfactory exchange of
letters with Gorst, offered the post to Fergusson, nobody's first
choice but acceptable all round, who took it.

The exchange with Gorst turned partly on the labour
question, where his claims to independence were so vehemently
expressed that Salisbury felt 'it would be quite impossible to
put him at the head of a department, where the labour question
is constantly cropping up—and where he would have frequent
opportunities for driving us into a corner',[3] and Smith agreed
that 'it would have been madness to "endorse" his independent
attitude by promotion'.[4] The exchange also illustrated
Salisbury's notions of the requirements of party loyalty and
the conditions for a successful career, which, acting on Smiths'
advice, he explained as part of his 'parental efforts'[5] to Gorst:

> I entertain—as everybody must do—the very highest
> estimate of your abilities; and I have seen with great sorrow

[1] Smith to Salisbury, 3 September 1891. Salisbury MSS. H. W. Lucy agreed
with Smith's estimate of Gorst's value in the House describing him as the 'utility
man of the Treasury Bench'. *A Diary of the Salisbury Parliament 1886–1892*
(London, 1892), pp. 153–4, and one backbencher at least wrote of his performance
in glowing terms. Sir Richard Temple, *Letters and Character Sketches from the House
of Commons*, ed. Sir R. C. Temple (London, 1912), pp. 465–6.
[2] Salisbury to Balfour, 19 September 1891. Balfour MSS. B.M. Add. MSS
49689/120–1.
[3] Salisbury to Balfour. *Ibid.*
[4] Smith to Salisbury, 17 September 1891. Salisbury MSS.
[5] Salisbury to Smith, 15 September 1891. Hambleden MSS Ser. II. 8.

the impediments you have thrown in your own way. I
do not attempt to lay down any rule as to the amount of
independence in his public action that a member of
Government or a supporter of a Government may reason-
ably claim, without acting incompatibly with those
designations. It is a mere question of prudence. You
complain that you have not got on to the extent your
abilities justified you in expecting. In order to secure the
general support and confidence of a political party,
something is more necessary than ability—and that is the
general confidence that the party can rely upon you to
stand by them at a pinch. No one can lay down by what
acts, or by what abstinence from action, this confidence
is to be won. I only express the fear, which what I heard
in the Session suggested to me—and what you now tell me
confirms—that your action on two or three occasions has
seriously qualified the confidence which your great powers
should otherwise inspire.[1]

To which admonition Gorst replied that there was one point
on which Salisbury was very much mistaken:

Upon this labour question, I have not at all lost the
confidence of the Conservative party either in the House
of Commons or the country. But I fear many of your
colleagues are wholly out of touch with their party and
with public opinion upon the subject. Nor am I unwilling to act cordially with members of the Cabinet; it is
some of them who from foolish jealousy will not act with
me. . . . But I care a great deal more about this question
than I do about offices and seats, and if my political leaders
leave me without sympathy or advice I am compelled to
proceed by my own poor light in the best way I can.[2]

Salisbury in turn explained that he had not said that the
dissatisfaction with Gorst rose wholly or in the main out of
labour questions, and while he agreed that these questions
were very much more important than offices, or seats 'yet those
who are acting together in a Government must have regard
to each other's opinions on this and on other questions'.[3]

Gorst never learned this lesson, and his failure excluded him

[1] Salisbury to Gorst, 7 September 1891. Salisbury MSS.
[2] Gorst to Salisbury, 10 September 1891. Salisbury MSS.
[3] Salisbury to Gorst, 12 September 1891. Salisbury MSS.

from promotion to the Cabinet under Salisbury and from office altogether under Balfour. It was his character and his unwillingness to suppress unorthodox opinions that undid him. But conscious as he was of his own abilities, he felt throughout his career that social prejudice was responsible. As party agent in the 1870s, he could not get on with the whips, country gentlemen all, and turned down Disraeli's offer of an undersecretaryship as being an inadequate reward for his services, an action he later regretted.[1] In his position a period of loyal and relatively humble administrative industry might have consolidated his claims: he preferred the luxury of independent action, but bitterly resented the cost. Independence was especially a luxury for him since he had not established a practice at the Bar before entering politics, and money was always a problem. It created bad feeling between himself and Smith, as Chairman of the Central Committee, after he had returned to be party agent in 1880,[2] at a time when his disagreement with the old school of the party managers and his alliance with Lord Randolph Churchill were giving further evidence of the difficulties of working harmoniously with him or of relying on his sense of loyalty to the front bench. After the fall of Churchill he was part of no recognized grouping which might have exacted recognition of his claims, but depended entirely on his personal qualifications. Yet his penchant for talking out of turn remained. He attacked his own government on labour legislation in 1891 and in the same year made a speech in Ireland on denominational education without consulting Balfour and against his declared policy, which prompted Balfour to speculate whether he did not in fact want to be turned out, either in order to take up 'the old 4th party game' or because he meant to rat and turn Home Rule. In either case Balfour was tempted to forestall him by kicking him out.[3] Nor did he become any easier to work

---

[1] H. J. Hanham, *Elections and Party Management. Politics in the Time of Disraeli and Gladstone* (London, 1959), pp. 361–5. He asked to be considered for the secretaryship to the Treasury in 1876 on the grounds that he was 'the only person engaged in the party management in 1874 to whom our accession to office has brought no political advancement as yet'. Gorst to Disraeli, 30 March 1876. Disraeli MSS, Box A.

[2] Balfour to Salisbury, 23 January 1881. Salisbury MSS.

[3] Balfour to Salisbury, 23 September 1891. Salisbury MSS. Salisbury did not think it worth taking any action against him: 'Two of the ordinary objects of

with. As Vice President of the Council for Education in the Administration of 1895, Gorst presided over the Poor Law Schools Committee, one of whose members described him as 'so able and so hasty that the elements soon make a blaze, and another called his conduct 'undignified and very near ungentlemanly'.[1] His chief, the Duke of Devonshire, also found him difficult to work with and there were the perennial troubles about speeches and letters to the press which did not follow the government line.[2] He was finally dropped on the formation of the new ministry in 1902, and retired with a pension, having refused the Governorship of the Isle of Man, which was no doubt intended to remove him from the House.[3]

Gorst's case illustrates the dilemmas of leadership: he was an embarrassment in office, but at once too dangerous and too useful to leave out. He was thus excluded from the Postmaster Generalship in 1891 because of his opinions, only to be given the more important post of Financial Secretary to the Treasury later in the same year, in the reshuffle following the death of Smith, because of his abilities. As Goschen told Salisbury the post was difficult to fill:

> I have no really good man in my eye. A double set of qualifications are wanted, one for the official, the other for the parliamentary work. For the former you want a strong man, a good business man if possible (I don't mean reared in business, but with an aptitude for business) and a man who can get on decently with the Civil Service. For the latter you want, especially in these days, a man with tact, or with sufficient parliamentary position to be able to carry things through. I mention all this as you say you have no sufficient knowledge of what is wanted to form a judgement. I would take Gorst as a strong man who I understand has not got on badly with the India people, and who has much dexterity, if not tact, in the House. I know of many objections. I might have a

punishment cannot be aimed at in this case—reformation of the offender, and a warning to others like him. There is no chance of reforming the offender and there are no others like him in the government.' Salisbury to Balfour, 24 September 1891. Balfour MSS, B.M. Add. MSS 49689/128–9.

[1] Mrs Barnett and the Rev. Brooke Lambert, quoted in W. H. G. Armytage, *A. J. Mundella 1825–1897* (London, 1951), p. 309.

[2] Letters from the Duke of Devonshire to Salisbury, 13 September 1896; 6 May 1899; 9 August 1899. Salisbury MSS.

[3] H. W. Lucy, *The Balfourian Parliament 1900–1905* (London, 1906), p. 202.

great deal of trouble with him: yet he would be less dangerous than at the Post Office.

And after running over the possible candidates he concluded 'No, whatever we decide on, I have no decently satisfactory solution except in regard to Gorst and Ridley[1] of whom the former is risky, and the latter probably unwilling to come.'[2] Even Balfour who had been itching to turn Gorst out a month or so earlier, told Salisbury not to be afraid 'that I shall find him difficult to get on with if you make him Secretary to the Treasury. *He* knows nothing about my views of his Irish and Indian escapades: and the man himself . . . dangerous as I think him, I have always been able personally to get on with.'[3] While he did not reach the Cabinet in the next ministry, the scarcity of available talent again overcame other considerations and put him into a senior post concerned with the politically sensitive subject of education. Gorst was the ablest of the outsiders who failed to get what they considered their due reward from the party. In this he was undoubtedly hampered by his social position, not in the sense that he was passed over from aristocratic prejudice, but because he lacked the financial security necessary to support his eight children and his independent opinions. What was more important still was the nature of those opinions, which were consistent in theme from his early speeches on employers liability and merchant shipping[4] to his later writings on the need for social reform.[5] He believed in 'Tory democracy', believed that is that the Conservative party was the most likely instrument of popular welfare. But in the end he came to the conclusion that this was not so: 'Since the death of Mr Disraeli the leaders of the Tory party have been always too weak to protect the interests of the workers against any fixed determination of the capitalists.'[6] A conclusion that

[1] Sir Matthew White Ridley, Bart. M.P. North Northumberland, 1868–85, Lancashire North Blackpool Div., 1886–1900. 1878–80 Under-secretary Home Office, 1885–6 Financial Secretary to the Treasury. 1895–1900 Home Secretary. Raised to peerage 1900. Landowner in Northumberland, director and Chairman of North Eastern Railway, and responsible for the development of Blyth.

[2] Goschen to Salisbury, 22 October 1891. Salisbury MSS.

[3] Balfour to Salisbury, 2 November 1891. Salisbury MSS.

[4] See 3 *Hansard* CCXXV, 107, CCXXXIX, 1053.

[5] 'Social Reform: The Obligation of the Tory party', *The Nineteenth Century;* 1903, vol. 53, pp. 519–33, and 'Government and Reform', *Fortnightly Review,* 1905, vol. 83, pp. 843–54.

[6] J. E. Gorst, *The Children of the Nation. How their health and vigour should be promoted by the State* (London, 1906), p. 221.

echoed Churchill's despairing cry: 'I am afraid it is an idle
schoolboy's dream to suppose that the Tories can legislate, as I
did stupidly. They can govern and make war and increase
taxation "à merveille", but legislation is not their province in a
democratic constitution.'[1]

The failure both of Churchill and of Gorst was partly due to
faults of character, but these faults were magnified by the
strains of the genuine political dilemma in which they found
themselves. Churchill's political position in 1885 had been
created by exploiting dissatisfaction both with the parliamentary leadership and with the organization of the party.
When this dissatisfaction had been relieved by his own assumption of the leadership and by the reorganization of the party
in 1886, he had no secure base from which to operate. While
he had many supporters in parliament and outside, they were
in no sense an organized political force, and to achieve his
ends Churchill needed patience, judgement and tact. These
powers he lacked and he found himself no match for Salisbury
in the inner politics of the Cabinet.[2] While Gorst had been
an important factor in Churchill's success, he himself had no
pretensions to being a popular leader. In so far as he could
throw political weight behind his opinions, it was in the rôle
of candid friend, as the type of able backbencher who can
express the discontent of his less articulate fellows and expose
the shortcomings of his own front bench. This rôle he was
admirably equipped to play and in it he might have exercised
considerable influence on the actions of the Government. But
he wanted and needed office, and what he could not do was
to accept office, still play the candid friend and expect to be
promoted. And this is just what he did. He might not be
consciously disloyal as Balfour thought,[3] but the nagging sense
that his abilities and services had neither been adequately
recognized nor rewarded certainly undermined his judgement
and his willingness to abide by what Balfour called 'the ordinary

[1] Churchill to Salisbury, 8 November 1886. Salisbury MSS.
[2] The comparison between Churchill's position and Chamberlain's is instructive.
Chamberlain's political dilemmas were more acute and trying, but he never lost
sight of the essential source of his strength, his independent electoral base. See
M. C. Hurst, *Joseph Chamberlain and West Midland Politics 1886–1895* (Oxford,
1962), and 'Joseph Chamberlain and the Conservatives and the succession to John
Bright, 1886–89', *Historical Journal*, vol. 7, no. 1, 1964, pp. 64–93.
[3] Balfour to Salisbury, 28 September 1891. Salisbury MSS.

rules of honour which regulate the relations between colleagues.'

Gorst in fact fell between two stools, between being a loyal colleague and being too dangerous to leave out. His parliamentary dexterity proved useful as it was, and had he been able to restrain the public expression of his 'dangerous' opinions, his abilities would have won him a place in the Cabinet. Though the number of outsiders who reached the Cabinet under the Cecils was small, it is quite clear that their administrative skills and business capacity were much relied upon. W. H. Smith became the sheet anchor of the ministry in the 1886 parliament, Goschen the leading figure on finance, C. T. Ritchie[1] carried through the reform of local government, and W. L. Jackson was a key man both in Treasury and Irish business. In a sense none of these men represented any threat to the political position of the Cecils. They were not 'popular' politicians in the style of Churchill or Chamberlain: they were unsuccessful as orators—Smith was described as a 'plain faced man who could hardly string two words together'—they had no popular following and did not compete or even take part in the social side of politics. It might be argued that they were simply used, and that any outsider who would not subordinate his own opinions was excluded. But there is a difference between the public expression of controversial views by members of a government and the internal discussions of the Cabinet. To accept the restraints of collective responsibility did not necessarily imply unwillingness or inability to express opinions in private. The harmonious relations between Salisbury and Smith, for instance, rested not on subordination but on mutual respect, a common feeling of distaste for the changes they saw around them,[2] a wide area of agreement on the issues confronting

---

[1] Charles Thomson Ritchie. M.P. Tower Hamlets, 1874–85; St George-in-the-East, 1885–92; Croydon, 1895–1905. 1885–6 Parliamentary Secretary to the Admiralty. 1886–92 President of the Local Government Board. 1895–1900 President of the Board of Trade. 1900–2 Home Secretary. 1902–3 Chancellor of the Exchequer. Raised to the peerage 1905. Merchant and Jute Spinner.

[2] Thus, for instance, Salisbury's reply to an offer from Smith to resign (5 February 1889, Hambleden MSS, II 5): '. . . if you had heard the general expression of consternation with which the apparent failure of your health was watched by the principal men of the party, you would have no doubt that in their judgement your retirement from the lead in the House of Commons would be one of the heaviest blows that could befall it.

'I agree in all you say as to the gravity of our present condition. We are in a state of bloodless civil war. No common principles, no respect for common institutions or traditions, unite the various groups of politicians, who are struggling

them, and the willingness to accommodate their differences.

Nor does what we know of Salisbury's manner of conducting business suggest anything of the autocrat. Indeed Hicks Beach thought him too permissive: 'Certainly as Prime Minister he did not exercise the control over his colleagues, either in or out of the Cabinet, that Lord Beaconsfield did. . . . Lord Beaconsfield kept a watchful eye on all his colleagues. . . . Lord Salisbury left them very much to themselves unless they consulted him. I have known Lord Beaconsfield enforce his own view on the Cabinet after all its members but one had expressed a different opinion: Lord Salisbury frequently allowed important matters to be decided by a small majority of votes, even against his own opinion.'[1]

That bankers, merchants, stationers and manufacturers sat in such cabinets, occupied key positions and took charge of important legislation, suggests that the aristocratic predominance may have been more numerical than influential. That all those who sat in the seats of power arrived at their opinions and pursued their policies within a network of pressures and constraints and not simply as a reflex of their own social positions and interests; that these pressures and constraints may have been more important in determining the outcome than the character of the decision makers; that leadership in fact bore a tolerably close resemblance to following from in front, these are the points that must finally and briefly be considered, if the importance of the social character of the parliamentary party and leadership are to be seen in perspective.

III

Salisbury himself had no doubts as to what leadership entailed. In 1880 he wrote to Balfour to justify Northcote's tactics in trying to detach the Whig rank and file from Gladstone: 'The leader, even of a diminished party, must behave as the arbitrator between its various sections: and if he has fair ground for hoping to attract a new section, they must come within the scope of the arbitration.'[2]

for power. To loot somebody or something is the common object under a thick varnish of pious phrases, so that our lines are not cast in pleasant places.'
[1] Lady Gwendolen Cecil, *Life of Robert, Marquis of Salisbury* (London, 1931), vol. III, p. 169.
[2] Salisbury to Balfour, 5 October 1880. Balfour MSS, B.M. Add. MSS. 49688/33-5.

Studies such as those of Curtis on Irish policy and Dunbabin[1] on the reform of local government, have demonstrated the complex process of manœuvre and compromise by which decisions on policy were arrived at. The attitudes of allies and opponents, the feasible administrative alternatives, the scarce resources of money and parliamentary time, all entered into an equation that had to come out in the agreement of ministers and the compliance of followers. The agreement of ministers was not easily arrived at and the compliance of followers could by no means be taken for granted. For quite apart from the alliance with the Liberal Unionists, which was the most obvious parliamentary factor to modify Government policy, the Conservative party itself was a coalition, both socially and politically. Some issues such as Ireland or the South African war had a centripetal effect: they emphasized the common sentiments and assumptions of the different sections of the party. Though even here special interests such as those of the Irish landlords and the Ulster protestants could seriously hamper the leaders, and their manner of carrying out agreed policies could create uneasiness and even disgust, as in the case of the Parnell Commission or the army contract scandals in the Boer war, which were soon reflected in parliamentary difficulties. But there were other issues that were centrifugal in the sense that there was no fundamental agreement within the party and in fact the views of various sections were diametrically opposed. On labour questions and social reform Manchester liberals confronted Tory democrats; on fiscal matters the remnants of the country party were reinforced by the growing body of industrial protectionists against the entrenched orthodoxy of Free Trade. Even on issues where the battle lines were not so clearly drawn, shades of opinion were apt to make their appearance. The Established Church had many loyal adherents, forming perhaps the largest section in the party, but enthusiasm for its privileges was by no means universal. Such Scots, Welsh and Catholic members as there were had no great cause to bless it, and one English member went so far as to resign the Whip in 1899 in protest against a bill for the partial relief of the rates of clerical tithe-payers.

[1] J. P. D. Dunbabin, 'The Politics of the Establishment of County Councils', *Historical Journal*, vol. 6, no. 2, 1963.

Education was a subject ministers touched at their peril. The advocates of free education and of increased technical instruction fell foul of the defenders of the voluntary schools, while Balfour's greatest constructive achievement, the Education Act of 1902, probably did more than anything else to drive away non-conformists and put the stuffing back into the Liberal party. Even Temperance had its advocates in the party, and since members were sensitive not only to the attitudes of their own supporters but also to the issues which might stir their opponents to vigorous action against them, the range of opinion which had to be taken into account was a wide one, and almost any course of action was likely to incur some loss. The methods of consultation between the Whips and the leader of the Commons, by which the ministers made their prudential calculus, are well illustrated by Lord Chilston's studies of his grandfather and of W. H. Smith,[1] which give an idea of how often leadership consisted in anticipating the feelings and accommodating the interests of followers.

The cohesion of the party thus depended to some extent on which kind of issue happened to be to the fore, and to some extent on the skill and tact with which the Government conducted itself. Not only the Unionist alliance, but the Conservative party itself was in danger of disintegration whenever the focus shifted from Irish and Imperial affairs to social questions. Whether an issue became prominent or not was hardly within the control of politicians: conditions in Ireland or South African or Britain dictated what problems they had to deal with. The advantages conferred by leadership were some degree of control over the manner and timing of the attempted solution. There can be little doubt that Salisbury's position enabled him to delay and modify innovations to which he was opposed: there can be equally little doubt that his position rested on the fact that the dominant issues confronting his governments were ones on which his own views and sentiments were widely shared within his party. The consensual foundations of his authority were demonstrated by the fate of Balfour: he could delay but not prevent even by the most tortuous arbitration the split over the fiscal question: loyal

[1] Viscount Chilston, *Chief Whip. The Political Life and Times of Aretas Akers-Douglas, 1st Viscount Chilston* (London, 1961), and *W. H. Smith* (London, 1965).

colleagues of twenty years simply deserted him. He could hold on to office to ensure that his answers to the problems of education, defence, and Ireland were the ones adopted, but only at the price of a further disintegration in the instrument of his power, the crumbling of the foundations of the Hotel Cecil.[1] For the demoralization and disintegration of the party were not only the product of centrifugal issues: they were accelerated by the disastrous performance of the Government in the South African War. As the most astringent critic within the party put it:

> Neither the priests of Birmingham nor the Levites of Hatfield, neither the disciples of Blenheim, nor the links of North Berwick have availed. Souls, Cecils, sycophants and Socialists are alike found wanting, and there has arisen the most profound exasperation with the Ministry which, when so well provided, has done so ill.[2]

Such exasperation found a ready target in the personnel of the Ministry. The distribution of offices always provoked discontent, and those promoted had to justify themselves, as Salisbury had known when he chose Balfour as Irish secretary and later as leader of the Commons;[3] if he had later any doubts that this was still the case, Bowles was there to dispel them:

> Your letter of 3rd inst. seems to invite my opinion of the Admiralty appointments, and I will therefore give it frankly.
>   I think them unsatisfactory and unfortunate, and rather calculated to increase than to allay, the anxieties of those interested in the Navy. I am not aware that Lord Selborne has any experience in naval administration, and Mr Arnold-Forster's interest has been shown rather in the Army and the marines.

---

[1] Balfour's dilemmas are described at length in A. M. Gollin, *Balfour's Burden* (London, 1965).

[2] Thomas Gibson Bowles, *The Tory Government and the War by a Tory M.P.* (London, 1901). Bowles was M.P. for Salford in 1885, and for King's Lynn from 1892–1906, and again as a Liberal in 1910, proprietor of *Vanity Fair*, a master mariner, and one of a handful of backbenchers who conducted a guerilla opposition to the Liberal Government of 1892. Like his ally Bartley, quoted above, he was disappointed by the absence of reward for these activities.

[3] 'It will make you a target for very jealous and exacting criticism', he told Balfour on the latter occasion. 'But I do not think you can avoid or refuse it as matters stand.' Salisbury to Balfour, 14, 15, 16 October 1891. Balfour MSS, B.M. Add. MSS 49689, quoted in Curtis, *Coercion and Conciliation*, p. 378.

I should think it even more unfortunate if, as the newspapers suggest, you intend to add to the three nephews and a son-in-law now occupying most important and highly paid posts, your son Lord Cranborne, who would thus make the sixth member of the family in the Government.

The Party is full of murmurs at the marked preference reserved for Liberal Unionists and relatives; and though the Party is long-suffering and the majority large, a too contemptuous treatment of it might provoke disaffection and accidents.[1]

Whether Salisbury's habitual distaste for the business of party management, his growing weariness, his preference for those about him whom he knew and trusted, constituted contempt or not, they certainly resulted in appointments which did nothing to appease and much to exacerbate the wounded feelings of the faithful. Salisbury might have argued with some justice that it was as difficult as it had always been to find suitable candidates,[2] and that the members of his family were no worse than the alternatives. But that was not good enough: for the charge of nepotism to lose its sting they had to be better. To Salisbury himself, acutely aware of the unpleasantness of office and the limited power it bestowed, one nephew more or less probably signified little. But this was an attitude hardly to be understood, let alone accepted, by the Gorsts, Bowles's and Bartleys of the party. Nor was it an attitude that Salisbury could afford. With every additional member of the family accommodated, the Hotel Cecil came nearer to collapse, until Balfour was finally reduced to shoring it up with timbers from the old Whig houses.[3]

[1] Thomas Gibson Bowles to Salisbury, 5 November 1900. Salisbury MSS.

[2] As the disintegration proceeded it became more difficult still. Five of the nine candidates considered by Balfour for the War Office in 1903 refused to take it. See Albert Tucker, 'The Issue of Army Reform in the Unionist Government 1903–5', *Historical Journal*, vol. 9, no. 1, 1966, pp. 92–3.

[3] For permission to consult and quote from papers in their possession or custody I have to thank the Marquis of Salisbury (the Salisbury MSS at Christ Church, Oxford), the Hon. David Smith (the Hambleden MSS at the National Register of Archives), the National Trust (the Disraeli MSS at Hughenden Manor, Bucks), and the Trustees of the British Museum (the Balfour MSS).

TABLE A
SOCIAL STRUCTURE OF PARLIAMENTARY GROUPS

percentage of each group in

Parliamentary Group	Landed Classes	Industry and Commerce	Professional Public Service	Others	N
1885/6 Old	54·8	28·7	15·2	1·4	153
1885 New	34·1	34·2	26·5	5·1	117
1886 New	36·7	27·5	29·2	6·7	120
1892 New	41·9	32·0	19·6	6·0	81
1895 New	36·0	28·0	24·9	10·9	136
1900 New	28·7	42·5	18·1	10·6	94
TOTALS	39·6	31·4	22·2	6·6	701

TABLE B
SOCIAL COMPOSITION OF PARLIAMENTS
percentage

GROUP	PARLIAMENT					
	1885	1886	1892	1895	1900	1906
Landed Classes	45·8	43·3	46·2	41·2	38·5	40·1
Industry & Commerce	31·1	29·5	28·1	28·3	32·0	31·5
Professional & Public Service	19·9	23·2	20·7	23·2	21·3	19·6
Others	2·9	4·0	4·7	7·3	8·6	8·4
N	270	370	298	381	368	143

TABLE C
TURNOVER OF PARLIAMENTARY GROUPS
PARLIAMENT

GROUP	1885	1886	1892	1895	1900	post-1906*
1885/6 Old	153	143	71	55	47	19
1885 New	117	107	66	54	33	9
1886 New	—	120	80	69	45	8
1892 New	—	—	81	67	51	21
1895 New	—	—	—	136	98	37
1900 New	—	—	—	—	94	49
TOTAL	270	370	298	381	368	143
No. of Cons. seats at General Election	250	316	268	341	334	(134)

* Includes all members of Parliamentary party 1885–1905 who sat in later parliaments, but this was not until 1910 in many cases.

TABLE D
AGE OF ENTRY AND LENGTH OF PARLIAMENTARY CAREER FOR MAJOR SOCIAL CATEGORIES
percentage

			AGE OF ENTRY		PARLIAMENTARY LENGTH OF CAREER	
			21–40	*41+*	*1–15 yrs*	*16 yrs+*
Landed	1.	Peerage	89	11	61	39
Classes	2.	Gentry	66	34	52	48
Industry and	3.	Dynasties	53	47	70	30
Commerce	4.	Second Generation	33	67	73	27
	5.	Self-made	13	87	74	26
Professional Men	6.		38	62	71	29
TOTAL			50	50	66	34

TABLE E
MEMBERS OF PARLIAMENT, 1885–1905,
holding office at any time in political career, by highest office held only

OFFICE	Landed Classes	Industry and Commerce	Professional and Public Service	Other	Total
CABINET	23	5	7	—	35
Non-Cabinet	9	—	3	—	12
Junior Minister	13	4	4	—	21
Whips	15	—	—	—	15
Law Offices	1	—	16	—	17
TOTALS	61	9	30	—	100

Trinity College in the Age of Peel

B^Y a pleasant chance the span of Peel's lifetime coincides almost exactly with a distinct and significant period in the history of Trinity College. He was born in 1788, two years after a famous incident from which the revival of the College from the eighteenth century has often been dated. Within two years of his death in 1850 the impetus to reform of the sort which that incident had given had almost expired, and the first of the Royal Commissions on the University, appointed by Peel's successor as Prime Minister, Lord John Russell, made its report. The period is characterized by a flavour of conservative reform in the College not unlike that favoured by Peel for the State. Not surprisingly, its history reflects many of the themes of the general history of these times. More boastfully it may be claimed that these themes were themselves not uninfluenced by the ideals and achievements of Trinity men, more perhaps than at any time before or since. For these reasons the subject may fairly claim a place among the essays written to honour one who has been a life-long student of Peel and servant of Trinity College.[1]

The Master of Trinity College is appointed by the Crown —according to prevailing attitudes with regard to Crown appointments. None of the Masters during Peel's lifetime were unworthy men; but it may perhaps be suggested that in every instance except that of William Whewell, appointed

---

[1] There is a short history of the College by G. M. Trevelyan, *Trinity College. An Historical Sketch* (Cambridge, 1943). See also D. A. Winstanley, *Unreformed Cambridge* (Cambridge, 1935), and *Early Victorian Cambridge* (Cambridge, 1940). I am grateful to Professor J. P. C. Roach and Professor G. F. A. Best for their comments on an early draft of this essay.

by Peel himself, the choice was influenced more by considerations of connection than of merit.

John Hinchcliffe, Master of Trinity when Peel was born, came up to the College from Westminster School in 1750 and became a Fellow in 1755. He spent seven years as an assistant master at Westminster School, and became acquainted with the Duke of Grafton who took him under his wing. He was Head Master of Westminster for three months in 1764, resigning through ill health to become tutor to the Duke of Devonshire. In 1766 Grafton presented him to the living of Greenwich and got him made chaplain to the king. On Robert Smith's death in 1768 he was made Master of Trinity, and in the following year, Bishop of Peterborough—giving up Greenwich, but not Trinity. The Duke of Newcastle had tried to get his friend and agent in Trinity, James Backhouse, made Master, but in 1768 the Duke of Grafton was more important than the Duke of Newcastle, and his influence prevailed. Hinchcliffe supported the ministry in the early stages of the American War, but later changed his mind and spoke against it in the House of Lords. Neither this nor his advocacy of a measure of relief for Roman Catholics was popular in court circles, and it was thought dangerous that so unsuitable a character should continue to hold such an influential position as Master of Trinity; he might put wrong ideas in the young men's heads. In 1789, therefore, he was offered the Deanery of Durham on condition that he resigned the Mastership; his bishopric he was allowed to keep.

Thomas Postlethwaite was appointed by Pitt to succeed him on the advice of Dr Richard Farmer, Master of Emmanuel, who told him that it would 'oblige the society'.[1] It certainly did so more than the appointment of the evangelical Dr Isaac Milner, President of Queens', would have done. Milner tried desperately, both in 1789 and 1798, to get the job in order to eradicate what he considered to be the last refuge of Jacobinism in the University. On both occasions, fortunately, he was thwarted, and he had to content himself with the Deanery of Carlisle. Postlethwaite had come up from St Bees Grammar School as a subsizar; he held many college offices, and was

---

[1] Quoted by H. R. Luard in *The Trident* (The College Magazine), March 1890, p. 12.

W

popular, though the most notorious event of his reign, when he seemed to have broken his promise of a lay fellowship to Richard Porson, cost him some of his popularity.[1]

He was succeeded after his death in 1798 by William Lort Mansel.   Like Postlethwaite, whose pupil he had been, Mansel had spent most of his life in Cambridge since he came up from Gloucester Grammar School in 1770, though he had married after becoming Vicar of Chesterton in 1788.   He numbered the Duke of Gloucester and Spencer Perceval among his pupils in Trinity and it was on Perceval's recommendation that he was made Master of Trinity 'in order that his strong discipline might correct some abuses which had crept into its administration'.[2]   He was a friend of Pitt's who was often in the Lodge.   He was made Bishop of Bristol by Perceval in 1808, but he continued to live in Cambridge.   Mansel had a large family including two sons named after their godfathers, Gloucester and Spencer Perceval,[3] and six daughters on whose behalf he gave what was for those days an unusual amount of entertainment in the Lodge; five of them married Trinity men.

Christopher Wordsworth succeeded him on his death in 1820. Like his elder brother William, Christopher was at Hawkshead Grammar School and came up to Trinity in 1792.   He became a Fellow in 1798, and was tutor to Charles Manners Sutton, who became Speaker of the House of Commons and whose father became Archbishop of Canterbury.   It was a connection which stood Wordsworth in good stead.   Both men became his patrons and he was presented to many livings, eventually becoming Chaplain to the Archbishop and Chaplain to the Speaker.   He was made Master of Trinity by Lord Liverpool on the recommendation of the Archbishop, though many people, including the Chancellor, the Duke of Gloucester, had expected that J. H. Monk, a Fellow of the College and Regius Professor of Greek, would get the job.   Wordsworth had three sons, two of them becoming Fellows and two of them

---

[1] Two fellowships were exempt from the rule that tenure was conditional upon becoming ordained within seven years of taking the M.A. degree.   They were nominally intended for students of civil law and medicine, and were in the gift of the Master.   For the quarrel between Postlethwaite and Porson see M. L. Clarke, *Richard Porson* (Cambridge, 1937), pp. 31–40.

[2] *D.N.B.*

[3] He is said to have gone deaf for a year after the shock of hearing of Perceval's assassination.

Bishops. One of them, Christopher, became headmaster of Harrow in his youth, and for some time his father seems to have hoped that he would succeed him as Master of Trinity.

In 1841, however, there was a better man available, and it was Peel who saw to it that he was sent to Trinity Lodge. It is doubtful whether a more suitable man than William Whewell could have been found, but his appointment, like those of his predecessors, was not without its political flavour.

The Mastership of Trinity was at this time a life appointment, and Christopher Wordsworth, a High Tory in matters of Church and State, was determined not to resign his office, even though it was becoming increasingly uncongenial to him, until he could be sure that his successor would be chosen by the Crown on advice less reckless than that he believed the Whigs would offer. So he held on while Melbourne was in office, but promptly resigned when Peel replaced him in 1841. It was entirely in accordance with the practice of the past that rumours of the impending vacancy should cause Whewell's friends to urge him to interrupt his honeymoon in the Lakes to solicit the appointment from Peel in London.[1] But it was characteristic of the new Prime Minister and an augury for the future that such solicitation should have been unnecessary. On the advice of the Archbishop of Canterbury and of Blomfield, Bishop of London and formerly Fellow of Trinity, Peel had already recommended Whewell to the Queen as 'a general favourite among all who have had intercourse with him from his good temper and easy and conciliatory manners. Though not *peculiarly* eminent as a divine (less so at least than a writer on scientific and philosophical subjects), his works manifest a deep sense of the importance of religion and sound religious views'.[2] 'It will always be satisfactory both to you and to

---

[1] Mrs Stair Douglas, *The Life of William Whewell, D.D.* (London, 1881), p. 226.

[2] *The Letters of Queen Victoria*, 1st series, ed. A. C. Benson and Viscount Esher (London, 1907), vol. I, pp. 437–8. Blomfield wrote to Peel on 21 September 1841, 'Mr Whewell is a man of extraordinary powers of mind, and his Bridgewater treatise evinces the soundness of his general religious views. I have some doubt whether he possesses a sufficient staple of divinity to qualify him for the difficult task which I foresee he will have to undertake, of combating or checking the extravagances of the Oxford Tractarians which are beginning to make themselves felt at Cambridge. If he should be appointed to the Mastership I hope he will feel the necessity of devoting himself somewhat less to science, and more to theology. He will easily master any subject to which he applies his mind.' C. S. Parker, *Sir Robert Peel* (London, 1899), vol. III, pp. 422–3.

myself,' Peel wrote to Whewell, 'to reflect that I named you to the Queen for the Mastership without any solicitation, and previously to the expression of any wish on your part.'[1]

Whatever may have been the practice in the previous hundred years, during this period elections to Fellowships were uninfluenced by political, though perhaps not always by personal, considerations. The Statutes provided for sixty Fellowships which were tenable for life on condition of remaining celibate and of taking holy orders within seven years of proceeding to the degree of Master of Arts. Vacancies caused by death or by resignation were filled at the annual election in October. Fellows were entitled to free rooms and commons, and to various payments rendered trivial by the decline in the value of money since they were fixed by the Elizabethan Statutes. Since the seventeenth century, however, it had been the practice to divide the surplus income for each year among the Master and Fellows according to an established scale whereby the Master at one extreme got fifteen times the sum received by the minor Fellows at the other. This surplus varied considerably. In 1788 £2,000 was divided, the Master receiving £150, and the minor Fellows £10. In 1800 and 1810 £12,000 was divided, in 1820 £24,000, in 1830 £15,000, in 1840 £16,000 and in 1850 £20,000. In 1817 no less than £32,000 was divided, but the sum fell to £10,000 in 1823 and did not rise again to £20,000 until 1846. In the golden year of 1817 the majority of the Fellows received £400 each but in 1823 their share fell as low as £125.[2]

There were still, in the eighteenth and early nineteenth centuries, relatively few established posts in the College and the University by which this variable income could be supplemented. As far as the College is concerned, there were

---

[1] Stair Douglas, *William Whewell*, p. 227. On 22 October 1841, F. D. Maurice wrote to Julius Hare, 'I was very glad to see Whewell's appointment announced; more as it had been rumoured that Lord Lyndhurst was struggling hard to get in one of his supporters, and even wished to go out of the College. I should hope this was a calumny; at all events, it is proved that Peel will not be under such influences. Whewell's marriage to the member of a Whig family, some of whom are making themselves rather busy against the Ministry, increases the merit of the appointment.' *The Life of F. D. Maurice*, ed. F. Maurice (London, 1884), vol. I, pp. 320-1. Whewell's wife was one of the Marshalls of Leeds; see W. G. Rimmer, *Marshalls of Leeds, Flax-Spinners* (Cambridge, 1960).

[2] There is a convenient account of the dividend system in Winstanley, *Early Victorian Cambridge*, Appendix A.

the offices of Master, Vice-Master, the Deans, Bursars, Tutors and Chaplains, the Librarian, the Steward and the Pandoxator.[1] Private coaching, though frowned upon officially, could be profitable. The sixteen Fellows who held the office of College Preacher were allowed to retain their Fellowships together with ecclesiastical preferment of a limited amount, but otherwise acceptance of a living entailed forfeiting a Fellowship. For those who were content to remain bachelor clergymen, however, a Fellowship of Trinity provided a tolerable livelihood.

On the whole, however, and in spite of the fact that Fellowships could be held for life, they seem generally to have been considered either as a temporary means of securing independence of their families for the very young, or as a means to better ends for them when they became older.

And there are some reasons for suspecting that before the revival of the University in the early nineteenth century, the majority of Fellows were glad to get away from the place as soon as the succession to a living enabled them to leave and get married. Cooped up with nothing to do, in buildings however stately, they got on each other's nerves, or developed a degree of eccentricity to which few even of the bachelor Fellows would nowadays aspire. Gunning has a famous description of the senior Fellows of Trinity at the end of the eighteenth century: James Backhouse, 'like most of the Seniority, . . . considered a man of gallantry; but Cambridge not being the scene of his *amours*, he was not thought so immoral as the rest'; Thomas Wilson the Bursar, horrified one night to discover that the lady he was addressing at the Great Gate and inviting to come to his rooms was not one with whom he had an assignation, but Mrs Hinchcliffe, the Master's wife; John Higgs and Thomas Spencer, too mad to be allowed to stay in College but who were brought back whenever the Master wanted their votes. William Pugh, employed to make a catalogue of the University Library, was dismissed when he was found to be reading the books instead, and, driven frantic by his dismissal, was found rushing about the streets breaking

[1] The Pandoxator had charge of the College brewhouse and bakehouse. In 1800 the Vice-Master's stipend was £60, the Senior Dean's £50, the Junior Dean's £42, the Junior Bursar's £50, and the Steward's £40. (Bursar's MS notes of the Meetings of the Seniority, the Board composed of the Master and the eight senior Fellows who ruled the College. The formal decisions of this Board were recorded in the Conclusion Book.)

the lamps and shouting, 'Death to the villain Marat! destruction to Robespierre!' He also had to be sent away for a time, but he recovered, and had a fine reputation as an examiner for scholarships and fellowships. 'His judgement was considered extremely good,' Adam Sedgwick recorded, 'and in the Fellowship Examination his opinion was preferred to that of most other examiners.'[1] James Lambert, says Gunning, 'was never addicted to those vices for which at that time the Seniors of Trinity were so notorious; but, when in College attended closely to literary pursuits'.[2] But it was James Lambert who described to George Crabbe the loneliness and melancholy which might afflict even the most studious fellow and which Crabbe referred to in his poem *The Borough*:

> Books cannot always please, however good;
> Minds are not ever craving for their food;
> But sleep will soon the weary soul prepare
> For cares tomorrow that were this day's care.

The academic career for life was as yet something which hardly existed; the University was still small, its concerns extremely narrow, and the careers it offered in consequence relatively few. In theory it was mainly concerned with teaching—and hardly at all with research. It was part of the ecclesiastical structure of the country, not an end in itself:[3] a jumping-off ground, rather than a place in which to live and work for the whole of one's life. So much so, indeed, that Professor Pryme thought it worth while saying of Peter Paul Dobree, Fellow of Trinity and Regius Professor of Greek, that he valued his Fellowship 'not merely for its emoluments but for the opportunities which a college residence afforded him of pursuing his researches'.[4] Most people in the eighteenth century had regarded Fellowships in much the same way as jobs elsewhere—freeholds existing for the benefit of their owners

---

[1] Quoted in J. W. Clark, *Cambridge. Brief Historical and Descriptive Notes* (London, 1890), p. 324.

[2] Henry Gunning, *Reminiscences of the University, Town, and County of Cambridge* (London, 1854), vol. II, pp. 58, 113–21.

[3] In a sermon on Commencement Sunday, 30 June 1822, Monk reminded his congregation that they belonged to: 'An Institution whose professed object is the support of true religion by educating able persons for Christ's ministry.' Printed under the title *The Duty of Attention to the Original Objects of Academical Institutions*.

[4] George Pryme, *Autobiographic Recollections* (Cambridge and London, 1870), p. 151.

rather than as the means whereby necessary functions were performed for society.   It is an attitude which it is easier now to scorn than to understand, but it was one to which the thought and institutions and structure of eighteenth-century English society lent powerful support.   But the day would dawn when all these things would alter and such attitudes become extremely harmful if persisted in.   That day dawned in Trinity College in 1786 with a row over the methods used in the Fellowship election of that year, a row which seems to have inaugurated an important and continuous movement of reform.   The quarrel may have begun, however, for the quite simple reason that some of the younger Fellows were disappointed that one of their friends was not elected that year, and, in their disappointment, discovering that one of the Seniors had returned to College too late to examine the candidates but only in time to vote, presented a formal protest to the Master complaining of this neglect of statutory obligations.

The Master and Seniors reacted as one might expect, with surprise and indignation that their edicts and authority should be questioned by those whose place was not to govern, but to be governed.   The ten signatories, however, were not to be cowed by a mere haughty reflection upon their behaviour in the Conclusion Book, and an order that they should withdraw their protest.   They persisted to the extent of taking it up to the Visitor, and getting the whole issue judged by the Lord Chancellor.   Thurlow produced a statesmanlike verdict, asking the ten signatories to withdraw the imputation of dishonesty which their protest implied, and the Seniors to withdraw their rebuke.   The Juniors were prepared to do no more than regret that their memorial appeared to be offensive to the Seniority, and the Seniority in consequence refused to remove their admonition from the Conclusion Book, where it remains.

It was from this episode in the reign of Bishop Hinchcliffe that many commentators, impressed with the character of the College in the early nineteenth century, dated its revival.   In the reign of Hinchcliffe's successor, Thomas Postlethwaite, a public written examination for Fellowships took the place of the individual examination of the candidates by the Seniors in their rooms (a system, it may be noted, which had been introduced by Bentley in the early part of the century as an improvement on the public *viva voce* examination in the chapel)[1]. Bentley's system, like many other institutions in the eighteenth century, had worked when the people involved had wanted it to do so: Richard Cumberland's account of his examination in 1752 suggests that it could work stringently enough.[2] But once a *public* system was established, and once—and this is more important—the atmosphere had been created in which it was expected that the system should work properly, the accidents of personality began to be ruled out, and a satisfactory working of the system could be relied upon. The extent to which this new system was the responsibility of Postlethwaite, or of such men as Thomas Jones who was one of the ten signatories in 1786 and became Head Tutor in 1787, is less important than the fact that it was established. The factors which might help to prevent the best men being elected were now drastically limited. Such an obstacle as the restriction of the number of Fellowships which might be held at any one time by men who came from certain parts of the country, which hampered other colleges, had not existed in Trinity since 1560,[3] and the danger that the College would be swamped by Westminsters who claimed certain priorities had been quite dramatically removed in the time of Hinchcliffe. And there was an additional consideration. The recovery of the college finances under the Bursarships of Stephen Whisson and James Lambert from the severe blows they had suffered in Bentley's time, together with the gift of £12,000 by John Piggott in 1810 and 1811—the triumph of the Bursarship of John Hailstone—enabled the College to improve the value of its livings at the same time as it was made more unusual for them to be held with Fellowships, and helped to promote the circulation of Fellowships, and to ensure that only those stayed on who wanted to do so for academic reasons.[4] In the past, part of the trouble had been that many stayed

---

[1] J. H. Monk, *The Life of Richard Bentley, D.D.* (London, 1830), p. 124.

[2] *Memoirs of Richard Cumberland* (London, 1806), pp. 106–9.

[3] The earliest statutes had restricted the number of fellowships that could be held at one time by the natives of any county. These restrictions were removed in the statutes of 1560 which remained in force until 1844; they were never restored. Thomas Jones himself migrated to Trinity from St John's because his chances of being elected to a Fellowship there were diminished by such restrictions.

[4] At the instigation of Pryme and Monk it was agreed to use the Pigott benefaction to increase the value of small livings already in the gift of the College

only because they had nowhere else they could afford to go to.[1]

But, whatever the causes may have been, the results of all this, in the shape of a remarkable and distinguished body of Fellows in the first decades of the nineteenth century, are undeniable. Fellows of Trinity were prominent in the Royal Society, the Geological Society, the Philological Society, and the British Association. The distinction of Newton's College in the fields of Mathematics and Natural Sciences was maintained by the work of Sedgwick, Whewell, Airy, Sheepshanks, and Peacock.[2] Classical studies were represented by Blomfield, Monk, Dobree, and Scholefield. In literary, philosophical, philological and historical scholarship also some of the leading men of the day were Fellows of Trinity.[3] Finding nourishment in Kant and Coleridge rather than in the dry bones of Locke and Paley which had been fed to them as undergraduates, Hare and Thirlwall, Sedgwick and Whewell, foremost in England in German scholarship, led the attack on utilitarian thinking which is one of the characteristic intellectual developments of the time, a development with which their pupils of the generation of Tennyson, Hallam, and Sterling were in deep sympathy.[4] Lyndhurst, Macaulay and Praed, Tindal,

rather than to buy more livings. It was also at their suggestion that the augmentation was restricted to those livings with a population of more than eight hundred, and that it should be conditional upon the incumbent residing for a certain number of months in the year. Pryme, *Autobiographic Recollections*, p. 101.

[1] Pryme tells the sad story of John Davies who had wanted to marry as a young man. He did not receive the offer of a suitable living until he was fifty-two, by which time he had decided it was too late to change his way of life.

> 'He deemed too much of life gone by:
> Fate had dissolv'd each early tie,
> And left no wish, but here to die.'

Pryme, *Autobiographic Recollections*, p. 102.

[2] Considerable attention is now being given to the work of these men. See for example, W. F. Cannon, 'Scientists and Broad Churchmen: an Early Victorian Intellectual Network', *Journal of British Studies*, vol. IV, pt. 1 (November 1964), and 'The Role of the Cambridge Movement in Early Nineteenth-Century Science', *Ithaca*, 26 VIII—2 IX 1962; also R. Robson and W. F. Cannon, 'William Whewell, F.R.S.', *Notes and Records of the Royal Society of London*, vol. 19, no. 2 (December 1964).

[3] See, for example, Duncan Forbes, *The Liberal Anglican Idea of History* (Cambridge, 1952); Hans Aarsleff, 'The Early History of the *Oxford English Dictionary*,' *Bulletin of the New York Public Library*, vol. 66, no. 7 (September, 1962).

[4] In his *Discourse on the Studies of the University of Cambridge*, first delivered as a commemoration sermon in the College Chapel in December 1832, Sedgwick said, 'Utilitarian philosophy, in destroying the domination of the moral feelings, offends at once both against the law of honour and the law of God. It rises not for an instant above the world; allows not the expansion of a single lofty sentiment; and its natural tendency is to harden the hearts and debase the moral practice of mankind.' (5 ed., Cambridge and London, 1850), p. 74.

Parke and Shaw-Lefevre are perhaps the most prominent of those who used their fellowships as a prelude to a public, rather than an academic, career.

At this point the undergraduates may at last be brought on the stage, associating them with the reigns of Mansel and Wordsworth. It is then that undergraduates leading a life still recognizable in that of their successors begin to appear; it is then that they begin to be bothered about, both because there were now men in the place who were prepared to do so, and because their number made it impossible any longer to ignore them. Also by their conduct—good and bad—they force themselves upon the attention of the historian.

Since the late eighteenth century Trinity has been the largest college at Cambridge.[1] The numbers of undergraduates admitted taking every tenth year from 1781 to 1851 are as follows: 41, 42, 46, 64, 107, 152, 135, 148.[2] A complete analysis of the schools from which these men came would be tedious to read and difficult to interpret. But, for what the numbers are worth, it may be mentioned that of the 41 men admitted in 1801, whose schools are known, 12 came from Eton, 4 from Westminster, 4 from Charterhouse, and the rest from 17 schools. In 1811, 64 men were admitted, 46 from 24 schools, ranging from Westminster (7) Harrow (6) and Eton (4) to other schools which sent one pupil each, for example, Macclesfield, Tiverton, Kendal, Heversham, and Ponder's End. Of the 85 admitted from known schools in 1821, 12 were from Westminster, 10 from Eton, 7 from Harrow, 6 from Leeds; Oakington, Lynn, Sheffield, Ormskirk, Shrewsbury, Walthamstow and Braintree are among the schools sending one boy each. There were some schools, Richmond and Bury, Tiverton and Norwich, for example, which were as regularly represented as Eton and Harrow, though less strongly, and there are some grounds for suspecting that such schools

[1] The sight of the College at dinner or at Chapel was one of the tourist attractions of Cambridge. Tennyson said that the line 'Six hundred maidens clad in purest white' in 'The Princess' was taken from the striking memory of the white-surpliced undergraduates in Trinity Chapel. *Alfred Lord Tennyson, a Memoir by his son* (New ed., London, 1905), p. 544.

[2] *Admissions to Trinity College, Cambridge*, edited by W. W. Rouse Ball and J. A. Venn, 5 vols (London 1911–16). Matriculations in the University for the same years have been estimated as, 155, 190, 150, 240, 455, 435, 430, 445. J. A. Venn, *Oxford and Cambridge Matriculations 1544–1906* (Cambridge, 1908).

may have found it easier to get their boys in here at this time than would have been the case later in the century.

A completely satisfactory explanation of the increase in numbers would inevitably be complicated. Increase in population, new social habits, new demands of society, all had their effect. A more local reason for the increase in the number admitted to Trinity may have been a succession of remarkable tutors beginning with Thomas Jones in 1787. *Tutor eximius* is his proud epitaph in the Ante-Chapel.

> The wild unbroken boy he led, not drove,
> And changed coercion for paternal love.
> By mildness won, youth found resistance vain,
> Bound in a silken, yet a snapless chain.
> Around his sacred tomb th'ingenuous band
> Of sorrowing pupils oft shall pensive stand,
> Shall hail the Tutor faithful to his trust,
> Revere his memory, and bedew his dust.[1]

Other notable tutors in the period were Monk, Whewell, Peacock, Hudson, Perry, and Thorp; of Peacock—'Gentleman' Peacock, as he was known to his pupils—one grateful pupil wrote: 'Never was there a Tutor of Trinity as I imagine more affectionately remembered by his pupils.'[2]

In 1755 the number of tutors had been reduced to two; between 1801 and 1822 the undergraduates were organized on two 'sides' and a third 'side' was added in 1822. The tutors

---

[1] Elegy by Robert Dealtry written after Jones's death. Printed in J. W. Clark and T. McKenny Hughes *The Life and Letters of the Reverend Adam Sedgwick*, vol. I, p. 75 (Cambridge 1890). It was the pleasant custom then for pupils to pin copies of laudatory verses to the coffins of the Fellows which lay in state in the Hall before being carried in procession to the Chapel for the funeral service.

> 'Farewell blest shade! departed saint adieu!
> O more than friend! than father! fare thee well!
> How much I lov'd thee once, how mourn thee now,
> A griev'd and broken heart alone can tell.'

Printed with a description of the funeral of Stephen Whisson in 1783, in J. Nichols, *Literary anecdotes of the Eighteenth Century* vol. III, p. 657; quoted in Winstanley, *Unreformed Cambridge*, p. 383.

[2] John Allen to W. H. Thompson, 25 November 1858. Trin. Coll. Add. MSS, b.49. An old member of the College, M. W. Thompson, wrote to the Master in 1874, 'My recollection of Peacock, J. M. Heath, and yourself is very clear and my loyalty amounts to this that if I had fifty sons and could afford it I would enter them all at Trinity on "Peacock's side".' *Ibid.* See also *Personal Remembrances of Sir Frederick Pollock* (London, 1887), vol. I, pp. 40, 77; and *Alma Mater; or Seven Years at the University of Cambridge. By a Trinity Man* (J. M. F. Wright) (London, 1827), vol. I, p. 177.

were responsible not so much for looking after their pupils generally as for teaching them personally or employing an assistant tutor to do so. The pastoral side of their job was only beginning to develop when people like Jones and Sheepshank, Peacock and Thirlwall and Hare in particular began to break down the rather rigid barrier which separated the Fellows from the undergraduates, a barrier of which Tennyson was to complain bitterly.[1] In addition to being reduced to some semblance of order in this way, the undergraduates were increasingly controlled in another. In 1790 annual college examinations for first and second year men had been introduced and in 1818 an examination for third year men was started. 'The wonderful effects of these institutions,' said Monk, who was responsible for the examination introduced in 1818, 'in exciting industry and emulation among the young men, and exalting the character of the College, are such as must have even surpassed the hopes of their promoters.'[2]

And just as the reform of the Fellowship examination seems to have had quite sudden results in the shape of an unusually distinguished body of Fellows, so this examination for undergraduates, coupled with the new tutors and assistant tutors, seems to have stimulated a flow of the most brilliant undergraduates—many of those already mentioned as Fellows may be mentioned again here, together with such men as Babbage, Tennyson, Hallam, Kinglake, Malden, Monckton Milnes, Thackeray, Lytton, Fitzgerald, Spedding, Trench, Sterling, and Buller. These are some of the brightest stars in the galaxy of these years—the first years of the Union and the Apostles, the time of the Speculative Society and the True Blue Club, the Ghost Club and the Extractors, and the

---

[1] Describing his undergraduate days to the Master on a return visit to the College Tennyson said, 'there was a want of love in Cambridge then', and remarked that relations between dons and undergraduates had become much easier since then. His own tutor was the formidable Whewell for whom he had a great respect. Tennyson came to regret the bitterness of his *Lines on Cambridge of 1830*:

> '. . . Your manner sorts
> Not with this age wherefrom ye stand apart,
> . . . You that do profess to teach
> And teach us nothing, feeding not the heart.'

Tennyson. A Memoir by his son, p. 58.

[2] J. H. Monk, *Life of Richard Bentley*, p. 667; see also Pryme, *Autobiographic Recollections*, pp. 90–2.

beginnings of organized sport.[1] And there are other indications of the distinction of the College at this time. Sixteen
of the Senior Wranglers between 1800 and 1851 came from
Trinity; between the foundation of the Classical Tripos in 1824
and 1851 the Senior Classic was on twenty occasions a Trinity
man. In the same period 22 out of 27 Craven Scholarships,
71 out of 100 Chancellor's Classical Medals and 94 of the 105
Smith's Prizes were won by Trinity men. In the first thirty-
seven years of its existence the Chancellor's Prize for English
verse was won eighteen times by members of the College,
ranging from Whewell on *Boadicea* to Tennyson on *Timbuctoo*.[2]

It was a brilliant generation, and knew it. Moultrie who
belonged to it, described it in a long autobiographical poem.

> . . . not in vain
> Spent I the spring and seed-time of my youth
> Beneath thy reverend towers;—no slender gain
> I count it to have known whom I have known,
> And with the noblest spirits of my day
> Beheld the dawn of manhood; not ill timed
> My sojourn in thy courts—for 'twas my lot
> To know a generation nobler far
> Than that which went before it—more athirst
> For knowledge—more intent on loftiest schemes
> And purposes of good—and if more prone
> To daring speculation, apt to tread
> More venturous paths—yet purer from the stain
> Of gross and sensual vice—which among those
> Our predecessors in the steep ascent
> Of academic honour, still had been
> Too oft allied with genius. . . .[3]

---

[1] See among many other sources, Pryme, *Autobiographic Recollections*; *Alma Mater*;
or, Seven Years at the University of Cambridge. By a Trinity Man; Percy Cradock,
Recollections of the Cambridge Union (Cambridge [Bowes & Bowes] 1953); and the
biographies of many of the leading figures of this time. Whewell was President,
and Thirlwall Secretary, of the Union, when it was suppressed by the Vice-
Chancellor in 1817 because of suspected subversive tendencies.

[2] Macaulay and Praed were successful competitors for this prize. Hallam was
unsuccessful; his verses on *Timbuctoo* contained a description of Coleridge whom
he had visited at Highgate.

> 'a good old man,
> Most eloquent, who spake of things divine'

Tennyson. A Memoir by his son; p. 42 n. 1.

[3] John Moultrie, *The Dream of Life*, printed in the edition of his poems by Der-
went Coleridge (London, 1876). Moultrie came up in 1819.

The general improvement was noticed also by James Losh, an old Trinity man who came up in 1822 to make arrangements for his son to come into residence in October. He remarked on the paving and lighting of the streets, the amount of building that had gone on, particularly of small houses built to provide lodgings for the large number of young men who could no longer be housed in college now that their number was almost doubled. 'There is clearly much less form and much more information amongst the Senior part of the University than there was in my time,' he noted, 'And I was glad to learn that drinking is nearly given up by the more genteel part of the young men, tho' I fear that gambling and other kinds of dissipation still retain their ground.'[1]

From their diaries and letters, and from other poems in the same vein as Moultrie's, a strong impression is derived of the spirit of these undergraduate years, 'the dawn-golden times' that lived and glowed in the memories of many others besides Tennyson. The adulation of their heroes Coleridge and Wordsworth is noticed time and again.[2] 'Though it is now two o'clock, and I am bed-ward disposed,' wrote the future Dean Alford in his diary for 19 December, 1830, 'I must stop to relate a most glorious evening spent in the company of and in conversation with Wordsworth. It was at Spedding's rooms; present—Wordsworth, Spedding, Blakesley, Thompson, Tennant, Brookfield, and myself. If I remember rightly the first thing we spoke of was the great work of Coleridge.' There follows a long description of the other topics covered— the state of religion in the University, De Quincey, Kant, the general state of the country, the effects of revolution, Wordsworth's fear of the increasing desire for reform and of a reign of terror in England, the 'exceeding importance of the middle or resisting classes', the way the press incited the people, 'and

---

[1] *The Diaries and Correspondence of James Losh*, ed. E. Hughes, vol. 1, p. 154, Surtees Society vol. CLXXI (London, 1962).

[2] 'Coleridge and Wordsworth were our principal divinities, and Hare and Thirlwall were regarded as their prophets; or rather in this celestial hierarchy I should have put Shakespeare at the top of all, and I should have found a lofty pedestal for Kant and Goëthe.' *Autobiography and Letters of Charles Merivale, Dean of Ely*, ed. J. A. Merivale (Oxford, 1898), p. 98. Merivale was a Johnian, but also an Apostle. R. C. Trench described his friends as 'that gallant band of Platonico-Wordsworthian-Coleridgian-anti-Utilitarians'. R. C. Trench, *Letters and Memorials*, vol. I (London, 1888), p. 10. See also the letters to Trench from John Sterling which are printed in the same volume, esp. pp. 8–9, 119.

the shameful temporizing and fear of the magistrates'. 'I count it one of the proud passages of my life,' Alford concluded, 'to have met and conversed with Wordsworth.'[1] Of an earlier encounter Alford's friend John Allen had recorded quite simply, '*Virgilium vidi!* This day I saw William Wordsworth'.[2]

Along with this went their disgust with utilitarianism and their gratitude for the teaching of its enemies Hare and Whewell and Sedgwick, and for the friendships made among the Apostles—a society which had more influence on the minds of some of its members than the more formal teaching of the College, which they found too dry and mathematical for their more poetic natures.[3] The romantic yearning for the colour and chivalry of medieval life as they and Scott imagined it was present in its ripest form in Whewell's pupil Kenelm Digby, the author of *The Broad Stone of Honour*, who as an undergraduate kept vigil all night in King's College Chapel—a more appropriate setting, certainly, for such an exercise than the classical interior given to his own College chapel in the Age of Reason.[4] Equally characteristic are the generous and liberal sentiments that involved Sterling and Hallam, Trench and Tennyson, in a vain attempt to restore constitutional government in Spain in 1830,[5] and, in violent contrast with what

[1] *Life, Journals and Letters of Henry Alford, D.D.* (London, 1874), pp. 62–5.

[2] MS Diary of John Allen in the Library of Trinity College, 20 November 1830. For Allen see R. M. Grier, *John Allen*, *A Memoir* (London, 1889), and A. O. Allen, *John Allen and His Friends* (London, n.d.). The quotations in these books from Allen's diary are sometimes wrongly dated and transcribed.

[3] For the Apostles, see F. M. Brookfield, *The Cambridge 'Apostles'* (London, 1906), and also the memoirs of Trench, Maurice, Tennyson, Sterling, Merivale, among others. Anti-utilitarianism seems to have been a fashion of the late 'twenties. F. D. Maurice records that when he came up in 1825 'Among the younger and cleverer undergraduates of the day, especially in Trinity, Benthamism was the prevalent faith . . . I, in a small society of which I was a member, defended Coleridge's metaphysics and Wordsworth's poetry against the Utilitarian teaching.' *Life of F. D. Maurice*, vol. I, p. 176. In an earlier generation, Charles Austin converted Macaulay from Toryism but not to Utilitarianism. G. O. Trevelyan, *Life and Letters of Lord Macaulay*. Macaulay came up to Trinity in 1818, and was elected to a Fellowship in 1824.

[4] Julius Hare described *The Broad Stone of Honour* as 'that noble manual for gentlemen, that volume which, had I a son, I would place in his hands, charging him, though such prompting words would be needless, to love it next to his Bible'. A. J. C. Hare, *Memorials of a Quiet Life* (London, 1872), vol. I, p. 197. See also B. Holland, *Memoir of Kenelm Henry Digby* (London, 1919).

[5] The most famous account of this episode is in Carlyle's *Life of John Sterling*. See also Trench, *Letters and Memorials*, vol. I, and the Memoir of Tennyson by his son.

would have been expected of undergraduates of the generation of Bishop Watson of Llandaff, the soul-searchings and emotional outpourings worthy of their Oxford contemporaries, and the scrupulosity of conscience that compelled John Allen, who refused to have an easy chair in his rooms, to confess: 'I am often afraid that when I think of becoming a clergyman, I am not wholly without thoughts of entering the Church as it were for a maintenance.'[1]

The increased number of undergraduates, and probably also their increased high spirits, also increased the amount of trouble they gave to those who had charge over them. In 1799 Lort Mansel as Vice-Chancellor had attempted to impose some order in the matter of dress, denouncing what he called *togatum ocreatumque genus*.[2] In 1812 the Master and Seniors of Trinity struck a blow in the battle between breeches and trousers that was then going on by declaring that under-graduates who appeared in Hall or in Chapel in pantaloons or trousers would be deemed absent and liable to the consequent penalties. But it was a losing battle. Airy, who came up in 1819, had been advised by an old-fashioned friend that breeches were the thing. 'The struggle between the old dress and the trowsers customary in society was still going on,' he wrote, 'but almost terminated, and I was one of the very few freshmen who retained the old habiliments. This made me in some measure distinguishable; however, at the end of my first three terms I laid these aside.'[3]

But there are more serious problems than the clothes under-graduates choose to wear, and Lort Mansel and Christopher Wordsworth were both conscious of them and inclined by temperament to deal with them. In 1798 the king had congratulated Pitt on being able to find someone as suitable as Mansel to 'restore discipline in that great seminary, and a more correct attachment to the Church of England and the

[1] MS Diary, 10 September 1830. 'After Chapel Thackeray came up—expressed some doubts of Xt being =with God, read over St Matthew together and he was convinced.' *Ibid.*, 7 February 1830.

[2] Pryme, *Autobiographic Recollections*, p. 43. Mansel once punished Althorp for walking across the grass in loose pantaloons by depriving him of ale and pudding for a fortnight. D. Le Marchant, *Memoir of John Charles, Viscount Althorp* (London, 1876), p. 73 n. See also *Alma Mater*, etc., vol. I, p. 10.

[3] *Autobiography of Sir George Biddell Airy*, ed. Wilfrid Airy (Cambridge, 1896), p. 23.

British constitution than the young men educated there for some time have been supposed to possess'.[1] Hinchcliffe had been tempted away from Trinity with the Deanery of Durham because he was thought to have failed in this respect; Christopher Wordsworth was brought back to the College after a long absence in 1820 because of his reputation as a disciplinarian. He had neither the inclination nor the opportunity to bury his talents. The first problem that he took up was the result of the increased number of undergraduates, the majority of whom could not be accommodated in College and were living in lodgings, exposed to all the temptations of the town. The University itself had made some attempt to cope with this situation in 1818 by appointing two pro-proctors and by imposing all sorts of conditions on the lodging houses where undergraduates lived. But Wordsworth had a better answer than that, and in 1820 suggested to the Seniority that the College should build a large number of new sets of college rooms. All sorts of questions were involved, ranging from what would happen to Mr Pugh's coal-hole and the Fellows' stables to whether the College would be able to afford it. Discussion of the matter occupied and divided the College until 1823, when at last the Master won his case, and the first stone of the new court was laid on the King's birthday by Wordsworth's former pupil and present patron, Manners Sutton, Speaker of the House of Commons.[2]

The Master had won over the Fellows on this occasion, though there was a row the day after because he thought some

---

[1] George III to Pitt, 13 May 1798; quoted in a typescript Life of Mansel in the College Library, p. 89, Trinity had a reputation as a Whig college. Erskine, Grey, Melbourne, and Althorp were members. Prizes were offered annually for a declamation on the glories of the Revolution settlement and an essay on William III. The essay prize was once won by Macaulay, and Pryme claimed that he was converted from Toryism by reading for it. (*Autobiographic Recollections*, p. 59.) In 1830 Wilberforce said that Trinity would be a suitable corrective influence on a boy with excessively Tory inclinations (quoted in *English Historical Documents*, Vol. XI, p. 696, [London, 1959].) The exclusion of *The Times* from the Combination Room in 1832 showed that there were limits to the liberalism of the Fellows. (*History of* The Times, vol. I, p. 276, (London, 1935.) Many Fellows deserted liberalism after Gladstone's conversion to Home Rule. (J. P. C. Roach, 'Liberalism and the Victorian Intelligentsia' *Cambridge Historical Journal*, vol. XIII pt. i (1957), pp. 58–81.)

[2] The Court was built by the fashionable architect William Wilkins. He produced two designs, one in the classical style, and the other in what he called his 'Monastic Style'. The Seniority chose the latter. Another significant feature of the building was that the Gothic window frames were made of cast iron.

of the junior Fellows had incited the undergraduates to boycott the dinner in Hall as a way of expressing their dissatisfaction at not being invited to stay and hear the speeches and see the Fellows drink their wine. For the same purpose of disciplining the undergraduates the College agreed to build new lecture-rooms and increase the accommodation in the Chapel (providing the Deans with high seats from which they could keep a watchful eye on proceedings).[1] But there were other occasions when the Master's imperious interpretation of his duties in the College succeeded in provoking many of the Fellows, the most important of them being the episode in 1834 when he summarily dismissed Connop Thirlwall from his post as Whewell's assistant tutor for venturing to express public disagreement with his views on compulsory chapel.

As Peel knew to his cost, Cambridge was not the only university in which the problems of church and state, church and dissent, caused trouble in the 'twenties and 'thirties of the nineteenth century. But the local manifestation of this issue arose out of the controversy over the possibility of admitting dissenters to degrees in the University. In the course of a pamphlet issued in this controversy, Thirlwall had denied the essentially religious character of the College as an institution of the established church, concerned with teaching its doctrines and seeing that its members observed its practices. Without consultation, and as if his position in this matter were no more than that of a private person, he published an attack on the system of compulsory attendance at Chapel, denying its spiritual value and repudiating angrily the suggestion that it was justified as a means to the end of disciplining the undergraduates.[2]

---

[1] In 1797 the stipends of the discipline officers had been increased, though not that of the Junior Bursar. In 1817 it was agreed to employ two extra markers to check the attendance of undergraduates at Chapel. *Seniority Minutes*, 3 June 1797, and 12 December 1817.

[2] C. Thirlwall, *A Letter to the Rev. T. Turton on the admission of Dissenters to Academical Degrees* (Cambridge, 1834). To the claim that 'the alternative was between compulsory religion or no religion at all', Thirlwall replied: 'The difference is too subtle for my grasp.' Trevelyan, *Trinity College*, p. 95, n. 1. The claim was made by the Master's son Christopher. There is an interesting passage on the nature of a university in his pamphlet on the *Admission of Dissenters to Graduate in the University of Cambridge* (Cambridge, 1834), p. 5. 'What then is the title and definition of an English University? Call them, if you will, as they call themselves, "seminaries of sound learning and religious education". Call them even, as they are called by the Dissenters, "National seminaries of Education": but call them not Scientific Institutions, or Literary Academies: the names are honourable but they are not descriptive of the English Universities. The Universities of

He thus succeeded in rousing the Master on two of the principles he held most sacred, and the result was a bitter quarrel in which both sides were guilty of conduct more inspired by anger than a politic regard for the welfare of the college.

Thirlwall was certainly wrong in thinking it consonant with his duties as an officer of the College to make so public an attack on one of its most central institutions. Even those like Julius Hare and Whewell himself who might have been inclined by friendship or temperament to stand by him, recognised the rashness of his conduct. Influenced by neither of these considerations, and inspired by a profoundly Tory faith in the Church of England and all established institutions, the Master reacted violently and without consulting even Whewell, who protested vigorously against his conduct, though on the original point at issue his position was probably nearer that of Wordsworth than that of his assistant tutor.[1]

The episode made the Master even more unpopular with many of the Fellows than he was already, and increasingly he was driven to lead a lonely—if self-righteous—life in the Lodge. Compulsory chapel was not abolished for many years to come: indeed it provoked another less serious, though more amusing incident during this Mastership. In 1838 the undergraduates reacted against the order of the Master and Seniors that they should attend chapel eight instead of five times a week by forming a Society for the Prevention of Cruelty to Undergraduates which published lists in Cambridge and in London of the weekly attendance of the Fellows at Chapel, classified according to the categories of the Tripos.[2] The lists were

England have produced, are producing, and still, by God's blessing, hope to produce men eminent in every department of literature and science: but this is neither their sole, nor is it their primary and characteristic object. Give them rather a financial and commercial character and call them the banks and depositories of the best, the living, hopes of the parents of England, for the loan of which the receivers are responsible, and which they are bound and anxious to restore with accumulated interest.'

[1] Thirlwall believed that the Master had been advised in this affair by Hugh James Rose, a former member of the College. There is no proof of this, but Rose had preached a High-Church sermon in Great St Mary's on Whitsunday 1834 in which the affair is alluded to. J. W. Clark, *Old Friends in Cambridge and Elsewhere* (London, 1900), p. 121, n. 1.; Winstanley, *Early Victorian Cambridge*, p. 75, n. 5.

[2] There are copies of these lists in the College Libary, together with verses published at the time, and the Bible given to Perry (afterwards Bishop of Melbourne) for being the Fellow who (other than the Deans) attended the Chapel most often. The Bible is embossed with the arms of the Society, which were the arms of the College supported by two undergraduates rampant.

revealing, and the verses composed for the occasion both
atrocious and scurrilous;[1] but the tactic produced no other
result. The College was not likely in 1839, or for some time
to come, to do things simply because undergraduates wanted
them done.

Certainly nothing of the sort was to be expected of Wordsworth's successor as Master, William Whewell. Already as a
tutor he was well known for the firmness with which he kept his
pupils in their subordinate place. As Master he was to
become legendary for his authoritarian attitude in his dealings
with undergraduates and Fellows alike. When he was
appointed the College was still governed by the statutes of
1560. In the 1830s in Trinity as elsewhere there were signs
that members of such corporations were anxious to slacken the
restrictive bonds of the ancient statutes they had promised to
observe, and to seek for redress at the hands of Parliament.
Whewell was among the leaders of this movement and he
took up the question at once on becoming Master. The
result was the revised statutes of 1844. Significantly enough
they were still written in Latin—the last to be so—for they
departed from the old ways in no very dramatic fashion. 'We
are to make a revision, not new statutes', the Master had
written in 1842, 'we are to deal reverently with the existing
statutes and not to deviate from them except so far as is requisite to bring the statutes and the practice into accordance'.[2]
And, perhaps in order to make sure that as few problems as
possible were raised, the Master instructed the Seniors to keep
their deliberations confidential from the other Fellows; they
should be a 'Privy Council, and ought not to communicate to
others our proceedings'.[3]

A more reverent reform would be difficult to imagine. Only
one statute—*De Comoediis ludisque in Natalitia Christi exhibendis*—
disappeared entirely. A few features of others that had become

---

[1] One of the chief organizers of the Society was Charles Tindal, son of Sir
Nicholas Tindal, former Fellow and afterwards Chief Justice of the Common
Pleas. In a letter to his father he disassociated the Society from the scurrilous
and blasphemous verses which he ascribed to J. B. Hume, 'son of Joseph Hume
(the radical politician) whose presence, I regret to say, disgraces this College'.

[2] Stair Douglas, *William Whewell*, p. 256.

[3] Winstanley, *Early Victorian Cambridge*, p. 191, quoting the manuscript Diary of
J. Romilly (15 February 1842) which is in the Cambridge University Library.

merely quaint and had long been ignored were also removed; but enough survived. Spears, swords, and daggers were still not to be carried in College or in the town except by leave of the Master, and all members of the College were to dress 'solis vestibus et ornatu Presbyteris et viris ... Ecclesiasticis congruentibus'. The Fellowship examination was restricted to scholars of the College, and a not completely successful attempt was made to define the visitatorial powers in the College of the Bishop of Ely. 'None of the changes made were of fundamental importance,' Winstanley wrote, 'and no regard had been paid to the more serious criticisms of the outside world.'[1]

Whewell's aim had been achieved, and in 1846 the College celebrated the third centenary of its foundation with statutes little changed since 1560. In the light of the changes which had taken place by the time of the fourth centenary it is difficult to believe that anyone, however much he might be given to wishful thinking, could have had much confidence that the position established in 1844 could be maintained for long. It is true that a generation born in the eighteenth century was likely to think of statutes as more sacred things than their successors have done, and would be inclined to expect that the new statutes would last for more than twenty years when the old ones had served for almost three hundred. Change and instability were to be the characteristics and very condition of life of the world of their successors, and have given to institutions both inside and outside the University something of a transitory nature. But the inevitability of change had been so little expected by their predecessors that it had been thought possible to regulate by statute changeable only by the Sovereign, the most minute aspects of the daily lives of institutions such as this.

Nevertheless, there were those who had doubts, and who can only have been disappointed at what was done. Two Fellows of Trinity, B. D. Walsh and George Peacock,[2] had analysed in minute detail the old statutes of the colleges and the University in relation to their present practice, and had pointed to many glaring and ludicrous discrepancies. But they suggested

[1] Winstanley, *Early Victorian Cambridge*, pp. 195–6.
[2] B. D. Walsh, *An Historical Account of the University of Cambridge and its Colleges* (London, 1837); G. Peacock, *Observations on the Statutes of the University of Cambridge* (London, 1841).

also that for some there was more to reforming the statutes than cutting away dead wood. There were questions to be raised about the very nature and purpose of the colleges and of university education which could not be avoided for ever. The problems underlying the controversy between Christopher Wordsworth and Connop Thirlwall had not yet been squarely faced, but it was perhaps already sensed that the opposing points of view were fundamentally irreconcilable. Just as dissenters from the national religion could only be admitted to full membership of the state if the nature and purposes of the state were differently defined from what they had been before the concession, so also could they only be reckoned full members of a college or a university if the nature and purposes of these institutions too were differently defined. And if they were differently defined, much that had been insisted on or taken for granted in the past would become without logical foundation. Compulsory attendance at chapel, the obligation on Fellows to take orders and to remain celibate, subscription to the thirty-nine articles as a necessary pre-condition to admission to a degree, are perhaps the most obvious things which were brought in question. But other matters would soon be raised, most notably perhaps that of the whole nature and content of the curriculum. Could the colleges remain as it were seminaries without an agreed syllabus? How was a man to teach a subject of which the basis and the content was being questioned? Was the inculcation of doubts an adequate substitute for the indoctrination of certainties: were not the young and immature by definition in need of certainty and incapable of coping with doubt?

Whewell was one of those who took a leading part in the scientific revival of early nineteenth-century England, and in Cambridge he was largely responsible for the foundation of the Natural Sciences Tripos. As a Tutor he had sometimes regretted the extent to which his duties to his pupils got in the way of his research and writing. 'My tutorship hangs about the neck of my theories in a wonderful manner,' he once wrote, 'I mean in the manner of a millstone and not of a mistress.'[1] But however interested he might be in scientific advance, he

[1] I. Todhunter, *W. Whewell, D.D. An Account of his Writings*, (2 vols London, 1876), vol. II, p. 62.

had no doubt that the main function of the College and the University was teaching and not research. And although his importance in the movement for broadening the Cambridge syllabus has long been recognized, perhaps less well known are his views on the unsuitability for didactic purposes of subjects which were unsettled.[1] They are views which once again raised problems which went so deep as perhaps to be insoluble, and like the others already mentioned, were calculated in the context of mid-nineteenth-century England to provoke points of view which were perhaps in the last resort irreconcilable. They had been ignored by those who revised the statutes of Trinity College in 1844, but they were not allowed to remain unconsidered for much longer. The Royal Commission appointed by Lord John Russell in the year of Peel's death made sure of that.

[1] See Owen Chadwick, *Westcott and the University* (Cambridge, 1962), for an excellent brief account of the controversy over the nature of a university at this time.

had no doubt that the main function of the College and the University was to keep, and not to remunerate. And although the importance in the argument of the small body must largely be qualitative, few recruits of pretence be well to wise as his view on the usual office, do hence purpose of a project which were indicated. They may have taken even what men professors whenas so dropt, perhaps to be builded; and the manully values mentioned were abandoned in the last text or interested earnest country England to promote a state, even which up open is in the last act the common body. They had been bound in the proportioned elements of Trinity College, that all they were so allowed to remain unremunerated not honest the Royal Commission appointed by Lord John in the first year of ... added more, and of ...

Index